Negro Heritage Library

NEGRO HERITAGE LIBRARY

A

Martin Luther King

Treasury

including STRIDE TOWARD FREEDOM · STRENGTH TO LOVE

AN APPEAL TO THE PRESIDENT OF THE UNITED STATES
AND
THE DAYS OF MARTIN LUTHER KING, JR., *A Photographic Diary*

Photographs by ROLAND MITCHELL

M. W. LADS
New York – Philadelphia

FIRST EDITION

PHOTOGRAPHS: On page 37 and 97 copyright © 1958 by Wide World Photos; on pages 40–41, 43, 44, 47, 48, 50, 55, 58, 77, 82, copyright © 1958 by Dan Weiner; page 138 United Press International Photos; page 141 Southern Christian Leadership Conference; page 256 Feingold (Denver-Hilton); pages 258–287 by Roland Mitchell, copyright © 1964 Educational Heritage, Inc.

Designed by Harold Franklin

PRINTED IN THE UNITED STATES OF AMERICA BY
GOODWAY, INC., PHILADELPHIA, PA.

DEDICATION

TO THE present generation of Negro youth
and generations yet unborn;
that they might discover the dynamics
of the contemporary non-violent revolution:
the spirit of *love*—
actualized in the human personality—
through which their children
and their children's children
will rise up and call their name
"blessed."

MARTIN LUTHER KING, JR.

M. W. LADS — OFFICERS

Chairman
MILTON WOLK

President
DONALD WOLK

Vice President
BERYL WOLK

Secretary
PAUL R. ROSEN, Esq.

Treasurer
JOHN J. GALLAGHER, JR.

A NOTE FROM THE PUBLISHERS

THE NEGRO HERITAGE LIBRARY is M. W. Lads' response to a major historical, social and psychological necessity of our times. There is little question that the Negro has emerged as the dominant figure on the American scene today, and yet he remains a stranger to most white Americans and often to himself as well.

Too many Americans, Negro and white, have scant knowledge of the fact that the Negro has a proud heritage of notable achievement. This ignorance—and euphemisms serve no valid purpose here—is easily explained. The standard texts on the history of America and the Western world, the very sources from which we have drawn our knowledge of Man and Society, have consistently excluded the Negro's contribution. I submit that this omission has been a significant factor in the perpetuation of white prejudice and the distortion of Negro self-esteem. An honest reckoning of the Negro's contribution to the building of our society is long overdue.

Accordingly, we have set ourselves the combined tasks of:

strengthening the Negro's confidence and assurance
that he *has* historical roots deep
within the soil of Western civilization, and

restoring to History those missing pages whose absence
has crippled America's ability to understand the Negro,
hence retarding fulfillment of the American ideal of equal justice
to all men, regardless of race, creed, color or national origin.

This can only be done by a truthful and accurate recounting of the Negro's remarkable story. It is our hope that the content of these volumes will serve this high purpose.

Table of Contents

Foreword

AS I WRITE THESE LINES, Martin King is beginning his third day in the St. John's County Jail, a few miles north of St. Augustine, Florida. He is charged with having violated Florida's "undesirable guest statute" because he attempted to be served at one of the ancient city's rigidly segregated restaurants. No foreword could be more expressive and more meaningful than the simple fact of his imprisonment on this charge.

More than a decade has passed since Dr. King, a young Baptist minister called to his first pastorate, arrived in Montgomery, Alabama. A disciple of Mohandas K. Gandhi's *"satyagraha,"* he was firmly convinced that the concept that had led to Indian independence could, in time, be applied to the southern grass-roots protest movement. Gandhi himself had foreseen this eventuality when, in 1936, he had prophesied that "it may be through the Negroes that the unadulterated message of non-violence will be delivered to the world."

But even King, with all his hard-won faith in the Gandhian method of passive resistance, did not seriously believe that southern Negroes were yet ready to accept the demanding discipline of non-violence as a way of life. "When I went to Montgomery as a pastor," he wrote in 1958, "I had not the slightest idea that I would later become involved in a crisis in which nonviolent resistance would be applicable." It took the Montgomery bus boycott that began in the fall of 1955 to prove to him that non-violence was as morally imperative and as tactically sound in the streets of the Alabama capital as it had been, a quarter of a century earlier, on the Salt March to the Sea.

By the end of 1956, when the Supreme Court ended bus segregation in Montgomery forever, King was exhorting American Negroes, in the best Gandhian rhetoric, to adopt non-violence as their exclusive form of social protest. "We will take direct action against injustices without waiting for other agencies to act," he proclaimed. "We will not obey unjust laws or submit to unjust practices. We will do this peacefully, openly, cheerfully because our aim is to persuade."

He saw clearly that the course he was charting was a dangerous one. "It may mean going to jail," he warned. "If such is the case the resister must be willing to fill the jail houses of the South. It may even mean physical death. But if physical death is the price that a man must pay, to free his children and his white brethren from a permanent death of the spirit, then nothing could be more redemptive."

Few would now gainsay that the Negro Revolution began when Mrs. Rosa Parks, a Montgomery seamstress, quietly but firmly refused to obey the order of a bus driver to give up her seat to a white man. But it took something more than anger to transform an act born of fatigue, bitterness and frustration into the catalyst that inaugurated what is undoubtedly the most dynamic moral crusade of this or any other time. That something was Martin Luther King.

That King is an accident of time, place and circumstance may be superficially true. But he is no more—or less—an accident than Abraham Lincoln, Winston Churchill or Gandhi himself. Significantly, he is extremely fond of quoting Tom Paine's axiom that "there is no power like the power of an idea whose time has come." Since all change is the result of ideas that are put to work by men fortunate enough to arrive on stage at a time when fruition is possible, history, in this sense, may only be recorded coincidence.

But there is, of course, more to it than that. Even if one rejects Toynbee's cyclical theory, it is difficult to ascribe man's painful but steady progress toward truth and understanding to fortunate happenstance. If we are to maintain any faith in the ability of one man or one hundred million men to alter established courses, if we are unwilling to accept the deterministic concept of uncontrollable forces sweeping us headlong toward some dark and mysterious goal, if we believe that the individual, solitary or in concert, can influence his own destiny, then we must welcome a Martin Luther King as some evidence that our most cherished life concepts still have validity.

For he is not only a symbol of social protest, important as that function may be. Likewise, he is not a putative martyr who seeks, by the sheer offering of his own body, to produce the shining example that touches and motivates men. Nor is he an isolated mystic who, sitting cross-legged upon the ground, whispers occasional cryptic messages which only those closest to him can hear and only those schooled in interpreting enigma can understand.

But if he is neither symbol nor martyr nor mystic, then just what is he? I do not claim any magic key to his complex personality, yet like so many people who have come into close if sporadic contact with him, I sense that I know him well. That this almost intuitive feeling may be wholly illusory I readily concede, but since some judgment is called for, I am quite willing to proffer one for what it is worth.

First of all, it must be emphasized that there are as many Martin Kings as there are roles for him to play. To those who read his books, he is a colorful, often inspired and always moving writer. His audiences, whether in rural Georgia or urban Massachusetts, regard him as a superb orator who speaks to tenant farmers much the same as he does to university professors. As for his parishioners, they find him a sensitive and dedicated pastor who regards his ministry as his principal concern.

But it is as a leader that he merits our most serious consideration. In a very real sense, he is the result of a natural selection that can only occur when masses of oppressed people are set in motion by the application of a simple theory to bewildering factual situations. Under such circumstances, the man who suggests the theory and is capable of superintending its application with any degree of effectiveness may find himself, often to his utter dismay, imprisoned in the isolation of leadership. Like Alfred de Vigny's Moïse, he stands alone, unable even to sleep like other men.

When the "walk of freedom" succeeded in breaking bus segregation in Montgomery, King burst upon the national scene. To millions of Negroes he represented a latter-day Moses who, with an occasional assist from Thoreau and Gandhi, had demonstrated that new methods might solve age-old problems. Whether he liked it or not—and I am not at all sure that he does—he was suddenly in full command of a non-violent army marching through the wilderness. As he put it, "I simply responded to the call of the people for a spokesman."

He is, by the very nature of his role, a lonely, introspective man. Still, it is vital that he, his philosophy and his objectives be understood by the greatest number of people. This collection, bringing together as it does most of his previously published works, will do much to give his ideas a wide and diverse circulation. Should they find a more catholic acceptance than they presently enjoy, it is just possible that Dr. King's most fervent dream—the establishment of the beloved community—may yet become a reality.

"The past decade," he writes in *Strength To Love,* "has been a most exciting one. In spite of the tensions and uncertainties of this period something profoundly meaningful is taking place. Old systems of exploitation and oppression are passing away; new systems of justice and equality are being born. In a real sense, this is a great time to be alive. Therefore, I'm not yet discouraged about the future. Granted that the easygoing optimism of yesterday is impossible. Granted that we face a world crisis which leaves us standing so often amid the surging murmur of life's restless sea. But every crisis has both its dangers and its opportunities. It can spell either salvation or doom. In a dark, confused world the Kingdom of God may yet reign in the hearts of men."

Believing as I do in the Melvillian conviction that, like the white whale, evil is both unconquering and unconquerable, I accept non-violence in the same manner as I do Billy Budd. So long as evil can be contained by good, so long as there are other cheeks to be turned, so long as men strive for right in the face of unpunished wrong, then Dr. King's dream is worthy of being shared. If we truly stand on the threshold of a new age, it is only because we have signified our willingness, however begrudging, to adopt non-violent solutions to our most intense problems. Whether we cross over into Canaan or not will depend in large measure on our ability to subscribe to *satyagraha* as "a commitment to a way of life." Dr. King has made his choice—the next step is ours.

WILLIAM M. KUNSTLER

June 13, 1964

BOOK ONE

STRIDE TOWARD FREEDOM

The Montgomery Story

PREFACE

THIS BOOK IS an account of a few years that changed the life of a Southern community, told from the point of view of one of the participants. Although it attempts to interpret what happened it does not purport to be a detailed survey of the historical and sociological aspects of the Montgomery story. It is therefore limited in scope and its point of view is inevitably personal.

While the nature of this account causes me to make frequent use of the pronoun "I," in every important part of the story it should be "we." This is not a drama with only one actor. More precisely it is the chronicle of 50,000 Negroes who took to heart the principles of non-violence, who learned to fight for their rights with the weapon of love, and who, in the process, acquired a new estimate of their own human worth. It is the story of Negro leaders of many faiths and divided allegiances, who came together in the bond of a cause they knew was right. And of the Negro followers, many of them beyond middle age, who walked to work and home again as much as twelve miles a day for over a year rather than submit to the discourtesies and humiliation of segregated buses. The majority of the Negroes who took part in the year-long boycott of Montgomery's buses were poor and untutored; but they understood the essence of the Montgomery movement. One elderly woman summed it up for the rest. When asked after several weeks of walking whether she was tired, she answered, "My feets is tired, but my soul is at rest."

There is another side to the picture: it is the white community of Montgomery, long led or intimidated by a few extremists, that finally turned in disgust on the perpetrators of crime in the name of segregation. The change should not be exaggerated. The White Citizens Council is still active. Confessed bombers still win their freedom in the courts. And opposition to integration is still the rule. Yet by the end of the bus struggle it was clear that the vast majority of Montgomery's whites preferred peace and law to the excesses performed in the name of segregation. And even though the many saw segregation as right because it was the tradition, there were always the courageous few who saw the injustice in segregation and fought against it side by side with the Negroes.

Since Montgomery, a gallant bus protest has been conducted in Tallahassee, and efforts to integrate buses have spread to many other Southern communities. Negroes throughout the South have begun to take up in earnest their right to register and vote. Little Rock has occurred, and Negro children have walked with fortitude through the ranks of white students—often hostile and jeering—at Central High School. How much the Montgomery movement helped to give strength and new courage to Negroes elsewhere, and how much Montgomery and

Little Rock and Tallahassee were all results of the same causes, is a matter for future historians. Whatever the final estimate, it is already clear that Montgomery was a part of something much larger than itself.

The problem of acknowledgments in a work of this sort is immense. How can one acknowledge 50,000 individual contributions? Yet the book would not be complete without the author's thanks to some of the many people who made it possible.

I am deeply grateful to Theodore Brown, Charles Gomillion, Lewis Wade Jones, and Harris Wofford for significant suggestions and real encouragement. They are not responsible for my failure to accomplish all for which they must have hoped.

I am also indebted to my teacher and friend George D. Kelsey, who has given me valuable and stimulating suggestions.

I am sincerely grateful to my close associates, Mrs. Jo Ann Robinson and Fred D. Gray, for a painstaking and detailed reading of the entire manuscript.

My thanks also go to my friend L. D. Reddick who has read the manuscript and provided both suggestions and materials of rare usefulness. I am especially grateful to Mrs. Hermine Popper of Harper & Brothers, who with great competence rendered invaluable editorial assistance.

I am indebted to my secretary, Mrs. Maude Ballou, who continually encouraged me to persevere in this work and with great toil transferred my hand written pages to typewritten copy.

I thank, too, my collegemate Elliot Finley and his wife Genevieve, who provided a quiet and comfortable home where most of these words were written.

I owe a special debt of gratitude to the press—especially to Ted Poston of the *New York Post*, Abel Plenn of *The New York Times*, and Norman Walton of *The Negro History Bulletin*—whose reports of Montgomery provided invaluable resources and stimulants to my memory.

I am deeply grateful to the members of the Dexter Avenue Baptist Church, without whose patience, loyalty, and encouragement the completion of this work would not have been possible.

Most of all I am indebted to my wife Coretta, without whose love, sacrifices, and loyalty neither life nor work would bring fulfillment. She has given me words of consolation when I needed them most and a well-ordered home where Christian love is a reality. To her the book is dedicated.

MARTIN LUTHER KING, JR.

Montgomery, Alabama
May, 1958

CHAPTER I

RETURN TO THE SOUTH

On a cool Saturday afternoon in January 1954, I set out to drive from Atlanta, Georgia, to Montgomery, Alabama. It was a clear wintry day. The Metropolitan Opera was on the radio with a performance of one of my favorite operas—Donizetti's *Lucia di Lammermoor*. So with the beauty of the countryside, the inspiration of Donizetti's inimitable music, and the splendor of the skies, the usual monotony that accompanies a relatively long drive—especially when one is alone—was dispelled in pleasant diversions.

After a few hours I drove through rich and fertile farmlands to the sharp bend in the Alabama River on whose shores Montgomery stands. Although I had passed through the city before, I had never been there on a real visit. Now I would have the opportunity to spend a few days in this beautiful little city, one of the oldest in the United States.

Not long after I arrived a friend took me to see the Dexter Avenue Baptist Church where I was to preach the following morning. A solid brick structure erected in Reconstruction days, it stood at one corner of a handsome square not far from the center of town. As we drove up to the church I noticed diagonally across the square a stately white building of impressive proportions and arresting beauty, the State Capitol. The present building was erected in 1851, and its high-domed central portion is one of the finest examples of classical Georgian architecture in America. Here on January 7, 1861, Alabama voted to secede from the Union, and on February 18, on the steps of the portico, Jeffer-

son Davis took his oath of office as President of the Confederate States. It is for this reason that Montgomery has been known across the years as the Cradle of the Confederacy. Here the first Confederate flag was made and unfurled. One could see many of the patterns of the old Confederacy and the antebellum tradition persisting in Montgomery today, alongside the lively evidence of modern economic development.

I was to see this imposing reminder of the Confederacy from the steps of the Dexter Avenue Baptist Church many times in the following years; for my visit in January proved to be a prelude to my coming to live in Montgomery.

The previous August of 1953, after being in school twenty-one years without a break, I had reached the satisfying moment of completing the residential requirements for the Ph.D. degree. The major job that remained was to write my doctoral thesis. In the meantime I had felt that it would be wise to start considering a job so that I could be placed at least by September 1954. Two churches in the East—one in Massachusetts and one in New York—had expressed an interest in calling me. Three colleges had offered me attractive and challenging posts—one a teaching post, one a deanship, and the other an administrative position. In the midst of thinking about each of these positions, I had received a letter from the officers of the Dexter Avenue Baptist Church of Montgomery, saying that they were without a pastor and that they would be glad to have me preach when I was again in that section of the country. The officers who extended the invitation had heard of me through my father in Atlanta and other ministerial friends. I had written immediately saying that I would be home in Atlanta for the Christmas holidays, and that I would be happy to come to Montgomery to preach one Sunday in January.

The church was comparatively small, with a membership of around three hundred people, but it occupied a central place in the community. Many influential and respected citizens—professional people with substantial incomes—were among its members. Moreover it had a long tradition of an educated ministry. Some of the nation's best-trained Negro ministers had held pastorates there.

That Saturday evening as I began going over my sermon, I was aware of a certain anxiety. Although I had preached many times before—having served as associate pastor of my father's church in Atlanta for four years, and having done all of the preaching there for three successive summers—I was very conscious this time that I was on trial. How could I best impress the congregation? Since the membership was educated and intelligent, should I attempt to interest it with a display of scholarship? Or should I preach just as I had always done, depending finally on the inspiration of the spirit of God? I decided to follow the latter course. I said to my-

self, "Keep Martin Luther King in the background and God in the foreground and everything will be all right. Remember you are a channel of the gospel and not the source."

At eleven o'clock on Sunday I was in the pulpit, delivering my sermon before a large congregation. My topic was: "The Three Dimensions of a Complete Life." The congregation was receptive, and I left with the feeling that God had used me well, and that here was a fine church with challenging possibilities. Later in the day the pulpit committee talked to me concerning many business details of the church, and asked me if I would accept the pastorate in the event they saw fit to call me. After answering that I would give such a call my most prayerful and serious consideration, I left Montgomery for Atlanta, and then took a flight back to Boston.

About a month later I received an air-mail, special-delivery letter from Montgomery, telling me that I had been unanimously called to the pastorate of the Dexter Avenue Baptist Church. I was very happy to have this offer, but I did not answer immediately; for I was to fly to Detroit the next morning for a preaching engagement the following Sunday.

It was one of those turbulent days in which the clouds hovered' low, but as the plane lifted itself above the weather, the choppiness of the flight soon passed. As I watched the silvery sheets of clouds below and the deep dark shadow of the blue above, I faced up to the problem of what to do about the several offers that had come my way. At this time I was torn in two directions. On the one hand I was inclined toward the pastorate; on the other hand, toward educational work. Which way should I go? And if I accepted a church, should it be one in the South, with all the tragic implications of segregation, or one of the two available pulpits in the North?

As far back as I could remember, I had resented segregation, and had asked my parents urgent and pointed questions about it. While I was still too young for school I had already learned something about discrimination. For three or four years my inseparable playmates had been two white boys whose parents ran a store across the street from our home in Atlanta. Then something began to happen. When I went across the street to get them, their parents would say that they couldn't play. They weren't hostile; they just made excuses. Finally I asked my mother about it.

Every parent at some time faces the problem of explaining the facts of life to his child. Just as inevitably, for the Negro parent, the moment comes when he must explain to his offspring the facts of segregation. My mother took me on her lap and began by telling me about slavery and how it had ended with the Civil War. She tried to explain the divided system of the South—the segregated schools, restaurants, theaters, housing; the white and colored signs on drinking fountains, waiting rooms, lavatories—as a social condition rather than a natural order. Then she said the words that almost every Negro hears before he can yet understand the injustice that makes them necessary: "You are as good as anyone."

My mother, as the daughter of a successful minister, had grown up in comparative comfort. She had been sent to the best available school and college and had, in general, been protected from the worst blights of discrimination. But my father, a sharecropper's son, had met its brutalities at first hand, and had begun to strike back at an early age. With his fearless honesty and his robust, dynamic presence, his words commanded attention.

I remembered a trip to a downtown shoestore with Father when I was still small. We had sat down in the first empty seats at the front of the store. A young white clerk came up and murmured politely:

"I'll be happy to wait on you if you'll just move to those seats in the rear."

My father answered, "There's nothing wrong with these seats. We're quite comfortable here."

"Sorry," said the clerk, "but you'll have to move."

"We'll either buy shoes sitting here," my father retorted, "or we won't buy shoes at all." Whereupon he took me by the hand and walked out of the store. This was the first time I had ever seen my father so angry. I still remember walking down the street beside him as he muttered, "I don't care how long I have to live with this system, I will never accept it."

And he never has. I remembered riding with him another day when he accidentally drove past a stop sign. A policeman pulled up to the car and said:

"All right, boy, pull over and let me see your license."

My father replied indignantly, "I'm no boy." Then, pointing to me, "This is a boy. I'm a man, and until you call me one, I will not listen to you."

The policeman was so shocked that he wrote the ticket up nervously, and left the scene as quickly as possible.

From before I was born, my father had refused to ride the city buses, after witnessing a brutal attack on a load of Negro passengers. He had led the fight in Atlanta to equalize teachers' salaries, and had been instrumental in the elimination of Jim Crow elevators in the courthouse. As pastor of the Ebenezer Baptist Church, where he still presides over a congregation of four thousand, he had wielded great influence in the Negro community, and had perhaps won the grudging respect of the whites. At any rate, they had never attacked him physically, a fact that filled my brother and sister and me with wonder as we grew up in this tension-packed atmosphere.

With this heritage, it is not surprising that I had also learned to abhor segregation, considering it both rationally inexplicable and morally unjustifiable. As a teenager I had never been able to accept the fact of having to go to the back of a bus or sit in the segregated section of a train. The first time that I had been seated behind a curtain in a dining car, I felt as if the curtain had been dropped on my selfhood. Having the usual growing boy's pleasure in movies, I had yet gone to a downtown theater in Atlanta only once. The experience of having to enter a rear door and sit in a filthy peanut gallery was so obnoxious that I could not enjoy the picture. I could never adjust to the separate waiting rooms, separate eating places, separate rest rooms, partly because the separate was always unequal, and partly because the very idea of separation did something to my sense of dignity and self-respect.

Now, I thought, as the plane carried me toward Detroit, I have a chance to escape from the long night of segregation. Can I return to a society that condones a system I have abhorred since childhood?

These questions were still unanswered when I returned to Boston. I discussed them with my wife, Coretta (we had been married less than a year), to find that she too was hesitant about returning South. We discussed the all-important question of raising children in the bonds of segregation. We reviewed our own growth in the South, and the many advantages that we had been deprived of as a result of segregation. The question of my wife's musical career came up. She was certain that a Northern city would afford a greater opportunity for continued study than any city in the deep South. For several days we talked and thought and prayed over each of these matters. Finally we agreed that, in spite of the disadvantages and inevitable sacrifices, our greatest service could be rendered in our native South. We came to the conclusion that we had something of a moral obligation to return—at least for a few years.

The South, after all, was our home. Despite its shortcomings we loved it as home, and had a real desire to do something about the problems that we had felt so keenly as youngsters. We never wanted to be considered detached spectators. Since racial discrimination was most intense in the South, we felt that some of the Negroes who had received a portion of their training in other sections of the country should return to share their broader contacts and educational experience in its solution. Moreover, despite having to sacrifice much of the cultural life we loved, despite the existence of Jim Crow which kept reminding us at all times of the color of our skin, we had the feeling that something remarkable was unfolding in the South, and we wanted to be on hand to witness it. The region had marvelous possibilities, and once it came to itself and removed the blight of racial segregation, it would experience a moral, political, and economic boom hardly paralleled by any other section of the country.

With this decision my inclination toward the pastorate temporarily won out over my desire to teach, and I decided to accept the call to Dexter for a few years and satisfy my fondness for scholarship later by turning to the teaching field. I sent a telegram to Montgomery that I would be down in three weeks to discuss details.

So I went back to Montgomery. After exploring arrangements with the officers, I accepted the pastorate. Because of my desire to spend at least four more months of intensive work on my doctoral thesis, I asked for and was granted the condition that I would not be required to take up the full-time pastorate until September 1, 1954. I agreed, however, to come down to Montgomery at least once a month to keep things running smoothly during this interim period. On a Sunday in May 1954 I preached my first sermon as minister of the Dexter Avenue Baptist Church, and for the next four months I commuted by plane between Boston and Montgomery.

On my July trip I was accompanied by Coretta. Montgomery was not unfamiliar to her, for her home was just 80 miles away, in the little town of Marion, Alabama. There her father, Obie Scott, though born on a farm, had made a success in business, operating a trucking concern, a combination filling station and grocery store, and a chicken farm. Despite the reprisals and physical threats of his white competitors, he had dared to make a decent living for his family, and to maintain an abiding faith in the future. Coretta had lived in Marion until she left to attend Antioch College in Yellow Springs, Ohio. Having inherited a talent for music from her mother, Bernice Scott, as well as the strength of quiet determination, she had then gone on with the aid of a scholarship to work her way through the New England Conservatory in Boston. It was in Boston that I had met and fallen in love with the attractive young singer whose gentle manner and air of repose did not disguise her lively spirit. And although we had returned to Marion on June 18, 1953, to be married by my father on the Scotts' spacious lawn, it was in Boston that we had begun our married life together.

So on the July visit Coretta looked at Montgomery with fresh eyes. Since her teens she had breathed the free air of unsegregated colleges, and stayed as a welcome guest in white homes. Now in preparation for our long-term return to the South, she visited the Negro section of town where we would be living without choice. She saw the Negroes crowded into the backs of segregated buses and knew that she would be riding there too. But on the same visit she was introduced to the church and cordially received by its fine congregation. And with her sense of optimism and balance, which were to be my constant support in the days to come, she placed her faith on the side of the opportunities and the challenge for Christian service that were offered by Dexter and the Montgomery community.

On September 1, 1954, we moved into the parsonage and I began my full-time pastorate. The first months were busy with the usual chores of getting to know a new house, a new job, a new city. There were old friendships to pick up and new ones to be made, and little time to look beyond our private lives to the general community around us. And although we had come back to the South with the hope of playing a part in the changes we knew were on the horizon, we had no notion yet of how the changes would come about, and no inkling that in little more than a year we would be involved in a movement that was to alter Montgomery forever and to have repercussions throughout the world.

CHAPTER II

MONTGOMERY BEFORE THE PROTEST

THE CHURCH WORK was stimulating from the beginning. The first few weeks in the autumn of 1954 were spent formulating a program that would be meaningful to this particular congregation. I was anxious to change the impression in the community that Dexter was a sort of silk-stocking church catering only to a certain class. Often it was referred to as the "big folks' church." Revolting against this idea, I was convinced that worship at its best is a social experience with people of all levels of life coming together to realize their oneness and unity under God. Whenever the church, consciously or unconsciously, caters to one class it loses the spiritual force of the "whosoever will, let him come" doctrine, and is in danger of becoming little more than a social club with a thin veneer of religiosity.

I was also concerned with broadening the auxiliary program of the church. These activities, when I arrived, consisted chiefly of the Sunday School, where adults and children assembled to study the tenets of Christianity and the Bible; the Baptist Training Union, designed to develop Christian leadership; and the Missionary Society, which carried the message of the church into the community. Among the new functions I decided to recommend were a committee to revitalize religious education; a social service committee to channel and invigorate services to the sick and needy; a social and political action committee; a committee to raise and administer scholarship funds for high school graduates; and a cultural committee to give encouragement to promising artists.

Since many points in the new program represented a definite departure from the traditional way of doing things, I was somewhat dubious about its acceptance. I therefore presented my recommendations to the church with some trepidation; but, to my surprise, they were heartily approved. The response and coöperation of the members from this moment on was impressive. Almost immediately the membership began to grow, and the financial report for the first six months revealed that the income of the church had almost tripled over previous years. The various new committees were functioning well, and the program of religious education was characterized by sturdy growth.

For several months I had to divide my efforts between completing my thesis and carrying out my duties with the church. I rose every morning at five-thirty and spent three hours writing the thesis, returning to it late at night for another three hours. The remainder of the day was given to church work, including, besides the weekly service, marriages, funerals, and personal conferences. One day each week was given over to visiting and praying with members who were either sick or otherwise confined to their homes.

A great deal of time in the early days was also occupied with getting to know all the members of the congregation. This entailed visiting them at home and attending the various auxiliary meetings of the church. Almost every week I attended from five to ten such group meetings, and most of my early evenings were consumed in this fashion. I was also spending a minimum of fifteen hours a week in preparing my Sunday sermon. I usually began an outline on Tuesday. On Wednesday I did the necessary research and thought of illustrative material and life situations that would give the sermon practical content. On Friday I began writing, and usually finished the writing on Saturday night.

I still found additional time to take an immediate interest in the larger community of Montgomery. The city's economic life was heavily influenced by the presence there of the Maxwell and Gunter Air Force bases. According to the annual report of the Montgomery Chamber of Commerce, these two bases channeled a total of $58 million into Montgomery's business economy during 1955. One in every fourteen employed civilians in Montgomery worked at these bases, and approximately one in every seven families was an air force family, either civilian or military. Four thousand families living outside base reservations occupied homes in the city. Yet ironically, although the bases, which contributed so much to the economic life of the community, were fully integrated, the city around them adhered to a rigorous pattern of racial segregation. One could not help wishing that the vast economic power of the federal agencies were being used for the good of race relations in Montgomery.

Modern Montgomery is a prominent market for cotton, livestock, yellow pine, and hardwood lumber, and is one of the nation's important centers for the manufacture of commercial fertilizer. It has the largest cattle market east of Fort Worth, Texas, and south of the Ohio River, marketing approximately $30 million worth of cattle annually. But there is a dearth of heavy industry. This lack of industry is one of the reasons why so many Negroes go into domestic service: 63 percent of the Negro women workers in Montgomery are domestics, and 48 percent of the Negro men are laborers or domestic workers. It is also probably one of the factors in the appalling gap between the living conditions of the whites and the Negroes. In 1950 the median income for the approximately 70,000 white people of Montgomery was $1730, compared with $970 for the 50,000 Negroes. Ninety-four percent of the white families in Montgomery have flush toilets inside their homes, while only 31 percent of the Negro families enjoy such facilities. Aside, then, from the problem of segregation itself, with its effects on every aspect of Negro life, it was clear that Montgomery's Negroes were also the victims of severe economic deprivation.

The two communities moved, as it were, along separate channels. The schools of course were segregated; and the United States Supreme Court decision on school integration, handed down in May 1954, appeared to have no effect on Montgomery's determination to keep them that way. If a white man and a Negro wanted to ride in a taxi together, they could not have done so, since by law white operators served white passengers exclusively and Negroes rode in a separate system confined to them. True, Negroes and whites met as employers and employees, and they rode to work together at either ends of the same buses, with a sharp line of separation between the two groups. They used the same shopping centers, though Negroes were sometimes forced to wait until all the whites had been served, and they were seldom given the dignity of courtesy titles. In several sections of town, Negro and white residential neighborhoods adjoined, and in others they interlocked like the fingers of two hands. But each section turned its back on its neighbor and faced into its own community for its social and cultural life.

There were no integrated professional organizations of physicians, lawyers, teachers, and so forth; and even when such professionals shared membership in national organizations, they went their separate ways at home. No interracial ministerial alliance existed in Montgomery. There was no local Urban League to bring Negro and white together on an interracial board, and the active membership of the Montgomery Chapter of the National Association for the Advancement of Colored People (NAACP) was entirely Negro. The largest institution of higher learning in Montgomery was the all-Negro Alabama State College, mainly devoted to teacher-training, with a faculty of almost 200 and a student body of approximately 2000. Although the faculty had included such nationally known figures as Horace Mann Bond and Charles H. Thompson, and the college still exerted a lively cultural influence on both city and state, it drew few local white visitors to its handsome campus. In fact, the local chapter of the Alabama Council on Human Relations alone in Montgomery brought the two races together in mutual efforts to solve shared problems.

Alabama law and its administration had worked to keep Negro voting down to a minimum. By 1940 there were not more than 2000 Negro voters in all Alabama. Today the number is closer to 50,000, but although this represents progress, it is still less than 10 percent of all Negroes of voting age in the state. In 1954 there were some 30,000 Negroes of voting age in Montgomery County, but only a few more than 2000 were registered. This low figure was in part the result of the Ne-

groes' own lack of interest or persistence in surmounting the barriers erected against them; but the barriers were themselves formidable. Alabama law gives the registrars wide discretionary powers. At the registration office are separate lines and separate tables for voters according to race. The registrars servicing Negro lines move at a noticeably leisurely pace, so that of fifty Negroes in line, as few as fifteen may be reached by the end of the day. All voters are required to fill out a long questionnaire as a test of eligibility. Often Negroes fill out the questionnaire at several different times before they have been informed that they have done so successfully. In the light of these facts it was not surprising to find that there was no Negro in public office in either the city or the county of Montgomery.

As an expression of my concern with such problems as these, one of the first committees that I set up in my church was designed to keep the congregation intelligently informed on the social, political, and economic situations. The duties of the Social and Political Action Committee were, among others, to keep before the congregation the importance of the NAACP and the necessity of being registered voters, and—during state and national elections—to sponsor forums and mass meetings to discuss the major issues. I sought members for this committee who had already evinced an interest in social problems, and who had some prior experience in this area. Fortunately this was not a difficult task, for Dexter had several members who were deeply concerned with community problems, and who accepted with alacrity. Interestingly enough, two members of this committee—Mrs. Jo Ann Robinson and Rufus Lewis—were among the first people to become prominent in the bus boycott that was soon to mobilize the latent strength of Montgomery's Negro community.

As the year passed I saw impressive results from the work of this committee. By the first of November it was publishing a bi-weekly newsletter, SAPAC, which was distributed to every member of the church and proved to be of great value in placing major social and political issues before the church members. Under the committee's auspices a voting clinic had trained almost every unregistered member of the congregation in the pitfalls of discriminatory registration procedures. By November 1955, in my annual report to the membership, I was able to say that "the work of this committee has been superb, and every member of Dexter has felt its influence. Through the work of this committee many persons have become registered voters, and Dexter has led all other churches in Montgomery in contributions to the NAACP."

After having started the program of the church on its way, I joined the local branch of the NAACP and began to take an active interest in implementing its program in the community itself. Besides raising money through my church, I made several speeches for the NAACP in Montgomery and elsewhere. Less than a year after I joined the branch I was elected to the executive committee. By attending most of the monthly meetings I was brought face to face with some of the racial problems that plagued the community, especially those involving the courts.

Before my arrival in Montgomery, and for several years after, most of the local NAACP's energies and funds were devoted to the defense of Jeremiah Reeves. Reeves, a drummer in a Negro band, had been arrested at the age of sixteen, accused of raping a white woman. One of the authorities had led him to the death chamber, threatening that if he did not confess at once he would burn there later. His confession, extracted under this duress, was later retracted, and for the remaining seven years that his case, and his life, dragged on, he continued to deny not only the charge of rape but the accusation of having had sexual relations at all with his white accuser.

The NAACP hired the lawyers and raised the money for Reeve's defense. In the local court he was found guilty and condemned to death. The conviction was upheld in a series of appeals through the Alabama courts. The case was appealed to the United States Supreme Court on two occasions. The first time, the Court reversed the decision and turned it back to the State Supreme Court for rehearing. The second time, the United States Supreme Court agreed to hear the case but later dismissed it, thus leaving the Alabama Court free to electrocute. After the failure of a final appeal to the Governor to commute the sentence, the police officials kept their promise. On March 28, 1958, Reeves was electrocuted.

The Reeves case was typical of the unequal justice of Southern courts. In the years that he sat in jail, several white men in Alabama had also been charged with rape; but their accusers were Negro girls. They were seldom arrested; if arrested, they were soon released by the Grand Jury; none was ever brought to trial. For good reason the Negroes of the South had learned to fear and mistrust the white man's justice.

Around the time that I started working with the NAACP the Alabama Council on Human Relations also caught my attention. This interracial group was concerned with human relations in the State of Alabama and employed educational methods to achieve its purpose. An affiliate of the Southern Regional Council, and the successor to the Alabama Inter-Racial Committee, the Council on Human Relations sought to attain through research and action equal opportunity for all the people of Alabama. Its basic philosophy recognized "that all men are created equal under God. Interpreted into the life of our nation, this means that each individual is endowed with the right of equal opportunity to contribute to and share in the life of our nation. No individual or group of individuals has the privilege to limit this right in any way."

I joined this organization, and attended most of the monthly meetings of the Montgomery Chapter, which were held in the meeting room of my church. After working with the Council for a few months I was elected to the office of vice-president, and served in this capacity until other responsibilities intervened. The president of the Council was Rev. Ray Wadley, the young white minister of St. Mark's Methodist Church. A native Southerner, he was later shifted to a small, back-woods community after his congregation protested his activities in the field of race relations. Two other prominent white members of the Council were Revs. Thomas P. Thrasher and Robert Graetz, both of whom were to be prominent in the subsequent bus struggle.

Although the Montgomery Council never had a large membership, it played an important role. As the only truly interracial group in Montgomery, it served to keep the desperately needed channels of communication open between the races. Men often hate each other because they fear each other; they fear each other because they do not know each other; they do not know each other because they cannot communicate; they cannot communicate because they are separated. In providing an avenue of communication, the Council was fulfilling a necessary condition for better race relations in the South.

I was surprised to learn that many people found my dual interest in the NAACP and the Council inconsistent. Many Negroes felt that integration could come only through legislation and court action—the chief emphasis of the NAACP. Many white people felt that integration could come only through education—the chief emphasis of the Council on Human Relations. How could one give his allegiance to two organizations whose approaches and methods seemed so diametrically opposed?

This question betrayed an assumption that there was only one approach to the solution of the race problem. On the contrary I felt that both approaches were necessary. Through education we seek to change attitudes; through legislation and court orders we seek to regulate behavior. Through education we seek to change internal feelings (prejudice, hate, etc.); through legislation and court orders we seek to control the external effects of those feelings. Through education we seek to break down the spiritual barriers to integration; through legislation and court orders we seek to break down the physical barriers to integration. One method is not a substitute for the other, but a meaningful and necessary supplement. Anyone who starts out with the conviction that the road to racial justice is only one lane wide will inevitably create a traffic jam and make the journey infinitely longer. My work with the NAACP and the Alabama Council on Human Relations grew out of the conviction that both organizations met a real need in the community, and each carried out its work at a high level of dignity and wisdom.

As time went on, I discovered several things in the Negro community which needed to be remedied before any real social progress could be effected. First, there was an appalling lack of unity among the leaders. Several civic groups existed, each at loggerheads with the other. There was the organization known as the Progressive Democrats headed by E. D. Nixon. There was the Citizens Committee headed by Rufus Lewis. There was the

Women's Political Council headed by Mrs. Mary Fair Burks and Jo Ann Robinson. There was the NAACP headed by R. L. Matthews. Smaller groups further divided the Negro community. While the heads of each of these organizations were able and dedicated leaders with common aims, their separate allegiances made it difficult for them to come together on the basis of a higher unity.

Many people sensed the effects of this crippling factionalism. Early in 1955 some influential leaders attempted to solve the problem by organizing a group which finally came to be known as the Citizens Coördinating Committee. I can remember the anticipation with which I attended the first meeting of this group, feeling that here the Negro community had an answer to a problem that had stood too long as a stumbling block to social progress. Soon, however, my hopes were shattered. Due to a lack of tenacity on the part of the leaders and of active interest on the part of the citizens in general, the Citizens Coördinating Committee finally dissolved. With the breakdown of this promising undertaking, it appeared that the tragic division in the Negro community could be cured only by some divine miracle.

But not only was the community faced with competing leadership; it was also crippled by the indifference of the educated group. This indifference expressed itself in a lack of participation in any move toward better racial conditions, and a sort of tacit acceptance of things as they were. To be sure, there were always some educated people who stood in the forefront of the struggle for racial justice—but they were exceptions. The vast majority were indifferent and complacent.

Some of this lack of concern had its basis in fear. Many of the educated group were employed in vulnerable positions, and a forthright stand in the area of racial justice might result in the loss of a job. So rather than jeopardize their economic security, many steered clear of any move toward altering the status quo. This, however, was not the whole story. Too much of the inaction was due to sheer apathy. Even in areas—such as voting—where they would not really be accused of tampering with the established order, the educated group had an indifference that for a period appeared incurable.

The apparent apathy of the Negro ministers presented a special problem. A faithful few had always shown a deep concern for social problems, but too many had remained aloof from the area of social responsibility. Much of this indifference, it is true, stemmed from a sincere feeling that ministers were not supposed to get mixed up in such earthly, temporal matters as social and economic improvement; they were to "preach the gospel," and keep men's minds centered on "the heavenly." But however sincere, this view of religion, I felt, was too confined.

Certainly, otherworldly concerns have a deep and significant place in all religions worthy of the name. Any religion that is completely earthbound sells its birthright for a mess of naturalistic pottage. Religion, at its best, deals not only with man's preliminary concerns but with his inescapable ultimate concern. When religion overlooks this basic fact it is reduced to a mere ethical system in which eternity is absorbed into time and God is relegated to a sort of meaningless figment of the human imagination.

But a religion true to its nature must also be concerned about man's social conditions. Religion deals with both earth and heaven, both time and eternity. Religion operates not only on the vertical plane but also on the horizontal. It seeks not only to integrate men with God but to integrate men with men and each man with himself. This means, at bottom, that the Christian gospel is a two-way road. On the one hand it seeks to change the souls of men, and thereby unite them with God; on the other hand it seeks to change the environmental conditions of men so that the soul will have a chance after it is changed. Any religion that professes to be concerned with the souls of men and is not concerned with the slums that damn them, the economic conditions that strangle them, and the social conditions that cripple them is a dry-as-dust religion. Such a religion is the kind the Marxists like to see—an opiate of the people.

Another striking fact about Montgomery's Negro community was the apparent passivity of the majority of the uneducated. While there were always some who struck out against segregation, the largest number accepted it without apparent protest. Not only did they seem resigned to segregation per se; they also accepted the abuses and indignities which came with it. My predecessor at the Dexter Avenue Baptist Church—Rev. Vernon Johns—tells of an incident that illustrates the attitude of the people at this time. One day he boarded a bus and sat in one of the front seats reserved for whites only. The bus driver demanded that he move back. Mr. Johns refused. The operator then ordered him off the bus. Again Mr. Johns refused, until the driver agreed to return his fare. Before leaving, Mr. Johns stood in the aisle and asked how many of his people would follow him off the bus in protest. Not a single person responded. A few days later when he chided a woman who had been on the bus for not joining his protest, she quoted her fellow passengers as saying: "You ought to knowed better."

Some of the passivity of the uneducated could, like that of the educated, be attributed to the fear of economic reprisals. Dependent on the white community, they dared not protest against unjust racial conditions for fear of losing their jobs. But perhaps an even more basic force at work was their corroding sense of inferiority, which often expressed itself in a lack of self-respect. Many unconsciously wondered whether they actually deserved any better conditions. Their minds and souls were so conditioned to the system

of segregation that they submissively adjusted themselves to things as they were. This is the ultimate tragedy of segregation. It not only harms one physically but injures one spiritually. It scars the soul and degrades the personality. It inflicts the segregated with a false sense of inferiority, while confirming the segregator in a false estimate of his own superiority. It is a system which forever stares the segregated in the face, saying: "You are less than . . ." "You are not equal to . . ." The system of segregation itself was responsible for much of the passivity of the Negroes of Montgomery.

So I found the Negro community the victim of a threefold malady—factionalism among the leaders, indifference in the educated group, and passivity in the uneducated. All of these conditions had almost persuaded me that no lasting social reform could ever be achieved in Montgomery.

Beneath the surface, however, there was a ground swell of discontent. Such men as Vernon Johns and E. D. Nixon had never tired of keeping the problem before the conscience of the community. When others had feared to speak, they had spoken with courage. When others had dared not take a stand, they had stood with valor and determination.

Vernon Johns, now the director of Maryland State Baptist Center, was a brilliant preacher with a creative mind and an incredibly retentive memory. It was not unusual for him to quote from the classics of literature and philosophy for hours without ever referring to a manuscript. A fearless man, he never allowed an injustice to come to his attention without speaking out against it. When he was still pastor, hardly a Sunday passed that he did not lash out against complacency. He often chided the congregation for sitting up so proudly with their many academic degrees, and yet lacking the very thing that degrees should confer, that is, self-respect. One of his basic theses was that any individual who submitted willingly to injustice did not really deserve more justice.

Johns loved to farm and live close to nature. He agreed with Booker T. Washington that "no race can prosper till it learns there is as much dignity in tilling a field as in writing a poem." Johns also felt, as Washington did, that the Negro must lift himself by his own bootstraps, and that one of the best ways to do this was by gaining an economic stronghold. Considering it a tragedy that the Negro produced so little of what he consumed, he consistently urged the Negroes of Montgomery to pool their economic resources. As a result, a few enterprising individuals came together in 1953, under Johns's influence, and organized Farm and City Enterprises—a coöperative supermarket which has today developed into a thriving business. This was a *tour de force* in a community that had generally been abysmally slow to move.

Like Vernon Johns, E. D. Nixon had always been a foe of injustice. You could look at the face of this tall, dark-skinned, graying man and tell that he was a fighter. In his work as a Pullman porter—a job he still holds—he was in close contact with organized labor. He had served as state president of the NAACP and also as president of the Montgomery branch. Through each of these mediums E. D. Nixon worked fearlessly to achieve the rights of his people, and to rouse the Negroes from their apathy. Thanks to his efforts, hundreds of Negroes had been encouraged to register at the polls. As the result of his fearless stand, he was one of the chief voices of the Negro community in the area of civil rights, a symbol of the hopes and aspirations of the long oppressed people of the State of Alabama.

So through the work of men like Johns and Nixon there had developed beneath the surface a slow fire of discontent, fed by the continuing indignities and inequities to which the Negroes were subjected. These were the fearless men who created the atmosphere for the social revolution that was slowly developing in the Cradle of the Confederacy.

But this discontent was still latent in 1954. At that time both Negroes and whites accepted the well-established patterns of segregation as a matter of fact. Hardly anyone challenged the system. Montgomery was an easy-going town; it could even have been described as a peaceful town. But the peace was achieved at the cost of human servitude.

Many months later, an influential white citizen of Montgomery was to protest to me:

"Over the years we have had such peaceful and harmonious race relations here. Why have you and your associates come in to destroy this long tradition?"

My reply was simple: "Sir," I said, "you have never had real peace in Montgomery. You have had a sort of negative peace in which the Negro too often accepted his state of subordination. But this is not true peace. True peace is not merely the absence of tension; it is the presence of justice. The tension we see in Montgomery today is the necessary tension that comes when the oppressed rise up and start to move forward toward a permanent, positive peace."

I went on to speculate that this was what Jesus meant when he said: "I have not come to bring peace, but a sword." Certainly Jesus did not mean that he came to bring a physical sword. He seems to have been saying in substance: "I have not come to bring this old negative peace with its deadening passivity. I have come to lash out against such a peace. Whenever I come, a conflict is precipitated between the old and the new. Whenever I come, a division sets in between justice and injustice. I have come to bring a positive peace which is the presence of justice, love, yea, even the Kingdom of God."

The racial peace which had existed in Montgomery was not a Christian peace. It was a pagan peace and it had been bought at too great a price.

One place where the peace had long been precarious was on the city-wide buses. Here the Negro was daily reminded of the indignities of segregation. There were no Negro drivers, and although some of the white men who drove the buses were courteous, all too many were abusive and vituperative. It was not uncommon to hear them referring to Negro passengers as "niggers," "black cows," and "black apes." Frequently Negroes paid their fares at the front door, and then were forced to get off and reboard the bus at the rear. Often the bus pulled off with the Negro's dime in the box before he had had time to reach the rear door.

An even more humiliating practice was the custom of forcing Negroes to stand over empty seats reserved for "whites only." Even if the bus had no white passengers, and Negroes were packed throughout, they were prohibited from sitting in the first four seats (which held ten persons). But the practice went further. If white passengers were already occupying all of their reserved seats and additional white people boarded the bus, Negroes sitting in the unreserved section immediately behind the whites were asked to stand so that the whites could be seated. If the Negroes refused to stand and move back, they were arrested. In most instances the Negroes submitted without protest. Occasionally, however, there were those, like Vernon Johns, who refused.

A few months after my arrival a fifteen-year-old high school girl, Claudette Colvin, was pulled off a bus, handcuffed, and taken to jail because she refused to give up her seat for a white passenger. This atrocity seemed to arouse the Negro community. There was talk of boycotting the buses in protest. A citizens committee was formed to talk with the manager of the bus company and the City Commission, demanding a statement of policy on seating and more courtesy from the drivers.

I was asked to serve on this committee. We met one afternoon in March 1955 in the office of J. E. Bagley, manager of the Montgomery City Lines. Dave Birmingham, the police commissioner at the time, represented the city commission. Both men were quite pleasant, and expressed deep concern over what had happened. Bagley went so far as to admit that the bus operator was wrong in having Miss Colvin arrested, and promised to reprimand him. Commissioner Birmingham agreed to have the city attorney give a definite statement on the seating policy of the city. We left the meeting hopeful; but nothing happened. The same old patterns of humiliation continued. The city attorney never clarified the law. Claudette Colvin was convicted with a suspended sentence.

But despite the fact that the city commission and the bus company did not act, something else had begun to happen. The long repressed feelings of resentment on the part of the Negroes had begun to stir. The fear and apathy which had for so long cast a shadow on the life of the Negro community were gradually fading before a new spirit of courage and self-respect. The inaction of the city and bus officials after the Colvin case would make it necessary for them in a few months to meet another committee, infinitely more determined. Next time they would face a committee supported by the longings and aspirations of nearly 50,000 people, tired people who had come to see that it is ultimately more honorable to walk the streets in dignity than to ride the buses in humiliation.

CHAPTER III

THE DECISIVE ARREST

On December 1, 1955, an attractive Negro seamstress, Mrs. Rosa Parks, boarded the Cleveland Avenue Bus in downtown Montgomery. She was returning home after her regular day's work in the Montgomery Fair —a leading department store. Tired from long hours on her feet, Mrs. Parks sat down in the first seat behind the section reserved for whites. Not long after she took her seat, the bus operator ordered her, along with three other Negro passengers, to move back in order to accommodate boarding white passengers. By this time every seat in the bus was taken. This meant that if Mrs. Parks followed the driver's command she would have to stand while a white male passenger, who had just boarded the bus, would sit. The other three Negro passengers immediately complied with the driver's request. But Mrs. Parks quietly refused. The result was her arrest.

There was to be much speculation about why Mrs. Parks did not obey the driver. Many people in the white community argued that she had been "planted" by the NAACP in order to lay the groundwork for a test case, and at first glance that explanation seemed plausible, since she was a former secretary of the local branch of the NAACP. So persistent and persuasive was this argument that it convinced many reporters from all over the country. Later on, when I was having press conferences three times a week—in order to accommodate the reporters and journalists who came to Montgomery from all over the world—the invariable first question was: "Did the NAACP start the bus boycott?"

But the accusation was totally unwarranted, as the testimony of both Mrs. Parks and the officials of the NAACP revealed. Actually, no one can understand the action of Mrs. Parks unless he realizes that eventually the cup of endurance runs over, and the human personality cries out, "I can take it no longer." Mrs. Parks's refusal to move back was her intrepid affirmation that she had had enough. It was an individual expression of a timeless longing for human dignity and freedom. She was not "planted" there by the NAACP, or any other organization; she was planted there by her personal sense of dignity and self-respect. She was anchored to that seat by the accumulated indignities of days gone by and the boundless aspirations of generations yet unborn. She was a victim of both the forces of history and the forces of destiny. She had been tracked down by the *Zeitgeist*—the spirit of the time.

Fortunately, Mrs. Parks was ideal for the role assigned to her by history. She was a charming person with a radiant personality, soft spoken and calm in all situations. Her character was impeccable and her dedication deep-rooted. All of these traits together made her one of the most respected people in the Negro community.

Only E. D. Nixon—the signer of Mrs. Parks's bond—and one or two other persons were aware of the arrest when it occurred early Thursday evening. Later in the evening the word got around to a few influential women of the community, mostly members of the Women's Political Council. After a series of telephone calls back and forth they agreed that the Negroes should boycott the buses.

They immediately suggested the idea to Nixon, and he readily concurred. In his usual courageous manner he agreed to spearhead the idea.

Early Friday morning, December 2, Nixon called me. He was so caught up in what he was about to say that he forgot to greet me with the usual "hello" but plunged immediately into the story of what had happened to Mrs. Parks the night before. I listened, deeply shocked, as he described the humiliating incident. "We have taken this type of thing too long already," Nixon concluded, his voice trembling. "I feel that the time has come to boycott the buses. Only through a boycott can we make it clear to the white folks that we will not accept this type of treatment any longer."

I agreed at once that some protest was necessary, and that the boycott method would be an effective one.

Just before calling me Nixon had discussed the idea with Rev. Ralph Abernathy, the young minister of Montgomery's First Baptist Church who was to become one of the central figures in the protest, and one of my closest associates. Abernathy also felt a bus boycott was our best course of action. So for thirty or forty minutes the three of us telephoned back and forth concerning plans and strategy. Nixon suggested that we call a meeting of all the ministers and civic leaders the same evening in order to get their thinking on the proposal, and I offered my church as the meeting place. The three of us got busy immediately. With the sanction of Rev. H. H. Hubbard—president of the Baptist Ministerial Alliance—Abernathy and I began calling all of the Baptist ministers. Since most of the Methodist ministers were attending a denominational meeting in one of the local churches that afternoon, it was possible for Abernathy to get the announcement to all of them simultaneously. Nixon reached Mrs. A. W. West—the widow of a prominent dentist—and enlisted her assistance in getting word to the civic leaders.

By early afternoon the arrest of Mrs. Parks was becoming public knowledge. Word of it spread around the community like uncontrolled fire. Telephones began to ring in almost rhythmic succession. By two o'clock an enthusiastic group had mimeographed leaflets concerning the arrest and the proposed boycott, and by evening these had been widely circulated.

As the hour for the evening meeting arrived, I approached the doors of the church with some apprehension, wondering how many of the leaders would respond to our call. Fortunately, it was one of those pleasant winter nights of unseasonable warmth, and to our relief, almost everybody who had been invited was on hand. More than forty people, from every segment of Negro life, were crowded into the large church meeting room.

I saw physicians, schoolteachers, lawyers, businessmen, postal workers, union leaders, and clergymen. Virtually every organization of the Negro community was represented.

The largest number there was from the Christian ministry. Having left so many civic meetings in the past sadly disappointed by the dearth of ministers participating, I was filled with joy when I entered the church and found so many of them there; for then I knew that something unusual was about to happen.

Had E. D. Nixon been present, he would probably have been automatically selected to preside, but he had had to leave town earlier in the afternoon for his regular run on the railroad. In his absence, we concluded that Rev. L. Roy Bennett—as president of the Interdenominational Ministerial Alliance—was the logical person to take the chair. He agreed and was seated, his tall, erect figure dominating the room.

The meeting opened around seven-thirty with H. H. Hubbard leading a brief devotional period. Then Bennett moved into action, explaining the purpose of the gathering. With excited gestures he reported on Mrs. Parks's resistance and her arrest. He presented the proposal that the Negro citizens of Montgomery should boycott the buses on Monday in protest. "Now is the time to move," he concluded. "This is no time to talk; it is time to act."

So seriously did Bennett take his "no time to talk" admonition that for quite a while he refused to allow anyone to make a suggestion or even raise a question, insisting that we should move on and appoint committees to implement the proposal. This approach aroused the opposition of most of those present, and created a temporary uproar. For almost forty-five minutes the confusion persisted. Voices rose high, and many people threatened to leave if they could not raise questions and offer suggestions. It looked for a time as though the movement had come to an end before it began. But finally, in the face of this blistering protest, Bennett agreed to open the meeting to discussion.

Immediately questions began to spring up from the floor. Several people wanted further clarification of Mrs. Parks's actions and arrest. Then came the more practical questions. How long would the protest last? How would the idea be further disseminated throughout the community? How would the people be transported to and from their jobs?

As we listened to the lively discussion, we were heartened to notice that, despite the lack of coherence in the meeting, not once did anyone question the validity or desirability of the boycott itself. It seemed to be the unanimous sense of the group that the boycott should take place.

The ministers endorsed the plan with enthusiasm, and promised to go to their congregations on Sunday morning and drive home their approval of the projected one-day protest. Their coöperation was significant, since virtually all of the influential Negro ministers of the city were present. It was decided that we should hold a city-wide mass meeting on Monday night, December 5, to determine how long we would abstain from riding the buses. Rev. A. W. Wilson—minister of the

The fingerprinting of Mrs. Rosa Parks, whose refusal to move back in a bus and subsequent arrest touched off the Montgomery bus protest. *"She was anchored to that seat by the accumulated indignities of days gone by and the boundless aspirations of generations yet unborn."*

Holt Street Baptist Church—offered his church, which was ideal as a meeting place because of its size and central location. The group agreed that additional leaflets should be distributed on Saturday, and the chairman appointed a committee, including myself, to prepare the statement.

Our committee went to work while the meeting was still in progress. The final message was shorter than the one that had appeared on the first leaflets, but the substance was the same. It read as follows:

Don't ride the bus to work, to town, to school, or any place Monday, December 5.

Another Negro woman has been arrested and put in jail because she refused to give up her bus seat.

Don't ride the buses to work, to town, to school, or anywhere on Monday. If you work, take a cab, or share a ride, or walk.

Come to a mass meeting, Monday at 7:00 P.M., at the Holt Street Baptist Church for further instruction.

After finishing the statement the committee began to mimeograph it on the church machine; but since it was late, I volunteered to have the job completed early Saturday morning.

The final question before the meeting concerned transportation. It was agreed that we should try to get the Negro taxi companies of the city—eighteen in number, with approximately 210 taxis—to transport the people for the same price that they were currently paying on the bus. A committee was appointed to make this contact, with Rev. W. J. Powell, minister of the Old Ship A.M.E. Zion Church, as chairman.

With these responsibilities before us the meeting closed. We left with our hearts caught up in a great idea. The hours were moving fast. The clock on the wall read almost midnight, but the clock in our souls revealed that it was daybreak.

I was so excited that I slept very little that night, and early the next morning I was on my way to the church to get the leaflets out. By nine o'clock the church secretary had finished mimeographing the 7000 leaflets and by eleven o'clock an army of women and young people had taken them off to distribute by hand.

Those on the committee that was to contact the taxi companies got to work early Saturday afternoon. They worked assiduously, and by evening they had reached practically all of the companies, and triumphantly reported that everyone of them so far had agreed to coöperate with the proposed boycott by transporting the passengers to and from work for the regular ten-cent bus fare.

Meanwhile our efforts to get the word across to the Negro community were abetted in an unexpected way. A maid who could not read very well came into possession of one of the unsigned appeals that had been distributed Friday afternoon. Apparently not knowing what the leaflet said, she gave it to her employer. As soon as the white employer received the notice she turned it over to the local newspaper, and the *Montgomery Advertiser* made the contents of the leaflet a front-page story on Saturday morning. It appears that the *Advertiser* printed the story in order to let the white community know what the Negroes were up to; but the whole thing turned out to the Negroes' advantage, since it served to bring the information to hundreds who had not previously heard of the plan. By Sunday afternoon word had spread to practically every Negro citizen of Montgomery. Only a few people who lived in remote areas had not heard of it.

After a heavy day of work, I went home late Sunday afternoon and sat down to read the morning paper. There was a long article on the proposed boycott. Implicit throughout the article, I noticed, was the idea that the Negroes were preparing to use the same approach to their problem as the White Citizens Councils used. This suggested parallel had serious implications. The White Citizens Councils, which had had their birth in Mississippi a few months after the Supreme Court's school decision, had come into being to preserve segregation. The Councils had multiplied rapidly throughout the South, purporting to achieve their ends by the legal maneuvers of "interposition" and "nullification." Unfortunately, however, the actions of some of these Councils extended far beyond the bounds of the law. Their methods were the methods of open and covert terror, brutal intimidation, and threats of starvation to Negro men, women, and children. They took open economic reprisals against whites who dared to protest their defiance of the law, and the aim of their boycotts was not merely to impress their victims but to destroy them if possible.

Disturbed by the fact that our pending action was being equated with the boycott methods of the White Citizens Councils, I was forced for the first time to think seriously on the nature of the boycott. Up to this time I had uncritically accepted this method as our best course of action. Now certain doubts began to bother me. Were we following an ethi-

E. D. Nixon, veteran fighter for the cause of justice in Montgomery, who proposed the protest ". . . 'I feel that the time has come to boycott the buses. Only through a boycott can we make it clear to the white folks that we will not accept this type treatment any longer.' "

cal course of action? Is the boycott method basically unchristian? Isn't it a negative approach to the solution of a problem? Is it true that we would be following the course of some of the White Citizens Councils? Even if lasting practical results came from such a boycott, would immoral means justify moral ends? Each of these questions demanded honest answers.

I had to recognize that the boycott method could be used to unethical and unchristian ends. I had to concede, further, that this was the method used so often by the White Citizens Councils to deprive many Negroes, as well as white persons of good will, of the basic necessities of life. But certainly, I said to myself, our pending actions could not be interpreted in this light. Our purposes were altogether different. We would use this method to give birth to justice and freedom, and also to urge men to comply with the law of the land; the White Citizens Councils used it to perpetuate the reign of injustice and human servitude, and urged men to defy the law of the land. I reasoned, therefore, that the word "boycott" was really a misnomer for our proposed action. A boycott suggests an economic squeeze, leaving one bogged down in a negative. But we were concerned with the positive. Our concern would not be to put the bus company out of business, but to put justice in business.

As I thought further I came to see that what we were really doing was withdrawing our coöperation from an evil system, rather than merely withdrawing our economic support from the bus company. The bus company, being an external expression of the system, would naturally suffer, but the basic aim was to refuse to coöperate with evil. At this point I began to think about Thoreau's *Essay on Civil Disobedience*. I remembered how, as a college student, I had been moved when I first read this work. I became convinced that what we were preparing to do in Montgomery was related to what Thoreau had expressed. We were simply saying to the white community, "We can no longer lend our coöperation to an evil system."

Something began to say to me, "He who passively accepts evil is as much involved in it as he who helps to perpetrate it. He who accepts evil without protesting against it is really coöperating with it." When oppressed people willingly accept their oppression they only serve to give the oppressor a convenient justification for his acts. Often the oppressor goes along unaware of the evil involved in his oppression so long as the oppressed accepts it. So in order to be true to one's conscience and true to God, a righteous man has no alternative but to refuse to coöperate with an evil system. This I felt was the nature of our action. From this moment on I conceived of our movement as an act of massive non-coöperation. From then on I rarely used the word "boycott."

Wearied, but no longer doubtful about the morality of our proposed protest, I saw that the evening had arrived unnoticed. After several telephone calls I prepared to retire early. But soon after I was in bed our two-week-old daughter—Yolanda Denise—began crying; and shortly after that the telephone started ringing again. Clearly condemned to stay awake for some time longer, I used the time to think about other things. My wife and I discussed the possible success of the protest. Frankly, I still had doubts. Even though the word had gotten around amazingly well and the ministers had given the plan such crucial support, I still wondered whether the people had enough courage to follow through. I had seen so many admirable ventures fall through in Montgomery. Why should this be an exception? Coretta and I finally agreed that if we could get 60 percent coöperation the protest would be a success.

Around midnight a call from one of the committee members informed me that every Negro taxi company in Montgomery had agreed to support the protest on Monday morning. Whatever our prospects of success, I was deeply encouraged by the untiring work that had been done by the ministers and civic leaders. This in itself was a unique accomplishment.

After the midnight call the phone stopped ringing. Just a few minutes earlier "Yoki" had stopped crying. Wearily, I said good night to Coretta, and with a strange mixture of hope and anxiety, I fell asleep.

CHAPTER IV

THE DAY OF DAYS,

DECEMBER 5

MY WIFE AND I awoke earlier than usual on Monday morning. We were up and fully dressed by five-thirty. The day for the protest had arrived, and we were determined to see the first act of this unfolding drama. I was still saying that if we could get 60 percent coöperation the venture would be a success.

Fortunately, a bus stop was just five feet from our house. This meant that we could observe the opening stages from our front window. The first bus was to pass around six o'clock. And so we waited through an interminable half hour. I was in the kitchen drinking my coffee when I heard Coretta cry, "Martin, Martin, come quickly!" I put down my cup and ran toward the living room. As I approached the front window Coretta pointed joyfully to a slowly moving bus: "Darling, it's empty!" I could hardly believe what I saw. I knew that the South Jackson line, which ran past our house, carried more Negro passengers than any other line in Montgomery, and that this first bus was usually filled with domestic workers going to their jobs. Would all of the other buses follow the pattern that had been set by the first? Eagerly we waited for the next bus. In fifteen minutes it rolled down the street, and, like the first, it was empty. A third bus appeared, and it too was empty of all but two white passengers.

I jumped in my car and for almost an hour I cruised down every major street and examined every passing bus. During this hour, at the peak of the morning traffic, I saw no more than eight Negro passengers riding the buses. By this time I was jubilant. Instead of the 60 percent coöperation we had hoped for, it was becoming apparent that we had reached almost 100 percent. A miracle had taken place. The once dormant and quiescent Negro community was now fully awake.

All day long it continued. At the afternoon peak the buses were still as empty of Negro passengers as they had been in the morning. Students of Alabama State College, who usually kept the South Jackson bus crowded, were cheerfully walking or thumbing rides. Job holders had either found other means of transportation or made their way on foot. While some rode in cabs or private cars, others used less conventional means. Men were seen riding mules to work, and more than one horse-drawn buggy drove the streets of Montgomery that day.

During the rush hours the sidewalks were crowded with laborers and domestic workers, many of them well past middle age, trudging patiently to their jobs and home again, sometimes as much as twelve miles. They knew why they walked, and the knowledge was evident in the way they carried themselves. And as I watched them I knew that there is nothing more majestic than the determined cour-

age of individuals willing to suffer and sacrifice for their freedom and dignity.

Many spectators had gathered at the bus stops to watch what was happening. At first they stood quietly, but as the day progressed they began to cheer the empty buses and laugh and make jokes. Noisy youngsters

Week after week, crowds like the one below came together to sing and pray, to renew their courage, and to hear suggestions from their leaders. *"If you will protest courageously, and yet with dignity and Christian love, when the history books are written in future generations, the historians will have to pause and say, 'There lived a great people—a black people—who injected new meaning and dignity into the views of civilization.'"*

could be heard singing out, "No riders today." Trailing each bus through the Negro section were two policemen on motorcycles, assigned by the city commissioners, who claimed that Negro "goon squads" had been organized to keep other Negroes from riding the buses. In the course of the day the police succeeded in making one arrest. A college student who was helping an elderly woman across the street was charged with "intimidating passengers." But the "goon squads" existed only in the commission's imagination. No one was threatened or intimidated for riding the buses; the only harassment anyone faced was that of his own conscience.

Around nine-thirty in the morning I tore myself from the action of the city streets and headed for the crowded police court. Here Mrs. Parks was being tried for disobeying the city segregation ordinance. Her attorney, Fred D. Gray—the brilliant young Negro who later became the chief counsel for the protest movement—was on hand to defend her. After the judge heard the arguments, he found Mrs. Parks guilty and fined her ten dollars and court costs (a total of fourteen dollars). She appealed the case. This was one of the first clear-cut instances in which a Negro had been convicted for disobeying the segregation law. In the past, either cases like this had been dismissed or the people involved had been charged with disorderly conduct. So in a real sense the arrest and conviction of Mrs. Parks had a twofold impact: it was a precipitating factor to arouse the Negroes to positive action; and it was a test of the validity of the segregation law itself. I am sure that supporters of such prosecutions would have acted otherwise if they had had the prescience to look beyond the moment.

E. D. Nixon, and Rev. E. N. French—then minister of the Hilliard Chapel A.M.E. Zion Church—discussed the need for some organization to guide and direct the protest. Up to this time things had moved forward more or less spontaneously. These men were wise enough to see that the moment had now come for a clearer order and direction.

Meanwhile Roy Bennett had called several people together at three o'clock to make plans for the evening mass meeting. Everyone present was elated by the tremendous success that had already attended the protest. But beneath this feeling was the question, where do we go from here? When E. D. Nixon reported on his discussion with Abernathy and French earlier in the day, and their suggestions for an *ad hoc* organization, the group responded enthusiastically. The next job was to elect the officers for the new organization.

As soon as Bennett had opened the nominations for president, Rufus Lewis spoke from the far corner of the room: "Mr. Chairman, I would like to nominate Reverend M. L. King for president." The motion was seconded and carried, and in a matter of minutes I was unanimously elected.

The action had caught me unawares. It had happened so quickly that I did not even have time to think it through. It is probable that if I had, I would have declined the nomination. Just three weeks before, several members of the local chapter of the NAACP had urged me to run for the presidency of that organization, assuring me that I was certain of election. After my wife and I had discussed the matter, we agreed that I should not then take on any heavy community responsibili-

Leaving Mrs. Parks's trial, Ralph Abernathy,

Ralph Abernathy, ". . . *the young minister of Montgomery's First Baptist Church who was to become one of the central figures in the protest, and one of my closest associates.*"

ties, since I had so recently finished my thesis, and needed to give more attention to my church work. But on this occasion events had moved too fast.

The election of the remaining officers was speedily completed: Rev. L. Roy Bennett, vice-president; Rev. U. J. Fields, recording secretary; Rev. E. N. French, corresponding secretary; Mrs. Erna A. Dungee, financial secretary; Mr. E. D. Nixon, treasurer. It was then agreed that all those present would con-

M. L. King, Robert Graetz and Ralph Abernathy in prayer. *". . . an early recruit to the executive committee was Rev. Robert Graetz . . . This boyish-looking white minister of the Negro Trinity Lutheran Church was a constant reminder to us in the trying months of the protest that many white people as well as Negroes were applying the 'love-thy-neighbor-as-thyself' teachings . . ."*

stitute the executive board of the new organization. This board would serve as the coördinating agency of the whole movement. It was a well-balanced group, including ministers of all denominations, schoolteachers, businessmen, and two lawyers.

The new organization needed a name, and several were suggested. Someone proposed the Negro Citizens Committee; but this was rejected because it resembled too closely the White Citizens Council. Other suggestions were made and dismissed until finally Ralph Abernathy offered a name that was agreeable to all—the Montgomery Improvement Association (MIA).

With these organizational matters behind us, we turned to a discussion of the evening meeting. Several people, not wanting the re-

porters to know our future moves, suggested that we just sing and pray; if there were specific recommendations to be made to the people, these could be mimeographed and passed out secretly during the meeting. This, they felt, would leave the reporters in the dark. Others urged that something should be done to conceal the true identity of the leaders, feeling that if no particular name was revealed it would be safer for all involved. After a rather lengthy discussion, E. D. Nixon rose impatiently:

"We are acting like little boys," he said. "Somebody's name will have to be known, and if we are afraid we might just as well fold up right now. We must also be men enough to discuss our recommendations in the open; this idea of secretly passing something around on paper is a lot of bunk. The white folks are eventually going to find it out anyway. We'd better decide now if we are going to be fearless men or scared boys."

With this forthright statement the air was cleared. Nobody would again suggest that we try to conceal our identity or avoid facing the issue head on. Nixon's courageous affirmation had given new heart to those who were about to be crippled by fear.

It was unanimously agreed that the protest should continue until certain demands were met, and that a committee under the chairmanship of Ralph Abernathy would draw up these demands in the form of a resolution and present them to the evening mass meeting for approval. We worked out the remainder of the program quickly. Bennett would preside and I would make the main address. Remarks by a few other speakers, along with Scripture reading, prayer, hymns, and collection, would round out the program.

Immediately the resolution committee set to drafting its statement. Despite our satisfaction at the success of the protest so far, we were still concerned. Would the evening meeting be well attended? Could we hope that the fortitude and enthusiasm of the Negro community would survive more than one such day of hardship? Someone suggested that perhaps we should reconsider our decision to continue the protest. "Would it not be better," said the speaker, "to call off the protest while it is still a success rather than let it go on a few more days and fizzle out? We have already proved our united strength to the white community. If we stop now we can get anything we want from the bus company, simply because they will have the feeling that we can do it again. But if we continue, and most of the people return to the buses tomorrow or the next day, the white people will laugh at us, and we will end up getting nothing." This argument was so convincing that we almost resolved to end the protest. But we finally agreed to let the mass meeting—which was only about an hour off—be our guide. If the meeting was well attended and the people were enthusiastic, we would continue; otherwise we would call off the protest that night.

I went home for the first time since seven that morning, and found Coretta relaxing from a long day of telephone calls and general excitement. After we had brought each other up to date on the day's developments, I told her, somewhat hesitantly—not knowing what her reaction would be—that I had been elected president of the new association. I need not have worried. Naturally surprised, she still saw that since the responsibility had fallen on me, I had no alternative but to accept it. She did not need to be told that we would now have even less time together, and she seemed undisturbed at the possible danger to all of us in my new position. "You know," she said quietly, "that whatever you do, you have my backing."

Reassured, I went to my study and closed the door. The minutes were passing fast. It was now six-thirty, and I had to leave no later than six-fifty to get to the meeting. This meant that I had only twenty minutes to prepare the most decisive speech of my life. As I thought of the limited time before me and the possible implications of this speech, I became possessed by fear. Each week I needed at least fifteen hours to prepare my Sunday sermon. Now I was faced with the inescapable task of preparing, in almost no time at all, a speech that was expected to give a sense of direction to a people imbued with a new and still unplumbed passion for justice. I was also conscious that reporters and television men would be there with their pencils and sound cameras poised to record my words and send them across the nation.

I was now almost overcome, obsessed by a feeling of inadequacy. In this state of anxiety, I had already wasted five minutes of the original twenty. With nothing left but faith in a power whose matchless strength stands over against the frailties and inadequacies of human nature, I turned to God in prayer. My words were brief and simple, asking God to restore my balance and to be with me in a time when I needed His guidance more than ever.

With less than fifteen minutes left, I began preparing an outline. In the midst of this, however, I faced a new and sobering dilemma: How could I make a speech that would be militant enough to keep my people aroused to positive action and yet moderate enough to keep this fervor within controllable and Christian bounds? I knew that many of the Negro people were victims of bitterness that could easily rise to flood proportions. What could I say to keep them courageous and prepared for positive action and yet devoid of hate and resentment? Could the militant and the moderate be combined in a single speech?

I decided that I had to face the challenge head on, and attempt to combine two apparent irreconcilables. I would seek to arouse the group to action by insisting that their self-respect was at stake and that if they accepted such injustices without protesting, they would betray their own sense of dignity and the eternal edicts of God Himself. But I would balance this with a strong affirmation of the Christian doctrine of love. By the time I had sketched an outline of the speech in my mind, my time was up. Without stopping to eat supper (I had not eaten since morning) I said good-by to Coretta and drove to the Holt Street Church.

Within five blocks of the church I noticed a traffic jam. Cars were lined up as far as I could see on both sides of the street. It was a moment before it occurred to me that all of these cars were headed for the mass meeting. I had to park at least four blocks from the church, and as I started walking I noticed that hundreds of people were standing outside. In the dark night, police cars circled

M. L. King and a supporter. *"I could hear voices saying: 'We are with you all the way, Reverend.'"*

slowly around the area, surveying the orderly, patient, and good-humored crowd. The three or four thousand people who could not get into the church were to stand cheerfully throughout the evening listening to the proceedings on the loud-speakers that had been set up outside for their benefit. And when, near the end of the meeting, these speakers were silenced at the request of the white people in surrounding neighborhoods, the crowd would still remain quietly, content simply to be present.

It took fully fifteen minutes to push my way through to the pastor's study, where Dr.

Wilson told me that the church had been packed since five o'clock. By now my doubts concerning the continued success of our venture were dispelled. The question of calling off the protest was now academic. The enthusiasm of these thousands of people swept everything along like an onrushing tidal wave.

It was some time before the remaining speakers could push their way to the rostrum through the tightly packed church. When the meeting began it was almost half an hour late. The opening hymn was the old familiar "Onward Christian Soldiers," and when that mammoth audience stood to sing, the voices outside swelling the chorus in the church, there was a mighty ring like the glad echo of heaven itself.

Rev. W. F. Alford, minister of the Beulah Baptist Church, led the congregation in prayer, followed by a reading of the Scripture by Rev. U. J. Fields, minister of the Bell Street Baptist Church. Then the chairman in-

troduced me. As the audience applauded, I rose and stood before the pulpit. Television cameras began to shoot from all sides. The crowd grew quiet.

Without manuscript or notes, I told the story of what had happened to Mrs. Parks. Then I reviewed the long history of abuses and insults that Negro citizens had experienced on the city buses. "But there comes a time," I said, "that people get tired. We are here this evening to say to those who have mistreated us so long that we are tired—tired of being segregated and humiliated; tired of being kicked about by the brutal feet of oppression." The congregation met this statement with fervent applause. "We had no alternative but to protest," I continued. "For

At a central pickup station, Negroes, young and old, wait to be driven home in the voluntary car pool. *"The once dormant and quiescent Negro community was now fully awake . . . as I watched them I knew that there is nothing more majestic than the determined courage of individuals willing to suffer and sacrifice for their freedom and dignity."*

many years, we have shown amazing patience. We have sometimes given our white brothers the feeling that we liked the way we were being treated. But we come here tonight to be saved from that patience that makes us patient with anything less than freedom and justice." Again the audience interrupted with applause.

Briefly I justified our actions, both morally and legally. "One of the great glories of democracy is the right to protest for right." Comparing our methods with those of the White Citizens Councils and the Ku Klux Klan, I pointed out that while "these organizations are protesting for the perpetuation of injustice in the community, we are protesting for the birth of justice in the community. Their methods lead to violence and lawlessness. But in our protest there will be no cross burnings. No white person will be taken from his home by a hooded Negro mob and brutally murdered. There will be no threats and intimidation. We will be guided by the highest principles of law and order."

With this groundwork for militant action, I moved on to words of caution. I urged the people not to force anybody to refrain from riding the buses. "Our method will be that of persuasion, not coercion. We will only say to the people, 'Let your conscience be your guide.' " Emphasizing the Christian doctrine of love, "our actions must be guided by the deepest principles of our Christian faith. Love must be our regulating ideal. Once again we must hear the words of Jesus echoing across the centuries: 'Love your enemies, bless them that curse you, and pray for them that despitefully use you.' If we fail to do this our protest will end up as a meaningless drama on the stage of history, and its memory will be shrouded with the ugly garments of shame. In spite of the mistreatment that we have confronted we must not become bitter,

and end up by hating our white brothers. As Booker T. Washington said, 'Let no man pull you so low as to make you hate him.' " Once more the audience responded enthusiastically.

Then came my closing statement. "If you will protest courageously, and yet with dignity and Christian love, when the history books are written in future generations, the historians will have to pause and say, 'There lived a great people—a black people—who injected new meaning and dignity into the veins of civilization.' This is our challenge and our overwhelming responsibility." As I took my seat the people rose to their feet and applauded. I was thankful to God that the message had gotten over and that the task of combining the militant and the moderate had been at least partially accomplished. The people had been as enthusiastic when I urged them to love as they were when I urged them to protest.

As I sat listening to the continued applause I realized that this speech had evoked more response than any speech or sermon I had ever delivered, and yet it was virtually unprepared. I came to see for the first time what the older preachers meant when they said, "Open your mouth and God will speak for you." While I would not let this experience tempt me to overlook the need for continued preparation, it would always remind me that God can transform man's weakness into his glorious opportunity.

When Mrs. Parks was introduced from the rostrum by E. N. French, the audience responded by giving her a standing ovation. She was their heroine. They saw in her courageous person the symbol of their hopes and aspirations.

Now the time had come for the all-important resolution. Ralph Abernathy read the words slowly and forcefully. The main substance of the resolution called upon the Negroes not to resume riding the buses until (1) courteous treatment by the bus operators was guaranteed; (2) passengers were seated on a first-come, first-served basis—Negroes seated from the back of the bus toward the front while whites seated from the front toward the back; (3) Negro bus operators were employed on predominantly Negro routes. At the words "All in favor of the motion stand," every person to a man stood up, and those who were already standing raised their hands. Cheers began to ring out from both inside and outside. The motion was carried unanimously. The people had expressed their determination not to ride the buses until conditions were changed.

At this point I had to leave the meeting and rush to the other side of town to speak at a YMCA banquet. As I drove away my heart was full. I had never seen such enthusiasm for freedom. And yet this enthusiasm was tempered by amazing self-discipline. The unity of purpose and *esprit de corps* of these people had been indescribably moving. No historian would ever be able fully to describe this meeting and no sociologist would ever be able to interpret it adequately. One had to be a part of the experience really to understand it.

At the Ben Moore Hotel, as the elevator slowly moved up to the roof garden where the banquet was being held, I said to myself, the victory is already won, no matter how long we struggle to attain the three points of the resolution. It is a victory infinitely larger than the bus situation. The real victory was in the mass meeting, where thousands of black people stood revealed with a new sense of dignity and destiny.

Many will inevitably raise the question, why did this event take place in Montgomery, Alabama, in 1955? Some have suggested that the Supreme Court decision on school desegregation, handed down less than two years before, had given new hope of eventual justice to Negroes everywhere, and fired them with the necessary spark of encouragement to rise against their oppression. But although this might help to explain why the protest occurred when it did, it cannot explain why it happened in Montgomery.

Certainly, there is a partial explanation in the long history of injustice on the buses of Montgomery. The bus protest did not spring into being full grown as Athena sprang from the head of Zeus; it was the culmination of a slowly developing process. Mrs. Parks's arrest was the precipitating factor rather than the cause of the protest. The cause lay deep in the record of similar injustices. Almost everybody could point to an unfortunate episode that he himself had experienced or seen.

But there comes a time when people get tired of being trampled by oppression. There comes a time when people get tired of being plunged into the abyss of exploitation and nagging injustice. The story of Montgomery is the story of 50,000 such Negroes who were willing to substitute tired feet for tired souls, and walk the streets of Montgomery until the walls of segregation were finally battered by the forces of justice.

But neither is this the whole explanation. Negroes in other communities confronted conditions equally as bad, and often worse. So we cannot explain the Montgomery story merely in terms of the abuses that Negroes suffered there. Moreover, it cannot be explained by a preëxistent unity among the leaders, since we have seen that the Montgomery Negro community prior to the protest was marked by divided leadership, indifference, and complacency. Nor can it be explained by the appearance upon the scene of new leadership. The Montgomery story would have taken place if the leaders of the protest had never been born.

So every rational explanation breaks down at some point. There is something about the protest that is suprarational; it cannot be explained without a divine dimension. Some may call it a principle of concretion, with Alfred N. Whitehead; or a process of integration, with Henry N. Wieman; or Being-itself, with Paul Tillich; or a personal God. Whatever the name, some extrahuman force labors to create a harmony out of the discords of the universe. There is a creative power that works to pull down mountains of evil and level hilltops of injustice. God still works through history His wonders to perform. It seems as though God had decided to use Montgomery as the proving ground for the struggle and triumph of freedom and justice in America. And what better place for it than the leading symbol of the Old South? It is one of the splendid ironies of our day that Montgomery, the Cradle of the Confederacy, is being transformed into Montgomery, the cradle of freedom and justice.

The day of days, Monday, December 5, 1955, was drawing to a close. We all prepared to go to our homes, not yet fully aware of what had happened. The deliberations of that brisk, cool night in December will not be forgotten. That night we were starting a movement that would gain national recognition; whose echoes would ring in the ears of people of every nation; a movement that would astound the oppressor, and bring new hope to the oppressed. That night was Montgomery's moment in history.

A bus in operation during the protest. *"I could hardly believe what I saw . . . Instead of the 60 percent cooperation we had hoped for, it was becoming apparent that we had reached almost 100 percent."*

CHAPTER V

THE MOVEMENT GATHERS MOMENTUM

AFTER ASCENDING the mountain on Monday night, I woke up Tuesday morning urgently aware that I had to leave the heights and come back to earth. I was faced with a number of organizational decisions. The movement could no longer continue without careful planning.

I began to think of the various committees necessary to give the movement guidance and direction. First we needed a more permanent transportation committee, since the problem of getting the ex-bus riders about the city was paramount. I knew that we could not work out any system that would solve all the transportation problems of the nearly 17,500 Negroes who had formerly ridden the buses twice daily; even the most effective system that we could devise would still leave almost everyone walking a little more than he had done formerly. But a well-worked-out system could do a good deal to alleviate the problem.

We would also need to raise money to carry on the protest. Therefore, a finance committee was necessary. Since we would be having regular mass meetings, there must be a program committee for these occasions. And then, I reasoned, from time to time strategic decisions would have to be made; we needed the best minds of the association to think them through and then make recommendations to the executive board. So I felt that a strategy committee was essential.

With all of these things in mind I called a meeting of the executive board for Wednesday at ten o'clock in one of the larger rooms of the Alabama Negro Baptist Center. Every board member was present to applaud the report that after almost two and a half days the protest was still more than 99 percent effective. There followed the appointment of the various committees. Because of the relatively small number on the executive board, it was necessary to place several people on more than one committee. As in all organizations, the problem of conflicting egos was involved, and the selections were guided by the desire to assure that the people on each committee could work well together. Rufus Lewis agreed to be chairman of the transportation committee, and Rev. R. J. Glasco, our host for the morning, chairman of the finance committee. The executive board was expanded to make it a broad cross section of the Negro community. (See 'MONTGOMERY IMPROVEMENT ASSOCIATION' for list of members of the executive board and its committees.)

The members of the strategy committee were appointed a few days later. This new committee brought together a dozen men and women who had already provided strong leadership in the early days of the protest, and whose clear thinking and courageous guidance were to be the inestimable help in the difficult decisions that still lay ahead. Besides the indispensable E. D. Nixon and our brilliant legal strategist, Fred Gray, the committee included Roy Bennett, who had chaired the first meeting to organize the protest and was to continue to give the movement his loyal support until he was transferred to a pastorate in California. H. H. Hubbard and A. W. Wilson, both Baptist ministers, represented the largest Negro congregations in Montgomery. Hubbard's stately presence brought a sense of security to every meeting that he attended; and his colleague, Wilson, who has held key positions in the Alabama Baptist State Convention, contributed his fine talent as an organizer and administrator.

Mrs. Euretta Adair, the wife of a prominent Montgomery physician, was a one-time faculty member of Tuskegee Institute who combined a rich academic background with a passion for social betterment. The current academic world was represented by Jo Ann Robinson and J. E. Pierce, both faculty members of Alabama State College, who had never allowed their secure positions to make them indifferent to the problems of the people. Rufus Lewis, a businessman who had also had a long interest in the Negroes' struggle for first-class citizenship, was to display his conscientiousness and coöperative spirit as first chairman of the transportation committee. When, after several months, the need for extending the MIA's activities into such areas as voting became apparent, he took the chairmanship of the new registration and voting committee, a responsibility which he still holds.

W. J. Powell and S. S. Seay, like Bennett, were ministers of the A.M.E. Zion Church. Powell brought a cool head and an even temper to the problems that confronted the strategy committee in these tempestuous days. S. S. Seay's was one of the few clerical voices that, in the years preceding the protest, had

lashed out against the injustices heaped on the Negro, and urged his people to a greater appreciation of their own worth. A dynamic preacher, his addresses from time to time at the weekly mass meetings raised the spirits of all who heard him.

The final member of the strategy committee was already in the forefront of the forces of protest. Ralph Abernathy was another of the few Negro clergymen who had long been active in civic affairs. Although he was then only twenty-nine, his devotion to the cause of freedom was already beyond question. With his short, stocky frame and his thoughtful expression, he looked older than his years. But a boyish smile always lurked beneath the surface of his face. Ralph's slow movements and slow, easy talk were deceptive. For he was an indefatigable worker and a sound thinker, possessed of a fertile mind. As a speaker, he was persuasive and dynamic, with the gift of laughing people into positive action. When things became languid around the mass meetings, Ralph Abernathy infused his audiences with new life and ardor. The people loved and respected him as a symbol of courage and strength.

From the beginning of the protest Ralph Abernathy was my closest associate and most trusted friend. We prayed together and made important decisions together. His ready good humor lightened many tense moments. Whenever I went out of town I always left him in charge of the important business of the association, knowing that it was in safe hands. After Bennett left Montgomery, Ralph became first vice-president of the MIA, and has held that position ever since with dignity and efficiency.

These were the people with whom, from the beginning, I worked most closely. As time went on others were added. Among these, an early recruit to the executive committee was Rev. Robert Graetz, whom I had first met in

the Council on Human Relations. This boyish-looking white minister of the Negro Trinity Lutheran Church was a constant reminder to us in the trying months of the protest that many white people as well as Negroes were applying the "love-thy-neighbor-as-thyself" teachings of Christianity in their daily lives. Other close associates who were later added to the board were Clarence W. Lee, a tall distinguished-looking mortician, whose sound business ability became a great asset to the organization, and Moses W. Jones, a prominent physician, who later became the second vice-president of the MIA.

We met at all hours, whenever a new emergency demanded attention. It was not unusual to find some of us talking things over in one of our homes at two-thirty in the morning. While our wives plied us with coffee, and joined the informal discussion, we laid plans and arrived at agreements on policy. No parliamentary rules were necessary in this small group; the rule of the majority was tacitly accepted.

In the early stages of the protest the problem of transportation demanded most of our attention. The labor and ingenuity that went into that task is one of the most interesting sides of the Montgomery story. For the first few days we had depended on the Negro taxi companies who had agreed to transport the people for the same ten-cent fare that they paid on the buses. Except for a few private cars that had been volunteered, these taxis had provided the only transportation. But during the first "negotiation meeting" that we were to hold with the city commission on

The protest leaders meet often and at all hours. S. S. Seay, H. H. Hubbard, M. L. King, and R. J. Glasco carry on at the end of an Executive Board meeting.

Thursday, December 8, Police Commissioner Sellers mentioned in passing that there was a law that limited the taxis to a minimum fare. I caught this hint and realized that Commissioner Sellers would probably use this point to stop the taxis from assisting in the protest.

At that moment I remembered that some time previously my good friend Rev. Theodore Jemison had led a bus boycott in Baton Rouge, Louisiana. Knowing that Jemison and his associates had set up an effective private car pool, I put in a long-distance call to ask him for suggestions for a similar pool in Montgomery. As I expected, his painstaking description of the Baton Rouge experience was invaluable. I passed on word of Sellers' remark and Jemison's advice to the transportation committee and suggested that we immediately begin setting up a pool in order to offset the confusion which could come if the taxis were eliminated from service.

Fortunately, a mass meeting was being held that night. There I asked all those who were willing to offer their cars to give us their names, addresses, telephone numbers, and the hours that they could drive, before leaving the meeting. The response was tremendous. More than a hundred and fifty signed slips volunteering their automobiles. Some who were not working offered to drive in the car pool all day; others volunteered a few hours before and after work. Practically all of the ministers offered to drive whenever they were needed.

On Friday afternoon, as I had predicted, the police commissioner issued an order to all of the cab companies reminding them that by law they had to charge a minimum fare of forty-five cents, and saying that failure to comply would be a legal offense. This brought an end to the cheap taxi service.

Our answer was to call hastily on our volunteers, who responded immediately. They started out simply by cruising the streets of Montgomery with no particular system. On

Saturday the ministers agreed to go to their pulpits the following day and seek additional recruits. Again the response was tremendous. With the new additions, the number of cars swelled to about three hundred.

The real job was just beginning—that of working out some system for these three hundred-odd automobiles, to replace their haphazard movement around the city. During the days that followed, the transportation committee worked every evening into the morning hours attempting to set up an adequate system. Several of Jemison's suggestions proved profitable. Finally, the decision was made to set up "dispatch" and "pick-up" stations, points at which passengers would assemble for transportation to their jobs and home again. The dispatch stations would be open from 6:00 to 10:00 A.M., and the pick-up stations from 3:00 to 7:00 P.M.

Next came the difficult task of selecting sites for the stations that would adequately cover the whole city. While most of us found it relatively easy to think of dispatch stations, since they would be in Negro sections of town, we discovered that we were at a loss in selecting pick-up stations. The problem was that the vast majority of those who had ridden the buses worked for white employers, and the pick-up stations would therefore have to be in white sections, of which we had little, if any, knowledge. Fortunately, however, we had two postal workers on the committee, who knew the city from end to end. With their assistance and the aid of a city map we began working with new facility.

At this time, R. J. Glasco was prominent on the transportation committee along with the chairman, Rufus Lewis. These men, with the assistance of the whole committee, worked assiduously to lay out the plan. By Tuesday, December 13, the system had been worked out. Thousands of mimeographed leaflets were distributed throughout the Negro community with a list of the forty-eight dispatch and the forty-two pick-up stations. Most of the dispatch stations were located at the Negro churches. These churches coöperated by opening their doors early each morning so that the waiting passengers could be seated, and many of them provided heat on cold mornings. Each of the private cars was assigned to one of the dispatch and one of the pick-up stations, the number of cars assigned to each station determined by the number of persons using it. By far the most heavily used station was a Negro-owned parking lot located in the downtown section of Montgomery. It was a combination pick-up and dispatch point.

In a few days this system was working astonishingly well. The white opposition was so impressed at this miracle of quick organization that they had to admit in a White Citizens Council meeting that the pool moved with "military precision." The MIA had worked out in a few nights a transportation problem that the bus company had grappled with for many years.

Despite this success, so profoundly had the spirit of the protest become a part of the people's lives that sometimes they even preferred to walk when a ride was available. The act of walking, for many, had become of symbolic importance. Once a pool driver stopped beside an elderly woman who was trudging along with obvious difficulty.

"Jump in, grandmother," he said. "You don't need to walk."

She waved him on. "I'm not walking for myself," she explained. "I'm walking for my children and my grandchildren." And she continued toward home on foot.

While the largest number of drivers were ministers, their ranks were augmented by housewives, teachers, businessmen, and unskilled laborers. At least three white men from the air bases drove in the pool during their off-duty hours. One of the most faithful drivers was Mrs. A. W. West, who had early shown her enthusiasm for the protest idea by helping to call the civic leaders to the first organizing meeting. Every morning she drove her large green Cadillac to her assigned dispatch station, and for several hours in the morning and again in the afternoon one could see this distinguished and handsome gray-haired chauffeur driving people to work and home again.

Another loyal driver was Jo Ann Robinson. Attractive, fair-skinned, and still youthful, Jo Ann came by her goodness naturally. She did not need to learn her nonviolence from any book. Apparently indefatigable, she, perhaps more than any other person, was active on every level of the protest. She took part in both the executive board and the strategy committee meetings. When the MIA newsletter was inaugurated a few months after the protest began, she became its editor. She was sure to be present whenever negotiations were in progress. And although she carried a full teaching load at Alabama State, she still found time to drive both morning and afternoon.

The ranks of our drivers were further swelled from an unforeseen source. Many white housewives, whatever their commitment to segregation, had no intention of being without their maids. And so every day they drove to the Negro sections to pick up their servants and returned them at night. Certainly, if selfishness was a part of the motive, in many cases affection for a faithful servant also played its part. There was some humor in the tacit understandings—and sometimes mutually accepted misunderstandings—between these white employers and their Negro servants. One old domestic, an influential matriarch to many young relatives in Montgomery, was asked by her wealthy employer, "Isn't this bus boycott terrible?"

The old lady responded: "Yes, ma'am, it sure is. And I just told all my young'uns that this kind of thing is white folks' business and we just stay off the buses till they get this whole thing settled."

As time moved on the pool continued to grow and expand. Rev. B. J. Simms, college professor and pastor of a Baptist church in Tuskegee, took over the chairmanship of the committee, adding his own creative ideas to the good work of his predecessor, Rufus Lewis. Soon the transportation office had grown to a staff of six. More than twenty-five people were employed as all-day drivers, working six days a week. In most of the stations, dispatchers were employed to keep things running smoothly and divide the passengers on the basis of the direction in which they were going. A chief dispatcher—Rev. J. H. Cherry—stationed at the downtown parking lot proved to be of inestimable value. Richard Harris, a Negro pharmacist, was also a great asset to the transportation system. From the office of his drugstore he dispatched cars by telephone from early morning till late evening. Visitors were always astonished to see this young energetic businessman standing with a telephone at his ear dispatching cars and filling a prescription simultaneously.

Finally, a fleet of more than fifteen new station wagons was added. Each of these 1956 cars was registered as the property of a different church, and the name of the sponsoring church was emblazoned on the front and side of each vehicle. As these "rolling churches" carried their spirited loads of passengers along to work, an occasional sound of hymn-singing came from their windows. Pedestrians who could find no room in the crowded vehicles waved as their own "church" passed by, and walked on with new heart.

Altogether the operation of the motor pool represented organization and coördination at their best. Reporters and visitors from all over the country looked upon the system as a unique accomplishment. But the job took money. For a while the MIA had been able to carry on through local contributions. Week after week, wealthy or poor, the Negroes of Montgomery gave what they could, even though sometimes there was only a dime or a quarter to put into the collection box. But as the pool grew and other expenses mounted, it was evident that we needed additional funds to carry on. The cost of running the MIA had increased to $5000 a month.

Fortunately the liberal coverage of the press had carried the word of our struggle across the world. Although we never made a public appeal for funds, contributions began to pour in from as far away as Tokyo. MIA leaders were invited to cities all over the country to appear in fund-raising meetings. Every day brought visitors bearing gifts, and every mail brought checks. Sometimes the gift was as large as $5000, sometimes only a single dollar bill, but altogether they added up to nearly $250,000.

The largest response came from church groups—particularly, though by no means only, Negro churches. Several ministerial associations contributed generously. It would be safe to say that churches in almost every city in the United States sent help. Labor, civic, and social groups were our stanch supporters, and in many communities new organizations were founded just to support the protest. Almost every branch of the NAACP responded generously to a letter from Roy Wilkins, the executive secretary, urging them to give moral and financial support to the movement; and this was only one of the many ways in which the NAACP was to lend its strength in the days ahead.

Contributions came from many individuals, too, both white and Negro, here and abroad. Often these were accompanied by letters that raised our spirits and helped to break the sense of isolation that surrounded us in our own community. From Pennsylvania came a check for a hundred dollars, along with a note in the spidery handwriting of an elderly gentlewoman: "Your work . . . is outstanding and unprecedented in the history of our country. Indeed, it is epoch-making and it should have a far-reaching effect. . . . 'Not by might, nor by power, but by my spirit, saith the Lord'— this might well be the motto of the Montgomery Improvement Association." A former federal judge wrote: "You have shown that decency and courage will eventually prevail. . . . The immediate issue has not been won as yet but such faith and determination is bound to be triumphant and the persecutors must themselves by this time come to realize that they are fighting a cruel but losing effort. The entire nation salutes you and prays for your early relief and victory."

From Singapore came the assurance that "what you are doing is a real inspiration to us here in the part of the world where the struggle between democracy and communism is raging." The crew of a ship at sea cabled: "We offer a prayer in sympathy in the fight for justice." And a Swiss woman whose "friends and husband do not understand" saved her own money to send us one of our largest individual contributions. "Since I have no possibility," she wrote, "to help you in an efficacious manner (this is such a bad

Rufus Lewis and B. J. Simms discuss transportation committee business. *In the early stages of the protest the problem of transportation demanded most of our attention . . . In a few days this system* [carpools] *was working astonishingly well . . . The MIA* [Montgomery Improvement Association] *had worked out in a few nights a transportation problem that the bus company had grappled with for many years."*

feeling, believe me) and I burningly would like to do just something, I send you these 500 dollars. . . . You would make me a very great pleasure, if you accepted, because what else could I do?"

Truly the Montgomery movement had spoken to a responsive world. But while these letters brought us much-needed encouragement, they were also the source of persistent frustration for me. The MIA lacked proper office facilities and staff, and due to the shortage of secretarial help most of the early letters had to go unanswered. Even financial contributions were often unacknowledged. The more I thought of my inability to cope with these matters, the more disturbed I became.

My frustration was augmented by the fact that for several weeks after the protest began, people were calling me at every hour of the day and night. The phone would start ringing as early as five o'clock in the morning and seldom stopped before midnight. Sometimes it was an ex-bus rider asking me to arrange to get her to work and back home at a certain hour. Sometimes it was a driver complaining about uncoöperative passengers or a passenger complaining about a temperamental driver. Sometimes a driver's car had broken down. Sometimes it was a maid who had been threatened with firing by her employer if she continued to stay off the buses, and sometimes a person who simply wanted to know where the nearest pick-up station was located. From time to time someone called to say that a certain driver was charging his passengers, and needed to be stopped before his acts jeopardized the legal status of the whole system.

We came to see the necessity of having a well-staffed office to face such problems as these. At first we attempted to run it with volunteer secretarial help. But this was not sufficient. So we hired a full-time secretary to do the regular work of the association, and set up a transportation office with a secretary to work directly in that area. As time went on the correspondence became so heavy and the transportation work so detailed that it was necessary to employ an office staff of ten persons. With the growth of the office staff and other administrative matters, the board finally supplied me with an executive assistant, Rev. R. J. Glasco. All of these steps—the hiring of office secretaries, setting up a transportation office, and the hiring of an executive assistant—served to lighten an almost unbearable load, and helped me to regain my bearings.

But the job of getting the movement going was not yet finished. There was still the task of finding permanent office space to house the MIA. This problem proved to be unexpectedly difficult, and we were forced to move no less than four times before we found a relatively permanent location.

The first office was in the Alabama Negro Baptist Center. Here we had access to two large rooms and also an assembly room for board meetings. Both location and facilities met our needs. As soon as we were settled there, however, the white officials of the Montgomery Baptist Association—the organization which supplied the largest amount of money for the operation of the center—called the trustees of the center into a conference and suggested that "for the good of the center" and "the good of the community" the MIA headquarters should be moved. Although it was never explicitly stated, we could discern an implicit threat to withdraw financial assistance if the request were not complied with immediately.

Seeing that we were almost out of doors, Rufus Lewis offered the MIA the use of his club—the Citizens Club. He set at our disposal a large room, which was usually used for banquets, and a small room for the transportation committee. But after we had been in the Citizens Club for a few weeks Mr. Lewis got word from reliable sources that if the MIA remained there his license would be revoked on the grounds that the club was being used as an office building. In this emergency the First Baptist Church offered its limited office space as a temporary abode.

Finally, we discovered that the new building of the Bricklayers Union had available space which would serve our purposes well. Here the white community could not force us out, since most of the members and all of the officers of the union that owned the building were Negroes. With this consideration in mind we decided to rent space there.

By then the office staff was exhausted. They had moved back and forth all over the city. In this continuous moving process some important letters had almost certainly been lost and significant records misplaced. But at least we now had an office with an air of permanence. For the first time we had enough space to work with a modicum of peace and security.

The biggest job in getting any movement off the ground is to keep together the people who form it. This task requires more than a common aim: it demands a philosophy that wins and holds the people's allegiance; and it depends upon open channels of communication between the people and their leaders. All of these elements were present in Montgomery.

From the beginning a basic philosophy guided the movement. This guiding principle has since been referred to variously as nonviolent resistance, noncoöperation, and passive resistance. But in the first days of the protest none of these expressions was mentioned; the phrase most often heard was "Christian love." It was the Sermon on the Mount, rather than a doctrine of passive resistance, that initially inspired the Negroes of Montgomery to dignified social action. It was Jesus of Nazareth that stirred the Negroes to protest with the creative weapon of love.

As the days unfolded, however, the inspiration of Mahatma Gandhi began to exert its influence. I had come to see early that the Christian doctrine of love operating through the Gandhian method of nonviolence was one of the most potent weapons available to the Negro in his struggle for freedom. About a week after the protest started, a white woman who understood and sympathized with the Negroes' efforts wrote a letter to the editor of the *Montgomery Advertiser* comparing the bus protest with the Gandhian movement in India. Miss Juliette Morgan, sensitive and frail, did not long survive the rejection and condemnation of the white community, but long before she died in the summer of 1957 the name of Mahatma Gandhi was well-known in Montgomery. People who had never heard of the little brown saint of India were now saying his name with an air of familiarity. Nonviolent resistance had emerged as the technique of the movement, while love stood as the regulating ideal. In other words, Christ furnished the spirit and motivation, while Gandhi furnished the method.

This philosophy was disseminated mainly through the regular mass meetings which were held in the various Negro churches of the city. For the first several months the meetings occurred twice a week—on Mondays and Thursdays—but in the fall of 1956 the number was reduced to one a week, a schedule that continues to this day. At the beginning of the protest these twice-a-week get-togethers were indispensable channels of communication, since Montgomery had neither a Negro-owned radio station nor a widely read Negro newspaper.

The meetings rotated from church to church. The speakers represented the various denominations, thus removing any grounds for sectarian jealousy. One of the glories of the Montgomery movement was that Baptists, Methodists, Lutherans, Presbyterians, Episcopalians, and others all came together with a willingness to transcend denominational lines. Although no Catholic priests were actively involved in the protest, many of their parishioners took part. All joined hands in the bond of Christian love. Thus the mass meetings accomplished on Monday and Thursday nights what the Christian Church had failed to accomplish on Sunday mornings.

The mass meetings also cut across class lines. The vast majority present were working people; yet there was always an appreciable number of professionals in the audience. Physicians, teachers, and lawyers sat or stood beside domestic workers and unskilled laborers. The Ph.D's and the no "D's" were bound together in a common venture. The so-called "big Negroes" who owned cars and had never ridden the buses came to know the maids and the laborers who rode the buses every day. Men and women who had been separated from each other by false standards of class were now singing and praying together in a common struggle for freedom and human dignity.

The meetings started at seven, but people came hours ahead of time to get a seat. It was not uncommon to find the churches completely filled by five in the afternoon. Some read papers and books while they waited; others joined in group singing. Usually the hymns preceding the meeting were unaccompanied lined tunes of low pitch and long meter. One could not help but be moved by these traditional songs, which brought to mind the long history of the Negro's suffering.

By the time the meeting started, virtually every space was taken, and hundreds often overflowed into the streets. Many latecomers learned to bring their own folding stools, and many others stayed away because they knew that it would be impossible to find a space. At first we tried to deal with this problem by having as many as five simultaneous meetings in different parts of the city, each with the same theme and pattern. For several weeks I made it a practice to appear at all five meetings, but this was a strenuous undertaking. Moreover, the people began to insist that they wanted to be together; so we soon went back to the one big meeting.

The evenings followed a simple pattern: songs, prayer, Scripture reading, opening remarks by the president, collection, reports from various committees, and a "pep talk." The latter was the main address of the evening, usually given by a different minister at each meeting. The "pep talk" acquired its rather undignified title during the early days of the protest, when the primary purpose was to give the people new "pep" and enthusiasm for the struggle ahead. Night after night the group was admonished to love rather than hate, and urged to be prepared to suffer violence if necessary but never to inflict it. Every "pep" speaker was asked to make nonviolence a central part of his theme.

Inevitably, a speaker would occasionally get out of hand. One minister, after lashing out against the whites in distinctly untheological terms, ended by referring to the extremists of the white community as "dirty crackers." After the meeting he was politely but firmly informed that his insulting phrases were out of place. But such instances of offensive language were surprisingly few.

In my weekly remarks as president, I

stressed that the use of violence in our struggle would be both impractical and immoral. To meet hate with retaliatory hate would do nothing but intensify the existence of evil in the universe. Hate begets hate; violence begets violence; toughness begets a greater toughness. We must meet the forces of hate with the power of love; we must meet physical force with soul force. Our aim must never be to defeat or humiliate the white man, but to win his friendship and understanding.

From the beginning the people responded to this philosophy with amazing ardor. To be sure, there were some who were slow to concur. Occasionally members of the executive board would say to me in private that we needed a more militant approach. They looked upon nonviolence as weak and compromising. Others felt that at least a modicum of violence would convince the white people that the Negroes meant business and were not afraid. A member of my church came to me one day and solemnly suggested that it would be to our advantage to "kill off" eight or ten white people. "This is the only language these white folks will understand," he said. "If we fail to do this they will think we're afraid. We must show them we're not afraid any longer." Besides, he thought, if a few white persons were killed the federal government would inevitably intervene and this, he was certain, would benefit us.

Still others felt that they could be nonviolent only if they were not attacked personally. They would say: "If nobody bothers me, I will bother nobody. If nobody hits me, I will hit nobody. But if I am hit, I will hit back." They thus drew a moral line between aggressive and retaliatory violence. But in spite of these honest disagreements, the vast majority were willing to try the experiment.

The very spirit of the meetings revealed their nature. The songs, the prayers, the Scripture readings, and the speeches were by and large nonviolent in tone. A favorite Scriptural passage was, "And now abideth faith, hope, love, these three; but the greatest of these is love." Another was the famous dialogue on forgiveness between Jesus and Peter: "Then came Peter to him, and said, Lord, how oft shall my brother sin against me, and I forgive him? till seven times? Jesus saith unto him, I say not unto thee, Until seven times: but, Until seventy times seven." For the mass meeting audiences, these Scriptural admonitions were not abstractions that came to them from a distance across the centuries; they had a personal and immediate meaning for them today.

Throughout, there was a surprising lack of bitterness, even when speakers referred to the latest white insult or act of terrorism. And when, later on, the MIA was to be faced with its only serious internal crisis, the people showed that they could handle dissension among themselves with equal restraint, refraining not only from physical violence but also from violence of spirit.

In a real sense, Montgomery's Negroes showed themselves willing to grapple with a new approach to the crisis in race relations. It is probably true that most of them did not believe in nonviolence as a philosophy of life, but because of their confidence in their leaders and because nonviolence was presented to them as a simple expression of Christianity in action, they were willing to use it as a technique. Admittedly, nonviolence in the truest sense is not a strategy that one uses simply because it is expedient at the moment; nonviolence is ultimately a way of life that men live by because of the sheer morality of its claim. But even granting this, the willingness to use nonviolence as a technique is a step forward. For he who goes this far is more likely to adopt nonviolence later as a way of life.

CHAPTER VI

PILGRIMAGE TO NONVIOLENCE

OFTEN THE QUESTION has arisen concerning my own intellectual pilgrimage to nonviolence. In order to get at this question it is necessary to go back to my early teens in Atlanta. I had grown up abhorring not only segregation but also the oppressive and barbarous acts that grew out of it. I had passed spots where Negroes had been savagely lynched, and had watched the Ku Klux Klan on its rides at night. I had seen police brutality with my own eyes, and watched Negroes receive the most tragic injustice in the courts. All of these things had done something to my growing personality. I had come perilously close to resenting all white people.

I had also learned that the inseparable twin of racial injustice was economic injustice. Although I came from a home of economic security and relative comfort, I could never get out of my mind the economic insecurity of many of my playmates and the tragic poverty of those living around me. During my late teens I worked two summers, against my father's wishes—he never wanted my brother and me to work around white people because of the oppressive conditions—in a plant that hired both Negroes and whites. Here I saw economic injustice firsthand, and realized that the poor white was exploited just as much as the Negro. Through these early experiences I grew up deeply conscious of the varieties of injustice in our society.

So when I went to Atlanta's Morehouse College as a freshman in 1944 my concern for racial and economic justice was already substantial. During my student days at Morehouse I read Thoreau's *Essay on Civil Disobedience* for the first time. Fascinated by the idea of refusing to coöperate with an evil system, I was so deeply moved that I reread the work several times. This was my first intellectual contact with the theory of non-violent resistance.

Not until I entered Crozer Theological Seminary in 1948, however, did I begin a serious intellectual quest for a method to eliminate social evil. Although my major interest was in the fields of theology and philosophy, I spent a great deal of time reading the works of the great social philosophers. I came early to Walter Rauschenbusch's *Christianity and the Social Crisis,* which left an indelible imprint on my thinking by giving me a theological basis for the social concern which had already grown up in me as a result of my early experiences. Of course there were points at which I differed with Rauschenbusch. I felt that he had fallen victim to the nineteenth-century "cult of inevitable progress" which led him to a superficial optimism concerning man's nature. Moreover, he came perilously close to identi-

fying the Kingdom of God with a particular social and economic system—a tendency which should never befall the Church. But in spite of these shortcomings Rauschenbusch had done a great service for the Christian Church by insisting that the gospel deals with the whole man, not only his soul but his body; not only his spiritual well-being but his material well-being. It has been my conviction ever since reading Rauschenbusch that any religion which professes to be concerned about the souls of men and is not concerned about the social and economic conditions that scar the soul, is a spiritually moribund religion only waiting for the day to be buried. It well has been said: "A religion that ends with the individual, ends."

After reading Rauschenbusch, I turned to a serious study of the social and ethical theories of the great philosophers, from Plato and Aristotle down to Rousseau, Hobbes,

Bentham, Mill, and Locke. All of these masters stimulated my thinking—such as it was—and, while finding things to question in each of them, I nevertheless learned a great deal from their study.

During the Christmas holidays of 1949 I decided to spend my spare time reading Karl Marx to try to understand the appeal of communism for many people. For the first time I carefully scrutinized *Das Kapital* and *The Communist Manifesto*. I also read some interpretive works on the thinking of Marx and Lenin. In reading such Communist writings I drew certain conclusions that have remained with me as convictions to this day. First I rejected their materialistic interpretation of history. Communism, avowedly secularistic and materialistic, has no place for God. This I could never accept, for as a Christian I believe that there is a creative personal power in this universe who is the ground and essence of all reality—a power that cannot be explained in materialistic terms. History is ultimately guided by spirit, not matter. Second, I strongly disagreed with communism's ethical relativism. Since for the Communist there is no divine government, no absolute moral order, there are no fixed, immutable principles; consequently almost anything—force, violence, murder, lying—is a justifiable means to the "millennial" end. This type of relativism was abhorrent to me. Constructive ends can never give absolute moral justification to destructive means, because in the final analysis the end is preëxistent in the mean. Third, I opposed communism's political totalitarianism. In communism the individual ends up in subjection to the state. True, the Marxist would argue that the state is an "interim" reality which is to be eliminated when the classless society emerges; but the state is the end while it lasts, and man only a means to that end. And if any man's so-called rights or liberties stand in the way of that end, they are simply swept aside. His liberties of expression, his freedom to vote, his freedom to listen to what news he likes or to choose his books are all restricted. Man becomes hardly more, in communism, than a depersonalized cog in the turning wheel of the state.

This deprecation of individual freedom was objectionable to me. I am convinced now, as I was then, that man is an end because he is a child of God. Man is not made for the state; the state is made for man. To deprive man of freedom is to relegate him to the status of a thing, rather than elevate him to the status of a person. Man must never be treated as a means to the end of the state, but always as an end within himself.

Yet, in spite of the fact that my response to communism was and is negative, and I considered it basically evil, there were points at which I found it challenging. The late Archbishop of Canterbury, William Temple, referred to communism as a Christian heresy. By this he meant that communism had laid hold of certain truths which are essential parts of the Christian view of things, but that it had bound up with them concepts and practices which no Christian could ever accept or profess. Communism challenged the late Archbishop and it should challenge every Christian—as it challenged me—to a growing concern about social justice. With all of its false assumptions and evil methods, communism grew as a protest against the hardships of the underprivileged. Communism in theory emphasized a classless society, and a concern for social justice, though the world knows from sad experience that in practice it created new classes and a new lexicon of injustice. The Christian ought always to be challenged by any protest against unfair treatment of the poor, for Christianity is itself such a protest, nowhere expressed more eloquently than in Jesus' words: "The Spirit of the Lord is upon me, because he hath anointed me to preach the gospel to the poor; he hath sent me to heal the broken-hearted, to preach deliverance to the captives, and recovering of sight to the blind, to set at liberty them that are bruised, to preach the acceptable year of the Lord."

I also sought systematic answers to Marx's critique of modern bourgeois culture. He presented capitalism as essentially a struggle between the owners of the productive resources and the workers, whom Marx regarded as the real producers. Marx interpreted economic forces as the dialectical process by which society moved from feudalism through capitalism to socialism, with the primary mechanism of this historical movement being the struggle between economic classes whose interests were irreconcilable. Obviously this theory left out of account the numerous and significant complexities—political, economic, moral, religious, and psychological—which played a vital role in shaping the constellation of institutions and ideas known today as Western civilization. Moreover, it was dated in the sense that the capitalism Marx wrote about bore only a partial resemblance to the capitalism we know in this country today.

But in spite of the shortcomings of his analysis, Marx had raised some basic questions. I was deeply concerned from my early teen days about the gulf between superfluous wealth and abject poverty, and my reading of Marx made me ever more conscious of this gulf. Although modern American capitalism had greatly reduced the gap through social reforms, there was still need for a better distribution of wealth. Moreover, Marx had revealed the danger of the profit motive as the sole basis of an economic system: capitalism is always in danger of inspiring men to be more concerned about making a living than making a life. We are prone to judge success by the index of our salaries or the size of our automobiles, rather than by the quality of our service and relationship to humanity—thus capitalism can lead to a practical materialism that is as pernicious as the materialism taught by communism.

In short, I read Marx as I read all of the influential historical thinkers—from a dialectical point of view, combining a partial yes and a partial no. In so far as Marx posited a metaphysical materialism, an ethical relativism, and a strangulating totalitarianism, I responded with an unambiguous "no"; but in so far as he pointed to weaknesses of traditional capitalism, contributed to the growth of a definite self-consciousness in the masses, and challenged the social conscience of the Christian churches, I responded with a definite "yes."

My reading of Marx also convinced me that truth is found neither in Marxism nor in traditional capitalism. Each represents a partial truth. Historically capitalism failed to see the truth in collective enterprise and Marxism failed to see the truth in individual enterprise. Nineteenth-century capitalism failed to see that life is social and Marxism failed and still fails to see that life is individual and personal. The Kingdom of God is neither the thesis of individual enterprise nor the antithesis of collective enterprise, but a synthesis which reconciles the truths of both.

During my stay at Crozer, I was also exposed for the first time to the pacifist position in a lecture by Dr. A. J. Muste. I was deeply moved by Dr. Muste's talk, but far from convinced of the practicability of his position. Like most of the students of Crozer, I felt that while war could never be a positive or absolute good, it could serve as a negative good in the sense of preventing the spread and growth of an evil force. War, horrible as it is, might be preferable to surrender to a totalitarian system—Nazi, Fascist, or Communist.

During this period I had about despaired of the power of love in solving social problems. Perhaps my faith in love was temporarily shaken by the philosophy of Nietzsche. I had been reading parts of *The Genealogy of Morals* and the whole of *The Will to Power*. Nietzsche's glorification of power—in his theory all life expressed the will to power—was an outgrowth of his contempt for ordinary morals. He attacked the whole of the Hebraic-Christian morality—with its virtues of piety and humility, its other-worldliness and its attitude toward suffering—as the glorification of weakness, as making virtues out of necessity and impotence. He looked to the development of a superman who would surpass man as man surpassed the ape.

Then one Sunday afternoon I traveled to Philadelphia to hear a sermon by Dr. Mordecai Johnson, president of Howard University. He was there to preach for the Fellowship House of Philadelphia. Dr. Johnson had just returned from a trip to India, and, to my great interest, he spoke of the life and teachings of Mahatma Gandhi. His message was so profound and electrifying that I left the meeting and bought a half-dozen books on Gandhi's life and works.

Like most people, I had heard of Gandhi, but I had never studied him seriously. As I read I became deeply fascinated by his campaigns of nonviolent resistance. I was particularly moved by the Salt March to the Sea and his numerous fasts. The whole concept of "Satyagraha" (*Satya* is truth which equals love, and *agraha* is force; "Satyagraha," therefore, means truth-force or love-force)

was profoundly significant to me. As I delved deeper into the philosophy Gandhi my skepticism concerning the power of love gradually diminished, and I came to see for the first time its potency in the area of social reform. Prior to reading Gandhi, I had about concluded that the ethics of Jesus were only effective in individual relationship. The "turn the other cheek" philosophy and the "love your enemies" philosophy were only valid, I felt, when individuals were in conflict with other individuals; when racial groups and nations were in conflict a more realistic approach seemed necessary. But after reading Gandhi, I saw how utterly mistaken I was.

Gandhi was probably the first person in history to lift the love ethic of Jesus above mere interaction between individuals to a powerful and effective social force on a large scale. Love for Gandhi was a potent instrument for social and collective transformation. It was in this Gandhian emphasis on love and nonviolence that I discovered the method for social reform that I had been seeking for so many months. The intellectual and moral satisfaction that I failed to gain from the utilitarianism of Bentham and Mill, the revolutionary methods of Marx and Lenin, the social-contracts theory of Hobbes, the "back to nature" optimism of Rousseau, and the superman philosophy of Nietzsche, I found in the nonviolent resistance philosophy of Gandhi. I came to feel that this was the only morally and practically sound method open to oppressed people in their struggle for freedom.

But my intellectual odyssey to nonviolence did not end here. During my last year in theological school, I began to read the works of Reinhold Niebuhr. The prophetic and realistic elements in Niebuhr's passionate style and profound thought were appealing to me, and I became so enamored of his social ethics that I almost fell into the trap of accepting uncritically everything he wrote.

About this time I read Niebuhr's critique of the pacifist position. Niebuhr had himself once been a member of the pacifist ranks. For several years, he had been national chairman of the Fellowship of Reconciliation. His break with pacifism came in the early thirties, and the first full statement of his criticism of pacifism was in *Moral Man and Immoral Society*. Here he argued that there was no intrinsic moral difference between violent and nonviolent resistance. The social consequences of the two methods were different, he contended, but the differences were in degree rather than kind. Later Niebuhr began emphasizing the irresponsibility of relying on nonviolent resistance when there was no ground for believing that it would be successful in preventing the spread of totalitarian tyranny. It could only be successful, he argued, if the groups against whom the resistance was taking place had some degree of moral conscience, as was the case of Gandhi's struggle against the British. Niebuhr's ultimate rejection of pacifism was based primarily on the doctrine of man. He argued that pacifism failed to do justice to the reformation doctrine of justification by faith, substituting for it a sectarian perfectionism which believes "that divine grace actually lifts men out of the sinful contradictions of history and establishes him above the sins of the world."

At first, Niebuhr's critique of pacifism left me in a state of confusion. As I continued to read, however, I came to see more and more the shortcomings of his position. For instance, many of his statements revealed that he interpreted pacifism as a sort of passive nonresistance to evil expressing naïve trust in the power of love. But this was a serious distortion. My study of Gandhi convinced me that true pacifism is not nonresistance to evil, but nonviolent resistance to evil. Between the two positions, there is a world of difference. Gandhi resisted evil with as much vigor and power as the violent resister, but he resisted with love instead of hate. True pacifism is not unrealistic submission to evil power, as Niebuhr contends. It is rather a courageous confrontation of evil by the power of love, in the faith that it is better to be the recipient of violence than the inflicter of it, since the latter only multiplies the existence of violence and bitterness in the universe, while the former may develop a sense of shame in the opponent, and thereby bring about a transformation and change of heart.

In spite of the fact that I found many things to be desired in Niebuhr's philosophy, there were several points at which he constructively influenced my thinking. Niebuhr's great contribution to contemporary theology is that he has refuted the false optimism characteristic of a great segment of Protestant liberalism, without falling into the anti-rationalism of the continental theologian Karl Barth, or the semi-fundamentalism of other dialectical theologians. Moreover, Niebuhr has extraordinary insight into human nature, especially the behavior of nations and social groups. He is keenly aware of the complexity of human motives and of the relation between morality and power. His theology is a persistent reminder of the reality of sin on every level of man's existence. These elements in Niebuhr's thinking helped me to recognize the illusions of a superficial optimism concerning human nature and the dangers of a false idealism. While I still believed a man's potential for good, Niebuhr made me realize his potential for evil as well. Moreover, Niebuhr helped me to recognize the complexity of man's social involvement and the glaring reality of collective evil.

Many pacifists, I felt, failed to see this. All too many had an unwarranted optimism concerning man and leaned unconsciously toward self-righteousness. It was my revolt against these attitudes under the influence of Niebuhr that accounts for the fact that in spite of my strong leaning toward pacifism, I never joined a pacifist organization. After reading Niebuhr, I tried to arrive at a realistic pacifism. In other words, I came to see the pacifist position not as sinless but as the lesser evil in the circumstances. I felt then, and I feel now, that the pacifist would have a greater appeal if he did not claim to be free from the moral dilemmas that the Christian nonpacifist confronts.

The next stage of my intellectual pilgrimage to nonviolence came during my doctoral studies at Boston University. Here I had the opportunity to talk to many exponents of nonviolence, both students and visitors to the campus. Boston University School of Theology, under the influence of Dean Walter Muelder and Professor Allen Knight Chalmers, had a deep sympathy for pacifism. Both Dean Muelder and Dr. Chalmers had a passion for social justice that stemmed, not from a superficial optimism, but from a deep faith in the possibilities of human beings when they allowed themselves to become co-workers with God. It was at Boston University that I came to see that Niebuhr had overemphasized the corruption of human nature. His pessimism concerning human nature was not balanced by an optimism concerning divine nature. He was so involved in diagnosing man's sickness of sin that he overlooked the cure of grace.

I studied philosophy and theology at Boston University under Edgar S. Brightman and L. Harold DeWolf. Both men greatly stimulated my thinking. It was mainly under these teachers that I studied personalistic philosophy—the theory that the clue to the meaning of ultimate reality is found in personality. This personal idealism remains today my basic philosophical position. Personalism's insistence that only personality—finite and infinite—is ultimately real strengthened me in two convictions: it gave me metaphysical and philosophical grounding for the idea of a personal God, and it gave me a metaphisical basis for the dignity and worth of all human personality.

Just before Dr. Brightman's death, I began studying the philosophy of Hegel with him. Although the course was mainly a study of Hegel's monumental work, *Phenomenology of Mind,* I spent my spare time reading his *Philosophy of History* and *Philosophy of Right.* There were points in Hegel's philosophy that I strongly disagreed with. For instance, his absolute idealism was rationally unsound to me because it tended to swallow up the many in the one. But there were other aspects of his thinking that I found stimulating. His contention that "truth is the whole" led me to a philosophical method of rational coherence. His analysis of the dialectical process, in spite of its shortcomings, helped me to see that growth comes through struggle.

In 1954 I ended my formal training with all of these relatively divergent intellectual forces converging into a positive social philosophy. One of the main tenets of this philosophy was the conviction that nonviolent resistance was one of the most potent weapons available to oppressed people in their quest for social justice. At this time, however, I had merely an intellectual understanding and appreciation of the position, with no firm determination to organize it in a socially effective situation.

When I went to Montgomery as a pastor, I had not the slightest idea that I would later become involved in a crisis in which nonviolent resistance would be applicable. I neither started the protest nor suggested it. I simply responded to the call of the people for a spokesman. When the protest began, my mind, consciously or unconsciously, was driven back to the Sermon on the Mount, with its sublime teachings on love, and the Gandhian method of nonviolent resistance. As the days unfolded, I came to see the power of nonviolence more and more. Living through the actual experience of the protest, nonviolence became more than a method to which I gave intellectual assent; it became a commitment to a way of life. Many of the things that I had not cleared up intellectually concerning nonviolence were now solved in the sphere of practical action.

Since the philosophy of nonviolence played such a positive role in the Montgomery Movement, it may be wise to turn to a brief discussion of some basic aspects of this philosophy.

First, it must be emphasized that nonviolent resistance is not a method for cowards; it does resist. If one uses this method because he is afraid or merely because he lacks the instruments of violence, he is not truly nonviolent. This is why Gandhi often said that if cowardice is the only alternative to violence, it is better to fight. He made this statement conscious of the fact that there is always another alternative: no individual or group need submit to any wrong, nor need they use violence to right the wrong; there is the way of nonviolent resistance. This is ultimately the way of the strong man. It is not a method of stagnant passivity. The phrase "passive resistance" often gives the false impression that this is a sort of "do-nothing method" in which the resister quietly and passively accepts evil. But nothing is further from the truth. For while the nonviolent resister is passive in the sense that he is not physically aggressive toward his opponent, his mind and emotions are always active, constantly seeking to persuade his opponent that he is wrong. The method is passive physically, but strongly active spiritually. It is not passive nonresistance to evil, it is active nonviolent resistance to evil.

A second basic fact that characterizes nonviolence is that it does not seek to defeat or humiliate the opponent, but to win his friendship and understanding. The nonviolent resister must often express his protest through noncoöperation or boycotts, but he realizes that these are not ends themselves; they are merely means to awaken a sense of moral shame in the opponent. The end is redemption and reconciliation. The aftermath of nonviolence is the creation of the beloved community, while the aftermath of violence is tragic bitterness.

A third characteristic of this method is that the attack is directed against forces of evil rather than against persons who happen to be doing the evil. It is evil that the nonviolent resister seeks to defeat, not the persons victimized by evil. If he is opposing racial injustice, the nonviolent resister has the vision to see that the basic tension is not between races. As I like to say to the people in Montgomery: "The tension in this city is not between white people and Negro people. The tension is, at bottom, between justice and injustice, between the forces of light and the forces of darkness. And if there is a victory, it will be a victory not merely for fifty thousand Negroes, but a victory for justice and the forces of light. We are out to defeat injustice and not white persons who may be unjust."

A fourth point that characterizes nonviolent resistance is a willingness to accept suffering without retaliation, to accept blows from the opponent without striking back.

"Rivers of blood may have to flow before we gain our freedom, but it must be our blood," Gandhi said to his countrymen. The nonviolent resister is willing to accept violence if necessary, but never to inflict it. He does not seek to dodge jail. If going to jail is necessary, he enters it "as a bridegroom enters the bride's chamber."

One may well ask: "What is the nonviolent resister's justification for this ordeal to which he invites men, for this mass political application of the ancient doctrine of turning the other cheek?" The answer is found in the realization that unearned suffering is redemptive. Suffering, the nonviolent resister realizes, has tremendous educational and transforming possibilities. "Things of fundamental importance to people are not secured by reason alone, but have to be purchased with their suffering," said Gandhi. He continues: "Suffering is infinitely more powerful than the law of the jungle for converting the opponent and opening his ears which are otherwise shut to the voice of reason."

A fifth point concerning nonviolent resistance is that it avoids not only external physical violence but also internal violence of spirit. The nonviolent resister not only refuses to shoot his opponent but he also refuses to hate him. At the center of nonviolence stands the principle of love. The nonviolent resister would contend that in the struggle for human dignity, the oppressed people of the world must not succumb to the temptation of becoming bitter or indulging in hate campaigns. To retaliate in kind would do nothing but intensify the existence of hate in the universe. Along the way of life, someone must have sense enough and morality enough to cut off the chain of hate. This can only be done by projecting the ethic of love to the center of our lives.

In speaking of love at this point, we are not referring to some sentimental or affectionate emotion. It would be nonsense to urge men to love their oppressors in an affectionate sense. Love in this connection means understanding, redemptive good will. Here the Greek language comes to our aid. There are three words for love in the Greek New Testament. First, there is *eros*. In Platonic philosophy *eros* meant the yearning of the soul for the realm of the divine. It has come now to mean a sort of aesthetic or romantic love. Second, there is *philia* which means intimate affection between personal friends. *Philia* denotes a sort of reciprocal love; the person loves because he is loved. When we speak of loving those who oppose us, we refer to neither *eros* nor *philia;* we speak of a love which is expressed in the Greek word *agape*. *Agape* means understanding, redeeming good will for all men. It is an overflowing love which is purely spontaneous, unmotivated, groundless, and creative. It is not set in motion by any quality or function of its object. It is the love of God operating in the human heart.

Agape is disinterested love. It is a love in which the individual seeks not his own good, but the good of his neighbor (I Cor. 10:24). *Agape* does not begin by discriminating between worthy and unworthy people, or any qualities people possess. It begins by loving others *for their sakes*. It is an entirely "neighbor-regarding concern for others," which discovers the neighbor in every man it meets. Therefore, *agape* makes no distinction between friend and enemy; it is directed toward both. If one loves an individual merely on account of his friendliness, he loves him for the sake of the benefits to be gained from the friendship, rather than for the friend's own sake. Consequently, the best way to assure one-self that Love is disinterested is to have love for the enemy-neighbor from whom you can expect no good in return, but only hostility and persecution.

Another basic point about *agape* is that it

springs from the *need* of the other person— his need for belonging to the best in the human family. The Samaritan who helped the Jew on the Jericho Road was "good" because he responded to the human need that he was presented with. God's love is eternal and fails not because man needs his love. St. Paul assures us that the loving act of redemption was done "while we were yet sinners"—that is, at the point of our greatest need for love. Since the white man's personality is greatly distorted by segregation, and his soul is greatly scarred, he needs the love of the Negro. The Negro must love the white man, because the white man needs his love to remove his tensions, insecurities, and fears.

Agape is not a weak, passive love. It is love in action. *Agape* is love seeking to preserve and create community. It is insistence on community even when one seeks to break it. *Agape* is a willingness to sacrifice in the interest of mutuality. *Agape* is a willingness to go to any length to restore community. It doesn't stop at the first mile, but it goes the second mile to restore community. It is a willingness to forgive, not seven times, but seventy times seven to restore community. The cross is the eternal expression of the length to which God will go in order to restore broken community. The resurrection is a symbol of God's triumph over all the forces that seek to block community. The Holy Spirit is the continuing community creating reality that moves through history. He who works against community is working against the whole of creation. Therefore, if I respond to hate with a reciprocal hate I do nothing but intensify the cleavage in broken community. I can only close the gap in broken community by meeting hate with love. If I meet hate with hate, I become depersonalized, because creation is so designed that my personality can only be fulfilled in the context of community. Booker T. Washington was right: "Let no man pull you so low as to make you hate him." When he pulls you that low he brings you to the point of working against community; he drags you to the point of defying creation, and thereby becoming depersonalized.

In the final analysis, *agape* means a recognition of the fact that all life is interrelated. All humanity is involved in a single process, and all men are brothers. To the degree that I harm my brother, no matter what he is doing to me, to that extent I am harming myself. For example, white men often refuse federal aid to education in order to avoid giving the Negro his rights; but because all men are brothers they cannot deny Negro children without harming their own. They end, all efforts to the contrary, by hurting themselves. Why is this? Because men are brothers. If you harm me, you harm yourself.

Love, *agape,* is the only cement that can hold this broken community together. When I am commanded to love, I am commanded to restore community, to resist injustice, and to meet the needs of my brothers.

A sixth basic fact about nonviolent resistance is that it is based on the conviction that the universe is on the side of justice. Consequently, the believer in nonviolence has deep faith in the future. This faith is another reason why the nonviolent resister can accept suffering without retaliation. For he knows that in his struggle for justice he has cosmic companionship. It is true that there are devout believers in nonviolence who find it difficult to believe in a personal God. But even these persons believe in the existence of some creative force that works for universal wholeness. Whether we call it an unconscious process, or impersonal Brahman, or a Personal Being of matchless power and infinite love, there is a creative force in this universe that works to bring the disconnected aspects of reality into a harmonious whole.

Pilgrimage to Nonviolence ☐ 73

CHAPTER VII

METHODS
OF THE OPPOSITION

IN SPITE OF THE FACT that the bus protest had been an immediate success, the city fathers—three in number, including the mayor—and the bus officials felt that it would fizzle out in a few days. They were certain that the first rainy day would find the Negroes back on the buses. Guided by this expectation, they refused to make any move toward the Negro community to determine what conditions needed to be met in order to rectify the situation. But the first rainy day came and passed and the buses remained empty.

In the meantime, the city fathers and the bus officials had expressed their first willingness to negotiate. Late Wednesday afternoon, December 7, Rev. Robert Hughes, executive director of the Alabama Council on Human Relations, called to say that he and two other members of the council—Rev. Thomas P. Thrasher, white rector of one of the leading Episcopal churches of the city, and Dr. H. Councill Trenholm, president of Alabama State College—had succeeded in getting the city fathers to consent to a meeting with the

Negro leaders and the bus officials the next morning at eleven o'clock.

At a special session of the MIA executive board a negotiating committee of twelve was appointed (See 'MONTGOMERY IMPROVEMENT ASSOCIATION') and I was chosen to serve as their spokesman. It was agreed that we would present to the meeting the same three proposals that had been adopted on the preceding Monday night: briefly, (1) a guarantee of courteous treatment; (2) passengers to be seated on a first-come first-served basis, the Negroes seating from the back; and (3) employment of Negro bus operators on predominantly Negro routes. The aim of these proposals was frankly no more than a temporary alleviation of the problem that we confronted. We never felt that the first-come first-served seating arrangement would provide a final solution, since this would eventually have to depend on a change in the law. We were sure, however, that the Rosa Parks case, which was now in the courts, provided the test that would ultimately bring about the defeat of bus segregation itself.

We arrived at the city hall about fifteen minutes before the hour set for the meeting. There we were directed to the Commissioners' Chamber, a room of moderate size, with the commissioners' table at one end and chairs arranged in front of it. We sat down near the front, and soon Thrasher, Hughes, and Trenholm came in and joined us. Two or three reporters were on hand and television cameras emphasized the importance of the occasion. Promptly at eleven the three commissioners—Mayor W. A. Gayle, Commissioner Clyde Sellers, and Commissioner Frank A. Parks—filed in and sat at the table facing us. They were joined by J. E. Bagley and Jack Crenshaw, representing the bus company, who took seats near one end of the table. Thus the lines appeared to be clearly drawn before the meeting began.

The mayor called the meeting to order, and invited Mr. Thrasher to make the opening statement. Thrasher—a man deeply dedicated to the ideal of Christian brotherhood—came to the front of the room and briefly presented the reasons why the Council on Human Relations had requested the meeting. He went on to express his faith in the ability of both sides to be reasonable and unemotional in all of the deliberations.

The mayor then turned to the Negro delegation and demanded: "Who is the spokesman?" When all eyes turned toward me, the mayor said: "All right, come forward and make your statement." In the glare of the television lights, I walked slowly toward the front of the room and took a seat at the opposite end of the table from Bagley and Crenshaw.

I opened by stating briefly why we found it necessary to "boycott" the buses. I made it clear that the arrest of Mrs. Parks was not the cause of the protest, but merely the precipitating factor. "Our action," I said, "is the culmination of a series of injustices and indignities that have existed over the years." I went on to cite many instances of discourtesy on the part of the bus drivers, and numerous occasions when Negro passengers had had to stand over empty seats. I emphasized that the Negroes had shown a great deal of patience, and had attempted to negotiate around the conference table on several occasions before to no avail.

After these background remarks I set forth the three requests and proceeded to explain each proposal in detail. I made it clear, for instance, that our request for a first-come, first-served seating arrangement, with Negroes loading from the back and whites from the front, was not something totally new for the South; other Southern cities—such as Nashville, Atlanta, and even Mobile, Alabama—followed this pattern, and each of them adhered as rigorously to a pattern of segregation as did Montgomery. As far as the request for a guarantee of courtesy from the drivers was concerned, "this is the least that any business can grant to its patrons," I said. And finally I pointed out that since the Negroes poured so much money into the pocketbook of the bus company, it was only fair for some of it to be returned to them in the form of jobs as operators on predominantly Negro routes. "The bus company admits," I reminded them, "that seventy-five percent of its patrons are colored; and it seems to me that it would be good business sense for the company to seek employees from the ranks of its largest patronage." I closed my remarks by assuring the commissioners that we planned to conduct the protest on the highest level of dignity and restraint, and I avowed that our aim was not to put the bus company out of business, but to achieve justice for ourselves as well as for the white man.

As soon as I finished the mayor opened the meeting to general discussion. Several members of the Negro delegation further elaborated on the three proposals. Then the commissioners and the attorney for the bus company began raising questions. They challenged the legality of the seating arrangement that we were proposing. They contended that the Negroes were demanding something that would violate the law. We answered by reiterating our previous argument that a first-come first-served seating arrangement could exist entirely within the segregation law, as it did in many Southern cities.

It soon became clear that Crenshaw, the attorney for the bus company, was our most stubborn opponent. Doggedly he sought to convince the group that there was no way to grant the suggested seating proposal without violating the city ordinance. The more Crenshaw talked, the more he won the city fathers to his position. Mayor Gayle and Commissioner Sellers became more and more intransigent. Eventually I saw that the meeting was getting nowhere, and suggested that we bring it to a close. Thereupon the mayor asked a few members of the Negro delegation to stay over with the officials of the bus company, in an attempt to come to some settlement.

As soon as the others had left we assembled around the conference table with Bagley, Crenshaw, and the two associate commissioners—Sellers and Parks. In the smaller group, with the press no longer recording every word, it seemed possible that some progress could at last be made. Soon after we had restated our position on seating, I heard Commissioner Parks say in a quiet voice,

"I don't see why we can't arrange to accept this seating proposal. We can work it within our segregation laws."

My hopes began to rise. But Parks had hardly closed his mouth before Crenshaw rejoined,

"But, Frank. I don't see how we can do it within the law. If it were legal I would be the first to go along with it; but it just isn't legal. The only way that it can be done is to change your segregation laws."

This put a quick end to my optimism. Lacking the resolution to stand firm on his conviction, Parks was readily dissuaded. Finally Crenshaw revealed the basis of his proposition:

"If we granted the Negroes these demands," he asserted, "they would go about boasting of a victory that they had won over the white people; and this we will not stand for."

Now, at least, Crenshaw's motives were out in the open. We tried to convince him that the Negroes had no such intention. We assured him that if the proposals were granted we would make it our primary business to restrain our people from proclaiming their victory. But none of these assurances moved him. Seeing the futility of continuing, I finally asked him to state specifically what the bus company would be willing to offer the Negroes. His answer was brief: "We will certainly be willing to guarantee courtesy. But we cannot change the seating arrangement because such a change would violate the law. And as far as bus drivers are concerned, we have no intention now or in the foreseeable future of hiring 'niggras.' "

Four hours of deliberation had come to an end without settlement.

I left the meeting despondent, but I soon saw that I was the victim of an unwarranted pessimism because I had started out with an unwarranted optimism. I had gone to the meeting with a great illusion. Feeling that our demands were moderate, I had assumed that they would be granted with little ques-

White Citizens Council in session. *"The members of the opposition . . . revealed that they did not know the Negroes with whom they were dealing . . . They were not aware that they were dealing with Negroes who had been freed from fear."*

tion; I had believed that the privileged would give up their privileges on request. This experience, however, taught me a lesson. I came to see that no one gives up his privileges without strong resistance. I saw further that the underlying purpose of segregation was to oppress and exploit the segregated, not simply to keep them apart. Even when we asked for justice *within* the segregation laws, the "powers that be" were not willing to grant it. Justice and equality, I saw, would never come while segregation remained, because the basic purpose of segregation was to perpetuate injustice and inequality.

Shortly after this first negotiating conference, I called a meeting of the executive board of the MIA to report the results. The members were disappointed, but agreed that we should stand firm on our three proposals. By this time someone had discovered that the Montgomery City Lines were owned by a company with headquarters in Chicago; this company—National City Lines, Inc.—operated buses in more than thirty-five cities. It was agreed that we should wire the president of the National City Lines stating our grievances, and urging him to come immediately, or send a representative, to Montgomery to negotiate further. Two days later the president replied that one of the company vice-presidents would be down in two or three days.

This favorable response gave us new hope, and we waited patiently for the representative from Chicago. After several days had passed and I had heard nothing, I began to wonder whether the company had backed out. In this state of uncertainty I received a call from one of my white friends on the morning of December 15, saying that he had heard from realiable sources that a Mr. C. K. Totten was in town from the National City Lines, and wondering whether I had talked to him. When I answered with obvious disappoint-

ment, my friend offered to check further. Sure enough, in about two hours he called me back to say that Totten was definitely in Montgomery and had been around for two or three days. It seemed strange to me that the bus official had been in town this long without trying to speak to anyone in the MIA, but I continued to wait for his call. The wait was in vain. I never heard from Mr. Totten.

In the meantime, the mayor sent word that he was calling a citizens committee to meet with the bus officials and Negro leaders on the morning of December 17. Over a week had passed since the first conference and the protest had still shown no signs of faltering.

The executive board of the MIA once more met to discuss our position. Again we agreed to stand firm on the three proposals. There was, however, this slight modification of the third point: considering the possibility that there were no imminent vacancies and taking into account the existence of certain priorities due to union regulations, it was agreed that we would not demand the immediate hiring of Negro bus drivers, but would settle for the willingness of the bus company to take applications from Negroes and hire some as soon as vacancies occurred.

Only a few people had assembled when we entered the conference room on Saturday morning, and these seemed exceptionally cordial. One of the first who came forward to greet us was Rev. Henry E. Russell, minister of the Trinity Presbyterian Church of Montgomery and brother of Senator Richard Russell of Georgia. I remember the heartiness of his smile and the warmth of his handclasp. Gradually, others came and they, too, appeared friendly. We began to hope that something better might come of this second meeting.

Just before the meeting opened I noticed an unfamiliar man entering the room with Bagley and Crenshaw. He was introduced as C. K. Totten of Chicago. He greeted each of us warmly, but said nothing of why he had not been in touch with our group. I also noticed two Negro citizens who were not on the committee appointed to represent the Negro community. I soon discovered that they were there on special invitation from the mayor. This made me rather suspicious of what was going on.

Finally, the mayor came in, followed by the two associate commissioners. By this time all were present: the three commissioners; four representatives from the bus company; the committee representing the Negro community; the two Negro men invited by the mayor; and the mayor's citizens committee, among them the Revs. Henry Parker, then minister of First Baptist Church, E. Stanley Frazier, then minister of St. James Methodist Church, and Henry Russell.

After summarizing the situation, the mayor called upon me to explain the Negroes' proposals. When I had finished he called on a representative from the bus company, and C. K. Totten rose to his feet.

As Totten stood up before the group I waited anxiously to hear what he would say. Because he came from outside, there was always a possibility that he would see the problem in a different light from his associates. Slowly and deliberately he spoke of each of our proposals. As he took them up one by one no doubt remained: he was taking the same position that the city commission and Crenshaw had held in the first meeting. If Totten could have miraculously acquired a Southern accent, and spoken without being seen, I would have sworn that he was Jack Crenshaw. I knew then that he had been "brainwashed" by the city commission and the bus officials.

As Totten continued, my indignation grew. I reflected bitterly that he had not even given the Negroes the courtesy of a hearing, in spite of the fact that we were the ones who had invited him to Montgomery. This was a difficult moment. Should I challenge his biased and one-sided presentation or let it pass? The question turned over and over in my mind. When he had finished, things were quiet for a moment. Then unable to restrain myself any longer I jumped to my feet and gave voice to my resentment: "Mr. Totten has not been fair in his assertions. He has made a statement that is completely biased. In spite of the fact that he was asked to come to Montgomery by the MIA, he has not done the Negro community the simple courtesy of hearing their grievances. The least that all of us can do in our deliberations is to be honest and fair." A chorus of amens could be heard from the Negro delegation. Neither the mayor nor C. K. Totten replied, but the latter shifted uncomfortably in his seat.

The meeting proceeded with statements from several of the citizens who had been invited by the mayor. I remember especially the words of Dr. Frazier—one of the most outspoken segregationists in the Methodist Church. Although I had heard his name and read his segregationist statements, I had never been in his presence. Now I saw a tall, distinguished-looking man, the quintessence of dignity. He was, I soon found, articulate and eloquent besides. He talked persuasively about the frailties and weaknesses of human nature. He made it clear that he felt the Negroes were wrong in boycotting the buses; and the even greater wrong, he contended, lay in the fact that the protest was being led by ministers of the gospel. The job of the minister, he averred, is to lead the souls of men to God, not to bring about confusion by getting tangled up in transitory social problems. He moved on to a brief discussion of the Christmas story. In evocative terms he talked of "God's unspeakable gift." He ended by saying that as we moved into the Christmas season, our minds and hearts should be turned toward the Babe of Bethlehem; and he urged the Negro ministers to leave the meeting determined to bring this boycott to a close and lead their people instead "to a glorious experience of the Christian faith."

Again I felt the need of answering. "We too know the Jesus that the minister just referred to," I said. "We have had an experience with him, and we believe firmly in the revelation of God in Jesus Christ. I can see no conflict between our devotion to Jesus Christ and our present action. In fact I see a necessary relationship. If one is truly devoted to the religion of Jesus he will seek to rid the earth of social evils. The gospel is social as well as personal. We are only doing in a minor way what Gandhi did in India; and certainly no one referred to him as an unrepentant sinner; he is considered by many a saint.

"We have been talking a great deal this morning about customs," I concluded. "It has been affirmed that any change in present conditions would mean going against the 'cherished customs' of our community. But if the customs are wrong we have every reason in the world to change them. The decision which we must make now is whether we will give our allegiance to outmoded and unjust customs or to the ethical demands of the universe. As Christians we owe our ultimate allegiance to God and His will, rather than to man and his folkways."

After a few more people had spoken, the mayor announced that he would appoint a small group from the citizens committee to meet with representatives from the MIA and the bus company. These groups were to work out some settlement and bring it back to him in the form of a recommendation. At first the mayor tried to stack the committee by appointing eight white people from the citizens committee, the two Negro men whom he had invited personally, and only three people from the MIA. But Jo Ann Robinson immediately took issue, insisting that the only equitable way to handle the problem was to appoint as many Negroes as whites. Thereupon the mayor reluctantly raised the number of Negroes to eight. He appointed Rev. Henry Parker chairman.

After the larger group had left the room, and Parker had called the new committee to order, Frazier asked permission to read a suggested solution to the seating problem. Its substance was that signs be placed on the buses clearly stating the section for each race to occupy. No more than ten spaces would be reserved for either race. In the event that whites or Negroes completely filled the seats in their section, the vacant seats beyond their prescribed area could be temporarily occupied so long as members of the opposite race did not board the bus. The members of the Negro group instantly rejected this idea, finding the idea of racial signs repugnant, and believing that acceptance would mean a step backward rather than forward.

Several of the white committeemen then suggested that we return to the buses, and come back after the Christmas holidays to work out a settlement. They contended that the white community would listen more sympathetically to our requests if we first called off the protest. Our response was again negative. We felt that all of our efforts would have been in vain if we called off the protest simply with the promise that something might be done about conditions later. By now considerable time had passed, and the chairman suggested that we adjourn and reassemble on Monday morning at ten.

At the close of the meeting I had my first opportunity to talk face to face with Totten.

Almost sheepishly he admitted that the plan we were offering was the one followed by the Mobile City Lines—another company owned by the National City Lines, Inc. "And as far as I am concerned," he said, "it would work very well in Montgomery. But the city commission seems to feel that it will not be acceptable." I was tempted to ask why he hadn't had the courage to say this in the general meeting when the commissioners were present, but I restrained myself, and the conversation ended on a friendly note.

As I drove home my mind went back to Frazier and his eloquence. How firmly he believed in the position he was taking. He would probably never change now; time-worn traditions had become too crystallized in his soul. The "isness" of segregation had for him become one with the "oughtness" of the moral law. Yet even though I totally disagreed with his point of view, and knew that history and religion had proven him wrong, I admired his sincerity and zeal. Why is it, I asked myself, that the whites who believe in integration are so often less eloquent, less positive, in their testimony than the segregationists? It is still one of the tragedies of human history that the "children of darkness" are frequently more determined and zealous than the "children of light."

Sunday, December 18, rolled away. At ten o'clock Monday morning we reassembled to continue our deliberations. Everyone was on hand and Parker was again presiding. Just after the meeting was called to order, I noticed a man who had not been present on Saturday and who, as far as I could remember, had not been appointed to the eight-man citizens committee by the Mayor. Someone next to me whispered, "That is Luther Ingalls—secretary of the Montgomery White Citizens Council."

As soon as the discussion period opened Ingalls stood up to make a statement. I immediately jumped to the floor and challenged his right to speak since he was not a member of the committee. "Furthermore," I continued, "we will never solve this problem so long as there are persons on the committee whose public pronouncements are anti-Negro."

At this Dr. Parker replied angrily: "He has just as much right to be on this committee as you do. You have a definite point of view and you are on it."

Thereupon the other white members of the committee began to lash out against me. They contended that I was the chief stumbling block to a real solution of the problem. A Mrs. Hipp said vehemently that I had insulted her by implying that she, along with other white members of the committee, had come to the meeting with a closed mind. I tried to make it clear that my statement applied only to those people whose public pronouncements were anti-Negro, and not to the committee as a whole, but to no avail. They continued to look at me as though I were the cause of the stalemate.

For a moment it appeared that I was alone. Nobody came to my rescue, until suddenly Ralph Abernathy was on the floor in my defense. He insisted that I spoke for the whole Negro delegation. He pointed out that since I was the spokesman for the group I naturally had to do most of the talking, but this did not mean that I did not have the support of the rest of the committee. As he continued, one could see obvious disappointment on the faces of the white committee members. By trying to convince the Negroes that I was the main obstacle to a solution they had hoped to divide us among ourselves. But Ralph's statement left no doubt. From this moment on the white group saw the futility of attempting to negotiate us into a compromise. A few more questions were raised and a few more suggestions were made; whereupon Parker brought the meeting to a close, promising to call another one later. But the other meeting was never called.

That Monday I went home with a heavy heart. I was weighted down by a terrible sense of guilt, remembering that on two or three occasions I had allowed myself to become angry and indignant. I had spoken hastily and resentfully. Yet I knew that this was no way to solve a problem. "You must not harbor anger," I admonished myself. "You must be willing to suffer the anger of the opponent, and yet not return anger. You must not become bitter. No matter how emotional your opponents are, you must be calm."

In this mood I went to the telephone and called Parker. He was obviously surprised to hear my voice. I told him that I was sorry about the misunderstanding that had come up in the meeting, and wanted to apologize if I was in any way responsible. He responded by seeking to justify the position he had taken. This led him into a discussion of the race problem in general and the bus situation in particular. He was certain that the Negroes had no basic justification for boycotting the buses, "since many white persons are treated just as discourteously as Negroes." As far as the general problem was concerned, he felt that Negroes all over were pushing things too fast, and this, he contended, could lead to nothing but trouble. I thanked him for talking to me, and the conversation ended.

One further attempt was made to reopen negotiations, thanks to the good offices of another group of white citizens. The Men of Montgomery was an organization composed of the most influential businessmen of the city. They had already begun to see the effects of the protest on trade, and realized

A motorcycle policeman trails a pool-car. *"The 'get-tough' policy turned out to be a series of arrests for minor and often imaginary traffic violations . . . Negro drivers in the car-pool were stopped throughout the city and questioned about their licenses, their insurance, their place of work."*

that a prolonged conflict could be disastrous. Moreover, their leaders were men of good will who abhorred the increasing tension they saw around them. This is not to imply that these men were stanch integrationists; far from it. Some of them believed firmly in segregation, and even those who did not would probably have agreed with Parker that the Negroes were "pushing things too fast." But at least they were open-minded enough to listen to another point of view and discuss the problem of race intelligently. Twice, a half a dozen of the Men of Montgomery met with a similar number from the MIA in an earnest effort to settle the protest, and I have no doubt that we would have come to a solution had it not been for the recalcitrance of the city commission. As it was, our joint effort petered out with no results.

After the opposition had failed to negotiate us into a compromise, it turned to subtler means for blocking the protest; namely, to conquer by dividing. False rumors were spread concerning the leaders of the movement. Negro workers were told by their white employers that their leaders were only concerned with making money out of the movement. Others were told that the Negro leaders rode big cars while they walked. During this period the rumor was spread that I had purchased a brand new Cadillac for myself and a Buick station wagon for my wife. Of course none of this was true.

Not only was there a conscious attempt to raise questions about the integrity of the Negro leaders, and thereby cause their followers to lose faith in them; there was also an attempt to divide the leaders among themselves. Prominent white citizens went to many of the older Negro ministers and said: "If there has to be a protest, you should be the leaders. It is a shame for you, who have been in the community for so many years, to have your own people overlook you and choose these young upstarts to lead them." Certain members of the white community tried to convince several of the other protest leaders that the problem could be solved if I were out of the picture. "If one of you," they would say, "took over the leadership, things would change overnight."

I almost broke down under the continual battering of this argument. I began to think that there might be some truth in it, and I also feared that some were being influenced by this argument. After two or three troubled days and nights of little sleep, I called a meeting of the executive board and offered my resignation. I told them that I would be the last person to want to stand in the way of a solution to the problem which plagued our community, and that maybe a more mature person could bring about a speedier conclusion. I suggested the names of two men who had worked closely with me and whose competence no one could question. I further assured the board that I would be as active in the background as I had been in the position of spokesman. But I had barely finished talking before board members began to urge me from every side to forget the idea of resignation. With a unanimous vote of confidence, they made it clear that they were well pleased with the way I was handling things, and that they would follow my leadership to the end.

Afterward, as I drove up to the parsonage, more at peace than I had been in some time, I could hear Coretta's high, true soprano through the living room window. In the back bedroom "Yoki," now more than a month old, was wide awake and busy discovering her fingers. I picked her up and walked to the front room, bouncing her in time to Coretta's song.

Such moments together had become rare.

We could never plan them, for I seldom knew from one hour to the next when I would be home. Many times Coretta saw her good meals grow dry in the oven when a sudden emergency kept me away. Yet she never complained, and she was always there when I needed her. "Yoki" and Beethoven, she said, kept her company when she was alone. Calm and unruffled, Coretta moved quietly about the business of keeping the household going. When I needed to talk things out, she was ready to listen, or to offer suggestions when I asked for them. Her fortitude was my strength. Afraid for me at times, she never allowed her fears to worry me or impede my work in the protest. And she seemed to have no fear for herself. Several times, in the months that followed, I sent her and "Yoki" to Atlanta to stay with my parents, or to Marion to stay with hers. But she never stayed long. "When I am away from this," she told a reporter, "I feel depressed and helpless." And so time and again she was back ahead of schedule.

The height of the attempt to conquer by dividing came on Sunday, January 22, when the city commissioners shocked the Negro community by announcing in the local newspaper that they had met with a group of prominent Negro ministers and worked out a settlement. The terms of the so-called "settlement" were: (1) a guarantee of courtesy; (2) a white reserved section at the front of the bus, and a Negro reserved section at the rear, with first-come, first-served obtaining for the unreserved, middle section; (3) special, all-Negro buses during the rush hours. Actually, except for the first provision, this "settlement" was nothing but a restatement of conditions that had existed prior to the protest. At some points it was a backward step. Nevertheless, many people were convinced the boycott was over.

It was soon clear that this announcement was a calculated design to get the Negroes back on the buses Sunday morning. The city commission felt certain that once a sizable number of Negroes began riding the buses, the boycott would end.

We were able to stave off the effects of this announcement by a set of interesting circumstances. Although the *Montgomery Advertiser* had apparently agreed to hold the story until Sunday morning, the Associated Press sent it out on Saturday evening. Carl T. Rowan, Negro editorial writer of the *Minneapolis Tribune,* caught the story as it came over the wires, and was amazed to learn that the Negroes had settled for such a "half loaf." Mr. Rowan had been to Montgomery a few weeks before to cover the boycott, and had established a close relationship with the MIA leaders. Around eight o'clock on Saturday evening, he called me long distance to verify the story. When he mentioned the meeting and settlement I was astonished, and when he spoke of three prominent Negro ministers present at the meeting I was even more puzzled. I told him that I knew nothing about the matter, and I began to wonder whether any of my associates had betrayed me and made an agreement in my absence. "But this can't be true," I said, "because I was in a strategy meeting this morning, and all of the 'prominent ministers' were there."

Rowan agreed to call Commissioner Sellers and get more detailed information. In about twenty minutes he phoned back to say that Sellers had confirmed the story but refused to give the names of the "prominent Negro ministers." Rowan had been able, however, to get their denominations from the commissioner. This clue was all I needed.

I asked several of my associates to come to my house immediately, and in less than thirty minutes they were all there. I told them the story, and we determined to get at the root of it before midnight. First we needed to find out if a group of Negro ministers had actually met with the city commission. Remembering the denominations that Rowan had mentioned, we started to track the identities down by a process of elimination. After about an hour of calling here and there we were able to identify the "three prominent Negro ministers." They were neither prominent nor were they members of the MIA.

It was now about eleven o'clock on Saturday night. Something had to be done to let the people know that the article they would read the next morning was false. I asked one group to call all the Negro ministers of the city and urge them to announce in church Sunday morning that the protest was still on. Another group joined me on a tour of the Negro night clubs and taverns to inform those present of the false settlement. For the first time I had a chance to see the inside of most of Montgomery's night spots. At one o'clock Sunday morning we were still making the announcement in clubs. As a result of our fast maneuvering, the word got around so well that the next day the buses were empty as usual.

I soon had a chance to talk to each of the "three prominent Negro ministers" personally. To a man they insisted that they had not agreed on any settlement. They asserted that they had been "hoodwinked" into the conference on the basis of a telephone invitation to join in a discussion of a new type of insurance for the city. All three publicly repudiated the commission's announcement.

With the failure of the attempted hoax, the city fathers lost face. Not only had they been outmaneuvered, but their veracity had been challenged. They were now desperate. Their answer was to embark on a "get-tough" policy. In obvious indignation, the mayor went on television and denounced the boycott. He threatened that the commission was going to "stop pussy-footing around with the boycott." The vast majority of white Montgomerians, he declared, did not care if a Negro ever rode the buses again, and he called upon the white employers to stop driving Negro employees to and from work. During this period all three city commissioners let it be known that they had joined the White Citizens Council.

The "get-tough" policy turned out to be a series of arrests for minor and often imaginary traffic violations. People who had never received a ticket were booked, and on several occasions taken to jail. Negro drivers in the car pool were stopped throughout the city and questioned about their licenses, their insurance, their place of work. The policemen made careful notes, apparently in the hope of building up subsequent cases. Some ex-bus riders, waiting to be picked up, were told that there was a law against hitchhiking; others were told that they would be arrested for vagrancy if they were found "milling around white neighborhoods."

Faced with these difficulties, the volunteer car pool began to weaken. Some drivers became afraid that their licenses would be revoked or their insurance canceled; others felt that they could no longer adhere to nonviolence under such circumstances. Many of the drivers quietly dropped out of the pool. It became more and more difficult to catch a ride. Complaints began to rise. From early morning to late at night my telephone rang and my doorbell was seldom silent. I began to have doubts about the ability of the Negro community to continue the struggle.

In an attempt to keep things together the ministers made special appeals at mass meetings, urging the people to stand fast. We assured the drivers in the car pool that we would stick with them through their difficulties. "We must remain together," we kept repeating, "for better or for worse, until this problem is solved."

I did not suspect that I myself was soon to face arrest as a result of the "get-tough" operation. One afternoon in the middle of January, after several hours of work at my church office, I started driving home with a friend, Robert Williams, and the church secretary, Mrs. Lilie Thomas. Before leaving the downtown district I decided to make a quick trip to the parking lot to pick up a few people going in my direction. As we entered the lot, I noticed four or five policemen questioning the drivers. I picked up three passengers and drove to the edge of the lot, where I was stopped by one of these officers. While he was asking to see my license and questioning me concerning the ownership of the car, I heard a policeman across the street say, "That's that damn King fellow."

Leaving the lot, I noticed two motorcycle policemen behind me. One was still following three blocks later. When I told Bob Williams that we were being trailed, he said, "Be sure that you follow every traffic regulation." Slowly and meticulously I drove toward home, with the motorcycle behind me. Finally, as I stopped to let the three passengers out, the policeman pulled up and said: "Get out, King; you are under arrest for speeding thirty miles an hour in a twenty-five mile zone." Without a question I got out of the car, telling Bob Williams and Mrs. Thomas to drive on and notify my wife. Soon a patrol car came, two policemen got out and searched me from top to bottom, put me in the car, and drove off.

As we drove off, presumably to the city jail, a feeling of panic began to come over me. I had always had the impression that the jail was in the downtown section of Montgomery.

Yet after riding for a while I noticed that we were going in a different direction. The more we rode the farther we were from the center of town. In a few minutes we turned into a dark and dingy street that I had never seen and headed under a desolate old bridge. By this time I was convinced that these men were carrying me to some faraway spot to dump me off. "But this couldn't be," I said to myself. "These men are officers of the law." Then I began to wonder whether they were driving me out to some waiting mob, planning to use the excuse later on that they had been overpowered. I found myself trembling within and without. Silently, I asked God to give me the strength to endure whatever came.

By this time we were passing under the bridge. I was sure now that I was going to meet my fateful hour on the other side. But as I looked up I noticed a glaring light in the distance, and soon I saw the words "Montgomery City Jail." I was so relieved that it was some time before I realized the irony of my position: going to jail at that moment seemed like going to some safe haven!

A policeman ushered me in. After depositing my things and giving the jailer the desired information, I was led to a dingy and odorous cell. As the big iron door swung open the jailer said to me: "All right, get on in there with all the others." For the moment strange gusts of emotion swept through me like cold winds on an open prairie. For the first time in my life I had been thrown behind bars.

As I entered the crowded cell, I recognized two acquaintances, one a teacher, who had also been arrested on pretexts connected with the protest. In the democracy of the jail they were packed together with vagrants and drunks and serious lawbreakers. One cellmate was in on a charge of assault and battery; another stood accused of collecting funds under false pretenses. But the democracy did not go so far as to break the rules of segregation. Here whites and Negroes languished in separate enclosures.

When I began to look around I was so appalled at the conditions I saw that I soon forgot my own predicament. I saw men lying on hard wood slats, and others resting on cots with torn-up mattresses. The toilet was in one corner of the cell without a semblance of an enclosure. I said to myself that no matter what these men had done, they shouldn't be treated like this.

They all gathered around to find out why I was there, and showed some surprise that the city had gone so far as to arrest me. Soon one man after another began talking to me about his reason for being in jail and asking if I could help him get out. After the third person had asked my help, I turned to the group and said: "Fellows, before I can assist in getting any of you out, I've got to get my ownself out." At this they laughed.

Shortly after, the jailer came to get me. As I left the cell, wondering where he was going to take me, one of the men called after me: "Don't forget us when you get out." I assured them that I would not forget. The jailer led me down a long corridor into a little room in the front of the jail. I thought for a moment that I was going to be bonded out, but I soon discovered my mistake. Curtly the jailer ordered me to be seated, and began rubbing my fingers on an ink pad. I was about to be fingerprinted like a criminal.

By this time the news of my arrest had spread over Montgomery, and a number of people had headed for the city jail. The first to arrive was my good friend Ralph Abernathy. He immediately sought to sign my bond, but the officials told him that he had to bring a certified statement from the court asserting that he owned a sufficient amount of property to sign a bond. Ralph pointed out that since it was almost six-thirty at night, the courthouse was already closed.

Indifferently, the official retorted: "Well, you will just have to wait till tomorrow morning."

Ralph then asked if he could see me.

The jailer replied: "No, you can't see him until ten o'clock tomorrow."

"Well, is it possible," said Abernathy, "to pay a cash bond?"

The jailer reluctantly answered yes. Ralph rushed to his church office a few blocks away to call someone who could produce the cash.

Meanwhile a number of people had assembled in front of the jail. Deacons and trustees of my church were coming from every side. Soon the crowd had become so large that the jailer began to panic. Rushing into the fingerprinting room he said: "King, you can go now," and before I could half get my coat on, he was ushering me out, released on my own bond. He returned my possessions and informed me that my trial would be held on Monday morning at eight-thirty.

As I walked out the front door and noticed the host of friends and well-wishers, I regained the courage that I had temporarily lost. I knew that I did not stand alone. After a brief statement to the crowd, I was driven home by one of my deacons. My wife greeted me with a kiss as I walked in the door. Inside, many members of my church and other friends were waiting anxiously to hear the outcome. Their words of encouragement gave me further assurance that I was not alone.

From that night on my commitment to the struggle for freedom was stronger than ever before. Before retiring I talked with Coretta, and, as usual, she gave me the reassurance that can only come from one who is as close to you as your own heartbeat. Yes, the night of injustice was dark: the "get-tough" policy was taking its toll. But in the darkness I could see a radiant star of unity.

CHAPTER VIII

THE VIOLENCE
OF DESPERATE MEN

AFTER THE "GET-TOUGH" policy failed to stop the movement the diehards became desperate, and we waited to see what their next move would be. Almost immediately after the protest started we had begun to receive threatening telephone calls and letters. Sporadic in the beginning, they increased as time went on. By the middle of January, they had risen to thirty and forty a day.

Postcards, often signed "KKK," said simply "get out of town or else." Many misspelled and crudely written letters presented religious half-truths to prove that "God do not intend the White People and the Negro to go to gather if he did we would be the same." Others enclosed mimeographed and printed materials combining anti-Semitic and anti-Negro sentiments. One of these contained a handwritten postscript: "You niggers are getting your self in a bad place. The Bible is strong for segregation as of the jews concerning other races. It is even for segregation between the 12 tribes of Isarael. We need and will have a Hitler to get our country straightened out." Many of the letters were unprintable catalogues of blasphemy and obscenity.

Meanwhile the telephone rang all day and most of the night. Often Coretta was alone in the house when the calls came, but the insulting voices did not spare her. Many times the person on the other end simply waited until we answered and then hung up. A large percentage of the calls had sexual themes. One woman, whose voice I soon came to recognize, telephoned day after day to hurl her sexual accusations at the Negro. Whenever I

tried to answer, as I frequently did in an effort to explain our case calmly, the caller would cut me off. Occasionally, we would leave the telephone off the hook, but we could not do this for long because we never knew when an important call would come in.

When these incidents started, I took them in stride, feeling that they were the work of a few hotheads who would soon be discouraged when they discovered that we would not fight back. But as the weeks passed, I began to see that many of the threats were in earnest. Soon I felt myself faltering and growing in fear. One day, a white friend told me that he had heard from reliable sources that plans were being made to take my life. For the first time I realized that something could happen to me.

One night at a mass meeting, I found myself saying: "If one day you find me sprawled out dead, I do not want you to retaliate with a single act of violence. I urge you to continue protesting with the same dignity and discipline you have shown so far." A strange silence came over the audience.

Afterward, to the anxious group that gathered around, I tried to make light of the incident by saying that my words had not grown from any specific cause, but were just a general statement of principle that should guide our actions in the event of any fatality. But Ralph Abernathy was not satisfied. As he drove me home that night, he said:

"Something is wrong. You are disturbed about something."

I tried to evade the issue by repeating what

I had just told the group at the church. But he persisted.

"Martin," he said, "You were not talking about some general principle. You had something specific in mind."

Unable to evade any longer, I admitted the truth. For the first time I told him about the threats that were harassing my family. I told him about the conversation with my white friend. I told him about the fears that were creeping up on my soul. Ralph tried to reassure me, but I was still afraid.

The threats continued. Almost every day someone warned me that he had overheard white men making plans to get rid of me. Almost every night I went to bed faced with the uncertainty of the next moment. In the morning I would look at Coretta and "Yoki" and say to myself: "They can be taken away from me at any moment; I can be taken away from them at any moment." For once I did not even share my thoughts with Coretta.

One night toward the end of January I settled into bed late, after a strenuous day. Coretta had already fallen asleep and just as I was about to doze off the telephone rang. An angry voice said, "Listen, nigger, we've taken all we want from you; before next week you'll be sorry you ever came to Montgomery." I hung up, but I couldn't sleep. It seemed that all of my fears had come down on me at once. I had reached the saturation point.

I got out of bed and began to walk the floor. Finally I went to the kitchen and heated a pot of coffee. I was ready to give up. With my cup of coffee sitting untouched before me I tried to think of a way to move out of the picture without appearing a coward. In this state of exhaustion, when my courage had all but gone, I decided to take my problem to God. With my head in my hands, I bowed over the kitchen table and prayed aloud. The words I spoke to God that mid-night are still vivid in my memory. "I am here taking a stand for what I believe is right. But now I am afraid. The people are looking to me for leadership, and if I stand before them without strength and courage, they too will falter. I am at the end of my powers. I have nothing left. I've come to the point where I can't face it alone."

At that moment I experienced the presence of the Divine as I had never experienced Him before. It seemed as though I could hear the quiet assurance of an inner voice saying: "Stand up for righteousness, stand up for truth; and God will be at your side forever." Almost at once my fears began to go. My uncertainty disappeared. I was ready to face anything.

Three nights later, on January 30, I left home a little before seven to attend our Monday evening mass meeting at the First Baptist Church. A member of my congregation, Mrs. Mary Lucy Williams, had come to the parsonage to keep my wife company in my absence. After putting the baby to bed, Coretta and Mrs. Williams went to the living room to look at television. About nine-thirty they heard a noise in front that sounded as though someone had thrown a brick. In a matter of seconds an explosion rocked the house. A bomb had gone off on the porch.

The sound was heard many blocks away, and word of the bombing reached the mass meeting almost instantly. Toward the close of the meeting, as I stood on the platform helping to take the collection, I noticed an usher rushing to give Ralph Abernathy a message. Abernathy turned and ran downstairs, soon to reappear with a worried look on his face. Several others rushed in and out of the church. People looked at me and then away; one or two seemed about to approach me and then changed their minds. An usher called me to the side of the platform, presumably to give me a message, but before I could get there S. S. Seay had sent him away. By now I was convinced that whatever had happened affected me. I called Ralph Abernathy, S. S. Seay, and E. N. French and asked them to tell me what was wrong. Ralph looked at Seay and French and then turned to me and said hesitantly:

"Your house has been bombed."

I asked if my wife and baby were all right. They said, "We are checking on that now."

Strangely enough, I accepted the word of the bombing calmly. My religious experience a few nights before had given me the strength to face it. I interrupted the collection and asked all present to give me their undivided attention. After telling them why I had to leave, I urged each person to go straight home after the meeting and adhere strictly to our philosophy of nonviolence. I admonished them not to become panicky and lose their heads. "Let us keep moving," I urged them, "with the faith that what we are doing is right, and with the even greater faith that God is with us in the struggle."

I was immediately driven home. As we neared the scene I noticed hundreds of people with angry faces in front of the house. The policemen were trying, in their usual rough manner, to clear the streets, but they were ignored by the crowd. One Negro was saying to a policeman, who was attempting to push him aside: "I ain't gonna move nowhere. That's the trouble now; you white folks is always pushin' us around. Now you got your '38 and I got mine; so let's battle it out." As I walked toward the front porch I realized that many people were armed. Nonviolent resistance was on the verge of being transformed into violence.

I rushed into the house to see if Coretta and "Yoki" were safe. When I walked into the bedroom and saw my wife and daughter uninjured, I drew my first full breath in many minutes. I learned that fortunately when Coretta and Mrs. Williams had heard the sound of something falling on the front porch, they had jumped up and run to the back of the house. If instead they had gone to the porch to investigate, the outcome might have been fatal. Coretta was neither bitter nor panicky. She had accepted the whole thing with unbelievable composure. As I noticed her calmness I became even more calm myself.

Mayor Gayle, Commissioner Sellers, and several white reporters had reached the house before I did and were standing in the dining room. After reassuring myself about my family's safety, I went to speak to them. Both Gayle and Sellers expressed their regret that "this unfortunate incident has taken place in our city." One of the trustees of my church, who is employed in the public school system of Montgomery, was standing beside me when the mayor and the commissioner spoke. Although in a vulnerable position, he turned to the mayor and said: "You may express your regrets, but you must face the fact that your public statements created the atmosphere for this bombing. This is the end result of your 'get-tough' policy." Neither Mayor Gayle nor Commissioner Sellers could reply.

By this time the crowd outside was getting out of hand. The policemen had failed to disperse them, and throngs of additional people were arriving every minute. The white reporters inside the house wanted to leave to get their stories on the wires, but they were afraid to face the angry crowd. The mayor and police commissioner, though they might not have admitted it, were very pale.

In this atmosphere I walked out to the porch and asked the crowd to come to order. In less than a moment there was complete silence. Quietly I told them that I was all right and that my wife and baby were all right. "Now let's not become panicky," I continued. "If you have weapons, take them home; if you do not have them, please do not seek to get them. We cannot solve this problem through retaliatory violence. We must meet violence with nonviolence. Remember the words of Jesus: 'He who lives by the sword will perish by the sword.' " I then urged them to leave peacefully. "We must love our white brothers," I said, "no matter what they do to us. We must make them know that we love them. Jesus still cries out in words that echo across the centuries: 'Love your enemies; bless them that curse you; pray for them that despitefully use you.' This is what we must live by. We must meet hate with love. Remember," I ended, "if I am stopped, this movement will not stop, because God is with the movement. Go home with this glowing faith and this radiant assurance."

As I finished speaking there were shouts of "Amen" and "God bless you." I could hear voices saying: "We are with you all the way, Reverend." I looked out over that vast throng of people and noticed tears on many faces.

After I finished, the police commissioner began to address the crowd. Immediately there were boos. Police officers tried to get the attention of the Negroes by saying, "Be quiet—the commissioner is speaking." To this the crowd responded with even louder boos. I came back to the edge of the porch and raised my hand for silence. "Remember what I just said. Let us hear the commissioner." In the ensuing lull, the commissioner

Ralph Abernathy's house after the bombers have finished. *"I looked at Ralph as he sat down beside me, stunned. Both his home and his church bombed in one night and I knew no words to comfort him."*

spoke and offered a reward to the person or persons who could report the offenders. Then the crowd began to disperse.

Things remained tense the whole of that night. The Negroes had had enough. They were ready to meet violence with violence. One policeman later told me that if a Negro had fallen over a brick that night a race riot would probably have broken out because the Negro would have been convinced that a white person had pushed him. This could well have been the darkest night in Montgomery's history. But something happened to avert it: The spirit of God was in our hearts; and a night that seemed destined to end in unleashed chaos came to a close in a majestic group demonstration of nonviolence.

After our many friends left the house late that evening, Coretta, "Yoki," and I were driven to the home of one of our church members to spend the night. I could not get to sleep. While I lay in that quiet front bedroom, with a distant street lamp throwing a reassuring glow through the curtained window, I began to think of the viciousness of people who would bomb my home. I could feel the anger rising when I realized that my wife and baby could have been killed. I thought about the city commissioners and all the statements that they had made about me and the Negro generally. I was once more on the verge of corroding hatred. And once more I caught myself and said: "You must not allow yourself to become bitter."

I tried to put myself in the place of the three commissioners. I said to myself these men are not bad men. They are misguided. They have fine reputations in the community. In their dealings with white people they are respectable and gentlemanly. They probably think they are right in their methods of dealing with Negroes. They say the things they

say about us and treat us as they do because they have been taught these things. From the cradle to the grave, it is instilled in them that the Negro is inferior. Their parents probably taught them that; the schools they attended taught them that; the books they read, even their churches and ministers, often taught them that; and above all the very concept of segregation teaches them that. The whole cultural tradition under which they have grown—a tradition blighted with more than 250 years of slavery and more than 90 years of segregation—teaches them that Negroes do not deserve certain things. So these men are merely the children of their culture. When they seek to preserve segregation they are seeking to preserve only what their local folkways have taught them was right.

Midnight had long since passed. Coretta and the baby were sound asleep. It was time for me too to get some rest. At about two-thirty I turned over in bed and fell into a dazed slumber. But the night was not yet over. Some time later Coretta and I were awakened by a slow, steady knocking at the front door. We looked at each other wordlessly in the dim light, and listened as the knocking began again. Through the window we could see the dark outline of a figure on the front porch. Our hosts were sound asleep in the back of the house, and we lay in the front, frozen into inaction. Eventually the sounds stopped and we saw a shadowy figure move across the porch and start down the steps to the street. I pulled myself out of bed, peered through the curtains, and recognized the stocky, reassuring back of Coretta's father.

Obie Scott had heard the news of the bombing over the radio in Marion, and had driven to Montgomery to take Coretta and "Yoki" home with him, "until this thing cools off." We talked together for some time, but although Coretta listened respectfully to her father's persuasions, she would not leave.

"I'm sorry, Dad," she said, "but I belong here with Martin." And so Obie Scott drove back to Marion alone.

Just two nights later, a stick of dynamite was thrown on the lawn of E. D. Nixon. Fortunately, again no one was hurt. Once more a large crowd of Negroes assembled, but they did not lose control. And so nonviolence had won its first and its second tests.

After the bombings, many of the officers of my church and other trusted friends urged me to hire a bodyguard and armed watchmen for my house. I tried to tell them that I had no fears now, and consequently needed no protection. But they were insistent, so I agreed to consider the question. I also went down to the sheriff's office and applied for a license to carry a gun in the car; but this was refused.

Meanwhile I reconsidered. How could I serve as one of the leaders of a nonviolent movement and at the same time use weapons of violence for my personal protection? Coretta and I talked the matter over for several days and finally agreed that arms were no solution. We decided then to get rid of the one weapon we owned. We tried to satisfy our friends by having floodlights mounted around the house, and hiring unarmed watchmen around the clock. I also promised that I would not travel around the city alone.

This was a comparatively easy promise to keep, thanks to our friend, Bob Williams, professor of music at Alabama State College and a former collegemate of mine at Morehouse. When I came to Montgomery, I had found him here, and from the moment the protest started he was seldom far from my side or Coretta's. He did most of my driving around Montgomery and accompanied me on several out-of-town trips. Whenever Coretta and "Yoki" went to Atlanta or Marion, he was always there to drive them down and to bring them back. Almost imperceptibly he had become my voluntary "bodyguard," though he carried no arms and could never have been as fierce as the name implied.

In this crisis the officers and members of my church were always nearby to lend their encouragement and active support. As I gradually lost my role as husband and father, having to be away from home for hours and sometimes days at a time, the women of the church came into the house to keep Coretta company. Often they volunteered to cook the meals and clean, or help with the baby. Many of the men took turns as watchmen, or drove me around when Bob Williams was not available. Nor did my congregation ever complain when the multiplicity of my new responsibilities caused me to lag in my pastoral duties. For months my day-to-day contact with my parishioners had almost ceased. I had become no more than a Sunday preacher. But my church willingly shared me with the community, and threw their own considerable resources of time and money into the struggle.

Our local white friends, too, came forward with their support. Often they called Coretta to say an encouraging word, and when the house was bombed several of them, known and unknown to us, came by to express their regret. Occasionally the mail would bring a letter from a white Montgomerian saying "Carry on, we are with you a hundred percent." Frequently these were simply signed "a white friend."

Interestingly enough, for some time after the bombings the threatening telephone calls slowed up. But this was only a lull; several months later they had begun again in full force. In order to sleep at night, it finally became necessary to apply for an unlisted number. This number was passed out to all the members of the church, the members of the MIA, and other friends across the coun-

gomery County Grand Jury was called to determine whether Negroes who were boycotting the buses were violating this law. After about a week of deliberations, the jury, composed of seventeen whites and one Negro, found the boycott illegal and indicted more than one hundred persons. My name, of course, was on the list.

At the time of the indictments I was at Fisk University in Nashville, giving a series of lectures. During this period I was talking to Montgomery on the phone at least three times a day in order to keep abreast of developments. Thus I heard of the indictments first in a telephone call from Ralph Abernathy, late Tuesday night, February 21. He said that the arrests were scheduled to begin the following morning. Knowing that he would be one of the first to be arrested, I assured him that I would be with him and the others in my prayers. As usual he was unperturbed. I told him that I would cut my trip short in Nashville and come to Montgomery the next day.

I booked an early morning flight. All night long I thought of the people in Montgomery. Would these mass arrests so frighten them that they would urge us to call off the protest? I knew how hard-pressed they had been. For more than thirteen weeks they had walked, and sacrificed, and worn down their cars. They had been harassed and intimidated on every hand. And now they faced arrest on top of all this. Would they become battle-weary, I wondered. Would they give up in despair? Would this be the end of our movement?

try. And although it had sometimes been suggested that our own group wss responsible for the threats, we never received another hostile call. Of course, the letters still came, but my secretaries were discreet enough to keep as many of them as possible from my attention.

When the opposition discovered that violence could not block the protest, they resorted to mass arrests. As early as January 9, a Montgomery attorney had called the attention of the press to an old state law against boycotts. He referred to Title 14, Section 54, which provides that when two or more persons enter into a conspiracy to prevent the operation of a lawful business, without just cause or legal excuse, they shall be guilty of a misdemeanor. On February 13 the Mont-

I arose early Wednesday morning, and notified the officials of Fisk that I had to leave ahead of time because of the situation in Montgomery. I flew to Atlanta to pick up my wife and daughter, whom I had left at my parents' home while I was in Nashville. My wife, my mother and father met me at the airport. I had told them about the indictments over the phone, and they had gotten additional information from a radio broadcast. Coretta showed her usual composure; but my parents' faces wore signs of deep perturbation.

My father, so unafraid for himself, had fallen into a constant state of terror for me and my family. Since the protest began he had beaten a path between Atlanta and Montgomery to be at our side. Many times he had sat in on our board meetings and never shown any doubt about the justice of our actions. Yet this stern and courageous man had reached the point where he could scarcely mention the protest without tears. My mother too had suffered. After the bombings she had had to take to bed under doctor's orders, and she was often ill later. Their expressions —even the way they walked, I realized as they came toward me at the airport—had begun to show the strain.

As we drove to their house, my father said that he thought it would be unwise for me to return to Montgomery now. "Although many others have been indicted," he said, "their main concern is to get you. They might even put you in jail without a bond." He went on to tell me that the law enforcement agencies in Montgomery had been trying to find something on my record in Atlanta which would make it possible to deport me from Alabama. They had gone to the Atlanta police department, and were disappointed when Chief Jenkins informed them that I did not have even a minor police record. "All of this shows," my father concluded, "that they are out to get you."

I listened to him attentively, and yet I knew that I could not follow his suggestion and stay in Atlanta. I was profoundly concerned about my parents. I was worried about their worry. I knew that if I continued the struggle I would be plagued by the pain that I was inflicting on them. But if I eased out now I would be plagued by my own conscience, reminding me that I lacked the moral courage to stand by a cause to the end. No one can understand my conflict who has not looked into the eyes of those he loves, knowing that he has no alternative but to take a dangerous stand that leaves them tormented.

My father told me that he had asked several trusted friends to come to the house in the early afternoon to discuss the whole issue. Feeling that this exchange of ideas might help to relieve his worries, I readily agreed to stay over and talk to them. Among those who came were A. T. Walden, a distinguished attorney; C. R. Yates and T. M. Alexander, both prominent businessmen; C. A. Scott, editor of *Atlanta Daily World;* Bishop Sherman L. Green of A. M. E. Church; Benjamin E. Mays, president of Morehouse College; and Rufus E. Clement, president of Atlanta University. Coretta and my mother joined us.

My father explained to the group that because of his respect for their judgment he was calling on them for advice on whether I should return to Montgomery. He gave them a brief history of the attempts that had been made to get me out of Montgomery. He admitted that the fear of what might happen to me had caused him and my mother many restless nights. He concluded by saying that he had talked to a liberal white attorney a few hours earlier, who had confirmed his feeling that I should not go back at this time.

There were murmurs of agreement in the room, and I listened as sympathetically and objectively as I could while two of the men gave their reasons for concurring. These were my elders, leaders among my people. Their words commanded respect. But soon I could not restrain myself any longer. "I must go back to Montgomery," I protested. "My friends and associates are being arrested. It would be the height of cowardice for me to stay away. I would rather be in jail ten years than desert my people now. I have begun the struggle, and I can't turn back. I have reached the point of no return." In the moment of silence that followed I heard my father break into tears. I looked at Dr. Mays, one of the great influences in my life. Perhaps he heard my unspoken plea. At any rate, he was soon defending my position strongly. Then others joined him in supporting me. They assured my father that things were not so bad as they seemed. Mr. Walden put through two calls on the spot to Thurgood Marshall, general counsel of the NAACP, and Arthur Shores, NAACP counsel in Alabama, both of whom assured him that I would have the best legal protection. In the face of all of these persuasions, my father began to be reconciled to my return to Montgomery.

After everybody had gone, Coretta and I went upstairs to our room and had a long talk. She, too, I was glad to find, had no doubt that I must go back immediately. With my own feelings reinforced by the opinions of others I trusted, and with my father's misgivings at rest, I felt better and more prepared to face the experience ahead.

Characteristically, my father, having withdrawn his objections to our return to Montgomery, decided to go along with us, unconcerned with any possible danger or unpleasantness to himself. He secured a driver and at six o'clock Thursday morning we were on the highway headed for Montgomery, arriving about nine. Before we could get out of the car, several television cameras were trained on us. The reporters had somehow discovered the time of our arrival. A few minutes later Ralph Abernathy, released on bail after his arrest the previous day, came to the house. With Ralph and my father, I set out for the county jail, several of my church members following after.

At the jail, an almost holiday atmosphere prevailed. On the way Ralph Abernathy told me how people had rushed down to get arrested the day before. No one, it seems, had been frightened. No one had tried to evade arrest. Many Negroes had gone voluntarily to the sheriff's office to see if their names were on the list, and were even disappointed when they were not. A once fear-ridden people had been transformed. Those who had previously trembled before the law were now proud to be arrested for the cause of freedom. With this feeling of solidarity around me, I walked with firm steps toward the rear of the jail. After I had received a number and had been photographed and fingerprinted, one of my church members paid my bond and I left for home.

The trial was set for March 19. Friends from all over the country came to Montgomery to be with us during the proceedings. Ministers from as far north as New York were present. Negro Congressman Charles C. Diggs (D-Mich.) was on hand. Scores of reporters representing publications in the United States, India, France, and England were there to cover the trial. More than five hundred Negroes stood in the halls and the streets surrounding the small courthouse. Several of them wore crosses on their lapels reading, "Father, forgive them."

Judge Eugene Carter brought the court to order, and after the necessary preliminaries the state called me up as the first defendant. For four days I sat in court listening to arguments and waiting for a verdict. William F. Thetford, solicitor for the state, was attempting to prove that I had disobeyed a law by organizing an illegal boycott. The defense attorneys—Arthur Shores, Peter Hall, Ozell

Billingsley, Fred Gray, Charles Langford, and Robert Carter—presented arguments to show that the prosecution's evidence was insufficient to prove that I had violated Alabama's anti-boycott law. Even if the state had proved such action, they asserted, no evidence was produced to show that the Negroes did not have just cause or legal excuse.

In all, twenty-eight witnesses were brought to the stand by the defense. I listened with a mixture of sadness and awe as these simple people—most of them unlettered—sat on the witness stand without fear and told their stories. They looked the solicitor and the judge in the eye with a courage and dignity to which there was no answer.

Perhaps the most touching testimony was that of Mrs. Stella Brooks. Her husband had climbed on a bus. After paying his fare he was ordered by the driver to get off and reboard by the back door. He looked through the crowded bus and seeing that there was no room in back he said that he would get off and walk if the driver would return his dime. The driver refused; an argument ensued; and the driver called the police. The policeman arrived, abusing Brooks, who still refused to leave the bus unlss his dime was returned. The policeman shot him. It happened so suddenly that everybody was dazed. Brooks died of his wounds.

Mrs. Martha Walker testified about the day when she was leading her blind husband from the bus. She had stepped down and as her husband was following the driver slammed the door and began to drive off.

Walker's leg was caught. Although Mrs. Walker called out, the driver failed to stop, and her husband was dragged some distance before he could free himself. She reported the incident, but the bus company did nothing about it.

The stories continued. Mrs. Sadie Brooks testified that she heard a Negro passenger threatened because he did not have the correct change. "The driver whipped out a pistol and drove the man off the bus." Mrs. Della Perkins described being called an "ugly black ape" by a driver.

I will always remember my delight when Mrs. Georgia Gilmore—an unlettered woman of unusual intelligence—told how an operator demanded that she get off the bus after paying her fare and board it again by the back door, and then drove away before she

The Associated Press news picture that led to reports of the author's collapse. ". . . *in the grip of an emotion I could not control, I said, 'Lord, I hope no one will have to die as a result of our struggle . . . But if anyone has to die, let it be me.' . . . So intense was the reaction that I could not go on . . . Finally with the help of my friends, I sat down.*"

could get there. She turned to Judge Carter and said: "When they count the money, they do not know Negro money from white money."

On Thursday afternoon, March 22, both sides rested. All eyes were turned toward Judge Carter, as with barely a pause he rendered his verdict; "I declare the defendant guilty of violating the state's anti-boycott law." The penalty was a fine of $500 and court costs, or 386 days at hard labor in the County of Montgomery. Then Judge Carter announced that he was giving a minimum penalty because of what I had done to prevent violence. In the cases of the other Negroes charged with the same violation—the number had now boiled down to 89—Judge Carter entered a continuance until a final appeal was complete in my case.

In a few minutes several friends had come up to sign my bond, and the lawyers had notified the judge that the case would be appealed. Many people stood around the courtroom in tears. Others walked out with their heads bowed. I came to the end of my trial with a feeling of sympathy for Judge Carter in his dilemma. To convict me he had to face the condemnation of the nation and world opinion; to acquit me he had to face the condemnation of the local community and those voters who kept him in office. Throughout the proceedings he had treated me with great courtesy, and he had rendered a verdict which he probably thought was the best way out. After the trial he left town for a "welcomed rest."

I left the courtroom with my wife at my side and a host of friends following. In front of the courthouse hundreds of Negroes and whites, including television cameramen and photographers, were waiting. As I waved my hand, they shouted: "God bless you," and began to sing, "We ain't gonna ride the buses no more."

Ordinarily, a person leaving a courtroom with a conviction behind him would wear a somber face. But I left with a smile. I knew that I was a convicted criminal, but I was proud of my crime. It was the crime of joining my people in a nonviolent protest against injustice. It was the crime of seeking to instill within my people a sense of dignity and self-respect. It was the crime of desiring for my people the inalienable rights of life, liberty, and the pursuit of happiness. It was above all the crime of seeking to convince my people that noncoöperation with evil is just as much a moral duty as is coöperation with good.

So ended another effort to halt the protest. Instead of stopping the movement, the opposition's tactics had only served to give it greater momentum, and to draw us closer together. What the opposition failed to see was that our mutual sufferings had wrapped us all in a single garment of destiny. What happened to one happened to all.

On that cloudy afternoon in March, Judge Carter had convicted more than Martin Luther King, Jr., Case No. 7399; he had convicted every Negro in Montgomery. It is no wonder that the movement couldn't be stopped. It was too large to be stopped. Its links were too well bound together in a powerfully effective chain. There is amazing power in unity. Where there is true unity, every effort to disunite only serves to strengthen the unity. This is what the opposition failed to see.

The members of the opposition had also revealed that they did not know the Negroes with whom they were dealing. They thought they were dealing with a group who could be cajoled or forced to do whatever the white man wanted them to do. They were not aware that they were dealing with Negroes who had been freed from fear. And so every move they made proved to be a mistake. It could not be otherwise, because their methods were geared to the "old Negro," and they were dealing with a "new Negro."

CHAPTER IX

DESEGREGATION AT LAST

Fʀᴏᴍ ᴛʜᴇ ʙᴇɢɪɴɴɪɴɢ of the bus protest most of the Negro leaders lived with the hope that a settlement would soon be worked out. Our demands were limited, moderate enough to permit adjustment within the segregation laws. Even the most conservative white person could go along with them, we reasoned. But as the days and months unfolded we discovered that our optimism was misplaced. The intransigence of the city commission, the crudeness of the "get-tough" policy, and the viciousness of the recent bombings convinced us all that an attack must be made upon bus segregation itself. Accordingly a suit was filed in the United States Federal District Court, asking for an end of bus segregation on the grounds that it was contrary to the Fourteenth Amendment. The court was also asked to stop the city commissioners from violating the civil rights of Negro motorists and pedestrians.

The hearing was set for May 11, 1956, before a three-judge federal court panel. It was a great relief to be in a federal court. Here the atmosphere of justice prevailed. No one can understand the feeling that comes to a Southern Negro on entering a federal court unless he sees with his own eyes and feels with his own soul the tragic sabotage of justice in the city and state courts of the South.

The Negro goes into these courts knowing that the cards are stacked against him. Here he is virtually certain to face a prejudiced jury or a biased judge, and is openly robbed with little hope of redress. But the Southern Negro goes into the federal court with the feeling that he has an honest chance of justice before the law.

Our suit was filed by the same attorneys who had acted for the defense before Judge Carter in the boycott case. This time they presented persuasive arguments against the constitutionality of segregation itself. Robert Carter of the legal staff of the NAACP argued against the validity of the old Plessy Doctrine. This doctrine, first promulgated by the United States Supreme Court in 1896, had given legal validity to the Southern institution of separate-but-equal facilities for Negroes and whites. In the area of education, the Supreme Court had already reversed this position in its historic decision of May 1954; but the Plessy Doctrine still remained as the rationale of segregation in other areas. This injustice and inconsistency in the segregation laws was the object of Bob Carter's brilliant attack. Meanwhile the city attorneys, throughout their argument, dwelt on a single theme: if bus segregation ended, Montgomery would become a battleground of violence and bloodshed.

After listening to these arguments for several hours, Judge Rives addressed the city attorneys. "Is it fair," he asked, "to command one man to surrender his constitutional rights, if they are his constitutional rights, in order to prevent another man from committing a crime?" At this I touched Ralph Abernathy, who was sitting on one side of me, and Vernon Johns (he was on a brief visit to Montgomery at this time), on the other side, and whispered: "It looks as though we might get a favorable verdict."

The judges deliberated for about three weeks. On June 4, 1956, they declared in a two-to-one decision, Judge Lynn of Birmingham dissenting, that the city bus segregation laws of Alabama were unconstitutional. The city attorneys immediately announced that they would appeal the case to the United States Supreme Court.

The battle was not yet won. We would have to walk and sacrifice for several more months, while the city appealed the case. But at least we could walk with new hope. Now it was only a matter of time.

Or so we thought. But almost on the heels of the court's decision, disaster threatened the movement from a new quarter. On June 11, Rev. U. J. Fields made a statement to the press claiming that he was resigning as recording secretary of the MIA. In his announcement the youthful, goateed pastor of the Bell Street Baptist Church, who had been an officer of the Association from the beginning, accused the members of "misusing money sent from all over the nation," and appropriating it "for their own purposes." Many of the leaders, he claimed, had taken on an air of "bigness" and had become "too egotistical and interested in perpetuating themselves." The Association, he said, no longer represented what he had stood for, and he was severing his relations with a movement in which "the many are exploited by the few."

I was out of the city when Fields released his statement. Coretta and I had driven to California with Ralph and Juanita Abernathy to attend some conferences, and to enjoy our first vacation together away from the daily tensions of the protest. Rev. R. J. Glasco, then administrative assistant at the MIA office, telephoned the news. Earlier in the evening Fields had come to the mass meeting indignant because the executive board had failed to re-elect him to office. When he brought the matter before the audience, he was further enraged by their almost unanimous approval of the board's action. He had left the meeting immediately to announce his "resignation" and prepare his attack on the MIA.

Although the news did not come entirely as a surprise, I realized the seriousness of the possible repercussions. While I was certain that there was no truth in Fields's charges, I knew that some people would believe them, and that many others would be left in a state of confusion. A charge of misappropriation of funds could cause a curtailment of contributions, thus hampering the car pool. Moreover, the white opposition would welcome this break as an opportunity to investigate our books with the ultimate aim of freezing our funds. I was also worried about how the Negroes of Montgomery might express their resentment against Fields.

My vacation had ended before it had well begun. I canceled the remainder of my engagements, promising to rejoin Coretta and the Abernathys later, and flew back to Montgomery. There I found, as I had expected, that emotions were running high. No one would speak in Fields's support, and so obviously distorted were his charges that even the local white press reported them with little enthusiasm. The Negroes were describing him as either a "fool" or a "black Judas." "I jest wish I could get my hands on him," said one indignant maid. The group of his own congregation had met and voted him out. (He was subsequently reinstated.) Everywhere in the Negro community sentiment mounted against him.

Fortunately by this time Fields had privately confessed to several people that he deeply regretted what he had done. Early on the morning of June 18 my telephone rang. Fields had learned that I was back in town, and wanted to see me. He arrived with a sober face, and went immediately to the point.

"I want you to know that I was not referring to you in my accusations. I have always had the greatest respect for your integrity and I still do. But there are some members of the MIA board that I don't care for at all. We never could get along."

I interrupted him. "You mean that your statements about the egotism of the leaders grew out of a personal conflict between you and one or two men on the board?"

"Yes," he admitted, "I guess that is true."

I asked him about the charge of misappropriation of funds, saying that if any such thing existed I wanted to know about it. With chagrin Fields answered:

"I confess that I don't know a single instance of misappropriation. All of those things I made up in a moment of anger. I felt that I had been mistreated by the board, and this was my way of retaliating."

By now it was clear that Fields was more to be pitied than scorned. I asked if he would be willing to make the same statements in the mass meeting that night. With some apprehension, he agreed.

People started assembling in front of the Beulah Baptist Church at three that afternoon. By five the church was filled. In the sweltering evening there was an unaccustomed atmosphere of bitterness. When Fields joined me on the rostrum at seven, the crowd muttered angrily, and I heard one voice call out, "Look at that devil sitting right next to Reverend King."

I had a double task ahead: one was to convince the people that there had been no misappropriation of funds and that the internal structure of the MIA was still stable; the other was to persuade them to forgive Fields for his errors and to give him a hearing. I plunged immediately into the first issue.

"I guess," I said, "that I know as much about the MIA as anyone in Montgomery, and I can truthfully say that I do not know of a single instance of misappropriation of funds. The finance committee of our Association is composed of honest men and women—persons whose integrity has been established over the years and whose character is above reproach. I have implicit faith in the finance committee and the ministers who have spoken at fund-raising meetings all over the country."

I denied the accusation of "bigness." "It is true," I said, "that some of the leaders have received national and international publicity, but only the shallow-minded are excited over publicity. Publicity is evanescent; it is here today and gone tomorrow. Today Autherine Lucy is showered with publicity; tomorrow it is Gus Courts. Today it is Emmet Till, tomorrow it is Martin Luther King. Then in another tomorrow it will be somebody else. Whoever falls in love with publicity is not fit to have it and will end up in misery.

"The honors and privileges," I continued, "that often come as a result of leadership constitute only one side of the picture. The greater the privileges, the greater the responsibilities and sacrifices."

So far the audience had listened sympathetically. But when I began to speak about Fields, they moved restlessly in their seats and I could hear a low murmur of disapproval. I expressed frank regret at Fields's statement. "Certainly it has created many unnecessary problems for us."

"You said it, Reverend," someone shouted.

"But," I continued, "we must meet this situation with the same dignity and discipline with which we have met so many difficult situations in the past. Let us never forget that we have committed ourselves to a way of nonviolence, and nonviolence means avoiding not only external physical violence but also internal violence of spirit. You not only refuse to shoot a man, but you refuse to hate him. Now in the spirit of our nonviolent movement I call upon you to forgive the Reverend Fields." I could see a few heads shaking in refusal, but I did not stop speaking. "We are all aware of the weaknesses of human nature. We have all made mistakes along the way of life, and we have all had moments when our emotions overpowered us. Now some of us are here this evening to stone one of our brothers because he has made a mistake." I paused a moment, and then spoke the words of Christ: "Let him who is without sin cast the first stone." With this a deep hush came across the audience.

In conclusion I recited the parable of the prodigal son. "Will we be like the unforgiving elder brother, or will we, in the spirit of Christ, follow the example of the loving and forgiving father?" As Fields rose to speak, instead of the boos and catcalls he had expected he was met with respectful silence. He began to pray. "Lord, help us to live in such a way from day to day, that even when we kneel to pray, our prayers will be for others. . . ." A great amen came from the audience. Then he asked forgiveness for his mistake, and assured the group that he had no evidence that money had been misused or misplaced by the MIA. By the time he had finished the group was deeply moved. He left the platform to solid applause.

So nonviolence triumphed again, and a situation that many had predicted would be the end of the MIA left it more united than ever in the spirit of tolerance.

The summer days gave way to the shorter cooler days of an Alabama autumn. The Supreme Court decision on our appeal was still pending. Meanwhile we were facing continued attempts to block the car pool. Insurance agents decided, almost overnight, to refuse to insure our station wagons, contending that the risk was too high. The liability insurance on our station wagons was canceled no less than four times within four months. (We had no trouble with the collision insurance because it was with a Negro company.)

Finally the company that held our liability insurance notified us that all the policies would be canceled as of September 15. A Northern friend who had read of our trouble wrote suggesting that we contact Lloyd's of London. A few days later I talked to T. M. Alexander, an insurance broker in Atlanta, who approved of the idea and agreed to make the contact for us. In a few days he was able to tell us that Lloyd's of London would take the insurance. From that moment on our insurance problems were solved.

But we were in for even greater difficulties. The city decided to take legal action against the car pool itself. On October 30, 1956, Mayor Gayle introduced a resolution instructing the city's legal department "to file such proceedings as it may deem proper to stop the operation of car pool or transportation systems growing out of the bus boycott." We tried to block this maneuver by filing a request in the federal court for an order restraining the city from interfering with the pool. But U.S. District Judge Frank M. Johnson refused to grant the request. Soon several of us received subpoenas; the city had filed the petition. The hearing was set for Tuesday, November 13.

The night before the hearing I had to go before the mass meeting to warn the people that the car pool would probably be enjoined. I knew that they had willingly suffered for nearly twelve months, but how could they function at all with the car pool destroyed? Could we ask them to walk back and forth every day to their jobs? And if not, would we then be forced to admit that the protest had failed in the end? For the first time in our long struggle together, I almost shrank from appearing before them.

The evening came, and I mustered up enough courage to tell them the truth. I tried,

however, to end on a note of hope. "This may well be," I said, "the darkest hour just before dawn. We have moved all of these months with the daring faith that God was with us in our struggle. The many experiences of days gone by have vindicated that faith in a most unexpected manner. We must go out with the same faith, the same conviction. We

The first non-segregated bus rides down the streets of Montgomery with Glenn Smiley, a white Southerner, sharing a seat with M. L. King. Ralph Abernathy (*in front*) and two other passengers enjoy the fruits of the year-long struggle. (*E. D. Nixon sat across the aisle.*)

must believe that a way will be made out of no way." But in spite of these words, I could feel the cold breeze of pessimism passing through the audience. It was a dark night—darker than a thousand midnights. It was a night in which the light of hope was about to fade away and the lamp of faith about to flicker. We went home with nothing before us but a cloud of uncertainty.

Tuesday morning found us in court, once again before Judge Carter. The city's petition was directed against the MIA and several churches and individuals. It asked the court to grant the city compensation for damages growing out of the car pool operation. The city contended that it had lost more than $15,000 as a result of the reduction in bus travel (the city receives 2 percent of the bus company revenues). It further alleged that the car pool was a "public nuisance" and a "private enterprise" operating without license fee or franchise. As the arguments unfolded the issue boiled down to this: Was the car pool a "private enterprise" operating without a franchise? Or was it a voluntary "share-a-ride" plan provided as a service by Negro churches without a profit?

As chief defendant I sat at the front table with the prosecuting and defense attorneys. Around twelve o'clock—during a brief recess—I noticed unusual commotion in the courtroom. Both Commissioner Sellers and Mayor Gayle were called to a back room, followed by two of the city attorneys. Several reporters moved excitedly in and out of the room.

I turned to Fred Gray and Peter Hall and said: "Something is wrong."

Before I could fully get these words out, Rex Thomas—a reporter for Associated Press—came up to me with a paper in his hand.

"Here is the decision that you have been waiting for. Read this release."

Quickly, with a mixture of anxiety and hope, I read these words: "The United States Supreme Court today affirmed a decision of a special three-judge U.S. District Court in declaring Alabama's state and local laws requiring segregation on buses unconstitutional. The Supreme Court acted without listening to any argument; it simply said 'the motion to affirm is granted and the Judgment is affirmed.' "

At this moment my heart began to throb with an inexpressible joy. The darkest hour of our struggle had indeed proved to be the first hour of victory. At once I told the news to the attorneys at the table. Then I rushed to the back of the room to tell my wife, Ralph Abernathy, and E. D. Nixon. Soon the word had spread to the whole courtroom. The faces of the Negroes showed that they had heard. "God Almighty has spoken from Washington, D.C.," said one joyful bystander.

After a few minutes Judge Carter called the court to order again, and we settled down to the case at hand for the remainder of the day. About five o'clock both sides rested, and the judge's decision came in a matter of minutes: As we had all expected, the city was granted a temporary injunction to halt the motor pool. But the decision was an anticlimax. Tuesday, November 13, 1956, will always remain an important and ironic date in the history of the Montgomery bus protest. On that day two historic decisions were rendered—one to do away with the pool; the other to remove the underlying conditions that made it necessary.

I rushed home and notified the press that I was calling the Negro citizens together on Wednesday night, November 14, to decide whether to call off the protest. In order to accommodate as many people as possible, two simultaneous meetings were scheduled, one on each side of town, with the speakers traveling from one meeting to the other. In the meantime, the executive board decided, on the advice of counsel, to recommend that the official protest be ended immediately, but that the return to the buses be delayed until the mandatory order arrived from the Supreme Court in Washington. It was expected in a few days.

The eight thousand men and women who crowded in and around the two churches were in high spirits. At the first meeting it was clear that the news of the decision had spread fast, and the opening hymn had a special note of joy. Reading the Scripture that night was Bob Graetz, who had chosen Paul's famous letter to the Corinthians: "Though I have all faith, so that I could remove mountains, and have not love, I am nothing. . . . Love suffereth long, and is kind. . . ."

When the slender blond minister came to the words: "When I was a child, I spoke as a child, I understood as a child, I thought as a child: but when I became a man, I put away childish things," the congregation burst into applause. Soon they were shouting and cheering and waving their handkerchiefs, as if to say that they knew they had come of age, had won new dignity. When Bob Graetz concluded: "And now abideth faith, hope, love, but the greatest of these is love," there was another spontaneous outburst. Only a people who had struggled to love in the midst of bitter conflict could have reacted in this fashion. I knew then that nonviolence, for all its difficulties, had won its way into our hearts.

Later Ralph Abernathy spoke. He told how a white newspaperman had reproached him for this outburst on the part of the congregation.

"Isn't it a little peculiar," the journalist had asked, "for people to interrupt the Scripture in that way?"

"Yes it is," Abernathy quoted himself in reply. "Just as it is peculiar for people to walk in the snow and rain when there are empty buses available; just as it is peculiar for people to pray for those who persecute them; just as it is peculiar for the Southern Negro to stand up and look a white man in the face as an equal." At this his audience laughed and shouted and applauded.

Each of the meetings accepted the recommendations of the executive board to call off the protest but refrain from riding the buses until the mandate reached Alabama.

That night the Ku Klux Klan rode. The radio had announced their plan to demonstrate throughout the Negro community, and threats of violence and new bombings were in the air. My mail was warning that "if you allow the niggers to go back on the buses and sit in the front seats we're going to burn down fifty houses in one night, including yours." Another letter cursed the Supreme Court and threatened "that damn Hugo Black": "When he comes back to Alabama we're going to hang you and him from the same tree."

Ordinarily, threats of Klan action were a signal to the Negroes to go into their houses, close the doors, pull the shades, or turn off the lights. Fearing death, they played dead. But this time they had prepared a surprise. When the Klan arrived—according to the newspapers "about forty carloads of robed and hooded members"—porch lights were on and doors open. As the Klan drove by, the Negroes behaved as though they were watching a circus parade. Concealing the effort it cost them, many walked about as usual; some simply watched from their steps; a few waved at the passing cars. After a few blocks, the Klan, nonplused, turned off into a sidestreet and disappeared into the night.

Soon we discovered that it was going to take the mandate more than four or five days to reach Montgomery. A reporter in contact with the clerk of the Court in Washington revealed that it would be closer to a month. This created a serious problem since the car pool was still enjoined. To meet this crisis we suggested that each area and street work out a coöperative "share-a-ride" plan. With S. S. Seay as skillful coördinator, the plan succeeded. The buses remained empty.

Meanwhile we went to work to prepare the people for integrated buses. In mass meeting after mass meeting we stressed nonviolence. The prevailing theme was that "we must not take this as a victory over the white man, but as a victory for justice and democracy." We hammered away at the point that "we must not go back on the buses and push people around unnecessarily boasting of our rights. We must simply sit where there is a vacant seat."

In several meetings we ran teaching sessions to school the people in nonviolent techniques. We lined up chairs in front of the altar to resemble a bus, with a driver's seat out front. From the audience we selected a dozen or so "actors" and assigned each one a role in a hypothetical situation. One man was driver and the others were white and Negro passengers. Both groups contained some hostile and some courteous characters. As the audience watched, the actors played out a scene of insult or violence. At the end of each scene the actors returned to the audience and another group took their place; and at the end of each session a general discussion followed.

Sometimes the person playing a white man put so much zeal into his performance that he had to be gently reproved from the sidelines. Often a Negro forgot his nonviolent role and struck back with vigor; whenever this happened we worked to rechannel his words and deeds in a nonviolent direction.

As the day for the mandate drew near, several MIA leaders went into the schools and urged the high school and college students to adhere to the way of nonviolence. We also distributed throughout the city a mimeographed list of "Suggestions for Integrating Buses." In preparing this text we had the assistance of the Rev. Glenn Smiley, a Southern-born white minister of the Fellowship of Reconciliation who was in Montgomery at the time.

INTEGRATED BUS SUGGESTIONS

This is a historic week because segregation on buses has now been declared unconstitutional. Within a few days the Supreme Court Mandate will reach Montgomery and you will be re-boarding *integrated* buses. This places upon us all a tremendous responsibility of maintaining, in face of what could be some unpleasantness, a calm and loving dignity befitting good citizens and members of our race. If there is violence in word or deed it must not be our people who commit it.

For your help and convenience the following suggestions are made. Will you read, study and memorize them so that our nonviolent determination may not be endangered. First, some general suggestions:

1. Not all white people are opposed to integrated buses. Accept good-will on the part of many.
2. The *whole* bus is now for the use of *all* people. Take a vacant seat.
3. Pray for guidance and commit yourself to complete non-violence in word and action as you enter the bus.
4. Demonstrate the calm dignity of our Montgomery people in your actions.
5. In all things observe ordinary rules of courtesy and good behavior.
6. Remember that this is not a victory for Negroes alone, but for all Montgomery and the South. Do not boast! Do not brag!
7. Be quiet but friendly; proud, but not arrogant; joyous, but not boisterous.
8. Be loving enough to absorb evil and

understanding enough to turn an enemy into a friend.

Now for some specific suggestions:

1. The bus driver is in charge of the bus and has been instructed to obey the law. Assume that he will coöperate in helping you occupy any vacant seat.
2. Do not deliberately sit by a white person, unless there is no other seat.
3. In sitting down by a person, white or colored, say "May I" or "Pardon me" as you sit. This is a common courtesy.
4. If cursed, do not curse back. If pushed, do not push back. If struck, do not strike back, but evidence love and goodwill at all times.
5. In case of an incident, talk as little as possible, and always in a quiet tone. Do not get up from your seat! Report all serious incidents to the bus driver.
6. For the first few days try to get on the bus with a friend in whose non-violence you have confidence. You can uphold one another by a glance or a prayer.
7. If another person is being molested, do not arise to go to his defense, but pray for the oppressor and use moral and spiritual force to carry on the struggle for justice.
8. According to your own ability and personality, do not be afraid to experiment with new and creative techniques for achieving reconciliation and social change.
9. If you feel you cannot take it, walk for another week or two. We have confidence in our people. GOD BLESS YOU ALL.

In spite of all of our efforts to prepare the Negroes for integrated buses, not a single white group would take the responsibility of preparing the white community. We tried to get the white ministerial alliance to make a simple statement calling for courtesy and Christian brotherhood, but in spite of the favorable response of a few ministers, Robert Graetz reported that the majority "dared not get involved in such a controversial issue." This was a deep disappointment. Although the white ministers as a group had been appallingly silent throughout the protest, I had still maintained the hope that they would take a stand once the decision was rendered. Yes, there were always a few; but they were far too rare.

The only white group that came near to making a positive statement was the Men of Montgomery, the businessmen who had already shown their good will in their earlier efforts to settle the protest. About ten days before the mandate came to Montgomery, a committee of the Men of Montgomery met with a group from the MIA and worked out a statement, calling for courtesy and nonviolence, to be issued jointly. When the statement was presented to the full membership of the Men of Montgomery, however, two or three members objected to it and, since unanimous approval was required, the release of the statement was blocked. Thus passed the one opportunity of the white community to take a positive stand for law and order.

Soon the reactionaries had taken over. A White Citizens Council leader threatened: "Any attempt to enforce this decision will lead to riot and bloodshed." One group suggested the establishment of a fleet of station wagons for a white pick-up service—an interesting proposal from those who had just succeeded in outlawing the Negro fleet! On December 18, the City Commissioners issued the following statement:

This decision in the bus case has had a tremendous impact on the customs of our people here in Montgomery. It is not an easy thing to live under a law recognized as constitutional for these many years and then have it suddenly overturned on the basis of psychology. . . . The City Commission, and we know our people are with us in this determination, will not yield one inch, but will do all in its power to oppose the integration of the Negro race with the white race in Montgomery, and will forever stand like a rock against social equality, inter-marriage, and mixing of the races under God's creation and plan.

On December 20, the bus integration order finally reached Montgomery. A mass meeting was immediately scheduled for that evening, to give the people final instructions before returning to the buses the following day. I called Mr. Bagley, manager of the bus company, and asked him to be sure to have service restored on all of the major lines. With evident relief, he agreed.

To the overflow crowd at the St. John A.M.E. Church I read the following message that I had carefully prepared in the afternoon:

For more than twelve months now, we, the Negro citizens of Montgomery, have been engaged in a nonviolent protest against injustices and indignities experienced on city buses. We came to see that, in the long run, it is more honorable to walk in dignity than ride in humiliation. So in a quiet dignified manner, we decided to substitute tired feet for tired souls, and walk the streets of Montgomery until the sagging walls of injustice had been crushed. . . .

These twelve months have not been easy. Our feet have often been tired. We have struggled against tremendous odds to maintain alternative transportation. We can remember days when unfavorable court decisions came upon us like tidal waves, leaving us treading the waters of despair. But amid all of this we have kept going with the faith that as we struggle, God struggles with us, and that the arc of the moral universe, although long, is bending toward justice. We have lived under the agony and darkness of Good Friday with the conviction that one day the heightened glow of Easter would emerge on the horizon. We have seen truth crucified and goodness buried, but we have kept going with the conviction that truth crushed to earth will rise again.

Now our faith seems to be vindicated. This morning the long awaited mandate from the United States Supreme Court concerning bus segregation came to Montgomery. This mandate expresses in terms that are crystal clear that segregation in public transportation is both legally and sociologically invalid. In the light of this mandate and the unanimous vote rendered by the Montgomery Improvement Association about a month ago, the year-old protest against city buses is officially called off, and the Negro citizens of Montgomery are urged to return to the buses tomorrow morning on a non-segregated basis.

I cannot close without giving just a word of caution. Our experience and growth during this past year of nonviolent protest has been such that we cannot be satisfied with a court "victory" over our white brothers. We must respond to the decision with an understanding of those who have oppressed us and with an appreciation of the new adjustments that the court order poses for them. We must be able to face up honestly to our own shortcomings. We must act in such a way as to make possible a coming together of white people and colored people on the basis of a real harmony of interests and understanding. We seek an integration based on mutual respect.

This is the time that we must evince calm dignity and wise restraint. Emotions must not run wild. Violence must not come from any of us, for if we become victimized with violent intents, we will have walked in vain, and our twelve months of glorious dignity will be transformed into an eve of gloomy catastrophe. As we go back to the buses let us be loving enough to turn an enemy into a friend. We must now move from protest to reconciliation. It is my firm conviction that God is working in Montgomery. Let all men of good-will, both Negro and white, continue to work with Him. With this dedication we will be able to emerge from the bleak and desolate midnight of man's inhumanity to man to the bright and glittering daybreak of freedom and justice.

The audience stood and cheered loudly. This was the moment toward which they had pressed for more than a year. The return to the buses, on an integrated basis, was a new beginning. But it was a conclusion, too, the end of an effort that had drawn Montgomery's Negroes together as never before. To many of those present the joy was not un-mixed. Some perhaps feared what might happen when they began to ride the buses again the next day. Others had found a spiritual strength in sacrifice to a cause; now the sacrifice was no longer necessary. Like many consummations, this one left a slight aftertaste of sadness.

At the close of the meeting I asked the ministers to stay over for a few minutes to urge them to ride the buses during the rush hours for the first few days. It was our feeling that their presence would give the Negro citizens courage and make them less likely to retaliate in case of insults. The ministers readily agreed. Accordingly, two were assigned to each bus line in the city, to ride mainly during the morning and afternoon rush. They were given suggestions as to how to handle situations of violence and urged to keep an accurate record of all incidents.

I had decided that after many months of struggling with my people for the goal of justice I should not sit back and watch, but should lead them back to the buses myself. I asked Ralph Abernathy, E. D. Nixon, and Glenn Smiley to join me in riding on the first integrated bus. They reached my house around 5:45 on Friday morning. Television cameras, photographers, and news reporters were hovering outside the door. At 5:55 we walked toward the bus stop, the cameras shooting, the reporters bombarding us with questions. Soon the bus appeared; the door opened, and I stepped on. The bus driver greeted me with a cordial smile. As I put my fare in the box he said:

"I believe you are Reverend King, aren't you?"

I answered: "Yes I am."

"We are glad to have you this morning," he said.

I thanked him and took my seat, smiling now too. Abernathy, Nixon, and Smiley followed, with several reporters and television men behind them. Glenn Smiley sat next to me. So I rode the first integrated bus in Montgomery with a white minister, and a native Southerner, as my seatmate.

Downtown we transferred to one of the buses that serviced the white residential section. As the white people boarded, many took seats as if nothing were going on. Others looked amazed to see Negroes sitting in front, and some appeared peeved to know that they either had to sit behind Negroes or stand. One elderly man stood up by the conductor, despite the fact that there were several vacant seats in the rear. When someone suggested to him that he sit in back, he responded: "I would rather die and go to hell than sit behind a nigger." A white woman unknowingly took a seat by a Negro. When she noticed her neighbor, she jumped up and said in a tone of obvious anger: "What are these niggers gonna do next?"

But despite such signs of hostility there were no major incidents on the first day. Many of the whites responded to the new system calmly. Several deliberately and with friendly smiles took seats beside Negroes. True, one Negro woman was slapped by a white man as she alighted, but she refused to retaliate. Later she said: "I could have broken that little fellow's neck all by myself, but I left the mass meeting last night determined to do what Reverend King asked." The *Montgomery Advertiser* reported at the end of the first day: "The calm but cautious acceptance of this significant change in Montgomery's way of life came without any major disturbance."

But the reactionaries were not in retreat. Many of them had predicted violence, and such predictions are always a conscious or unconscious invitation to action. When people,

especially in public office, talk about bloodshed as a concomitant of integration, they stir and arouse the hoodlums to acts of destruction, and often work under cover to bring them about. In Montgomery several public officials had predicted violence, and violence there had to be if they were to save face.

By December 28 the first few days of peaceful compliance had given way to a reign of terror. City buses were fired on throughout the city, especially in poorly lighted sections. A teenage girl was beaten by four or five white men as she alighted from a bus. A pregnant Negro woman was shot in the leg. Fearfully, many Negroes and whites refused to ride the buses. The city commission responded by suspending the night runs on city lines. No bus could begin a run after five o'clock, which meant that once again returning workers were without transportation. This was exactly what the violent elements wanted.

During this period a new effort was made to divide the Negroes. Handbills were distributed urging Negroes to rebel against me in particular and their leaders in general. These leaflets purported to come from "fed-up" Negroes, but virtually everyone knew that they were the work of white extremists. Referring to me as Luther, one leaflet said: "We get shot at while he rides. He is getting us in more trouble every day. Wake up. Run him out of town." Another one stated: "We been doing OK in Montgomery before outside preachers were born! Ask Reverend King's papa & Mamma if they like his doings—ask him if they going to help in Atlanta. Better quit him before it is too late!"

The KKK was in its element. One day it descended upon Montgomery in full regalia. But it seemed to have lost its spell. A college student who saw the Klansmen swarming the streets in their white costumes with red insignia went cheerfully on about her business, thinking that they were collecting for the United Fund. And one cold night a small

Negro boy was seen warming his hands at a burning cross.

On January 9, Ralph Abernathy and I went to Atlanta to prepare for a meeting of Negro leaders that I had called for the following day. In the middle of the night we were awakened by a telephone call from Ralph's wife, Juanita. I knew that only some new disaster would make her rouse us at two in the morning. When Ralph came back, his sober face told part of the story. "My home has been bombed," he said, "and three or four other explosions have been heard in the city, but Juanita doesn't know where yet." I asked about Juanita and their daughter. "Thank God, they are safe." Before we could talk any more, the telephone rang a second time. It was Juanita again, saying that the First Baptist Church had been hit. I looked at Ralph as he sat down beside me, stunned. Both his home and his church bombed in one night, and I knew no words to comfort him. There in the early morning hours we prayed to God together, asking for the power of endurance, the strength to carry on.

Between three and seven we received no less than fifteen calls. We finally learned that besides Ralph's home and church, Bob Graetz's home and three other Baptist churches—Bell Street, Hutchinson Street, and Mt. Olive—had all been hit. Worrying that this time the people might be goaded into striking back, I called a few ministers in Montgomery and urged them to do what they could to keep control. In the meantime, Ralph and I arranged to fly back, leaving the meeting of Southern leaders to begin without us.

From the Montgomery airport we drove directly to Ralph's house. The street was roped off, and hundreds of people stood staring at the ruins. The front porch had been almost completely destroyed, and things inside the house were scattered from top to bottom. Juanita, though shocked and pale, was fairly composed.

The rest of the morning was spent in a grim tour of the other bombings. The Bell Street and Mt. Olive Baptist churches had been almost completely destroyed. The other two churches were less severely damaged, but nevertheless faced great losses. The total damage to the four churches was estimated at $70,000. Bob Graetz's home had been a bomb target the previous summer, but had escaped serious damage. This time he was not so fortunate. The front of his house lay in ruins, and shattered glass throughout the interior showed the violence of the explosion. Assembled at each of the bombed sites was a large group of angry people; but with a restraint that I never ceased to wonder at, they held themselves under control.

The next morning, three important white agencies issued statements condemning the bombings. Grover Hall, the editor of the *Montgomery Advertiser,* wrote a strong editorial entitled "Is it safe to live in Montgomery?" in which he insisted that the issue had gone beyond the question of segregation *versus* integration. As I read Hall's strong statement I could not help admiring this brilliant but complex man who claimed to be a supporter of segregation but could not stomach the excesses performed in its name. Several white ministers denounced the bombing as unchristian and uncivilized, and all through the day their statement was repeated over television by the distinguished minister of the First Presbyterian Church, Rev. Merle Patterson. The Men of Montgomery, too, made known their unalterable opposition to the bombings. For the first time since the protest began, these influential whites were on public record on the side of law and order. Their stands gave us new confidence in the basic decency of the vast majority of whites in the community. Despite their commitment to segregation, it was clear that they were still law-abiding, and would never sanction the use of violence to preserve the system.

That afternoon, I returned to Atlanta to make at least an appearance at the meeting of Negro leaders. There I found an enthusiastic group of almost a hundred men from all over the South, committed to the idea of a Southern movement to implement the Supreme Court's decision against bus segregation through nonviolent means. Before adjourning they voted to form a permanent organization, the Southern Christian Leadership Conference, and elected me president, a position I still hold.

When I returned to Montgomery over the weekend I found the Negro community in low spirits. After the bombings the city commission had ordered all buses off the streets; and it now appeared that the city fathers would use this reign of violence as an excuse to cancel the bus company's franchise. As a result, many were coming to feel that all our gains had been lost; and I myself started to fear that we were in for another long struggle to get bus service renewed. I was also beginning to wonder whether the virulent leaflets that were bombarding the Negro community might be having their effect. Discouraged, and still revolted by the bombings, for some strange reason I began to feel a personal sense of guilt for everything that was happening.

In this mood I went to the mass meeting on Monday night. There for the first time, I broke down in public. I had invited the audience to join me in prayer, and had begun by asking God's guidance and direction in all our activities. Then, in the grip of an emotion I could not control, I said, "Lord, I hope no one will have to die as a result of our struggle for freedom in Montgomery. Certainly I don't want to die. But if anyone has to die, let it be me." The audience was in an uproar. Shouts and cries of "no, no" came from all

sides. So intense was the reaction, that I could not go on with my prayer. Two of my fellow ministers came to the pulpit and suggested that I take a seat. For a few minutes I stood with their arms around me, unable to move. Finally, with the help of my friends, I sat down. It was this scene that caused the press to report mistakenly that I had collapsed.

Unexpectedly, this episode brought me great relief. Many people came up to me after the meeting and many called the following day to assure me that we were all together until the end. For the next few days, the city was fairly quiet. Bus service was soon resumed, though still on a daytime schedule only.

Then another wave of terror hit. Early in the morning of January 28, the People's Service Station and Cab Stand was bombed, and another bomb fell at the home of Allen Robertson, a sixty-year-old Negro hospital worker. It was never discovered why these two victims had been singled out for attack. The same morning an unexploded bomb, crudely assembled from twelve sticks of dynamite, was found still smoldering on my porch.

I was staying with friends on the other side of town, and Coretta and "Yoki" were in Atlanta. So once more I heard the news first on the telephone. On my way home, I visited the other scenes of disaster nearby, and found to my relief that no one had been hurt. I noticed a police car driving away from the area with two Negroes on the rear seat. These men, I learned, were under arrest because they had challenged the police to their faces with having done nothing to catch the bombers. Both were later convicted of trying to "incite to riot." But there was no riot that day, although the crowds that had gathered around the damaged buildings were once again ready for violence. They were just waiting for a signal. Fortunately, the signal never came.

At home I addressed the crowd from my porch, where the mark of the bomb was clear. "We must not return violence under any condition. I know this is difficult advice to follow, especially since we have been the victims of no less than ten bombings. But this is the way of Christ; it is the way of the cross. We must somehow believe that unearned suffering is redemptive." Then, since it was Sunday morning, I urged the people to go home and get ready for church. Gradually they dispersed.

With these bombings the community came to see that Montgomery was fast being plunged into anarchy. Finally, the city began to investigate in earnest. Rewards of $4000 were offered for information leading to the arrest and conviction of the bombers. On January 31, the Negro community was surprised to hear that seven white men had been arrested in connection with the bombings. Detective J. D. Shows was given credit for apprehending them.

All of the men were released on bonds ranging from $250 to $13,000, and the city court passed the charges to the Montgomery County Grand Jury without testimony. The Grand Jury indicted five of the men and dropped charges against the other two.

The trial of the first two defendants, Raymond D. York and Sonny Kyle Livingston, came up in the Montgomery County Court, the same court where I had been tried in the anti-boycott case a year before, and with the same solicitor, William F. Thetford, in charge of the prosecution. With the Emmet Till case in Mississippi still fresh in our memories, the Negroes held little hope of conviction.

Several of us were subpoenaed as witnesses. On the opening day, we found the courtroom jammed with spectators, most of them white. In fact there was scarcely room for the Negroes. One could tell from the dress and manner of the whites that most of them were poor and uneducated, the kind that would find security in the Ku Klux Klan. As we entered they looked at us with undisguised hate.

The defense attorneys spent two days attempting to prove the innocence of their clients, arguing that the bombings had been carried out by the MIA in order to inspire new outside donations for their dwindling treasury. At the end of the second day I was called to the witness stand by the defense. For more than an hour I was questioned on things which had no relevance to the bombing case. The lawyers lifted statements of mine out of context to give the impression that I was a perpetrator of hate and violence. At many points they invented derogatory statements concerning white people, and attributed them to me.

On the other hand Mr. Thetford fought as diligently for a conviction as he had fought for mine a year earlier. He had an excellent case. The men had signed confessions. But in spite of all the evidence, the jury returned a verdict of not guilty. With their friends crowding around them, Raymond D. York and Sonny Kyle Livingston walked grinning out of the courtroom.

Justice had once more miscarried. But the diehards had made their last stand. The disturbances ceased abruptly. Desegregation on the buses proceeded smoothly. In a few weeks transportation was back to normal, and people of both races rode together wherever they pleased. The skies did not fall when integrated buses finally traveled the streets of Montgomery.

CHAPTER X

MONTGOMERY TODAY

"How are things in Montgomery today?" I am often asked. Everywhere I go people who have followed the reports of the bus protest in the newspapers or heard speakers tell about it wonder what the situation is now that bus desegregation has become a legal fact. They want to know whether the new pattern has been accepted by white as well as Negro residents of Montgomery, and whether there have been any other lasting effects of the great excitement that for over a year made the city front-page news throughout the nation and in many parts of the world.

At first, when this question was put to me, it was difficult to give a ready answer. Many things have to be considered in an appraisal of this sort, and not all of the effects are perceptible at once. But as the months passed after December 21, 1956, when bus segregation came to its official end, the answer became increasingly clear. "Better," I could say; "things are much better in Montgomery today."

On the buses Negroes, and white people too, now have the right to take any unoccupied seat anywhere. The younger Negroes—especially high school and college students—and the more educated and professional people exercise this new right freely. On the other hand, many of the elderly Negroes and those who work in domestic service still tend to take a rear seat, partly from timidity, partly from habit born of custom. On the bus lines that serve predominantly white neighborhoods, Negroes generally retire to the rear. On lines that serve predominantly Negro neighborhoods, the whites seem to seat themselves close to the driver—or stand. Yet it is not unusual to see white people sitting behind Negro passengers. Seldom do Negro and white passengers share a double seat; there appears to be a mutual disinclination to do so. And yet a few such cases, too, have been noticed.

Considering the thousands who use the public transportation system daily, there have been surprisingly few conflicts on the buses. But there have been some. Harsh words have been exchanged between Negro and white passengers scrambling for seats. In one case a white man struck a Negro woman with a wrench. She and her two female companions, forgetting nonviolence for the moment, overpowered him and struck him several sharp blows. The case went to court and the judge, fair-minded on this occasion, fined the man for disorderly conduct and did not even reprimand the women.

In another episode, a white woman claimed that a Negro man had attempted to take the seat beside her in order to get familiar with her. He was fined for disorderly conduct, although it appeared to be a case of her word against his. This was an isolated instance, however. More such situations had been expected, and some of us had feared that diehard opponents of desegregation might "plant" white women on buses so that they could make such complaints and stir up

trouble. Happily, our fears were misplaced.

Long before the final court order came through, the Montgomery City Lines had given up their policy of racial segregation and had begun to school their employees in proper behavior with all customers. The company removed from the buses all signs indicating segregation. The drivers, who were perhaps the chief irritants that "caused" the year-long protest, are no longer discourteous. Some of them are actively polite, saying "good morning" to their regular riders. Although the bus company had indicated at the end of the protest that they would be willing to accept applications from Negro drivers, the agreement has not to this day been put to the test.

We believe that our campaign of instruction and publicity before the first day of our return to the buses was an important factor in the comparative peace that followed. Our training sessions and mimeographed instructions had been successful in driving home the slogan, "If pushed, don't push back; if cursed, don't curse back." This time a soft answer did turn away wrath. Moreover, our effort to convince white bus riders and the white public in general that we did not intend to boast of our victory or to take over the buses apparently got across. The white people, knowing our attitude, had no reason to prepare for aggression or to assume a stiff posture of defense.

Race relations are better too in the city at large. After the sharp but brief flareup of bombings and shootings right after bus desegregation, the violence of the extremists came to an abrupt end. After the acquittal of the first two confessed bombers, the remainder were set free in an amnesty that also canceled the cases against the Negroes arrested under the anti-boycott law, with the provision that I pay the $500 fine lodged against me in court. I was reluctant to pay the fine, since such a step might appear to imply acceptance for the unjust equation of our actions with the brute violence of the bombers. Unfortunately, however, delay in transcribing the testimony in my case had caused it to be thrown out of court, which meant that any further legal action would have to be based on technicalities rather than on the merits of the issues. So I accepted the necessary compromise and paid.

Today the Negro citizen in Montgomery is respected in a way that he never was before. In the calm aftermath of the crisis many local white people are ready to say what they felt they could not afford to admit while the struggle was going on: "We've got to hand it to those Negroes. They had principles and they stuck to them and they stuck together. They organized and planned well." Others simply say, "We didn't think they had it in them." Again I believe that much of this residue of good will has come about because of our insistence on nonviolence. There are no

white homes in Montgomery that have lost or injured ones as a result of racial clashes over the buses. Casualties of war keep alive postwar bitterness; fortunately Montgomery's whites have no such casualties.

In the downtown stores today the business of the Negro customer is appreciated and he is treated courteously in most places. It is no longer unusual to hear the Negro addressed as Mr. or Mrs. Even the *Montgomery Advertiser* now makes it a policy to use courtesy titles in reference to Negroes in its pages.

The local labor movement has become somewhat more integrated than it was before the protest. Many union meetings are desegregated. And although there are also other factors at work, the improved general atmosphere may account in part for the election of eight Negroes to the joint AFL-CIO Executive Board for Southern Alabama.

Despite this picture of general improvement, it would be false to imply that the majority of white people in Montgomery have ceased to oppose integration. The opposite is closer to the truth. This city shares most of the fears of the state and the region, and there are still white citizens who react to the issue with all the raw emotions of patriots in a lost cause. Thus no move has yet been made to integrate the public schools in accordance with the now four-year-old directive of the United States Supreme Court. This is the big barrier currently erected. Here the segregationists seem determined to make an all-out stand. The rebels yell in Southern accents, "They shall not pass."

The two elements that are still most responsible for active segregationist sentiment are the newspapers and the politicians. Day in and day out the press is filled with stories of racial conflict, local and national. Any such disturbance in the North is played up here. Likewise the editorial pages constantly hammer at the Negro question. Readers are never permitted to forget that there is a war against "Yankees and race mixing."

The Alabama State Legislature, like most bodies of this sort in the Deep South, has passed many laws to delay or circumvent integration. Their effort to split up adjacent Macon County illustrates the extremes to which they are ready to go. In that county Negroes outnumber whites seven to one. If all eligibles were permitted to register and vote, the Negroes would inevitably share in some of the public offices. Moreover, Macon County contains the town where Booker T. Washington's famous Tuskegee Institute is located; there, thanks to Professor Charles Gomillion and the Tuskegee Civic Association, an energetic campaign for Negro registration and voting has been conducted. The State Legislature reacted first by redrawing the boundaries of Tuskegee so that almost all registered Negroes were outside the city limits; whereupon the Negroes instituted a boycott against the downtown stores that had supported or given tacit consent to the gerrymander. Next the governing body offered a referendum asking the voters of the state to authorize it, after due investigation, to split up Macon County itself, attaching slices to neighboring units, so that in every county of the area the white population would exceed the Negro. The voters assented, and the fate of Macon County now hangs in the balance of the investigating committee. Such agitation right next door to Montgomery has had its effect here. In turn, the success of the Montgomery bus protest has helped inspire the disfranchised Negroes of Macon County to pursue their campaign vigorously but without violence.

The state struck another blow at the Negro cause when it succeeded in persuading the Circuit Court to issue a temporary injunction against the NAACP in Alabama. This injunction, which became effective in June 1956—at the same time that several NAACP lawyers were successfully fighting our case against bus segregation in federal court—is still in effect.

The city commissioners of Montgomery have also passed several anti-Negro measures. New city ordinances make it a crime for Negroes and whites to play together or participate jointly in any sport or game, even checkers, or to use the same parks or playgrounds. A few years ago Montgomery had one or two Negroes on the city's baseball team, the Montgomery Rebels; this would no longer be possible. In the meantime, however, the complaint at the box office of "poor local support" has caused the franchise of the Montgomery Rebels to be sold to Knoxville. Under the new ordinances, a Negro man was arrested recently for merely walking through a "white" park; and a Negro family on a visit to the city was arrested when the father stopped to let his children look at the caged animals in the "white" zoo.

But the local courts are no longer so certain of their role. They remember too well what happened to their rulings on bus segregation when the United States Supreme Court reviewed them. They fear that the high court could also knock out other forms of segregation in public facilities if such cases should make their way to Washington. Accordingly, the local court dismissed the case of the Negro who had walked through the park, when he apologized for his "error." Moreover, the charge entered against other violators of segregation law is now merely "disorderly conduct," thus avoiding the possibility of a test case for appeal to the highest court of the land.

Politicians still get their loudest cheers from white audiences when they pledge an all-out fight against integration, but the listeners seem to be less inclined to pay for these comforting words. The Ku Klux Klan is virtually impotent and openly denounced on all sides, although to some extent opposition to the Klan is simply a convenient screen, since the White Citizens Councils have taken over most of the KKK's major objectives. Yet even the Councils appear to be slipping in Montgomery. Contributions have steadily declined since bus integration became a reality. That such organizations could not prevent this from happening was evidence to many of the dues-paying members that they could best use their own dollars otherwise.

Meanwhile, what of Montgomery's Negro community? Here too the experience of the protest has had its lasting and beneficial effects. Although the intense solidarity of the protest year has inevitably attenuated, there is still a feeling of closeness among the various classes and ages and religious denominations that was never present before. The increased self-respect of even the least sophisticated Negroes in Montgomery is evident in the way they dress and walk, in new standards of cleanliness and of general deportment. As one Negro janitor told a reporter from the North: "We got our heads up now, and we won't ever bow down again—no, sir—except before God!"

There has been a decline in heavy drinking. Statistics on crime and divorce indicate that both are on the wane. A nurse who owns a Negro hospital in Montgomery says that since the protest she has been able to go to church on Sunday mornings, something she had not been able to do for years. This means that Saturday nights are less belligerent than they used to be. There is a contagious spirit of friendliness and warmth; even the children seem to display a new sense of belonging.

The MIA has reduced its budget and staff, but it has broadened its focus and begun to address itself to other large areas of civic improvement. It has retained Fred Gray as full-time legal counsel to handle civil rights cases. It continues to conduct the once-a-week mass meetings, where, besides the religious program, voting clinics are held, and the speaker of the evening discusses the news and current issues of interest. Preceding the meetings a well-attended program of adult education demonstrates the Negroes' new concern with self-improvement.

The MIA has set forth a ten-point program entitled "Looking Forward," which envisions efforts in the fields of civic and political education, community relations, education for individual competence, improvement of economic status, health, recreation, law enforcement, public relations, cultural advancement, and spiritual enrichment. Parts of this long-range program are still on the drawing board; others are already in operation. Of most immediate importance, perhaps, is the continuing effort to promote registration and voting among all Negroes of voting age. This is still an arduous task; thanks chiefly to the persistent opposition of the white registrars, of the nearly 2000 Negroes sent to register locally in the last two years, barely 10 percent have succeeded in getting their names on the books of eligible voters.

Thus Montgomery's racial problems are still far from solved. Yet it is clear that things are much better than they were before December 5, 1955. Citizens have more mutual respect and more respect for themselves. Above all, our experience has shown that social change can take place without violence.

CHAPTER XI

WHERE DO WE GO FROM HERE?

THE BUS STRUGGLE in Montgomery, Alabama, is now history. As the integrated buses roll daily through the city they carry, along with their passengers, a meaning-crowded symbolism. Accord among the great majority of passengers is evidence of the basic good will of man for man and a portent of peace in the desegregated society to come. Occasional instances of discord among passengers are a reminder that in other areas of Montgomery life segregation yet obtains with all of its potential for group strife and personal conflict. Indeed, segregation is still a reality throughout the South.

Where do we go from here? Since the problem in Montgomery is merely symptomatic of the larger national problem, where do we go not only in Montgomery but all over the South and the nation? Forces maturing for years have given rise to the present crisis in race relations. What are these forces that have brought the crisis about? What will be the conclusion? Are we caught in a social and political impasse, or do we have at our disposal the creative resources to achieve the ideals of brotherhood and harmonious living?

The last half century has seen crucial changes in the life of the American Negro. The social upheavals of the two world wars, the great depression, and the spread of the automobile have made it both possible and necessary for the Negro to move away from his former isolation on the rural plantation. The decline of agriculture and the parallel growth of industry have drawn large numbers of Negroes to urban centers and brought about a gradual improvement in their economic status. New contacts have led to a broadened outlook and new possibilities for educational advance. All of these factors have conjoined to cause the Negro to take a fresh look at himself. His expanding life experiences have created within him a consciousness that he is an equal element in a larger social compound and accordingly should be given rights and privileges commensurate with his new responsibilities. Once plagued with a tragic sense of inferiority resulting from the crippling effects of slavery and segregation, the Negro has now been driven to reëvaluate himself. He has come to feel that he is somebody. His religion reveals to him that God loves all His children and that the important thing about a man is not "his specificity but his fundamentum"—not the texture of his hair or the color of his skin but his eternal worth to God.

This growing self-respect has inspired the Negro with a new determination to struggle and sacrifice until first-class citizenship becomes a reality. This is the true meaning of the Montgomery Story. One can never understand the bus protest in Montgomery without understanding that there is a new Negro in the South, with a new sense of dignity and destiny.

Along with the Negro's changing image of himself has come an awakening moral consciousness on the part of millions of white Americans concerning segregation. Ever since the signing of the Declaration of Independence, America has manifested a schizophrenic personality on the question of race. She has been torn between selves—a self in which she has proudly professed democracy and a self in which she has sadly practiced the antithesis of democracy. The reality of segregation, like slavery, has always had to confront the ideals of democracy and Christianity. Indeed, segregation and discrimination are strange paradoxes in a nation founded on the principle that all men are created equal. This contradiction has disturbed the consciences of whites both North and South, and has caused many of them to see that segregation is basically evil.

Climaxing this process was the Supreme Court's decision outlawing segregation in the public schools. For all men of good will May 17, 1954, marked a joyous end to the long night of enforced segregation. In unequivocal language the Court affirmed that "separate but equal" facilities are inherently unequal, and that to segregate a child on the basic of his race is to deny that child equal protection of the law. This decision brought hope to millions of disinherited Negroes who had formerly dared only to dream of freedom. It further enhanced the Negro's sense of dignity and gave him even greater determination to achieve justice.

This determination of Negro Americans to win freedom from all forms of oppression springs from the same deep longing that motivates oppressed peoples all over the world. The rumblings of discontent in Asia and Africa are expressions of a quest for freedom and human dignity by people who have long been the victims of colonialism and imperialism. So in a real sense the racial crisis in America is a part of the larger world crisis.

But the numerous changes which have culminated in a new sense of dignity on the part of the Negro are not of themselves responsible for the present crisis. If all men accepted these historical changes in good faith there would be no crisis. The crisis developed when the collective pressures to achieve fair goals for the Negro met with tenacious and determined resistance. Then the emerging new order, based on the principle of democratic equalitarianism, came face to face with the older order, based on the principles of paternalism and subordination. The crisis was not produced by oustide agitators, NAACP'ers, Montgomery Protesters, or even the Supreme Court. The crisis developed, paradoxically, when the most sublime principles of American democracy—imperfectly realized for almost two centuries—began fulfilling themselves and met with the brutal resistance of forces seeking to contract and repress freedom's growth.

The resistance has risen at times to ominous proportions. Many states have reacted in open defiance. The legislative halls of the South still ring loud with such words as "interposition" and "nullification." Many public officials are using the power of their offices to defy the law of the land. Through their irresponsible actions, their inflammatory statements, and their dissemination of distortions and half-truths, they have succeeded in arousing abnormal fears and morbid antipathies within the minds of underprivileged and uneducated whites, leaving them in such a state of excitement and confusion that they are led to acts of meanness and violence that no normal person would commit.

This resistance to the emergence of the new order expresses itself in the resurgence of the Ku Klux Klan. Determined to preserve segregation at any cost, this organization employs methods that are crude and primitive. It draws its members from underprivileged groups who see in the Negro's rising status a political and economic threat. Although the Klan is impotent politically and openly denounced from all sides, it remains a dangerous force which thrives on racial and religious bigotry. Because of its past history, whenever the Klan moves there is fear of violence.

Then there are the White Citizens Councils. Since they occasionally recruit members from a higher social and economic level than the Klan, a halo of partial respectability hovers over them. But like the Klan they are determined to preserve segregation despite the law. Their weapons of threat, intimidation, and boycott are directed both against Negroes and against any whites who stand for justice. They demand absolute conformity from whites and abject submission from Negroes. The Citizens Councils often argue piously that they abhor violence, but their defiance of the law, their unethical methods, and their vitriolic public pronouncements inevitably create the atmosphere in which violence thrives.

As a result of the Council's activities most white moderates in the South no longer feel free to discuss in public the issues involved in desegregation for fear of social ostracism and economic reprisals. What channels of communication had once existed between whites and Negroes have thus now been largely closed.

The present crisis in race relations has characteristics that come to the forefront in any period of social transition. The guardians of the staus quo lash out with denunciation against the person or organization that they consider most responsible for the emergence of the new order. Often this denunciation rises to major proportions. In the transition from slavery to restricted emancipation Abraham Lincoln was assassinated. In the present transition from segregation to desegregation the Supreme Court is castigated and the NAACP is maligned and subjected to extralegal reprisals.

As in other social crises the defenders of the status quo in the South argue that they were gradually solving their own problems until external pressure was brought to bear upon them. The familiar complaint in the South today is that the Supreme Court's decision on education has set us back a generation in race relations, that people of different races who had long lived at peace have now been turned against one another. But this is a misinterpretation of what is taking place. When a subject people moves toward freedom, they are not creating a cleavage, but are revealing the cleavage which apologists of the old order have sought to conceal. It is not the movement for integration which is creating a cleavage in the United States today. The depth of the cleavage that existed, the true nature of which the moderates failed to see and make clear, is being revealed by the resistance to integration.

During the crisis period, a desperate attempt is made by the extremists to influence the minds of the liberal forces in the ruling majority. So, for example, in the present transition white Southerners attempt to convince Northern whites that the Negroes are inherently criminal. They seek instances of Negro crime and juvenile delinquency in Northern communities and then say: "You see, the Negroes are problems to you. They create problems wherever they go." The accusation is made without reference to the true nature of the situation. Environmental problems of delinquency are interpreted as evidence of racial criminality. Crises arising in Northern schools are interpreted as proofs that Negores are inherently delinquent. The extremists do not recognize that these school problems are symptoms of urban dislocation, rather than expressions of racial deficiency. Criminality and delinquency are not racial; poverty and ignorance breed crime whatever the racial group may be.

In the attempt to influence the minds of Northern and Southern liberals, the segregationists are often subtle and skillful. Those who are too smart to argue for validity of segregation and racial inferiority on the basis of the Bible set forth their arguments on cultural and sociological grounds. The Negro is not ready for integration, they say; because of academic and cultural lags on the part of the Negro, the integration of schools will pull the white race down. They are never honest enough to admit that the academic and cultural lags in the Negro community are themselves the result of segregation and discrimination. The best way to solve any problem is to remove its cause. It is both rationally unsound and sociologically untenable to use the tragic effects of segregation as an argument for its continuation.

All of these calculated patterns—the defiance of Southern legislative bodies, the activities of White Supremacy organizations, and the distortions and rationalizations of the segregationists—have mounted up to massive resistance. This resistance grows out of the desperate attempt of the white South to perpetuate a system of human values that came into being under a feudalistic plantation system and which cannot survive in a day of growing urbanization and industrial expansion. These are the rock-bottom elements of the present crisis.

The schools of the South are the present storm center. Here the forces that stand for the best in our national life have been tragically ineffectual. A year after the Supreme Court had declared school segregation unconstitutional, it handed down a decree outlining the details by which integration should proceed "with all deliberate speed." While the Court did not set a definite deadline for the termination of this process, it did set a time for the beginning. It was clear that the Court had chosen this reasonable approach with the expectation that the forces of. good will will immediately get to work and prepare the communities for a smooth and peaceful transition.

But the forces of good will failed to come through. The Office of the President was appallingly silent, though just an occasional word from this powerful source, counseling the nation on the moral aspects of integration and the need for complying with the law, might have saved the South from much of its present confusion and terror. Other forces of justice also failed to act. It is true that immediately after the first decision was rendered, leading church, labor, and social welfare leaders issued statements upholding the decision, and many supporting resolutions were adopted by their organizations. But hardly a single group set forth an action program wherein their members could actively work to bring about a peaceable transition. Neither did they develop a plan whereby individuals in Southern communities who were willing to work for desegregation could receive organizational support in the face of economic reprisals and physical violence.

As a result of the failure of the moral forces of the nation to mobilize behind school integration, the forces of defeat were given the chance to organize and crystallize their opposition. While the good people stood silently and complacently by, the misguided people acted. If every church and synagogue had developed an action program; if every civic and social welfare organization, every labor union and educational institution, had worked out concrete plans for implementing their righteous resolutions; if the press, radio, and television had turned their powerful instruments in the direction of educating and elevating the people on this issue; if the President and the Congress had taken a forthright stand; if these things had happened, federal troops might not have been forced to walk the corridors of Central High School.

But it is still not too late to act. Every crisis has both its dangers and opportunities. It can spell either salvation or doom. In the present crisis America can achieve either racial justice or the ultimate social psychosis that can only lead to domestic suicide. The democratic ideal of freedom and equality will be fulfilled for all—or all human beings will share in the resulting social and spiritual doom. In short, this crisis has the potential for democracy's fulfillment or fascism's triumph; for social progress or retrogression. We can choose either to walk the high road of human brotherhood or to tread the low road of man's inhumanity to man.

History has thrust upon our generation an indescribably important destiny—to complete a process of democratization which our nation has too long developed too slowly, but which is our most powerful weapon for world respect and emulation. How we deal with this crucial situation will determine our moral health as individuals, our cultural health as a region, our political health as a nation, and our prestige as a leader of the free world. The future of America is bound up with the solution of the present crisis. The shape of the world today does not permit us the luxury of a faltering democracy. The United States cannot hope to attain the respect of the vital and growing colored nations of the world unless it remedies its racial problems at home. If America is to remain a first-class nation, it cannot have a second-class citizenship.

A solution of the present crisis will not take place unless men and women work for it. Human progress is neither automatic nor inevitable. Even a superficial look at history reveals that no social advance rolls in on the wheels of inevitability. Every step toward the goal of justice requires sacrifice, suffering, and struggle; the tireless exertions and passionate concern of dedicated individuals. Without persistent effort, time itself becomes an ally of the insurgent and primitive forces of irrational emotionalism and social destruction. This is no time for apathy or complacency. This is a time for vigorous and positive action.

It is the shame of the sunshine patriots if the foregoing paragraphs have a hollow sound, like an echo of countless political speeches. These things must be repeated time and again, for men forget quickly; but once said, they must be followed with a dynamic program, or else they become a refuge for those who shy from any action. If America is to respond creatively to the present crisis, many groups and agencies must rise above the reiteration of generalities and begin to take an active part in changing the face of their nation.

First, there is need for strong and aggressive leadership from the federal government. If the executive and legislative branches were as concerned about the protection of the citizenship rights of all people as the federal courts have been, the transition from a segregated to an integrated society would be much further along than it is today. The dearth of positive leadership from Washington is not confined to one political party. Both major parties have lagged in the service of justice. Many Democrats have betrayed it by capitulating to the undemocratic practices of the Southern Dixiecrats. Many Republicans have betrayed it by capitulating to the hypocrisy of right-wing Northerners.

In spite of the crucial role of the federal judiciary in this tense period of transition, the courts cannot do the job alone. The courts can clarify constitutional principles and remove the legal basis for segregation, but they cannot write laws, appoint administrators, or enforce justice on the local level.

The states and localities have the powers if they choose to exercise them. But the Southern states have made their policy clear. States' rights, they say in effect, include the right to abrogate power when it involves distasteful responsibilities, even to the Constitution of the United States, its amendments, and its judicial interpretation. So the power and the responsibility return by default to the federal government. It is up to all branches of the central government to accept the challenge.

Government action is not the whole answer to the present crisis, but it is an important partial answer. Morals cannot be legislated, but behavior can be regulated. The law cannot make an employer love me, but it can keep him from refusing to hire me because of the color of my skin. We must depend on religion and education to alter the errors of the heart and mind; but meanwhile it is an immoral act to compel a man to accept injustice until another man's heart is set straight. As the experience of several Northern states has shown, anti-discrimination laws can provide powerful sanctions against this kind of immorality.

Moreover, the law itself is a form of education. The words of the Supreme Court, of Congress, and of the Constitution are eloquent instructors. In fact, it would be a mistake to minimize the impact upon the South of the federal court orders and legislative and executive acts already in effect. Desegrega-tion of the armed services, for instance, has already had an immense, incalculable impact. Federal court decrees have altered transportation patterns, teachers' salaries, the use of recreational facilities, and myriad other matters. The habits if not the hearts of people have been and are being altered every day by federal action.

Another group with a vital role to play in the present crisis is the white Northern liberals. The racial issue that we confront in America is not a sectional but a national problem. The citizenship rights of Negroes cannot be flouted anywhere without impairing the rights of every other American. Injustice anywhere is a threat to justice everywhere. A breakdown of law in Alabama weakens the very foundations of lawful government in the other forty-seven states. The mere fact that we live in the United States means that we are caught in a network of inescapable mutuality. Therefore, no American can afford to be apathetic about the problem of racial justice. It is a problem that meets every man at his front door. The racial problem will be solved in America to the degree that every American considers himself personally confronted with it. Whether one lives in the heart of the Deep South or on the periphery of the North, the problem of injustice is his problem; it is his problem because it is America's problem.

There is a pressing need for a liberalism in the North which is truly liberal, a liberalism that firmly believes in integration in its own community as well as in the Deep South. It is one thing to agree that the goal of integration is morally and legally right; it is another thing to commit oneself positively and actively to the ideal of integration—the former is intellectual assent, the latter is actual belief. These are days that demand practices to match professions. This is no day to pay lip service to integration, we must pay *life* service to it.

Today in all too many Northern communities a sort of quasi-liberalism prevails, so bent on seeing all sides that it fails to become dedicated to any side. It is so objectively analytical that it is not subjectively committed. A true liberal will not be deterred by the propaganda and subtle words of those who say, "Slow up for a while; you are pushing things too fast." I am not calling for an end to sympathetic understanding and abiding patience; but neither sympathy nor patience should be used as excuses for indecisiveness. They must be guiding principles for all of our actions, rather than substitutes for action itself.

A significant role, in this tense period of transition, is assigned to the moderates of the white South. Unfortunately today, the leadership of the white South is by and large in the hands of close-minded extremists. These persons gain prominence and power by the dissemination of false ideas, and by appealing to the deepest fears and hates within the human mind. But they do not speak for the South; of that I am convinced. They speak only for a willful and vocal minority.

Even the most casual observer can see that the South has marvelous possibilities. It is rich in natural resources, blessed with the beauties of nature, and endowed with a native warmth of spirit. Yet in spite of these assets, it is retarded by a blight that debilitates not only the Negro but also the white man. Poor white men, women, and children, bearing the scars of ignorance, deprivation, and poverty, are evidence of the fact that harm to one is injury to all. Segregation has placed the whole South socially, education-

ally, and economically behind the rest of the nation.

Yet actually, there is no single "solid" South; there are at least three, geographically speaking. There is the South of compliance—Oklahoma, Kentucky, Kansas, Missouri, West Virginia, Delaware, and the District of Columbia. There is the wait-and-see South—Tennessee, Texas, North Carolina, Arkansas, and Florida. And there is the South of resistance—Georgia, Alabama, Mississippi, Louisiana, South Carolina, and Virginia.

Just as there are three Souths geographically, there are several Souths in terms of attitudes. A minority in each of these states would use almost any means, including physical violence, to preserve segregation. A majority, through tradition and custom, sincerely believe in segregation, but at the same time stand on the side of law and order. Hence, they are *willing* to comply with the law not because they feel it is sound but because it is the law. A third group, a growing minority, is working courageously and conscientiously to implement the law of the land. These people believe in the morality as well as the constitutionality of integration. Their still small voices often go unheard among the louder shouts of defiance, but they are actively in the field.

Furthermore there are in the white South millions of people of good will whose voices are yet unheard, whose course is yet unclear, and whose courageous acts are yet unseen. These persons are often silent today because of fear—fear of social, political, and economic reprisals. In the name of God, in the interest of human dignity, and for the cause of democracy these millions are called upon to gird their courage, to speak out, to offer the leadership that is needed. Still another South calls upon them: The colored South, the South of millions of Negroes whose sweat and blood has also built Dixie, who yearn for brotherhood and respect, who want to join hands with their white fellow Southerners to build a freer, happier land for all. If the moderates of the white South fail to act now, history will have to record that the greatest tragedy of this period of social transition was not the strident clamor of the bad people, but the appalling silence of the good people. Our generation will have to repent not only for the acts and words of the children of darkness but also for the fears and apathy of the children of light.

Who can best lead the South out of the social and economic quagmire? Her native sons. Those who were born and bred on her rich and fertile soil; those who love her because they were nurtured by her. Through love, patience, and understanding good will they can call their brothers to a way of noble living. This hour represents a great opportunity for the white moderates, if they will only speak the truth, obey the law, and suffer if necessary for what they know is right.

Still another agency of effective change today is the labor movement. Across the years the Negro has been a perpetual victim of economic exploitation. Prior to the Civil War the slaves worked under a system which offered neither compensation nor civil rights. Since emancipation the Negro American has continued to suffer under an essentially unreconstructed economy. He was freed without land or legal protection, and was made an outcast entitled only to the most menial jobs. Even the federal government that set him free failed to work out any long-range policy that would guarantee economic resources to a previously enslaved people—as much entitled to the land they had worked as were their former owners. The exploitation of the Negro population persisted through the Re-

construction period and continues down to the present day.

Labor unions can play a tremendous role in making economic justice a reality for the Negro. Trade unions are engaged in a struggle to advance the economic welfare of those American citizens whose wages are their livelihood. Since the American Negro is virtually nonexistent as the owner and manager of mass production industry, he must depend on the payment of wages for his economic survival.

There are in the United States 16.5 million members of approximately 150 bona fide trade unions. Of this number 142 are national and international affiliated organizations of the AFL-CIO. The unions forming the AFL-CIO include 1.3 million Negroes among their 13.5 million members. Only the combined religious institutions serving the Negro community can claim a greater membership of Negroes. The Negro then has the right to expect the resources of the American trade union movement to be used in assuring him—like all the rest of its members—of a proper place in American society. He has gained this right along with all the other workers whose mutual efforts have built this country's free and democratic trade unions.

Economic insecurity strangles the physical and cultural growth of its victims. Not only are millions deprived of formal education and proper health facilities but our most fundamental social unit—the family—is tortured, corrupted, and weakened by economic insufficiency. When a Negro man is inadequately paid, his wife must work to provide the simple necessities for the children. When a mother has to work she does violence to motherhood by depriving her children of her loving guidance and protection; often they are poorly cared for by others or by none— left to roam the streets unsupervised. It is not the Negro alone who is wronged by a disrupted society; many white families are in similar straits. The Negro mother leaves home to care for—and be a substitute mother for—white children, while the white mother works. In this strange irony lies the promise of future correction.

Both Negro and white workers are equally oppressed. For both, the living standards need to be raised to levels consistent with our national resources. Not logic but a hollow social distinction has separated the races. The economically depressed white accepts his poverty by telling himself that, if in no other respect, at least socially he is above the Negro. For this empty pride in a racial myth he has paid the crushing price of insecurity, hunger, ignorance, and hopelessness for himself and his children.

Strong ties must be made between those whites and Negroes who have problems in common. White and Negro workers have mutual aspirations for a fairer share of the products of industries and farms. Both seek job security, old-age security, health and welfare protection. The organized labor movement, which has contributed so much to the economic security and well-being of millions, must concentrate its powerful forces on bringing economic emancipation to white and Negro by organizing them together in social equality.

Certainly the labor movement has already made significant moves in this direction. Virtually every national or international union has clear policies of nondiscrimination, and the national leaders of AFL-CIO have proclaimed sincerely the ultimate objective of eliminating racial bias not only from the American labor movement but also from American society as a whole. But in spite of this stand, some unions, governed by the racist ethos, have contributed to the degraded economic status of the Negroes. Negroes have been barred from membership in certain unions, and denied apprenticeship training and vocational education. In every section of the country one can find local unions existing as a serious and vicious obstacle when the Negro seeks jobs or upgrading in employment. The AFL-CIO drive to organize the South has been virtually abandoned because of the massive resistance of a significant portion of the organized labor oligarchy, many of whom have been active in White Citizens Councils.

The existence of these conditions within the ranks of labor reveals that the job is a continuing one. The AFL-CIO must use all of the powerful forces at its command to enforce the principles it has professed. Labor leaders must continue to recognize that labor has a great stake in the struggle for civil rights, if only because the forces that are anti-Negro are usually anti-labor too. The current attacks on organized labor because of the misdeeds of a few malefactors should not blind us to labor's essential role in the present crisis.

The church too must face its historic obligation in this crisis. In the final analysis the problem of race is not a political but a moral issue. Indeed, as the Swedish economist Gunnar Myrdal has pointed out, the problem of race is America's greatest moral dilemma. This tragic dilemma presents the church with a great challenge. The broad universalism standing at the center of the gospel makes segregation morally unjustifiable. Racial segregation is a blatant denial of the unity which we have in Christ; for in Christ there is neither Jew nor Gentile, bond nor free, Negro nor white. Segregation scars the soul of both the segregator and the segregated. The segregator looks upon the segregated as a thing to be used, not a person to be respected.

Segregation substitutes an "I-it" relationship for the "I-thou" relationship. Thus it is utterly opposed to the noble teachings of our Judeo-Christian tradition.

It has always been the responsibility of the church to broaden horizons, challenge the status quo, and break the mores when necessary. The task of conquering segregation is an inescapable *must* confronting the church today.

There are several specific things that the church can do. First, it should try to get to the ideational roots of race hate, something that the law cannot accomplish. All race prejudice is based upon fears, suspicions, and misunderstandings, usually groundless. The church can be of immeasurable help in giving the popular mind direction here. Through its channels of religious education, the church can point out the irrationality of these beliefs. It can show that the idea of a superior or inferior race is a myth that has been completely refuted by anthropological evidence. It can show that Negroes are not innately inferior in academic, health, and moral standards. It can show that, when given equal opportunities, Negroes can demonstrate equal achievement.

The church can also do a great deal to reveal the true intentions of the Negro—that he is not seeking to dominate the nation, but simply wants the right to live as a first-class citizen, with all the responsibilities that good citizenship entails. The church can also help by mitigating the prevailing and irrational fears concerning intermarriage. It can say to men that marriage is an individual matter that must be decided on the merits of individual cases. Properly speaking, races do not marry; individuals marry. Marriage is a condition which requires the voluntary consent of two contracting parties, and either side can always say no. The church can reveal that the continual outcry concerning in-

termarriage is a distortion of the real issue. It can point out that the Negro's primary aim is to be the white man's brother, not his brother-in-law.

Another thing that the church can do to make the principle of brotherhood a reality is to keep men's minds and visions centered on God. Many of the problems America now confronts can be explained in terms of fear. There is not only the job of freeing the Negro from the bondage of segregation but also the responsibility of freeing his white brothers from the bondage of fears concerning integration. One of the best ways to rid oneself of fear is to center one's life in the will and purpose of God. "Perfect love casteth out fear."

When people think about race problems they are too often more concerned with men than with God. The question usually asked is: "What will my friends think if I am too friendly to Negroes or too liberal on the race question?" Men forget to ask: "What will God think?" And so they live in fear because they tend to seek social approval on the horizontal plane rather than spiritual devotion on the vertical plane.

The church must remind its worshipers that man finds greater security in devoting his life to the eternal demands of the Almighty God than in giving his ultimate allegiance to the transitory demands of man. The church must continually say to Christians, "Ye are a colony of heaven." True, man has a dual citizenry. He lives both in time and in eternity; both in heaven and on earth. But he owes his ultimate allegiance to God. It is this love for God and devotion to His will that casteth out fear.

A further effort that the church can make in attempting to solve the race problem is to take the lead in social reform. It is not enough for the church to be active in the realm of ideas; it must move out into the arena of social action. First, the church must remove the yoke of segregation from its own body. Only by doing this can it be effective in its attack on outside evils. Unfortunately, most of the major denominations still practice segregation in local churches, hospitals, schools, and other church institutions. It is appalling that the most segregated hour of Christian America is eleven o'clock on Sunday morning, the same hour when many are standing to sing, "In Christ there is no East nor West." Equally appalling is the fact that the most segregated school of the week is the Sunday School. How often the church has had a high blood count of creeds and an anemia of deeds! Dean Liston Pope of the Yale Divinity School rightly says in *The Kingdom beyond Caste:* "The church is the most segregated major institution in American society. It has lagged behind the Supreme Court as the conscience of the nation on questions of race, and it has fallen far behind trade unions, factories, schools, department stores, athletic gatherings and most other major areas of human association as far as the achievement of integration in its own life is concerned."

There has been some progress. Here and there churches are courageously making attacks on segregation, and actually integrating their congregations. The National Council of Churches has repeatedly condemned segregation and has requested its constituent denominations to do likewise. Most of the major denominations have endorsed that action. The Roman Catholic Church has declared, "Segregation is morally wrong and sinful." All this is admirable. But these stands are still far too few, and they move all too slowly down to the local churches in actual practice. The church has a schism in its own soul that it must close. It will be one of the tragedies of Christian history if a future Gibbon is able to say that at the height of the twentieth century the church proved to be one of the greatest bulwarks of segregated power.

The church must also become increasingly active in social action outside its doors. It must seek to keep channels of communication open between the Negro and white community. It must take an active stand against the injustice that Negroes confront in housing, education, police protection, and in city and state courts. It must exert its influence in the area of economic justice. As guardian of the moral and spiritual life of the community the church cannot look with indifference upon these glaring evils.

It is impossible to speak of the role of the church without referring to the ministers. Every minister of the gospel has a mandate to stand up courageously for righteousness, to proclaim the eternal verities of the gospel, and to lead men from the darkness of falsehood and fear to the light of truth and love.

In the South this mandate presents white ministers with a difficult choice. Many who believe segregation to be directly opposed to the will of God and the spirit of Christ are faced with the painful alternative of taking a vocal stand and being fired or staying quiet in order to remain in the situation and do some good. Pastors who have adopted the latter course feel that if they were forced out of their churches their successors would in all probability be segregationist, thus setting the Christian cause back. Many ministers have kept their peace not merely to save a job but because they feel that restraint is the best way to serve the cause of Christ in the South. In quiet unpublicized ways many of these ministers are making for a better day and helpfully molding minds of young people. These men should not be criticized.

In the final analysis every white minister in the South must decide for himself which course he will follow. There is no single right strategy. The important thing is for every minister to dedicate himself to the Christian ideal of brotherhood, and be sure that he is doing something positive to implement it. He must never allow the theory that it is better to remain quiet and help the cause to become a rationalization for doing nothing. Many ministers can do much more than they are doing and still hold their congregations. There is a great deal that ministers can achieve collectively. In every Southern city there should be interracial ministerial associations in which Negro and white ministers can come together in Christian fellowship and discuss common community problems. One of the most disappointing experiences of the Montgomery struggle was the fact that we could not get the white ministerial association to sit down with us and discuss our problem. With individual exceptions the white ministers, from whom I had naïvely expected so much, gave little.

Ministers can also collectively call for compliance with the law and a cessation of violence. This has been done by white ministers of Atlanta, Richmond, Dallas, and other cities, and not a single one has, to my knowledge, lost his job. It is difficult for a denomination to fire all of its ministers in a city. If ever the white ministers of the South decide to declare in a united voice the truth of the gospel on the question of race, the transition from a segregated to an integrated society will be infinitely smoother.

Any discussion of the role of the Christian minister today must ultimately emphasize the need for prophecy. Not every minister can be a prophet, but some must be prepared for the ordeals of this high calling and be willing to suffer courageously for righteousness. May the problem of race in America soon make hearts burn so that prophets will rise up, saying, "Thus saith the Lord," and cry out as Amos did, ". . . let justice roll down like waters, and righteousness like an ever-flowing stream."

Fortunately, a few in the South have already been willing to follow this prophetic way. I have nothing but praise for these ministers of the gospel of Jesus Christ and rabbis of the Jewish faith who have stood unflinchingly before threats and intimidations, inconvenience and unpopularity, even at times in physical danger, to declare the doctrine of the Fatherhood of God and the brotherhood of man. For such noble servants of God there is the consolation of the words of Jesus: "Blessed are ye, when men shall revile you, and persecute you, and shall say all manner of evil against you falsely, for my sake. Rejoice, and be exceeding glad: for great is your reward in heaven: for so persecuted they the prophets which were before you."

Here, then, is the hard challenge and the sublime opportunity: to let the spirit of Christ work toward fashioning a truly great Christian nation. If the church accepts the challenge with devotion and valor, the day will be speeded when men everywhere will recognize that they "are all one in Christ Jesus."

Finally, the Negro himself has a decisive role to play if integration is to become a reality. Indeed, if first-class citizenship is to become a reality for the Negro he must assume the primary responsibility for making it so. Integration is not some lavish dish that the federal government or the white liberal will pass out on a silver platter while the Negro merely furnishes the appetite. One of the most damaging effects of past segregation on the personality of the Negro may well be that he has been victimized with the delusion that others should be more concerned than himself about his citizenship rights.

In this period of social change, the Negro must come to see that there is much he himself can do about his plight. He may be un-educated or poverty-stricken, but these handicaps must not prevent him from seeing that he has within his being the power to alter his fate. The Negro can take direct action against injustice without waiting for the Government to act or a majority to agree with him or a court to rule in his favor.

Oppressed people deal with their oppression in three characteristic ways. One way is acquiescence: the oppressed resign themselves to their doom. They tacitly adjust themselves to oppression, and thereby become conditioned to it. In every movement toward freedom some of the oppressed prefer to remain oppressed. Almost 2800 years ago Moses set out to lead the children of Israel from the slavery of Egypt to the freedom of the promised land. He soon discovered that slaves do not always welcome their deliverers. They become accustomed to being slaves. They would rather bear those ills they have, as Shakespeare pointed out, than flee to others that they know not of. They prefer the "flesh-pots of Egypt" to the ordeals of emancipation.

There is such a thing as the freedom of exhaustion. Some people are so worn down by the yoke of oppression that they give up. A few years ago in the slum areas of Atlanta, a Negro guitarist used to sing almost daily: "Ben down so long that down don't bother me." This is the type of negative freedom and resignation that often engulfs the life of the oppressed.

But this is not the way out. To accept passively an unjust system is to coöperate with that system; thereby the oppressed become as evil as the oppressor. Noncoöperation with evil is as much a moral obligation as is coöperation with good. The oppressed must never allow the conscience of the oppressor to slumber. Religion reminds every man that he is his brother's keeper. To accept injustice or segregation passively is to say to the oppressor that his actions are morally right. It is a way of allowing his conscience to fall asleep. At this moment the oppressed fails to be his brother's keeper. So acquiescence—while often the easier way—is not the moral way. It is the way of the coward. The Negro cannot win the respect of his oppressor by acquiescing; he merely increases the oppressor's arrogance and contempt. Acquiescence is interpreted as proof of the Negro's inferiority. The Negro cannot win the respect of the white people of the South or the peoples of the world if he is willing to sell the future of his children for his personal and immediate comfort and safety.

A second way that oppressed people sometimes deal with oppression is to resort to physical violence and corroding hatred. Violence often brings about momentary results. Nations have frequently won their independence in battle. But in spite of temporary victories, violence never brings permanent peace. It solves no social problem; it merely creates new and more complicated ones.

Violence as a way of achieving racial justice is both impractical and immoral. It is impractical because it is a descending spiral ending in destruction for all. The old law of an eye for an eye leaves everybody blind. It is immoral because it seeks to humiliate the opponent rather than win his understanding; it seeks to annihilate rather than to convert. Violence is immoral because it thrives on hatred rather than love. It destroys community and makes brotherhood impossible. It leaves society in monologue rather than dialogue. Violence ends by defeating itself. It creates bitterness in the survivors and brutality in the destroyers. A voice echoes through time saying to every potential Peter, "Put up your sword." History is cluttered with the wreckage of nations that failed to follow this command.

If the American Negro and other victims of oppression succumb to the temptation of using violence in the struggle for freedom, future generations will be the recipients of a desolate night of bitterness, and our chief legacy to them will be an endless reign of meaningless chaos. Violence is not the way.

The third way open to oppressed people in their quest for freedom is the way of nonviolent resistance. Like the synthesis in Hegelian philosophy, the principle of nonviolent resistance seeks to reconcile the truths of two opposites—acquiescence and violence—while avoiding the extremes and immoralities of both. The nonviolent resister agrees with the person who acquiesces that one should not be physically aggressive toward his opponent; but he balances the equation by agreeing with the person of violence that evil must be resisted. He avoids the nonresistance of the former and the violent resistance of the latter. With nonviolent resistance, no individual or group need submit to any wrong, nor need anyone resort to violence in order to right a wrong.

It seems to me that this is the method that must guide the actions of the Negro in the present crisis in race relations. Through nonviolent resistance the Negro will be able to rise to the noble height of opposing the unjust system while loving the perpetrators of the system. The Negro must work passionately and unrelentingly for full stature as a citizen, but he must not use inferior methods to gain it. He must never come to terms with falsehood, malice, hate, or destruction.

Nonviolent resistance makes it possible for the Negro to remain in the South and struggle for his rights. The Negro's problem will not be solved by running away. He cannot listen to the glib suggestion of those who would urge him to migrate en masse to other sections of the country. By grasping his great opportunity in the South he can make a lasting contribution to the moral strength of the nation and set a sublime example of courage for generations yet unborn.

By nonviolent resistance, the Negro can also enlist all men of good will in his struggle for equality. The problem is not a purely racial one, with Negroes set against whites. In the end, it is not a struggle between people at all, but a tension between justice and injustice. Nonviolent resistance is not aimed against oppressors but against oppression. Under its banner consciences, not racial groups, are enlisted.

If the Negro is to achieve a goal of integration, he must organize himself into a militant and nonviolent mass movement. All three elements are indispensable. The movement for equality and justice càn only be a success if it has both a mass and militant character; the barriers to be overcome require both. Nonviolence is an imperative in order to bring about ultimate community.

A mass movement of a militant quality that is not at the same time committed to nonviolence tends to generate conflict, which in turn breeds anarchy. The support of the participants and the sympathy of the uncommitted are both inhibited by the threat that bloodshed will engulf the community. This reaction in turn encourages the opposition to threaten and resort to force. When, however, the mass movement repudiates violence while moving resolutely toward its goal, its opponents are revealed as the instigators and practitioners of violence if it occurs. Then public support is magnetically attracted to the advocates of nonviolence, while those who employ violence are literally disarmed by overwhelming sentiment against their stand.

Only through a nonviolent approach can the fears of the white community be mitigated. A guilt-ridden white minority lives in fear that if the Negro should ever attain power, he would act without restraint or pity to revenge the injustices and brutality of the years. It is something like a parent who continually mistreats a son. One day that parent raises his hand to strike the son, only to discover that the son is now as tall as he is. The parent is suddenly afraid—fearful that the son will use his new physical power to repay his parent for all the blows of the past.

The Negro, once a helpless child, has now grown up politically, culturally, and economically. Many white men fear retaliation. The job of the Negro is to show them that they have nothing to fear, that the Negro understands and forgives and is ready to forget the past. He must convince the white man that all he seeks is justice, *for both himself and the white man.* A mass movement exercising nonviolence is an object lesson in power under discipline, a demonstration to the white community that if such a movement attained a degree of strength, it would use its power creatively and not vengefully.

Nonviolence can touch men where the law cannot reach them. When the law regulates behavior it plays an indirect part in molding public sentiment. The enforcement of the law is itself a form of peaceful persuasion. But the law needs help. The courts can order desegregation of the public schools. But what can be done to mitigate the fears, to disperse the hatred, violence, and irrationality gathered around school integration, to take the initiative out of the hands of racial demagogues, to release respect for the law? In the end, for laws to be obeyed, men must believe they are right.

Here nonviolence comes in as the ultimate form of persuasion. It is the method which seeks to implement the just law by appealing to the conscience of the great decent majority who through blindness, fear, pride, or irrationality have allowed their consciences to sleep.

The nonviolent resisters can summarize their message in the following simple terms: We will take direct action against injustice without waiting for other agencies to act. We will not obey unjust laws or submit to unjust practices. We will do this peacefully, openly, cheerfully because our aim is to persuade. We adopt the means of nonviolence because our end is a community at peace with itself. We will try to pesuade with our words, but if our words fail, we will try to persuade with our acts. We will always be willing to talk and seek fair compromise, but we are ready to suffer when necessary and even risk our lives to become witness to the truth as we see it.

The way of nonviolence means a willingness to suffer and sacrifice. It may mean going to jail. If such is the case the resister must be willing to fill the jail houses of the South. It may even mean physical death. But if physical death is the price that a man must pay to free his children and his white brethren from a permanent death of the spirit, then nothing could be more redemptive.

What is the Negro's best defense against acts of violence inflicted upon him? As Dr. Kenneth Clark has said so eloquently, "His only defense is to meet every act of barbarity, illegality, cruelty and injustice toward an individual Negro with the fact that 100 more Negroes will present themselves in his place as potential victims." Every time one Negro school teacher is fired for believing in integration, a thousand others should be ready to take the same stand. If the oppressors bomb the home of one Negro for his protest, they must be made to realize that to press back the rising tide of the Negro's courage they will have to bomb hundreds more, and even then they will fail.

Faced with this dynamic unity, this amazing self-respect, this willingness to suffer, and this refusal to hit back, the oppressor will find, as oppressors have always found, that he is glutted with his own barbarity. Forced to stand before the world and his God splattered with the blood of his brother, he will call an end to his self-defeating massacre.

American Negroes must come to the point where they can say to their white brothers, paraphrasing the words of Gandhi: "We will match your capacity to inflict suffering with our capacity to endure suffering. We will meet your physical force with soul force. We will not hate you, but we cannot in all good conscience obey your unjust laws. Do to us what you will and we will still love you. Bomb our homes and threaten our children; send your hooded perpetrators of violence into our communities and drag us out on some wayside road, beating us and leaving us half dead, and we will still love you. But we will soon wear you down by our capacity to suffer. And in winning our freedom we will so appeal to your heart and conscience that we will win you in the process."

Realism impels me to admit that many Negroes will find it difficult to follow the path of nonviolence. Some will consider it senseless; some will argue that they have neither the strength nor the courage to join in such a mass demonstration of nonviolent action. As E. Franklin Frazier points out in *Black Bourgeoisie,* many Negroes are occupied in a middle-class struggle for status and prestige. They are more concerned about "conspicuous consumption" than about the cause of justice, and are probably not prepared for the ordeals and sacrifices involved in nonviolent action. Fortunately, however, the success of this method is not dependent on its unanimous acceptance. A few Negroes in every community, unswervingly committed to the nonviolent way, can persuade hundreds of others at least to use nonviolence as a technique and serve as the moral force to awaken the slumbering national conscience. Thoreau

was thinking of such a creative minority when he said: "I know this well, that if one thousand, if one hundred, if ten men whom I could name—if ten honest men only—aye, if one honest man, in the state of Massachusetts, ceasing to hold slaves, were actually to withdraw from the copartnership, and be locked up in the county jail therefore, it would be the abolition of slavery in America. For it matters not how small the beginning may seem to be, what is once well done is done forever."

Mahatma Gandhi never had more than one hundred persons absolutely committed to his philosophy. But with this small group of devoted followers, he galvanized the whole of India, and through a magnificent feat of nonviolence challenged the might of the British Empire and won freedom for his people.

This method of nonviolence will not work miracles overnight. Men are not easily moved from their mental ruts, their prejudiced and irrational feelings. When the underprivileged demand freedom, the privileged first react with bitterness and resistance. Even when the demands are couched in nonviolent terms, the initial response is the same. Nehru once remarked that the British were never so angry as when the Indians resisted them with nonviolence, that he never saw eyes so full of hate as those of the British troops to whom he turned the other cheek when they beat him with lathis. But nonviolent resistance at least changed the minds and hearts of the Indians, however impervious the British may have appeared. "We cast away our fear," says Nehru. And in the end the British not only granted freedom to India but came to have a new respect for the Indians. Today a mutual friendship based on complete equality exists between these two peoples within the Commonwealth.

In the South too, the initial white reaction to Negro resistance has been bitter. I do not predict that a similar happy ending will come to Montgomery in a few months, because integration is more complicated than independence. But I know that the Negroes of Montgomery are already walking straighter because of the protest. And I expect that this generation of Negro children throughout the United States will grow up stronger and better because of the courage, the dignity, and the suffering of the nine children of Little Rock, and their counterparts in Nashville, Clinton, and Sturges. And I believe that the white people of this country are being affected too, that beneath the surface this nation's conscience is being stirred.

The nonviolent approach does not immediately change the heart of the oppressor. It first does something to the hearts and souls of those committed to it. It gives them new self-respect; it calls up resources of strength and courage that they did not know they had. Finally it reaches the opponent and so stirs his conscience that reconciliation becomes a reality.

I suggest this approach because I think it is the only way to reëstablish the broken community. Court orders and federal enforcement agencies will be of inestimable value in achieving desegregation. But desegregation is only a partial, though necessary, step toward the ultimate goal which we seek to realize. Desegregation will break down the legal barriers, and bring men together physically. But something must happen so to touch the hearts and souls of men that they will come together, not because the law says it, but because it is natural and right. In other words, our ultimate goal is integration which is genuine intergroup and interpersonal living. Only through nonviolence can this goal be attained, for the aftermath of nonviolence is reconciliation and the creation of the beloved community.

It is becoming clear that the Negro is in for a season of suffering. As victories for civil rights mount in the federal courts, angry passions and deep prejudices are further aroused. The mountain of state and local segregation laws still stands. Negro leaders continue to be arrested and harassed under city ordinances, and their homes continue to be bombed. State laws continue to be enacted to circumvent integration. I pray that, recognizing the necessity of suffering, the Negro will make of it a virtue. To suffer in a righteous cause is to grow to our humanity's full stature. If only to save himself from bitterness, the Negro needs the vision to see the ordeals of this generation as the opportunity to transfigure himself and American society. If he has to go to jail for the cause of freedom, let him enter it in the fashion Gandhi urged his countrymen, "as the bridegroom enters the bride's chamber"—that is, with a little trepidation but with a great expectation.

Nonviolence is a way of humility and self-restraint. We Negroes talk a great deal about our rights, and rightly so. We proudly proclaim that three-fourths of the people of the world are colored. We have the privilege of watching in our generation the great drama of freedom and independence as it unfolds in Asia and Africa. All of these things are in line with the work of providence. We must be sure, however, that we accept them in the right spirit. In an effort to achieve freedom in America, Asia, and Africa we must not try to leap from a position of disadvantage to one of advantage, thus subverting justice. We must seek democracy and not the substitution of one tyranny for another. Our aim must never be to defeat or humiliate the white man. We must not become victimized with a philosophy of black supremacy. God is not interested merely in the freedom of black men, and brown men, and yellow men; God is interested in the freedom of the whole human race.

The nonviolent approach provides an answer to the long debated question of gradualism *versus* immediacy. On the one hand it prevents one from falling into the sort of patience which is an excuse for do-nothingism and escapism, ending up in standstillism. On the other hand it saves one from the irresponsible words which estrange without reconciling and the hasty judgment which is blind to the necessities of social process. It recognizes the need for moving towards the goal of justice with wise restraint and calm reasonableness. But it also recognizes the immorality of slowing up in the move toward justice and capitulating to the guardians of an unjust status quo. It recognizes that social change cannot come overnight. But it causes one to work as if it were a possibility the next morning.

Through nonviolence we avoid the temptation of taking on the psychology of victors. Thanks largely to the noble and invaluable work of the NAACP, we have won great victories in the federal courts. But we must not be self-satisfied. We must respond to every decision with an understanding of those who have opposed us, and with acceptance of the new adjustments that the court orders pose for them. We must act in such a way that our victories will be triumphs for good will in all men, white and Negro.

Nonviolence is essentially a positive concept. Its corollary must always be growth. On the one hand nonviolence requires noncoöperation with evil; on the other hand it requires coöperation with the constructive forces of good. Without this constructive aspect noncoöperation ends where it begins. Therefore, the Negro must get to work on a program with a broad range of positive goals.

One point in the Negro's program should be a plan to improve his own economic lot. Through the establishment of credit unions, savings and loan associations, and coöperative enterprises the Negro can greatly improve his economic status. He must develop habits of thrift and techniques of wise investment. He must not wait for the end of the segregation that lies at the basis of his economic deprivation; he must act now to lift himself up by his own bootstraps.

The constructive program ahead must include a campaign to get Negroes to register and vote. Certainly they face many external barriers. All types of underhand methods are still being used in the South to prevent the Negroes from voting, and the success of these efforts is not only unjust, it is a real embarrassment to the nation we love and must protect. The advocacy of free elections in Europe by American officials is hypocrisy when free elections are not held in great sections of America.

But external resistance is not the only present barrier to Negro voting. Apathy among the Negroes themselves is also a factor. Even when the polls are open to all, Negroes have shown themselves too slow to exercise their voting privileges. There must be a concerted effort on the part of Negro leaders to arouse their people from their apathetic indifference to this obligation of citizenship. In the past, apathy was a moral failure. Today, it is a form of moral and political suicide.

The constructive program ahead must include a vigorous attempt to improve the Negro's personal standards. It must be reiterated that the standards of the Negro as a group lag behind not because of an inherent inferiority, but because of the fact that segregation does exist. The "behavior deviants" within the Negro community stem from the economic deprivation, emotional frustration, and social isolation which are the inevitable concomitants of segregation. When the white man argues that segregation should continue because of the Negro's lagging standards, he fails to see that the standards lag because of segregation.

Yet Negroes must be honest enough to admit that our standards do often fall short. One of the sure signs of maturity is the ability to rise to the point of self-criticism. Whenever we are objects of criticism from white men, even though the criticisms are maliciously directed and mixed with half-truths, we must pick out the elements of truth and make them the basis of creative reconstruction. We must not let the fact that we are the victims of injustice lull us into abrogating responsibility for our own lives.

Our crime rate is far too high. Our level of cleanliness is frequently far too low. Too often those of us who are in the middle class live above our means, spend money on nonessentials and frivolities, and fail to give to serious causes, organizations, and educational institutions that so desperately need funds. We are too often loud and boisterous, and spend far too much on drink. Even the most poverty-stricken among us can purchase a ten-cent bar of soap; even the most uneducated among us can have high morals. Through community agencies and religious institutions Negro leaders must develop a positive program through which Negro youths can become adjusted to urban living and improve their general level of behavior. Since crime often grows out of a sense of futility and despair, Negro parents must be urged to give their children the love, attention, and sense of belonging that a segregated society deprives them of. By improving our standards here and now we will go a long way toward breaking down the arguments of the segregationist.

This then must be our present program: Nonviolent resistance to all forms of racial injustice, including state and local laws and practices, even when this means going to jail; and imaginative, bold, constructive action to end the demoralization caused by the legacy of slavery and segregation, inferior schools, slums, and second-class citizenship. The nonviolent struggle, if conducted with the dignity and courage already shown by the people of Montgomery and the children of Little Rock, will in itself help end the demoralization; but a new frontal assault on the poverty, disease, and ignorance of a people too long ignored by America's conscience will make victory more certain.

In short, we must work on two fronts. On the one hand, we must continue to resist the system of segregation which is the basic cause of our lagging standards; on the other hand we must work constructively to improve the standards themselves. There must be a rhythmic alternation between attacking the causes and healing the effects.

This is a great hour for the Negro. The challenge is here. To become the instruments of a great idea is a privilege that history gives only occasionally. Arnold Toynbee says in *A Study of History* that it may be the Negro who will give the new spiritual dynamic to Western civilization that it so desperately needs to survive. I hope this is possible. The spiritual power that the Negro can radiate to the world comes from love, understanding, good will, and nonviolence. It may even be possible for the Negro, through adherence to nonviolence, so to challenge the nations of the world that they will seriously seek an alternative to war and destruction. In a day when Sputniks and Explorers dash through outer space and guided ballistic missiles are carving highways of death through the stratosphere, nobody can win a war. Today the choice is no longer between violence and nonviolence. It is either nonviolence or nonexistence. The Negro may be God's appeal to this age—an age drifting rapidly to its doom. The eternal appeal takes the form of a warning: "All who take the sword will perish by the sword."

Eulogy for Martyred Children

THE REVEREND KING'S FAREWELL
TO THE VICTIMS OF THE BOMBING
AT THE 16TH STREET BAPTIST CHURCH,
BIRMINGHAM, ALABAMA,
ON SUNDAY, SEPTEMBER 15, 1963

THIS AFTERNOON we gather in the quiet of this sanctuary to pay our last tribute of respect to these three beautiful children of God. They entered the stage of history just a few years ago, and in the brief years that they were privileged to act on this mortal stage, they played their parts exceedingly well. Now the curtain falls; they move through the exit; the drama of their earthly life comes to a close. They are now committed back to that eternity from which they came.

These children—unoffending; innocent and beautiful—were the victims of one of the most vicious, heinous crimes ever perpetrated against humanity.

Yet they died nobly. They are the martyred heroines of a holy crusade for freedom and human dignity. So they have something to say to us in their death. They have something to say to every minister of the gospel who has remained silent behind the safe security of stained-glass windows. They have something to say to every politician who has fed his constituents the stale bread of hatred and the spoiled meat of racism. They have something to say to a federal government that has compromised with the undemocratic practices of southern Dixiecrats and the blatant hypocrisy of right-wing northern Republicans. They have something to say to every Negro who passively accepts the evil system of segregation, and stands on the sidelines in the midst of a mighty struggle for justice. They say to each of us, black and white alike, that we must substitute courage for caution. They say to us that we must be concerned not merely about *WHO* murdered them, but about the system, the way of life and the philosophy which *PRODUCED* the murderers. Their death says to us that we must work passionately and unrelentingly to make the American dream a reality.

So they did not die in vain. God still has a way of wringing good out of evil. History has proven over and over again that unmerited suffering is redemptive. The innocent blood of these little girls may well serve as the redemptive force that will bring new light to this dark city. The Holy Scripture says, "A little child shall lead them." The death of these little children may lead our whole southland from the low road of man's inhumanity to man to the high road of peace and brotherhood. These tragic deaths may lead our nation to substitute an aristocracy of character for an aristocracy of color. The spilt blood of these innocent girls may cause the whole citizenry of Birmingham to transform the negative extremes of a dark past into the positive extremes of a bright future. Indeed, this tragic event may cause the white south to come to terms with its conscience.

So in spite of the darkness of this hour we must not despair. We must not become bitter; nor must we harbor the desire to retaliate with violence. We must not lose faith in our white brothers. Somehow we must believe that the most misguided among them can learn to respect the dignity and worth of all human personality.

May I now say, a word to you the members of the bereaved families. It is almost impossible to say anything that can console you at this difficult hour and remove the deep clouds of disappointment which are floating in your mental skies. But I hope you can find a little consolation from; the universality of this experience. Death comes to every individual. There is an amazing democracy about death. It is not aristocracy for some of the people, but a democracy for all of the people. Kings die and beggars die; rich men die and poor men die; old people die and young people die; death comes to the innocent and it comes to the guilty. Death is the irreducible common denominator of all men.

I hope you can find some consolation from Christianity's affirmation that death is not the end. Death is not a period that ends the great sentence of life, but a comma that punctuates it to more lofty significance. Death is not a blind alley that leads the human race into a state of nothingness, but an open door which leads man into life eternal. Let this daring faith, this great invincible surmise, be your sustaining power during these trying days.

At times, life is hard, as hard as crucible steel. It has its bleak and painful moments. Like the ever-flowing waters of a river, life has its moments of drought and its moments of flood. Like the ever-changing cycle of the seasons, life has the soothing warmth of the summers and the piercing chill of its winters. But through it all, God walks with us. Never forget that God is able to lift you from fatigue of despair to the buoyancy of hope, and transform dark and desolate valleys into sunlit paths of inner peace.

Your children did not live long, but they lived well. The quantity of their lives was disturbingly small, but the quality of their lives was magnificently big. Where they died and what they were doing when death came will remain a marvelous tribute to each of you and an eternal epitaph to each of them. They died not in a den or dive nor were they hearing and telling filthy jokes at the time of their death. They died within the sacred walls of the Church after discussing a principle as eternal as love.

Shakespeare had Horatio utter some beautiful words over the dead body of Hamlet. I paraphrase these words today as I stand over the last remains of these lovely girls.

"Good-night sweet princesses; may the flight of angels take thee to thy eternal rest."

EPILOGUE: The doors of the Sixteenth Street Baptist Church re-opened on Sunday, June 7, 1964.

The "re-entry" sermon was preached by a white clergyman, the Reverend H. O. Hester, Secretary of the Department of Missions, Alabama Baptist Convention.

BOOK TWO

STRENGTH TO LOVE

PREFACE

IN THESE TURBULENT DAYS of uncertainty the evils of war and of economic and racial injustice threaten the very survival of the human race. Indeed, we live in a day of grave crisis. The sermons in this volume have the present crisis as their background; and they have been selected for this volume because, in one way or another, they deal with the personal and collective problems that the crisis presents. In these sermons I have sought to bring the Christian message to bear on the social evils that cloud our day and the personal witness and discipline required. All of these sermons were originally written for my former parishioners in the Dexter Avenue Baptist Church of Montgomery, Alabama, and my present parishioners in the Ebenezer Baptist Church of Atlanta, Georgia. Many of the sermons were later preached to congregations throughout the nation.

All of these sermons were preached during or after the bus protest in Montgomery, Alabama, and I have drawn a number of illustrations from that particular movement, some of which were included in my book *Stride Toward Freedom*. Three of the sermons—

"Love in Action," "Loving Your Enemies," and "Shattered Dreams"—were written while I was in Georgia jails. "Pilgrimage to Nonviolence" is a revision and updating of material which previously appeared in *The Christian Century* and *Stride Toward Freedom*. Although it is not a sermon, it has been included at the end of the volume at the specific urging of the publisher.

I have been rather reluctant to have a volume of sermons printed. My misgivings have grown out of the fact that a sermon is not an essay to be read but a discourse to be heard. It should be a convincing appeal to a listening congregation. Therefore, a sermon is directed toward the listening ear rather than the reading eye. While I have tried to rewrite these sermons for the eye, I am convinced that this venture could never be entirely successful. So even as this volume goes to press I have not altogether overcome my misgivings. But in deference to my former congregation, my present congregation, my close associates in the Southern Christian Leadership Conference, and my many friends across the nation who have asked for copies of individual sermons, I offer these discourses in the hope that a message may come to life for readers of these printed words.

I am happy to express my deep gratitude to many helpers. I am indebted to my close friend and Executive Assistant, Wyatt Tee Walker, a fine preacher in his own right, for reading the entire manuscript and offering valuable suggestions. I am also indebted to my teacher and friend, Samuel W. Williams, for helpful and stimulating suggestions. Charles L. Wallis gave valuable editorial assistance on the final manuscript. My thanks also go to my efficient secretary, Miss Dora E. McDonald, who constantly offered encouraging words and transferred my handwritten pages to typewritten copy. Most of all I must thank my devoted wife, Coretta, who has read the complete manuscript and given invaluable suggestions and inspiration. Her love and patience enabled her to be understanding in the face of my increased absence from her and our children while completing this volume.

MARTIN LUTHER KING, JR.

A TOUGH MIND
AND A TENDER HEART

And when he had called unto him his twelve disciples . . .

Now the names of the twelve apostles are these;
The first, Simon, who is called Peter, and Andrew his brother;
James, the son of Zebedee, and John his brother;

Philip, and Bartholomew; Thomas, and Matthew the publican;
James the son of Alphaeus, and Lebbaeus, whose surname was Thaddaeus;

Simon the Canaanite, and Judas Iscariot, who also betrayed him.

These twelve Jesus sent forth, and commanded them saying . . .

Behold, I send you forth as sheep in the midst of wolves:
be ye therefore wise as serpents, and harmless as doves.

Matthew 10

CHAPTER I

A FRENCH PHILOSOPHER SAID, "No man is strong unless he bears within his character antitheses strongly marked." The strong man holds in a living blend strongly marked opposites. Not ordinarily do men achieve this balance of opposites. The idealists are not usually realistic, and the realists are not usually idealistic. The militant are not generally known to be passive, nor the passive to be militant. Seldom are the humble self-assertive, or the self-assertive humble. But life at its best is a creative synthesis of opposites in fruitful harmony. The philosopher Hegel said that truth is found neither in the thesis nor the antithesis, but in an emergent synthesis which reconciles the two.

Jesus recognized the need for blending opposites. He knew that his disciples would face a difficult and hostile world, where they would confront the recalcitrance of political officials and the intransigence of the protectors of the old order. He knew that they would meet cold and arrogant men whose hearts had been hardened by the long winter of traditionalism. So he said to them, "Behold, I send you forth as sheep in the midst of wolves." And he gave them a formula for action: "Be ye therefore wise as serpents, and harmless as doves." It is pretty difficult to imagine a single person having, simultaneously, the characteristics of the serpent and the dove, but this is what Jesus expects. We must combine the toughness of the serpent and the softness of the dove, a tough mind and a tender heart.

ONE

Let us consider, first, the need for a tough

mind, characterized by incisive thinking, realistic appraisal, and decisive judgment. The tough mind is sharp and penetrating, breaking through the crust of legends and myths and sifting the true from the false. The tough-minded individual is astute and discerning. He has a strong, austere quality that makes for firmness of purpose and solidness of commitment.

Who doubts that this toughness of mind is one of man's greatest needs? Rarely do we find men who willingly engage in hard, solid thinking. There is an almost universal quest for easy answers and half-baked solutions. Nothing pains some people more than having to think.

This prevalent tendency toward softmindedness is found in man's unbelievable gullibility. Take our attitude toward advertisements. We are so easily led to purchase a product because television or radio advertisement pronounces it better than any other. Advertisers have long since learned that most people are softminded, and they capitalize on this susceptibility with skillful and effective slogans.

This undue gullibility is also seen in the tendency of many readers to accept the printed word of the press as final truth. Few people realize that even our authentic channels of information—the press, the platform, and in many instances the pulpit—do not give us objective and unbiased truth. Few people have the toughness of mind to judge critically and to discern the true from the false, the fact from the fiction. Our minds are constantly being invaded by legions of half-truths, prejudices, and false facts. One of the great needs of mankind is to be lifted above the morass of false propaganda.

Softminded individuals are prone to embrace all kinds of superstitions. Their minds are constantly invaded by irrational fears, which range from fear of Friday the thir-teenth to fear of a black cat crossing one's path. As the elevator made its upward climb in one of the large hotels of New York City, I noticed for the first time that there was no thirteenth floor—floor fourteen followed floor twelve. On inquiring from the elevator operator the reason for this omission, he said, "This practice is followed by most large hotels because of the fear of numerous people to stay on a thirteenth floor." Then he added, "The real foolishness of the fear is to be found in the fact that the fourteenth floor is actually the thirteenth." Such fears leave the soft mind haggard by day and haunted by night.

The softminded man always fears change. He feels security in the status quo, and he has an almost morbid fear of the new. For him, the greatest pain is the pain of a new idea. An elderly segregationist in the South is reported to have said, "I have come to see now that desegregation is inevitable. But I pray God that it will not take place until after I die." The softminded person always wants to freeze the moment and hold life in the gripping yoke of sameness.

Softmindedness often invades religion. This is why religion has sometimes rejected new truth with a dogmatic passion. Through edicts and bulls, inquisitions and excommunications, the church has attempted to prorogue truth and place an impenetrable stone wall in the path of the truth-seeker. The historical-philological criticism of the Bible is considered by the softminded as blasphemous, and reason is often looked upon as the exercise of a corrupt faculty. Softminded persons have revised the Beatitudes to read, "Blessed are the pure in ignorance: for they shall see God."

This has also led to a widespread belief that there is a conflict between science and religion. But this is not true. There may be a conflict between softminded religionists and toughminded scientists, but not between science and religion. Their respective worlds are different and their methods are dissimilar. Science investigates; religion interprets. Science gives man knowledge which is power; religion gives man wisdom which is control. Science deals mainly with facts; religion deals mainly with values. The two are not rivals. They are complementary. Science keeps religion from sinking into the valley of crippling irrationalism and paralyzing obscurantism. Religion prevents science from falling into the marsh of obsolete materialism and moral nihilism.

We do not need to look far to detect the dangers of softmindedness. Dictators, capitalizing on softmindedness, have led men to acts of barbarity and terror that are unthinkable in civilized society. Adolf Hitler realized that softmindedness was so prevalent among his followers that he said, "I use emotion for the many and reserve reason for the few." In *Mein Kampf* he asserted:

> By means of shrewd lies, unremittingly repeated, it is possible to make people believe that heaven is hell—and hell, heaven. . . . The greater the lie, the more readily will it be believed.

Softmindedness is one of the basic causes of race prejudice. The toughminded person always examines the facts before he reaches conclusions; in short, he postjudges. The tenderminded person reaches a conclusion before he has examined the first fact; in short, he prejudges and is prejudiced. Race prejudice is based on groundless fears, suspicions, and misunderstandings. There are those who are sufficiently softminded to believe in the superiority of the white race and the inferiority of the Negro race in spite of the toughminded research of anthropologists who

reveal the falsity of such a notion. There are softminded persons who argue that racial segregation should be perpetuated because Negroes lag behind in academic, health, and moral standards. They are not toughminded enough to realize that lagging standards are the result of segregation and discrimination. They do not recognize that it is rationally unsound and sociologically untenable to use the tragic effects of segregation as an argument for its continuation. Too many politicians in the South recognize this disease of softmindedness which engulfs their constituency. With insidious zeal, they make inflammatory statements and disseminate distortions and half-truths which arouse abnormal fears and morbid antipathies within the minds of uneducated and underprivileged whites, leaving them so confused that they are led to acts of meanness and violence which no normal person commits.

There is little hope for us until we become toughminded enough to break loose from the shackles of prejudice, half-truths, and downright ignorance. The shape of the world today does not permit us the luxury of softmindedness. A nation or a civilization that continues to produce softminded men purchases its own spiritual death on an installment plan.

TWO

But we must not stop with the cultivation of a tough mind. The gospel also demands a tender heart. Toughmindedness without tenderheartedness is cold and detached, leaving one's life in a perpetual winter devoid of the warmth of spring and the gentle heat of summer. What is more tragic than to see a person who has risen to the disciplined heights of toughmindedness but has at the same time sunk to the passionless depths of hardheartedness?

The hardhearted person never truly loves. He engages in a crass utilitarianism which values other people mainly according to their usefulness to him. He never experiences the beauty of friendship, because he is too cold to feel affection for another and is too self-centered to share another's joy and sorrow. He is an isolated island. No outpouring of love links him with the mainland of humanity.

The hardhearted person lacks the capacity for genuine compassion. He is unmoved by the pains and afflictions of his brothers. He passes unfortunate men every day, but he never really sees them. He gives dollars to a worthwhile charity, but he gives not of his spirit.

The hardhearted individual never sees people as people, but rather as mere objects or as impersonal cogs in an ever-turning wheel. In the vast wheel of industry, he sees men as hands. In the massive wheel of big city life, he sees men as digits in a multitude. In the deadly wheel of army life, he sees men as numbers in a regiment. He depersonalizes life.

Jesus frequently illustrated the characteristics of the hardhearted. The rich fool was condemned, not because he was not toughminded, but rather because he was not tenderhearted. Life for him was a mirror in which he saw only himself, and not a window through which he saw other selves. Dives went to hell, not because he was wealthy, but because he was not tenderhearted enough to see Lazarus and because he made no attempt to bridge the gulf between himself and his brother.

Jesus reminds us that the good life combines the toughness of the serpent and the tenderness of the dove. To have serpentlike qualities devoid of dovelike qualities is to be passionless, mean, and selfish. To have dovelike without serpentlike qualities is to be sentimental, anemic, and aimless. We must combine strongly marked antitheses.

We as Negroes must bring together toughmindedness and tenderheartedness, if we are to move creatively toward the goal of freedom and justice. Softminded individuals among us feel that the only way to deal with oppression is by adjusting to it. They acquiesce and resign themselves to segregation. They prefer to remain oppressed. When Moses led the children of Israel from the slavery of Egypt to the freedom of the Promised Land, he discovered that slaves do not always welcome their deliverers. They would rather bear those ills they have, as Shakespeare pointed out, than flee to others that they know not of. They prefer the "fleshpots of Egypt" to the ordeals of emancipation. But this is not the way out. Softminded acquiescence is cowardly. My friends, we cannot win the respect of the white people of the South or elsewhere if we are willing to trade the future of our children for our personal safety and comfort. Moreover, we must learn that passively to accept an unjust system is to cooperate with that system, and thereby to become a participant in its evil.

And there are hardhearted and bitter individuals among us who would combat the opponent with physical violence and corroding hatred. Violence brings only temporary victories; violence, by creating many more social problems than it solves, never brings permanent peace. I am convinced that if we succumb to the temptation to use violence in our struggle for freedom, unborn generations will be the recipients of a long and desolate night of bitterness, and our chief legacy to them will be a never-ending reign of chaos. A Voice, echoing through the corridors of time, says to every intemperate Peter, "Put up thy sword."[1] History is cluttered with the wreckage of nations that failed to follow Christ's command.

THREE

A third way is open in our quest for freedom, namely, nonviolent resistance, that combines toughmindedness and tenderheartedness and avoids the complacency and do-nothingness of the softminded and the violence and bitterness of the hardhearted. My belief is that this method must guide our action in the present crisis in race relations. Through nonviolent resistance we shall be able to oppose the unjust system and at the same time love the perpetrators of the system. We must work passionately and unrelentingly for full stature as citizens, but may it never be said, my friends, that to gain it we used the inferior methods of falsehood, malice, hate, and violence.

I would not conclude without applying the meaning of the text to the nature of God. The greatness of our God lies in the fact that he is both toughminded and tenderhearted. He has qualities both of austerity and of gentleness. The Bible, always clear in stressing both attributes of God, expresses his toughmindedness in his justice and wrath and his tenderheartedness in his love and grace. God has two outstretched arms. One is strong enough to surround us with justice, and one is gentle enough to embrace us with grace. On the one hand, God is a God of justice who punished Israel for her wayward deeds, and on the other hand, he is a forgiving father whose heart was filled with unutterable joy when the prodigal returned home.

I am thankful that we worship a God who is both toughminded and tenderhearted. If God were only toughminded, he would be a cold, passionless despot sitting in some far-off heaven "contemplating all," as Tennyson puts it in "The Palace of Art." He would be Aristotle's "unmoved mover," self-knowing, but not other-loving. But if God were only tenderhearted, he would be too soft and sentimental to function when things go wrong and incapable of controlling what he has made. He would be like H. G. Wells's lovable God in *God, the Invisible King,* who is strongly desirous of making a good world, but finds himself helpless before the surging powers of evil. God is neither hardhearted nor softminded. He is toughminded enough to transcend the world; he is tenderhearted enough to live in it. He does not leave us alone in our agonies and struggles. He seeks us in dark places and suffers with us and for us in our tragic prodigality.

At times we need to know that the Lord is a God of justice. When slumbering giants of injustice emerge in the earth, we need to know that there is a God of power who can cut them down like the grass and leave them withering like the green herb. When our most tireless efforts fail to stop the surging sweep of oppression, we need to know that in this universe is a God whose matchless strength is a fit contrast to the sordid weakness of man. But there are also times when we need to know that God possesses love and mercy. When we are staggered by the chilly winds of adversity and battered by the raging storms of disappointment and when through our folly and sin we stray into some destructive far country and are frustrated because of a strange feeling of homesickness, we need to know that there is Someone who loves us, cares for us, understands us, and will give us another chance. When days grow dark and nights grow dreary, we can be thankful that our God combines in his nature a creative synthesis of love and justice which will lead us through life's dark valleys and into sunlit pathways of hope and fulfillment.

CHAPTER II

TRANSFORMED NONCONFORMIST

"D O NOT CONFORM" is difficult advice in a generation when crowd pressures have unconsciously conditioned our minds and feet to move to the rhythmic drumbeat of the status quo. Many voices and forces urge us to choose the path of least resistance, and bid us never to fight for an unpopular cause and never to be found in a pathetic minority of two or three.

Even certain of our intellectual disciplines persuade us of the need to conform. Some philosophical sociologists suggest that morality is merely group consensus and that the folkways are the right ways. Some psychologists say that mental and emotional adjustment is the reward of thinking and acting like other people.

Success, recognition, and conformity are the bywords of the modern world where everyone seems to crave the anesthetizing security of being indentified with the majority.

ONE

In spite of this prevailing tendency to conform, we as Christians have a mandate to be nonconformists. The Apostle Paul, who knew the inner realities of the Christian faith, counseled, "be not conformed to this world: but be ye transformed by the renewing of your mind." We are called to be people of conviction, not conformity; of moral nobility, not social respectability. We are commanded to live differently and according to a higher loyalty.

I beseech you therefore, brethren, by the mercies of God,
that ye present your bodies a living sacrifice, holy,
acceptable unto God, which is your reasonable service.

And be not conformed to this world:
but be ye transformed by the renewing of your mind,
that ye may prove what is that good, and acceptable, and perfect, will of God.

Romans 12

Every true Christian is a citizen of two worlds, the world of time and the world of eternity. We are, paradoxically, in the world and yet not of the world. To the Philippian Christians, Paul wrote, "We are a colony of heaven."[2] They understood what he meant, for their city of Philippi was a Roman colony. When Rome wished to Romanize a province, she established a small colony of people who lived by Roman law and Roman customs and who, though in another country, held fast to their Roman allegiance. This powerful, creative minority spread the gospel of Roman culture. Although the analogy is imperfect—the Roman settlers lived within a framework of injustice and exploitation, that is, colonialism—the Apostle does point to the responsibility of Christians to imbue an unchristian world with the ideals of a higher and more noble order. Living in the colony of time, we are ultimately responsible to the empire of eternity. As Christians we must never surrender our supreme loyalty to any time-bound custom of earth-bound idea, for at the heart of our universe is a higher reality—God and his kingdom of love—to which we must be conformed.

This command not to conform comes, not only from Paul, but also from our Lord and Master, Jesus Christ, the world's most dedicated nonconformist, whose ethical nonconformity still challenges the conscience of mankind.

When an affluent society would coax us to believe that happiness consists in the size of our automobiles, the impressiveness of our houses, and the expensiveness of our clothes, Jesus reminds us, "A man's life consisteth not in the abundance of the things which he possesseth."[3]

When we would yield to the temptation of a world rife with sexual promiscuity and gone wild with a philosophy of self-expression, Jesus tells us that "whosoever looketh on a woman to lust after her hath committed adultery with her already in his heart."[4]

When we refuse to suffer for righteousness and choose to follow the path of comfort rather than conviction, we hear Jesus say, "Blessed are they which are persecuted for righteousness' sake: for theirs is the kingdom of heaven."[5]

When in our spiritual pride we boast of having reached the peak of moral excellence, Jesus warns, "The publicans and the harlots go into the kingdom of God before you."[6]

When we, through compassionless detachment and arrogant individualism, fail to respond to the needs of the underprivileged, the Master says, "Inasmuch as ye have done it unto one of the least of these my brethren, ye have done it unto me."[7]

When we allow the spark of revenge in our souls to flame up in hate toward our enemies, Jesus teaches, "Love your enemies, bless them that curse you, do good to them that hate you, and pray for them which despitefully use you, and persecute you."[8]

Everywhere and at all times, the love ethic of Jesus is a radiant light revealing the ugliness of our stale conformity.

In spite of this imperative demand to live differently, we have cultivated a mass mind and have moved from the extreme of rugged individualism to the even greater extreme of rugged collectivism. We are not makers of history; we are made by history. Longfellow said, "In this world a man must either be anvil or hammer,"[9] meaning that he is either a molder of society or is molded by society. Who doubts that today most men are anvils and are shaped by the patterns of the majority? Or to change the figure, most people, and Christians in particular, are thermometers that record or register the temperature of majority opinion, not thermostats that transform and regulate the temperature of society.

Many people fear nothing more terribly than to take a position which stands out sharply and clearly from the prevailing opinion. The tendency of most is to adopt a view that is so ambiguous that it will include everything and so popular that it will include everybody. Along with this has grown an inordinate worship of bigness. We live in an age of "jumboism" where men find security in that which is large and extensive—big cities, big buildings, big corporations. This worship of size has caused many to fear being identified with a minority idea. Not a few men, who cherish lofty and noble ideals, hide them under a bushel for fear of being called different. Many sincere white people in the South privately oppose segregation and discrimination, but they are apprehensive lest they be publicly condemned. Millions of citizens are deeply disturbed that the military-industrial complex too often shapes national policy, but they do not want to be considered unpatriotic. Countless loyal Americans honestly feel that a world body such as the United Nations should include even Red China, but they fear being called Communist sympathizers. A legion of thoughtful persons recognizes that traditional capitalism must continually undergo change if our great national wealth is to be more equitably distributed, but they are afraid their criticisms will make them seem un-American. Numerous decent, wholesome young persons permit themselves to become involved in unwholesome pursuits which they do not personally condone or even enjoy, because they are ashamed to say no when the gang says yes. How *few* people have the audacity to express publicly their convictions, and how *many* have allowed themselves to be "astronomically intimidated"!

Blind conformity makes us so suspicious of an individual who insists on saying what he really believes that we recklessly threaten his civil liberties. If a man, who believes vigorously in peace, is foolish enough to carry a sign in a public demonstration, or if a Southern white person, believing in the American dream of the dignity and worth of human personality, dares to invite a Negro into his home and join with him in his struggle for freedom, he is liable to be summoned before some legislative investigation body. He most certainly is a Communist if he espouses the cause of human brotherhood!

Thomas Jefferson wrote, "I have sworn upon the altar of God eternal hostility against every form of tyranny over the mind of man."[10] To the conformist and the shapers of the conformist mentality, this must surely sound like a most dangerous and radical doctrine. Have we permitted the lamp of independent thought and individualism to become so dim that were Jefferson to write and live by these words today we would find cause to harass and investigate him? If Americans permit thought-control, business-control, and freedom-control to continue, we shall surely move within the shadows of fascism.

TWO

Nowhere is the tragic tendency to conform more evident than in the church, an institution which has often served to crystallize, conserve, and even bless the patterns of majority opinion. The erstwhile sanction by the church of slavery, racial segregation, war, and economic exploitation is testimony to the fact that the church has hearkened more to the authority of the world than to the authority of God. Called to be the moral guardian of the community, the church at times has preserved that which is immoral and unethical. Called to combat social evils, it has remained silent behind stained-glass windows. Called to lead men on the highway of brotherhood and to summon them to rise above the narrow confines of race and class, it has enunciated and practiced racial exclusiveness.

We preachers have also been tempted by the enticing cult of conformity. Seduced by the success symbols of the world, we have measured our achievements by the size of our parsonage. We have become showmen to please the whims and caprices of the people. We preach comforting sermons and avoid saying anything from our pulpits which might disturb the respectable views of the comfortable members of our congregations. Have we ministers of Jesus Christ sacrificed truth on the altar of self-interest and, like Pilate, yielded our convictions to the demands of the crowd?

We need to recapture the gospel glow of the early Christians, who were nonconformists in the truest sense of the word and refused to shape their witness according to the mundane patterns of the world. Willingly they sacrificed fame, fortune, and life itself in behalf of a cause they knew to be right. Quantitatively small, they were qualitatively giants. Their powerful gospel put an end to such barbaric evils as infanticide and bloody gladiatorial contests. Finally, they captured the Roman Empire of Jesus Christ.

Gradually, however, the church became so entrenched in wealth and prestige that it began to dilute the strong demands of the gospel and to conform to the ways of the world. And ever since the church has been a weak and ineffectual trumpet making uncertain sounds. If the church of Jesus Christ is to regain once more its power, message, and authentic ring, it must conform only to the demands of the gospel.

The hope of a secure and livable world lies with disciplined nonconformists, who are dedicated to justice, peace, and brotherhood. The trailblazers in human, academic, scientific, and religious freedom have always been nonconformists. In any cause that concerns the progress of mankind, put your faith in the nonconformist!

In his essay "Self-Reliance" Emerson wrote, "Whoso would be a man must be a nonconformist." The Apostle Paul reminds us that whoso would be a Christian must also be a nonconformist. Any Christian who blindly accepts the opinions of the majority and in fear and timidity follows a path of expediency and social approval is a mental and spiritual slave. Mark well these words from the pen of James Russell Lowell:

They are slaves who fear to speak
For the fallen and the weak;
They are slaves who will not choose
Hatred, scoffing, and abuse,
Rather than in silence shrink
From the truth they needs must think;
They are slaves who dare not be
In the right with two or three.[11]

THREE

Nonconformity in itself, however, may not necessarily be good and may at times possess neither transforming nor redemptive power. Nonconformity per se contains no saving value, and may represent in some circumstances little more than a form of exhibition-ism. Paul in the latter half of the text offers a formula for constructive nonconformity: "Be ye transformed by the renewing of your mind."[12] Nonconformity is creative when it is controlled and directed by a transformed life and is constructive when it embraces a new mental outlook. By opening our lives to God in Christ we become new creatures. This experience, which Jesus spoke of as the new birth, is essential if we are to be transformed nonconformists and freed from the cold hard-heartedness and self-righteousness so often characteristic of nonconformity. Someone has said, "I love reforms but I hate reformers." A reformer may be an untransformed nonconformist whose rebellion against the evils of society has left him annoyingly rigid and unreasonably impatient.

Only through an inner spiritual transformation do we gain the strength to fight vigorously the evils of the world in a humble and loving spirit. The transformed nonconformist, moreover, never yields to the passive sort of patience which is an excuse to do nothing. And his very transformation saves him from speaking irresponsible words which estrange without reconciling and from making hasty judgments which are blind to the necessity of social process. He recognizes that social change will not come overnight, yet he works as though it is an imminent possibility.

This hour in history needs a dedicated circle of transformed nonconformists. Our planet teeters on the brink of atomic annihilation; dangerous passions of pride, hatred, and selfishness are enthroned in our lives; truth lies prostrate on the rugged hills of nameless calvaries; and men do reverence before the false gods of nationalism and materialism. The saving of our world from pending doom will come, not through the complacent adjustment of the conforming majority, but through the creative maladjustment of a nonconforming minority.

Some years ago Professor Bixler reminded

us of the danger of overstressing the well-adjusted life. Everybody passionately seeks to be well-adjusted. We must, of course, be well-adjusted if we are to avoid neurotic and schizophrenic personalities, but there are some things in our world to which men of goodwill must be maladjusted. I confess that I never intend to become adjusted to the evils of segregation and the crippling effects of discrimination, to the moral degeneracy of religious bigotry and the corroding effects of narrow sectarianism, to economic conditions that deprive men of work and food, and to the insanities of militarism and the self-defeating effects of physical violence.

Human salvation lies in the hands of the creatively maladjusted. We need today maladjusted men like Shadrach, Meshach, and Abednego, who, when ordered by King Nebuchadnezzar to bow before a golden image, said in unequivocal terms, "If it be so, our God whom we serve is able to deliver us. . . . But if not . . . we will not serve thy gods";[13] like Thomas Jefferson, who in an age adjusted to slavery wrote, "We hold these truths to be self-evident, that all men are created equal, that they are endowed by their Creator with certain unalienable Rights, that among these are Life, Liberty and the pursuit of Happiness";[14] like Abraham Lincoln, who had the wisdom to discern that this nation could not survive half slave and half free; and supremely like our Lord, who, in the midst of the intricate and fascinating military machinery of the Roman Empire, reminded his disciples that "they that take the sword shall perish with the sword."[15] Through such maladjustment an already decadent generation may be called to those things which make for peace.

Honesty impels me to admit that transformed nonconformity, which is always costly and never altogether comfortable, may mean walking through the valley of the shadow of suffering, losing a job, or having a six-year-old daughter ask, "Daddy, why do you have to go to jail so much?" But we are gravely mistaken to think that Christianity protects us from the pain and agony of mortal existence. Christianity has always insisted that the cross we bear precedes the crown we wear. To be a Christian, one must take up his cross, with all of its difficulties and agonizing and tragedy-packed content, and carry it until that very cross leaves its marks upon us and redeems us to that more excellent way which comes only through suffering.

In these days of worldwide confusion, there is a dire need for men and women who will courageously do battle for truth. We need Christians who will echo the words John Bunyan said to his jailer when, having spent twelve years in jail, he was promised freedom if he would agree to stop preaching:

> But if nothing will do, unless I make of my conscience a continual butchery and slaughter-shop, unless, putting out my own eyes, I commit me to the blind to lead me, as I doubt is desired by some, I have determined, the Almighty God being my help and shield, yet to suffer, if frail life might continue so long, even till the moss shall grow on mine eyebrows, rather than thus to violate my faith and principles.[16]

We must make a choice. Will we continue to march to the drumbeat of conformity and respectability, or will we, listening to the beat of a more distant drum, move to its echoing sounds? Will we march only to the music of time, or will we, risking criticism and abuse, march to the soul-saving music of eternity? More than ever before we are today challenged by the words of yesterday, "Be not conformed to this world: but be ye transformed by the renewing of your mind."

CHAPTER III

ON BEING A GOOD NEIGHBOR

I SHOULD LIKE to talk with you about a good man, whose exemplary life will always be a flashing light to plague the dozing conscience of mankind. His goodness was not found in a passive commitment to a particular creed, but in his active participation in a life-saving deed; not in a moral pilgrimage that reached its destination point, but in the love ethic by which he journeyed life's highway. He was good because he was a good neighbor.

The ethical concern of this man is expressed in a magnificent little story, which begins with a theological discussion on the meaning of eternal life and concludes in a concrete expression of compassion on a dangerous road. Jesus is asked a question by a man who had been trained in the details of Jewish law: "Master, what shall I do to inherit eternal life." The retort is prompt: "What is written in the law? how readest thou?" After a moment the lawyer recites articulately: "Thou shalt love the Lord thy God with all thy heart, and with all thy soul, and with all thy strength, and with all thy mind; and thy neighbour as thyself." Then comes the decisive word from Jesus: "Thou hast answered right: this do, and thou shalt live."

The lawyer was chagrined. "Why," the people might ask, "would an expert in law raise a question that even the novice can answer?" Desiring to justify himself and to show that Jesus' reply was far from conclusive, the lawyer asks, "And who is my neighbour?" The lawyer was now taking up the cudgels of debate that might have turned the conversation into an abstract theological discussion. But Jesus, determined not to be caught in the "paralysis of analysis," pulls the question from mid-air and places it on a dangerous curve between Jerusalem and Jericho.

He told the story of "a certain man" who went down from Jerusalem to Jericho and fell among robbers who stripped him, beat him, and, departing, left him half dead. By chance a certain priest appeared, but he passed by on the other side, and later a Levite also passed by. Finally, a certain Samaritan, a half-breed from a people with whom the Jews had no dealings, appeared. When he saw the wounded man, he was moved with compassion, administered first aid, placed him on his beast, "and brought him to an inn, and took care of him."

Who is my neighbor? "I do not know his name," says Jesus in essence. "He is anyone toward whom you are neighborly. He is anyone who lies in need at life's roadside. He is neither Jew nor Gentile; he is neither Russian nor American; he is neither Negro nor white. He is 'a certain man'—any needy man—on one of the numerous Jericho roads of life." So Jesus defines a neighbor, not in a theological definition, but in a life situation.

And, behold, a certain lawyer stood up, and tempted him, saying,
Master, what shall I do to inherit eternal life?

He said unto him, What is written in the law? how readest thou?
And he answering said, Thou shalt love the Lord thy God with all thy heart,
and with all thy soul, and with all thy strength,
and with all thy mind; and thy neighbor as thyself.

And he said unto him, Thou hast answered right: this do, and thou shalt live.

But he, willing to justify himself, said unto Jesus,
And who is my neighbor?

Luke 10

What constituted the goodness of the good Samaritan? Why will he always be an inspiring paragon of neighborly virtue? It seems to me that this man's goodness may be described in one word—altruism. The good Samaritan was altruistic to the core. What is altruism? The dictionary defines altruism as "regard for, and devotion to, the interest of others." The Samaritan was good because he made concern for others the first law of his life.

ONE

The Samaritan had the capacity for a *universal altruism*. He had a piercing insight into that which is beyond the eternal accidents of race, religion, and nationality. One of the great tragedies of man's long trek along the highway of history has been the limiting of neighborly concern to tribe, race, class, or nation. The God of early Old Testament days was a tribal god and the ethic was tribal. "Thou shalt not kill" meant "Thou shalt not kill a fellow Israelite, but for God's sake, kill a Philistine." Greek democracy embraced a certain aristocracy, but not the hordes of Greek slaves whose labors built the city-states. The universalism at the center of the Declaration of Independence has been shamefully negated by America's appalling tendency to substitute "some" for "all." Numerous people in the North and South still believe that the affirmation, "all men are created equal," means "All white men are created equal." Our unswerving devotion to monopolistic capitalism makes us more concerned about the economic security of the captains of industry than for the laboring men whose sweat and skills keep industry functioning.

What are the devastating consequences of this narrow, group-centered attitude? It means that one does not really mind what happens to the people outside his group. If an American is concerned only about his nation, he will not be concerned about the peoples of Asia, Africa, or South America. Is this not why nations engage in the madness of war without the slightest sense of penitence? Is this not why the murder of a citizen of your own nation is a crime, but the murder of the citizens of another nation in war is an act of heroic virtue? If manufacturers are concerned only in their personal interests, they will pass by on the other side while thousands of working people are stripped of their jobs and left displaced on some Jericho road as a result of automation, and they will judge every move toward a better distribution of wealth and a better life for the working man to be socialistic. If a white man is concerned only about his race, he will casually pass by the Negro who has been robbed of his personhood, stripped of his sense of dignity, and left dying on some wayside road.

A few years ago, when an automobile carrying several members of a Negro college basketball team had an accident on a Southern highway, three of the young men were severely injured. An ambulance was immediately called, but on arriving at the place of the accident, the driver, who was white, said without apology that it was not his policy to serve Negroes, and he drove away. The driver of a passing automobile graciously drove the boys to the nearest hospital, but the attending physician belligerently said, "We don't take niggers in this hospital." When the boys finally arrived at a "colored" hospital in a town some fifty miles from the scene of the accident, one was dead and the other two died thirty and fifty minutes later respectively. Probably all three could have been saved if they had been given immediate treatment. This is only one of thousands of inhuman incidents that occur daily in the South, an unbelievable expression of the barbaric consequences of any tribal-centered, national-centered, or racial-centered ethic.

The real tragedy of such narrow provincialism is that we see people as entities or merely as things. Too seldom do we see people in their true *humanness*. A spiritual myopia limits our vision to external accidents. We see men as Jews or Gentiles, Catholics or Protestants, Chinese or American, Negroes or whites. We fail to think of them as fellow human beings made from the same basic stuff as we, molded in the same divine image. The priest and the Levite saw only a bleeding body, not a human being like themselves. But the good Samaritan will always remind us to remove the cataracts of provincialism from our spiritual eyes and see men as men. If the Samaritan had considered the wounded man as a Jew first, he would not have stopped, for the Jews and the Samaritans had no dealings. He saw him as a human being first, who was a Jew only by accident. The good neighbor looks beyond the external accidents and discerns those inner qualities that make all men human and, therefore, brothers.

TWO

The Samaritan possessed the capacity for a *dangerous altruism*. He risked his life to save a brother. When we ask why the priest and the Levite did not stop to help the wounded man, numerous suggestions come to mind. Perhaps they could not delay their arrival at an important ecclesiastical meeting. Perhaps religious regulations demanded that they touch no human body for several hours prior to the performing of their temple functions. Or perhaps they were on their way to an organizational meeting of a Jericho Road Improvement Association. Certainly this would have been a real need, for it is not enough to aid a wounded man on the Jericho Road; it is also important to change the conditions which make robbery possible. Philanthropy is commendable, but it must not cause the philanthropist to overlook the circumstances of economic injustice which make philanthropy necessary. Maybe the priest and the Levite believed that it is better to cure injustice at the causal source than to get bogged down with a single individual effect.

These are probably reasons for their failure to stop, yet there is another possibility, often overlooked, that they were afraid. The Jericho Road was a dangerous road. When Mrs. King and I visited the Holy Land, we rented a car and drove from Jerusalem to Jericho. As we traveled slowly down that meandering, mountainous road, I said to my wife, "I can now understand why Jesus chose this road as the setting for his parable." Jerusalem is some two thousand feet above and Jericho one thousand feet below sea level. The descent is made in less than twenty miles. Many sudden curves provide likely places for ambushing and expose the traveler to unforeseen attacks. Long ago the road was known as the Bloody Pass. So it is possible that the Priest and the Levite were afraid that if they stopped, they too would be beaten. Perhaps the robbers were still nearby. Or maybe the wounded man on the ground was a faker, who wished to draw passing travelers to his side for quick and easy seizure. I imagine that the first question which the priest and the Levite asked was: "If I stop to help this man, what will happen to me?" But by the very nature of his concern, the good Samaritan reversed the question: "If I do not stop to help this man, what will happen to him?" The good Samaritan engaged in a dangerous altruism.

We so often ask, "What will happen to my job, my prestige, or my status if I take a stand on this issue? Will my home be bombed, will my life be threatened, or will I be jailed?" The good man always reverses the question. Albert Schweitzer did not ask, "What will happen to my prestige and security as a university professor and to my status as a Bach organist, if I work with the people of Africa?" but rather he asked, "What will happen to these millions of people who have been wounded by the forces of injustice, if I do not go to them?" Abraham Lincoln did not ask, "What will happen to me if I issue the Emancipation Proclamation and bring an end to chattel slavery?" but he asked, "What will happen to the Union and to millions of Negro people, if I fail to do it?" The Negro professional does not ask, "What will happen to my secure position, my middle-class status, or my personal safety, if I participate in the movement to end the system of segregation?" but "What will happen to the cause of justice and the masses of Negro people who have never experienced the warmth of economic security, if I do not participate actively and courageously in the movement?" The ultimate measure of a man is not where he stands in moments of comfort and convenience, but where he stands at times of challenge and controversy. The true neighbor will risk his position, his prestige, and even his life for the welfare of others. In dangerous valleys and hazardous pathways, he will lift some bruised and beaten brother to a higher and more noble life.

THREE

The Samaritan also possessed *excessive altruism*. With his own hands he bound the wounds of the man and then set him on his own beast. It would have been easier to pay an ambulance to take the unfortunate man to the hospital, rather than risk having his neatly trimmed suit stained with blood.

True altruism is more than the capacity to pity; it is the capacity to sympathize. Pity may represent little more than the impersonal concern which prompts the mailing of a check, but true sympathy is the personal concern which demands the giving of one's soul. Pity may arise from interest in an abstraction called humanity, but sympathy grows out of a concern for a particular needy human being who lies at life's roadside. Sympathy is fellow-feeling for the person in need—his pain, agony, and burdens. Our missionary efforts fail when they are based on pity, rather than true compassion. Instead of seeking to do something *with* the African and Asian peoples, we have too often sought only to do something *for* them. An expression of pity, devoid of genuine sympathy, leads to a new form of paternalism which no self-respecting person can accept. Dollars possess the potential for helping wounded children of God on life's Jericho Road, but unless those dollars are distributed by compassionate fingers they will enrich neither the giver nor the receiver. Millions of missionary dollars have gone to Africa from the hands of church people who would die a million deaths before they would permit a single African the privilege of worshiping in their congregation. Millions of Peace Corps dollars are being invested in Africa because of the votes of some men who fight unrelentingly to prevent African ambassadors from holding membership in their diplomatic clubs or establish residency in their particular neighborhoods. The Peace Corps will fail if it seeks to do something *for* the underprivileged peoples of the world; it will succeed if it seeks creatively to do something *with* them. It will fail as a negative gesture to defeat Communism; it will succeed only as a positive effort to wipe poverty, ignorance, and disease from the earth. Money devoid of love is like salt devoid of savor, good for nothing except to be trodden under the foot of men. True neighborliness requires personal concern. The Samaritan used his hands to bind up the wounds of the robbed man's body, and he also released an overflowing love to bind up the wounds of his broken spirit.

Another expression of the excessive altruism on the part of the Samaritan was his willingness to go far beyond the call of duty. After tending to the man's wounds, he put him on his beast, carried him to an inn, and left money for his care, making clear that if further financial needs arose he would gladly meet them. "Whatsoever thou spendest more, when I come again, I will repay thee." Stopping short of this, he would have more than fulfilled any possible rule concerning one's duty to a wounded stranger. He went beyond the second mile. His love was complete.

Dr. Harry Emerson Fosdick has made an impressive distinction between enforceable and unenforceable obligations. The former are regulated by the codes of society and the vigorous implementation of law-enforcement agencies. Breaking these obligations, spelled out on thousands of pages in law books, has filled numerous prisons. But unenforceable obligations are beyond the reach of the laws of society. They concern inner attitudes, genuine person-to-person relations, and expressions of compassion which law books cannot regulate and jails cannot rectify. Such obligations are met by one's commitment to an inner law, written on the heart. Man-made laws assure justice, but a higher law produces love. No code of conduct ever persuaded a father to love his children or a husband to show affection to his wife. The law court may force him to provide bread for the family, but it cannot make him provide the bread of love.

A good father is obedient to the unenforceable. The good Samaritan represents the conscience of mankind because he also was obedient to that which could not be enforced. No law in the world could have produced such unalloyed compassion, such genuine love, such thorough altruism.

In our nation today a mighty struggle is taking place. It is a struggle to conquer the reign of an evil monster called segregation and its inseparable twin called discrimination—a monster that has wandered through this land for well-nigh one hundred years, stripping millions of Negro people of their sense of dignity and robbing them of their birthright of freedom.

Let us never succumb to the temptation of believing that legislation and judicial decrees play only minor roles in solving this problem. Morality cannot be legislated, but behavior can be regulated. Judicial decrees may not change the heart, but they can restrain the heartless. The law cannot make an employer love an employee, but it can prevent him from refusing to hire me because of the color of my skin. The habits, if not the hearts, of people have been and are being altered every day by legislative acts, judicial decisions, and executive orders. Let us not be misled by those who argue that segregation cannot be ended by the force of law.

But acknowledging this, we must admit that the ultimate solution to the race problem lies in the willingness of men to obey the unenforceable. Court orders and federal enforcement agencies are of inestimable value in achieving desegregation, but desegregation is only a partial, though necessary, step toward the final goal which we seek to realize, genuine intergroup and interpersonal living. Desegregation will break down the legal barriers and bring men together physically, but something must touch the hearts and souls of men so that they will come together spiritu-

ally because it is natural and right. A vigorous enforcement of civil rights laws will bring an end to segregated public facilities which are barriers to a truly desegregated society, but it cannot bring an end to fears, prejudice, pride, and irrationality, which are the barriers to a truly integrated society. These dark and demonic responses will be removed only as men are possessed by the invisible, inner law which etches on their hearts the conviction that all men are brothers and that love is mankind's most potent weapon for personal and social transformation. True integration will be achieved by true neighbors who are willingly obedient to unenforceable obligations.

More than ever before, my friends, men of all races and nations are today challenged to be neighborly. The call for a worldwide good-neighbor policy is more than an ephemeral shibboleth; it is the call to a way of life which will transform our imminent cosmic elegy into a psalm of creative fulfillment. No longer can we afford the luxury of passing by on the other side. Such folly was once called moral failure; today it will lead to universal suicide. We cannot long survive spiritually separated in a world that is geographically together. In the final analysis, I must not ignore the wounded man on life's Jericho Road, because he is a part of me and I am a part of him. His agony diminishes me, and his salvation enlarges me.

In our quest to make neighborly love a reality, we have, in addition to the inspiring example of the good Samaritan, the magnanimous life of our Christ to guide us. His altruism was universal, for he thought of all men, even publicans and sinners, as brothers. His altruism was dangerous, for he willingly traveled hazardous roads in a cause he knew was right. His altruism was excessive, for he chose to die on Calvary, history's most magnificent expression of obedience to the unenforceable.

LOVE IN ACTION

And when they were come to the place,
which is called Calvary, there they crucified him . . .

Then said Jesus, Father, forgive them; for they know not what they do.
And they parted his raiment, and cast lots.

Luke 23

F<small>EW</small> W<small>ORDS</small> in the New Testament more clearly and solemnly express the magnanimity of Jesus' spirit than that sublime utterance from the cross, "Father, forgive them; for they know not what they do." This is love at its best.

We shall not fully understand the great meaning of Jesus' prayer unless we first notice that the text opens with the word "then." The verse immediately preceding reads thus: "And when they were come to the place, which is called Calvary, there they crucified him, and the malefactors, one on the right hand, and the other on the left." Then said Jesus, Father, forgive them. *Then*—when he was being plunged into the abyss of nagging agony. *Then*—when man had stooped to his worst. *Then*—when he was dying, a most ignominious death. *Then*—when the wicked hands of the creature had dared to crucify the only begotten Son of the Creator. Then said Jesus, "Father, forgive them." That "then" might well have been otherwise. He could have said, "Father, get even with them," or "Father, let loose the mighty thunderbolts of righteous wrath and destroy them," or "Father, open the flood gates of justice and permit the staggering avalanche of retribution to pour upon them." But none of these was his response. Though subjected to inexpressible agony, suffering excruciating pain, and despised and rejected, nevertheless, he cried, "Father, forgive them."

Let us take note of two basic lessons to be gleaned from this text.

ONE

First, it is a marvelous expression of Jesus' ability to match words with actions. One of the great tragedies of life is that men seldom bridge the gulf between practice and profession, between doing and saying. A persistent schizophrenia leaves so many of us tragically divided against ourselves. On the one hand, we proudly profess certain sublime and noble principles, but on the other hand, we sadly practice the very antithesis of those principles. How often are our lives characterized by a high blood pressure of creeds and an anemia of deeds! We talk eloquently about our commitment to the principles of Christianity, and yet our lives are saturated with the practices of paganism. We proclaim our devotion to democracy, but we sadly practice the very opposite of the democratic creed. We talk passionately about peace, and at the same time we assiduously prepare for war. We make our fervent pleas for the high road of justice, and then we tread unflinchingly the low road of injustice. This strange dichotomy, this agonizing gulf between the *ought* and the *is,* represents the tragic theme of man's earthly pilgrimage.

But in the life of Jesus we find that the gulf is bridged. Never in history was there a more sublime example of the consistency of word and deed. During his ministry in the sunny villages of Galilee, Jesus talked passionately about forgiveness. This strange doctrine awakened the questioning mind of Peter. "How oft," he asked,[17] "shall my brother sin against me, and I forgive him? till seven times?" Peter wanted to be legal and statistical. But Jesus responded by affirming that there is no limit to forgiveness. "I say not unto thee, Until seven times: but, Until seventy times seven." In other words, forgiveness is not a matter of quantity, but of quality. A man cannot forgive up to four hundred and ninety times without forgiveness becoming a part of the habit structure of his being. Forgiveness is not an occasional act; it is a permanent attitude.

Jesus also admonished his followers to love their enemies and to pray for them that despitefully used them. This teaching fell upon the ears of many of his hearers like a strange music from a foreign land. Their ears were not attuned to the tonal qualities of such amazing love. They had been taught to love their friends and hate their enemies. Their lives had been conditioned to seek redress in the time-honored tradition of retaliation. Yet Jesus taught them that only through a creative love for their enemies could they be children of their Father in heaven and also that love and forgiveness were absolute necessities for spiritual maturity.

The moment of testing emerges. Christ, the innocent Son of God, is stretched in painful agony on an uplifted cross. What place is there for love and forgiveness now? How will Jesus react? What will he say? The answer to these questions bursts forth in majestic splendor. Jesus lifts his thorn-crowned head and cries in words of cosmic proportions: "Father, forgive them; for they know not what they do." This was Jesus' finest hour; this was his heavenly response to his earthly rendezvous with destiny.

We sense the greatness of this prayer by contrasting it with nature, which caught in the finality of her own impersonal structure, does not forgive. In spite of the agonizing pleas of men trapped in the path of an onrushing hurricane or the anguishing cry of the builder falling from the scaffold, nature expresses only a cold, serene, and passionless indifference. She must honor everlastingly her fixed, immutable laws. When these laws are violated, she has no alternative except to follow inexorably her path of uniformity. Nature does not and cannot forgive.

Or contrast Jesus' prayer with the slowness of man to forgive. We live according to the philosophy that life is a matter of getting even and of saving face. We bow before the altar of revenge. Samson, eyeless at Gaza, prays fervently for his enemies—but only for their utter destruction. The potential beauty of human life is constantly made ugly by man's ever-recurring song of retaliation.

Or contrast the prayer with a society that is even less prone to forgive. Society must have its standards, norms, and mores. It must have its legal checks and judicial restraints. Those who fall below the standards and those who disobey the laws are often left in a dark abyss of condemnation and have no hope for a second chance. Ask an innocent young lady, who, after a moment of overriding passion, becomes the mother of an illegitimate child. She will tell you that society is slow to forgive. Ask a public official, who, in a moment's carelessness, betrays the public trust. He will tell you that society is slow to forgive. Go to any prison and ask the inhabitants, who have written shameful lines across the pages of their lives. From behind the bars they will tell you that society is slow to forgive. Make your way to death row and speak with the tragic victims of criminality. As they prepare to make their pathetic walk to the electric chair, their hopeless cry is that society will not forgive. Capital punishment is society's final assertion that it will not forgive.

Such is the persistent story of mortal life. The oceans of history are made turbulent by the ever-rising tides of revenge. Man has never risen above the injunction of the *lex talionis*: "Life for life, eye for eye, tooth for tooth, hand for hand, foot for foot."[18] In spite of the fact that the law of revenge solves no social problems, men continue to follow its disastrous leading. History is cluttered with the wreckage of nations and individuals that pursued this self-defeating path.

Jesus eloquently affirmed from the cross a higher law. He knew that the old eye-for-an-eye philosophy would leave everyone blind. He did not seek to overcome evil with evil. He overcame evil with good. Although crucified by hate, he responded with aggressive love.

What a magnificent lesson! Generations will rise and fall; men will continue to worship the god of revenge and bow before the altar of retaliation; but ever and again this noble lesson of Calvary will be a nagging reminder that only goodness can drive out evil and only love can conquer hate.

TWO

A second lesson comes to us from Jesus' prayer on the cross. It is an expression of Jesus' awareness of man's intellectual and spiritual blindness. "They know not what they do," said Jesus. Blindness was their trouble; enlightenment was their need. We must recognize that Jesus was nailed to the cross not simply by sin but also by blindness. The men who cried, "Crucify him," were not bad men but rather blind men. The jeering mob that lined the roadside which led to Calvary was composed not of evil people but of blind people. They knew not what they did. What a tragedy!

History reverberates with testimonies of this shameful tragedy. Centuries ago a sage named Socrates was forced to drink hemlock. The men who called for his death were not bad men with demonic blood running through their veins. On the contrary, they were sincere and respectable citizens of Greece. They genuinely thought that Socrates was an atheist because his idea of God had a philosophical depth that probed beyond traditional concepts. Not badness but blindness killed Socrates. Saul was not an evil-intentioned man when he persecuted Christians. He was a sincere, conscientious devotee of Israel's faith. He thought he was right. He persecuted Christians, not because he was devoid of integrity, but because he was devoid of enlightenment. The Christians who engaged in infamous persecutions and shameful inquistitions were not evil men but misguided men. The churchmen who felt that they had an edict from God to withstand the progress of science, whether in the form of a Copernican revolution or a Darwinian theory of natural selection, were not mischievous men but misinformed men. And so Christ's words from the cross are written in sharp-etched terms across some of the most inexpressible tragedies of history: "They know not what they do."

This tragic blindness expresses itself in many ominous ways in our own day. Some men still feel that war is the answer to the problems of the world. They are not evil people. On the contrary, they are good, respectable citizens whose ideas are robed in the garments of patriotism. They talk of brinkmanship and a balance of terror. They sincerely feel that a continuation of the arms race will be conducive to more beneficent than maleficent consequences. So they passionately call for bigger bombs, larger nuclear stockpiles, and faster ballistic missiles.

Wisdom born of experience should tell us that war is obsolete. There may have been a time when war served as a negative good by preventing the spread and growth of an evil force, but the destructive power of modern weapons eliminates even the possibility that war may serve as a negative good. If we assume that life is worth living and that man has a right to survival, then we must find an alternative to war. In a day when vehicles hurtle through outer space and guided ballistic missiles carve highways of death through the stratosphere, no nation can claim victory in war. A so-called limited war will leave little more than a calamitous legacy of human suffering, political turmoil, and spiritual disillusionment. A world war—God forbid!—will leave only smouldering ashes as a mute testimony of a human race whose folly led inexorably to untimely death. Yet there are those who sincerely feel that disarmament is an evil and international negotiation is an abominable waste of time. Our world is threatened by the grim prospect of atomic annihilation because there are still too many men who know not what they do.

Notice, too, how the truth of this text is revealed in race relations. Slavery in America was perpetuated not merely by human badness but also by human blindness. True, the causal basis for the system of slavery must to a large extent be traced back to the economic factor. Men convinced themselves that a system which was so economically profitable must be morally justifiable. They formulated elaborate theories of racial superiority. Their rationalizations clothed obvious wrongs in the beautiful garments of righteousness. This tragic attempt to give moral sanction to an economically profitable system gave birth to the doctrine of white supremacy. Religion and the Bible were cited to crystallize the status quo. Science was commandeered to prove the biological inferiority of the Negro. Even philosophical logic was manipulated to give intellectual credence to the system of slavery. Someone formulated the argument of the inferiority of the Negro according to the framework of an Aristotelian syllogism:

All men are made in the image of God;
God, as everyone knows, is not a Negro;
Therefore, the Negro is not a man.

So men conveniently twisted the insights of religion, science, and philosophy to give sanction to the doctrine of white supremacy. Soon this idea was imbedded in every textbook and preached in practically every pulpit. It became a structured part of the culture. And men then embraced this philosophy, not as the rationalization of a lie, but as the expression of a final truth. They sincerely came to believe that the Negro was inferior by nature and that slavery was ordained by God. In 1857, the system of slavery was given its greatest legal support by the deliberations of the Supreme Court of the United States in the Dred Scott decision. The Court affirmed that the Negro had no rights which the white man was bound to respect. The justices who rendered this decision were not wicked men. On the contrary, they were decent and dedicated men. But they were victims of spiritual and intellectual blindness. They knew not what they did. The whole system of slavery was largely perpetuated by sincere though spiritually ignorant persons.

This tragic blindness is also found in racial segregation, the not-too-distant cousin of slavery. Some of the most vigorous defenders of segregation are sincere in their beliefs and earnest in their motives. Although some men are segregationists merely for reasons of political expediency and economic gain, not all of the resistance to integration is the rearguard action of professional bigots. Some people feel that their attempt to preserve segregation is best for themselves, their children, and their nation. Many are good church people, anchored in the religious faith of their mothers and fathers. Pressed for a religious vindication for their conviction, they will even argue that God was the first segregationist. "Red birds and blue birds don't fly together," they contend. Their views about segregation, they insist, can be rationally explained and morally justified. Pressed for a justification of their belief in the inferiority of the Negro, they turn to some pseudo-scientific writing and argue that the Negro's brain is smaller than the white man's brain. They do not know, or they refuse to know, that the idea of an inferior or superior race has been refuted by the best evidence of the science of anthropology. Great anthropologists, like Ruth Benedict, Margaret Mead, and Melville J. Herskovits, agree that, although there may be inferior and superior individuals within all races, there is no superior or inferior race. And segregationists refuse to acknowledge that science has demonstrated that there are four types of blood and that these four types are found within every racial group. They blindly believe in the eternal validity of an evil called segregation and the timeless truth of a myth called white supremacy. What a tragedy! Millions of Negroes have been crucified by conscientious blindness. With Jesus on the cross, we must look lovingly at our oppressors and say, "Father, forgive them; for they know not what they do."

THREE

From all that I have attempted to say it should now be apparent that sincerity and conscientiousness in themselves are not enough. History has proven that these noble virtues may degenerate into tragic vices. Nothing in all the world is more dangerous than sincere ignorance and conscientious stupidity. Shakespeare wrote:

*For sweetest things turn sourest
            by their deeds;
Lilies that fester
            smell far worse than weeds.*[19]

As the chief moral guardian of the community, the church must implore men to be good and well-intentioned and must extol the virtues of kindheartedness and conscientiousness. But somewhere along the way the church must remind men that devoid of intelligence, goodness and conscientiousness will become brutal forces leading to shameful crucifixions. Never must the church tire of reminding men that they have a moral responsibility to be intelligent.

Must we not admit that the church has often overlooked this moral demand for enlightenment? At times it has talked as though ignorance were a virtue and intelligence a crime. Through its obscurantism, closemindedness, and obstinacy to new truth, the church has often unconsciously encouraged its worshipers to look askance upon intelligence.

But if we are to call ourselves Christians, we had better avoid intellectual and moral blindness. Throughout the New Testament we are reminded of the need for enlightenment. We are commanded to love God, not only with our hearts and souls, but also with our minds. When the Apostle Paul noticed the blindness of many of his opponents, he said, "I bear them record that they have a zeal for God, but not according to knowledge."[20] Over and again the Bible reminds us of the danger of zeal without knowledge and sincerity without intelligence.

So we have a mandate both to conquer sin and also to conquer ignorance. Modern man is presently having a rendezvous with chaos, not merely because of human badness, but also because of human stupidity. If Western civilization continues to degenerate until it, like twenty-four of its predecessors, falls hopelessly into a bottomless void, the cause will be not only its undeniable sinfulness, but also its appalling blindness. And if American democracy gradually disintegrates, it will be due as much to a lack of insight as to a lack of commitment to right. If modern man continues to flirt unhesitatingly with war and eventually transforms his earthly habitat into an inferno such as even the mind of Dante could not imagine, it will have resulted from downright badness and also from downright stupidity.

"They know not what they do," said Jesus. Blindness was their besetting trouble. And the crux of the matter lies here: we do not need to be blind. Unlike physical blindness that is usually inflicted upon individuals as a result of natural forces beyond their control, intellectual and moral blindness is a dilemma which man inflicts upon himself by his tragic misuse of freedom and his failure to use his mind to its fullest capacity. One day we will learn that the heart can never be totally right if the head is totally wrong. This is not to say that the head can be right if the heart is wrong. Only through the bringing together of head and heart—intelligence and goodness— shall man rise to a fulfillment of his true nature. Neither is this to say that one must be a philosopher or a possessor of extensive academic training before he can achieve the good life. I know many people of limited formal training who have amazing intelligence and foresight. The call for intelligence is a call for open-mindedness, sound judgment, and love for truth. It is a call for men to rise above the stagnation of closed-mindedness

and the paralysis of gullibility. One does not need to be a profound scholar to be open-minded, nor a keen academician to engage in an assiduous pursuit for truth.

Light has come into the world. A voice crying through the vista of time calls men to walk in the light. Man's earthly life will become a tragic cosmic elegy if he fails to heed this call. "This is the condemnation," says John, "that light is come into the world, and men loved darkness rather than light.[21]

Jesus was right about those men who crucified him. They knew not what they did. They were inflicted with a terrible blindness.

Every time I look at the cross I am reminded of the greatness of God and the redemptive power of Jesus Christ. I am reminded of the beauty of sacrificial love and the majesty of unswerving devotion to truth. It causes me to say with John Bowring:

In the cross of Christ I glory,
Towering o'er the wrecks of time;
All the light of sacred story
Gathers round its head sublime.

It would be wonderful were I to look at the cross and sense only such a sublime reaction. But somehow I can never turn my eyes from that cross without also realizing that it symbolizes a strange mixture of greatness and smallness, of good and evil. As I behold that uplifted cross I am reminded not only of the unlimited power of God, but also of the sordid weakness of man. I think not only of the radiance of the divine, but also of the tang of the human. I am reminded not only of Christ at his best, but of man at his worst.

We must see the cross as the magnificent symbol of love conquering hate and of light overcoming darkness. But in the midst of this glowing affirmation, let us never forget that our Lord and Master was nailed to that cross because of human blindness. Those who crucified him knew not what they did.

CHAPTER V

LOVING YOUR ENEMIES

PROBABLY NO ADMONITION of Jesus has been more difficult to follow than the command to "love your enemies." Some men have sincerely felt that its actual practice is not possible. It is easy, they say, to love those who love you, but how can one love those who openly and insidiously seek to defeat you? Others, like the philosopher Nietzsche, contend that Jesus' exhortation to love one's enemies is testimony to the fact that the Christian ethic is designed for the weak and cowardly, and not for the strong and courageous. Jesus, they say, was an impractical idealist.

In spite of these insistent questions and persistent objections, this command of Jesus challenges us with new urgency. Upheaval after upheaval has reminded us that modern man is traveling along a road called hate, in a journey that will bring us to destruction and damnation. Far from being the pious injunction of a Utopian dreamer, the command to love one's enemy is an absolute necessity for our survival. Love even for enemies is the key to the solution of the problems of our world. Jesus is not an impractical idealist; he is the practical realist.

I am certain that Jesus understood the difficulty inherent in the act of loving one's enemy. He never joined the ranks of those who talk glibly about the easiness of the moral life. He realized that every genuine expression of love grows out of a consistent and total surrender to God. So when Jesus said "Love your enemy," he was not unmindful of its stringent qualities. Yet he meant every word of it. Our responsibility as Christians is to discover the meaning of this command and seek passionately to live it out in our daily lives.

ONE

Let us be practical and ask the question, *How do we love our enemies?*

> Ye have heard that it hath been said,
> Thou shalt love thy neighbour, and hate thine enemy.
>
> But I say unto you,
> Love your enemies, bless them that curse you, do good to them that hate you,
> and pray for them which despitefully use you, and persecute you;
>
> That ye may be the children of your Father which is in Heaven:
> *for he maketh his sun to rise on the evil and on the good,*
> *and sendeth rain on the just and on the unjust.*
>
> Matthew 5

First, we must develop and maintain the capacity to forgive. He who is devoid of the power to forgive is devoid of the power to love. It is impossible even to begin the act of loving one's enemies without the prior acceptance of the necessity, over and over again, of forgiving those who inflict evil and injury upon us. It is also necessary to realize that the forgiving act must always be initiated by the person who has been wronged, the victim of some great hurt, the recipient of some tortuous injustice, the absorber of some terrible act of oppression. The wrongdoer may request forgiveness. He may come to himself, and, like the prodigal son, move up some dusty road, his heart palpitating with the desire for forgiveness. But only the injured neighbor, the loving father back home, can really pour out the warm waters of forgiveness.

Forgiveness does not mean ignoring what has been done or putting a false label on an evil act. It means, rather, that the evil act no longer remains as a barrier to the relationship. Forgiveness is a catalyst creating the atmosphere necessary for a fresh start and a new beginning. It is the lifting of a burden or the canceling of a debt. The words "I will forgive you, but I'll never forget what you've done" never explain the real nature of forgiveness. Certainly one can never forget, if that means erasing it totally from his mind. But when we forgive, we forget in the sense that the evil deed is no longer a mental block impeding a new relationship. Likewise, we can never say, "I will forgive you, but I won't have anything further to do with you." Forgiveness means reconciliation, a coming together again. Without this, no man can love his enemies. The degree to which we are able to forgive determines the degree to which we are able to love our enemies.

Second, we must recognize that the evil deed of the enemy-neighbor, the thing that hurts, never quite expresses all that he is. An element of goodness may be found even in our worst enemy. Each of us is something of a schizophrenic personality, tragically divided against ourselves. A persistent civil war rages within all of our lives. Something within us causes us to lament with Ovid, the Latin poet, "I see and approve the better things, but follow worse,"[22] or to agree with Plato that human personality is like a charioteer having two headstrong horses, each wanting to go in a different direction, or to repeat with the Apostle Paul, "The good that I would I do not: but the evil which I would not, that I do."[23]

This simply means that there is some good in the worst of us and some evil in the best of us. When we discover this, we are less prone to hate our enemies. When we look beneath the surface, beneath the impulsive evil deed, we see within our enemy-neighbor a measure of goodness and know that the viciousness and evilness of his acts are not quite representative of all that he is. We see him in a new light. We recognize that his hate grows out of fear, pride, ignorance, prejudice, and misunderstanding, but in spite of this, we know God's image is ineffably etched in his being. Then we love our enemies by realizing that they are not totally bad and that they are not beyond the reach of God's redemptive love.

Third, we must not seek to defeat or humiliate the enemy but to win his friendship and understanding. At times we are able to humilate our worst enemy. Inevitably, his weak moments come and we are able to thrust in his side the spear of defeat. But this we must not do. Every word and deed must contribute to an understanding with the enemy and release those vast reservoirs of goodwill which have been blocked by impenetrable walls of hate.

The meaning of love is not to be confused with some sentimental outpouring. Love is something much deeper than emotional bosh. Perhaps the Greek language can clear our confusion at this point. In the Greek New Testament are three words for love. The word *eros* is a sort of aesthetic or romantic love. In the Platonic dialogues *eros* is a yearning of the soul for the realm of the divine. The second word is *philia*, a reciprocal love and the intimate affection and friendship between friends. We love those whom we like, and we love because we are loved. The third word is *agape*, understanding and creative, redemptive goodwill for all men. An overflowing love which seeks nothing in return, *agape* is the love of God operating in the human heart. At this level, we love men not because we like them, nor because their ways appeal to us, nor even because they possess some type of divine spark; we love every man because God loves him. At this level, we love the person who does an evil deed, although we hate the deed that he does.

Now we can see what Jesus meant when he said, "Love your enemies." We should be happy that he did not say, "Like your enemies." It is almost impossible to like some people. "Like" is a sentimental and affectionate word. How can we be affectionate toward a person whose avowed aim is to crush our very being and place innumerable stumbling blocks in our path? How can we like a person who is threatening our children and bombing our homes? This is impossible. But Jesus recognized that *love* is greater than *like*. When Jesus bids us to love our enemies, he is speaking neither of *eros* nor *philia*; he is speaking of *agape*, understanding and creative, redemptive goodwill for all men. Only by following this way and responding with this type of love are we able to be children of our Father who is in heaven.

TWO

Let us move now from the practical *how* to the theoretical *why: Why should we love our enemies?* The first reason is fairly obvious. Returning hate for hate multiplies hate, adding deeper darkness to a night already devoid of stars. Darkness cannot drive out darkness; only light can do that. Hate cannot drive out hate; only love can do that. Hate multiplies hate, violence multiplies violence, and toughness multiplies toughness in a descending spiral of destruction. So when Jesus says "Love your enemies," he is setting forth a profound and ultimately inescapable admonition. Have we not come to such an impasse in the modern world that we must love our enemies—or else? The chain reaction of evil—hate begetting hate, wars producing more wars—must be broken, or we shall be plunged into the dark abyss of annihilation.

Another reason why we must love our enemies is that hate scars the soul and distorts the personality. Mindful that hate is an evil and dangerous force, we too often think of what it does to the person hated. This is understandable, for hate brings irreparable damage to its victims. We have seen its ugly consequences in the ignominious deaths brought to six million Jews by a hate-obsessed madman named Hitler, in the unspeakable violence inflicted upon Negroes by blood-thirsty mobs, in the dark horrors of war, and in the terrible indignities and injustices perpetrated against millions of God's children by unconscionable oppressors.

But there is another side which we must never overlook. Hate is just as injurious to the person who hates. Like an unchecked cancer, hate corrodes the personality and eats away its vital unity. Hate destroys a man's sense of values and his objectivity. It causes him to describe the beautiful as ugly and the ugly as beautiful, and to confuse the true with the false and the false with the true.

Dr. E. Franklin Frazier, in an interesting essay entitled "The Pathology of Race Prejudice," included several examples of white persons who were normal, amiable, and congenial in their day-to-day relationships with other white persons, but when they were challenged to think of Negroes as equals or even to discuss the question of racial injustice, they reacted with unbelievable irrationality and an abnormal unbalance. This happens when hate lingers in our minds. Psychiatrists report that many of the strange things that happen in the subconscious, many of our inner conflicts, are rooted in hate. They say, "Love or perish." Modern psychology recognizes what Jesus taught centuries ago: hate divides the personality and love in an amazing and inexorable way unites it.

A third reason why we should love our enemies is that love is the only force capable of transforming an enemy into a friend. We never get rid of an enemy by meeting hate with hate; we get rid of an enemy by getting rid of enmity. By its very nature, hate destroys and tears down; by its very nature, love creates and builds up. Love transforms with redemptive power.

Lincoln tried love and left for all history a magnificent drama of reconciliation. When he was campaigning for the presidency one of his archenemies was a man named Stanton. For some reason Stanton hated Lincoln. He used every ounce of his energy to degrade him in the eyes of the public. So deep rooted was Stanton's hate for Lincoln that he uttered unkind words about his physical appearance, and sought to embarrass him at every point with the bitterest diatribes. But in spite of this Lincoln was elected President of the United States. Then came the period when he had to select his cabinet which would consist of the persons who would be his most intimate associates in implementing his program. He started choosing men here and there for the various secretaryships. The day finally came for Lincoln to select a man to fill the all-important post of Secretary of War. Can you imagine whom Lincoln chose to fill this post? None other than the man named Stanton.

There was an immediate uproar in the inner circle when the news began to spread. Adviser after adviser was heard saying, "Mr. President, you are making a mistake. Do you know this man Stanton? Are you familiar with all of the ugly things he said about you? He is your enemy. He will seek to sabotage your program. Have you thought this through, Mr. President?" Mr. Lincoln's answer was terse and to the point: "Yes, I know Mr. Stanton. I am aware of all the terrible things he has said about me. But after looking over the nation, I find that he is the best man for the job." So Stanton became Abraham Lincoln's Secretary of War and rendered an invaluable service to his nation and his President. Not many years later Lincoln was assassinated. Many laudable things were said about him. Even today millions of people still adore him as the greatest of all Americans. H. G. Wells selected him as one of the six great men of history. But of all the great statements made about Abraham Lincoln, the words of Stanton remain among the greatest. Standing near the dead body of the man he once hated, Stanton referred to him as one of the greatest men that ever lived and said "he now belongs to the ages." If Lincoln had hated Stanton both men would have gone to their graves as bitter enemies. But through the power of love Lincoln transformed an enemy into a friend. It was this same attitude that made it possible for Lincoln to speak a kind word about the South during the Civil War when feeling was most bitter. Asked by a shocked bystander how he could do this, Lincoln said, "Madam, do I not destroy my enemies when I make them my friends?" This is the power of redemptive love.

We must hasten to say that these are not the ultimate reasons why we should love our enemies. An even more basic reason why we are commanded to love is expressed explicitly in Jesus' words, "Love your enemies . . . *that ye may be children of your Father which is in heaven.*" We are called to this difficult task in order to realize a unique relationship with God. We are potential sons of God. Through love that potentiality becomes actuality. We must love our enemies, because only by loving them can we know God and experience the beauty of his holiness.

The relevance of what I have said to the crisis in race relations should be readily apparent. There will be no permanent solution to the race problem until oppressed men develop the capacity to love their enemies. The darkness of racial injustice will be dispelled only by the light of forgiving love. For more than three centuries American Negroes have been battered by the iron rod of oppression, frustrated by day and bewildered by night by unbearable injustice, and burdened with the ugly weight of discrimination. Forced to live with these shameful conditions, we are tempted to become bitter and to retaliate with a corresponding hate. But if this happens, the new order we seek will be little more than a duplicate of the old order. We must in strength and humility meet hate with love.

Of course, this is not *practical*. Life is a matter of getting even, of hitting back, of dog eat dog. Am I saying that Jesus commands us to love those who hurt and oppress us? Do I sound like most preachers—idealistic and impractical? Maybe in some distant Utopia, you say, that idea will work, but not in the hard, cold world in which we live.

My friends, we have followed the so-called practical way for too long a time now, and it has led inexorably to deeper confusion and chaos. Time is cluttered with the wreckage of communities which surrendered to hatred and violence. For the salvation of our nation and the salvation of mankind, we must follow another way. This does not mean that we abandon our righteous efforts. With every ounce of our energy we must continue to rid this nation of the incubus of segregation. But we shall not in the process relinquish our privilege and our obligation to love. While abhorring segregation, we shall love the segregationist. This is the only way to create the beloved community.

To our most bitter opponents we say: "We shall match your capacity to inflict suffering by our capacity to endure suffering. We shall meet your physical force with soul force. Do to us what you will, and we shall continue to love you. We cannot in all good conscience obey your unjust laws, because nonco-operation with evil is as much a moral obligation as is co-operation with good. Throw us in jail, and we shall still love you. Bomb our homes and threaten our children, and we shall still love you. Send your hooded perpetrators of violence into our community at the midnight hour and beat us and leave us half dead, and we shall still love you. But be ye assured that we will wear you down by our capacity to suffer. One day we shall win freedom, but not only for ourselves. We shall so appeal to your heart and conscience that we shall win *you* in the process, and our victory will be a double victory."

Love is the most durable power in the world. This creative force, so beautifully exemplified in the life of our Christ, is the most potent instrument available in mankind's quest for peace and security. Napoleon Bonaparte, the great military genius, looking back over his years of conquest, is reported to have said: "Alexander, Caesar, Charlemagne and I have built great empires. But upon what did they depend? They depended on force. But centuries ago Jesus started an empire that was built on love, and even to this day millions will die for him." Who can doubt the veracity of these words. The great military leaders of the past have gone, and their empires have crumbled and burned to ashes. But the empire of Jesus, built solidly and majestically on the foundation of love, is still growing. It started with the small group of dedicated men, who, through the inspiration of their Lord, were able to shake the hinges from the gates of the Roman Empire, and carry the gospel into all the world. Today the vast earthly kingdom of Christ numbers more than 900,000,000 and covers every land and tribe. Today we hear again the promise of victory:

Jesus shall reign where'er the sun
Does his successive journeys run;
His kingdom stretch from shore to shore,
Till moon shall wax and wane no more.[24]

Another choir joyously responds:

In Christ there is no East or West,
In Him no South or North,
But one great Fellowship of Love
Throughout the whole wide earth.[25]

Jesus is eternally right. History is replete with the bleached bones of nations that refused to listen to him. May we in the twentieth century hear and follow his words—before it is too late. May we solemnly realize that we shall never be true sons of our heavenly Father until we love our enemies and pray for those who persecute us.

He was praying in a certain place,
and when he ceased, one of his disciples said to him,
"Lord, teach us to pray, as John taught his disciples."

And he said to them, "When you pray, say:
> *'Father, hallowed be thy name. Thy kingdom come.*

Give us each day our daily bread;

and forgive us our sins, for we ourselves forgive every one
who is indebted to us; and lead us not into temptation.'"

And he said to them, "Which of you who has a friend will go to
him at midnight and say to him, 'Friend, lend me three loaves;

for a friend of mine has arrived on a journey,
and I have nothing to set before him';

and he will answer from within,
'Do not bother me; the door is now shut, and my children are with me in bed;
I cannot get up and give you anything'?

I tell you,
though he will not get up and give him anything because he is his friend,
yet because of his importunity he will rise and give him whatever he needs.

And I tell you, Ask, and it will be given you;
seek and you will find; knock, and it will be opened to you.

Luke 11 RSV

CHAPTER VI

A KNOCK
AT
MIDNIGHT

ALTHOUGH THIS PARABLE is concerned with the power of persistent prayer, it may also serve as a basis for our thought concerning many contemporary problems and the role of the church in grappling with them. It is midnight in the parable; it is also midnight in our world, and the darkness is so deep that we can hardly see which way to turn.

ONE

It is midnight within the social order. On the international horizon nations are engaged in a colossal and bitter contest for supremacy. Two world wars have been fought within a generation, and the clouds of another war are dangerously low. Man now has atomic and nuclear weapons that could within seconds completely destroy the major cities of the world. Yet the arms race continues and nuclear tests still explode in the atmosphere, with the grim prospect that the very air we breathe will be poisoned by radioactive fallout. Will these circumstances and weapons bring the annihilation of the human race?

When confronted by midnight in the social order we have in the past turned to science for help. And little wonder! On so many occasions science has saved us. When we were in the midnight of physical limitation and material inconvenience, science lifted us to the bright morning of physical and material comfort. When we were in the midnight of crippling ignorance and superstition, science brought us to the daybreak of the free and open mind. When we were in the midnight of dread plagues and diseases, science, through surgery, sanitation, and the wonder drugs, ushered in the bright day of physical health, thereby prolonging our lives and making for greater security and physical well-being. How naturally we turn to science in a day when the problems of the world are so ghastly and ominous.

But alas! science cannot now rescue us, for even the scientist is lost in the terrible mid-night of our age. Indeed, science gave us the very instruments that threaten to bring universal suicide. So modern man faces a dreary and frightening midnight in the social order.

This midnight in man's external collective life is paralleled by midnight in his internal individual life. It is midnight within the psychological order. Everywhere paralyzing fears harrow people by day and haunt them by night. Deep clouds of anxiety and depression are suspended in our mental skies. More people are emotionally disturbed today than at any other time of human history. The psychopathic wards of our hospitals are crowded, and the most popular psychologists today are the psychoanalysts. Bestsellers in psychology are books such as *Man Against Himself, The Neurotic Personality of Our Times,* and *Modern Man in Search of a Soul.* Bestsellers in religion are such books as *Peace of Mind* and *Peace of Soul.* The popular clergyman preaches soothing sermons on "How to Be Happy" and "How to Relax." Some have been tempted to revise Jesus' command to read, "Go ye into all the world, keep your blood pressure down, and, lo, I will make you a well-adjusted personality." All of this is indicative that it is midnight within the inner lives of men and women.

It is also midnight within the moral order. At midnight colors lose their distinctiveness and become a sullen shade of gray. Moral principles have lost their distinctiveness. For modern man, absolute right and absolute wrong is a matter of what the majority is doing. Right and wrong are relative to likes and dislikes and the customs of a particular community. We have unconsciously applied Einstein's theory of relativity, which properly described the physical universe, to the moral and ethical realm.

Midnight is the hour when men desperately seek to obey the eleventh commandment, "Thou shalt not get caught." According to the ethic of midnight, the cardinal sin is to be caught and the cardinal virtue is to get by. It is all right to lie, but one must lie with real finesse. It is all right to steal, if one is so dignified that, if caught, the charge becomes embezzlement, not robbery. It is permissible even to hate, if one so dresses his hating in the garments of love that hating appears to be loving. The Darwinian concept of the survival of the fittest has been substituted by a philosophy of the survival of the slickest. This mentality has brought a tragic breakdown of moral standards, and the midnight of moral degeneration deepens.

TWO

As in a parable, so in our world today, the deep darkness of midnight is interrupted by the sound of a knock. On the door of the church millions of people knock. In this country the roll of church members is longer than ever before. More than one hundred and fifteen million people are at least paper members of some church or synagogue. This represents an increase of 100 per cent since 1929, although the population has increased by only 31 per cent.

Visitors to Soviet Russia, whose official policy is atheistic, report that the churches in that nation not only are crowded, but that attendance continues to grow. Harrison Salisbury, in an article in *The New York Times,* states that Communist officials are disturbed that so many young people express a growing interest in the church and religion. After forty years of the most vigorous efforts to suppress religion, the hierarchy of the Communist party now faces the inescapable fact that millions of people are knocking on the door of the church.

This numerical growth should not be over-emphasized. We must not be tempted to confuse spiritual power and large numbers. Jumboism, as someone has called it, is an utterly fallacious standard for measuring positive power. An increase in quantity does not automatically bring an increase in quality. A larger membership does not necessarily represent a correspondingly increased commitment to Christ. Almost always the creative, dedicated minority has made the world better. But although a numerical growth in church membership does not necessarily reflect a concomitant increase in ethical commitment, millions of people do feel that the church provides an answer to the deep confusion that encompasses their lives. It is still the one familiar landmark where the weary traveler by midnight comes. It is the one house which stands where it has always stood, the house to which the man traveling at midnight either comes or refuses to come. Some decide not to come. But the many who come and knock are desperately seeking a little bread to tide them over.

The traveler asks for three loaves of bread. He wants the bread of faith. In a generation of so many colossal disappointments, men have lost faith in God, faith in man, and faith in the future. Many feel as did William Wilberforce, who in 1801 said, "I dare not marry— the future is so unsettled," or as did William Pitt, who in 1806 said, "There is scarcely anything round us but ruin and despair." In the midst of staggering disillusionment, many cry for the bread of faith.

There is also a deep longing for the bread of hope. In the early years of this century many people did not hunger for this bread.

The days of the first telephones, automobiles, and airplanes gave them a radiant optimism. They worshiped at the shrine of inevitable progress. They believed that every new scientific achievement lifted man to higher levels of perfection. But then a series of tragic developments, revealing the selfishness and corruption of man, illustrated with frightening clarity the truth of Lord Acton's dictum, "Power tends to corrupt and absolute power corrupts absolutely."[26] This awful discovery led to one of the most colossal breakdowns of optimism in history. For so many people, young and old, the light of hope went out, and they roamed wearily in the dark chambers of pessimism. Many concluded that life has no meaning. Some agreed with the philosopher Schopenhauer that life is an endless pain with a painful end, and that life is a tragicomedy played over and over again with only slight changes in costume and scenery. Others cried out with Shakespeare's Macbeth that life

is a tale
Told by an idiot, full of sound and fury,
Signifying nothing.

But even in the inevitable moments when all seems hopeless, men know that without hope they cannot really live, and in agonizing desperation they cry for the bread of hope.

And there is the deep longing for the bread of love. Everybody wishes to love and to be loved. He who feels that he is not loved feels that he does not count. Much has happened in the modern world to make men feel that they do not belong. Living in a world which has become oppressively impersonal, many of us have come to feel that we are little more than numbers. Ralph Borsodi in an arresting picture of a world wherein numbers have replaced persons writes that the modern

mother is often maternity case No. 8434 and her child, after being fingerprinted and footprinted, becomes No. 8003, and that a funeral in a large city is an event in Parlor B with Class B flowers and decorations at which Preacher No. 14 officiates and Musician No. 84 sings Selection No. 174. Bewildered by this tendency to reduce man to a card in a vast index, man desperately searches for the bread of love.

THREE

When the man in the parable knocked on his friend's door and asked for the three loaves of bread, he received the impatient retort, "Do not bother me; the door is now shut, and my children are with me in bed; I cannot get up and give you anything." How often have men experienced a similar disappointment when at midnight they knock on the door of the church. Millions of Africans, patiently knocking on the door of the Christian church where they seek the bread of social justice, have either been altogether ignored or told to wait until later, which almost always means never. Millions of American Negroes, starving for the want of the bread of freedom, have knocked again and again on the door of so-called white churches, but they have usually been greeted by a cold indifference or a blatant hyprocrisy. Even the white religious leaders, who have a heartfelt desire to open the door and provide the bread, are often more cautious than courageous and more prone to follow the expedient than the ethical path. One of the shameful tragedies of history is that the very institution which should re-

180　□　STRENGTH TO LOVE

move man from the midnight of racial segregation participates in creating and perpetuating the midnight.

In the terrible midnight of war men have knocked on the door of the church to ask for the bread of peace, but the church has often disappointed them. What more pathetically reveals the irrelevancy of the church in present-day world affairs than its witness regarding war? In a world gone mad with arms buildups, chauvinistic passions, and imperialistic exploitation, the church has either endorsed these activities or remained appallingly silent. During the last two world wars, national churches even functioned as the ready lackeys of the state, sprinkling holy water upon the battleships and joining the mighty armies in singing, "Praise the Lord and pass the ammunition." A weary world, pleading desperately for peace, has often found the church morally sanctioning war.

And those who have gone to the church to seek the bread of economic justice have been left in the frustrating midnight of economic deprivation. In many instances the church has so aligned itself with the privileged classes and so defended the status quo that it has been unwilling to answer the knock at midnight. The Greek Church in Russia allied itself with the status quo and became so inextricably bound to the despotic czarist regime that it became impossible to be rid of the corrupt political and social system without being rid of the church. Such is the fate of every ecclesiastical organization that allies itself with things-as-they-are.

The church must be reminded that it is not the master or the servant of the state, but rather the conscience of the state. It must be the guide and the critic of the state, and never its tool. If the church does not recapture its prophetic zeal, it will become an irrelevant social club without moral or spiritual authority. If the church does not participate actively in the struggle for peace and for economic and racial justice, it will forfeit the loyalty of millions and cause men everywhere to say that it has atrophied its will. But if the church will free itself from the shackles of a deadening status quo, and, recovering its great historic mission, will speak and act fearlessly and insistently in terms of justice and peace, it will enkindle the imagination of mankind and fire the souls of men, imbuing them with a glowing and ardent love for truth, justice, and peace. Men far and near will know the church as a great fellowship of love that provides light and bread for lonely travelers at midnight.

While speaking of the laxity of the church, I must not overlook the fact that the so-called Negro church has also left men disappointed at midnight. I say so-called Negro church because ideally there can be no Negro or white church. It is to their everlasting shame that white Christians developed a system of racial segregation within the church, and inflicted so many indignities upon its Negro worshipers that they had to organize their own churches.

Two types of Negro churches have failed to provide bread. One burns with emotionalism, and the other freezes with classism. The former, reducing worship to entertainment, places more emphasis on volume than on content and confuses spirituality with muscularity. The danger in such a church is that the members may have more religion in their hands and feet than in their hearts and souls. At midnight this type of church has neither the vitality nor the relevant gospel to feed hungry souls.

The other type of Negro church that feeds no midnight traveler has developed a class system and boasts of its dignity, its membership of professional people, and its exclusiveness. In such a church the worship service is cold and meaningless, the music dull and un-inspiring, and the sermon little more than a homily on current events. If the pastor says too much about Jesus Christ, the members feel that he is robbing the pulpit of dignity. If the choir sings a Negro spiritual, the members claim an affront to their class status. This type of church tragically fails to recognize that worship at its best is a social experience in which people from all levels of life come together to affirm their oneness and unity under God. At midnight men are altogether ignored because of their limited education, or they are given bread that has been hardened by the winter of morbid class consciousness.

FOUR

In the parable we notice that after the man's initial disappointment, he continued to knock on his friend's door. Because of his importunity—his persistence—he finally persuaded his friend to open the door. Many men continue to knock on the door of the church at midnight, even after the church has so bitterly disappointed them, because they know the bread of life is there. The church today is challenged to proclaim God's Son, Jesus Christ, to be the hope of men in all of their complex personal and social problems. Many will continue to come in quest of answers to life's problems. Many young people who knock on the door are perplexed by the uncertainties of life, confused by daily disappointments, and disillusioned by the ambiguities of history. Some who come have been taken from their schools and careers and cast in the role of soldiers. We must provide them with the fresh bread of hope and imbue them with the conviction that God has the power to bring good out of evil. Some who come are tortured by a nagging guilt resulting from their wandering in the midnight of ethical relativism and their surrender to the doctrine of self-expression. We must lead them to Christ who will offer them the fresh bread of forgiveness. Some who knock are tormented by the fear of death as they move toward the evening of life. We must provide them with the bread of faith in immortality, so that they may realize that this earthly life is merely an embryonic prelude to a new awakening.

Midnight is a confusing hour when it is difficult to be faithful. The most inspiring word that the church may speak is that no midnight long remains. The weary traveler by midnight who asks for bread is really seeking the dawn. Our eternal message of hope is that dawn will come. Our slave foreparents realized this. They were never unmindful of the fact of midnight, for always there was the rawhide whip of the overseer and the auction block where families were torn asunder to remind them of its reality. When they thought of the agonizing darkness of midnight, they sang:

Oh, nobody knows de trouble I've seen;
Glory Hallelujah!

Sometimes I'm up, sometimes I'm down,
Oh, yes, Lord,

Sometimes I'm almost to de groun',
Oh, yes, Lord,

Oh, nobody knows de trouble I've seen,
Glory Hallelujah![27]

Encompassed by a staggering midnight but believing that morning would come, they sang:

I'm so glad trouble don't last alway.
O my Lord, O my Lord, what shall I do?[28]

Their positive belief in the dawn was the growing edge of hope that kept the slaves faithful amid the most barren and tragic circumstances.

Faith in the dawn arises from the faith that God is good and just. When one believes this, he knows that the contradictions of life are neither final nor ultimate. He can walk through the dark night with the radiant conviction that all things work together for good for those that love God. Even the most starless midnight may herald the dawn of some great fulfillment.

At the beginning of the bus boycott in Montgomery, Alabama, we set up a voluntary car pool to get the people to and from their jobs. For eleven long months our car pool functioned extraordinarily well. Then Mayor Gayle introduced a resolution instructing the city's legal department to file such proceedings as it might deem proper to stop the operation of the car pool or any transportation system growing out of the bus boycott. A hearing was set for Tuesday, November 13, 1956.

At our regular weekly mass meeting, scheduled the night before the hearing, I had the responsibility of warning the people that the car pool would probably be enjoined. I knew that they had willingly suffered for nearly twelve months, but could we now ask them to walk back and forth to their jobs? And if not, would we be forced to admit that the protest had failed? For the first time I almost shrank from appearing before them.

When the evening came, I mustered sufficient courage to tell them the truth. I tried, however, to conclude on a note of hope. "We have moved all of these months," I said, "in the daring faith that God is with us in our struggle. The many experiences of days gone by have vindicated that faith in a marvelous way. Tonight we must believe that a way will be made out of no way." Yet I could feel the cold breeze of pessimism pass over the audience. The night was darker than a thousand midnights. The light of hope was about to fade and the lamp of faith to flicker.

A few hours later, before Judge Carter, the city argued that we were operating a "private enterprise" without a franchise. Our lawyers argued brilliantly that the car pool was a voluntary "share-a-ride" plan provided without profit as a service by Negro churches. It became obvious that Judge Carter would rule in favor of the city.

At noon, during a brief recess, I noticed an unusual commotion in the courtroom. Mayor Gayle was called to the back room. Several reporters moved excitedly in and out of the room. Momentarily a reporter came to the table where, as chief defendant, I sat with the lawyers. "Here is the decision that you have been waiting for," he said. "Read this release."

In anxiety and hope, I read these words: "The United States Supreme Court today unanimously ruled bus segregation unconstitutional in Montgomery, Alabama." My heart throbbed with an inexpressible joy. The darkest hour of our struggle had become the first hour of victory. Someone shouted from the back of the courtroom, "God Almighty has spoken from Washington!"

The dawn will come. Disappointment, sorrow, and despair are born at midnight, but morning follows. "Weeping may endure for a night," says the Psalmist, "but joy cometh in the morning."[29] This faith adjourns the assemblies of hopelessness and brings new light into the dark chambers of pessimism.

CHAPTER VII

THE MAN WHO WAS A FOOL

And he spake a parable unto them,
saying, The ground of a certain rich man brought forth plentifully:

And he thought within himself, saying,
What shall I do, because I have no room where to bestow my fruits?

And he said, This will I do:
I will pull down my barns, and build greater;
and there will I bestow all my fruits and my goods.

And I will say to my soul,
Soul, thou hast much goods laid up for many years;
take thine ease, eat, drink, and be merry.

But God said unto him,
Thou fool, this night thy soul shall be required of thee:
then whose shall those things be, which thou hast provided?

Luke 12

I WOULD LIKE TO share with you a dramatic little story that is significantly relevant in its implications and profoundly meaningful in its conclusions. It is the story of a man who by all modern standards would be considered eminently successful. Yet Jesus called him a fool.

The central character in the drama is a "certain rich man," whose farm yielded such heavy crops that he decided to build new and larger barns, saying, "There will I bestow all my fruits and my goods. And I will say to my soul, Soul, thou hast much goods laid up for many years; take thine ease, eat, drink, and be merry." But God said to him, "Thou fool, this night thy soul shall be required of thee." And it was so. At the height of his prosperity, he died.

Think of this man. If he lived in our community today, he would be considered "a big shot." He would abound with social prestige and community respectability. He would be one of the privileged few in the economic power structure. And yet a Galilean peasant had the audacity to call him a fool.

Jesus did not call this man a fool merely because he possessed wealth. Jesus never made a sweeping indictment against wealth. Rather, he condemned the misuse of wealth.

Money, like any other force such as electricity, is amoral and can be used for either good or evil. It is true that Jesus commanded the rich young ruler to "sell all," but in this instance, as Dr. George A. Buttrick has said, Jesus was prescribing individual surgery, not making a universal diagnosis. Nothing in wealth is inherently vicious, and nothing in poverty is inherently virtuous.

Jesus did not condemn this man because he had made money in a dishonest fashion. Apparently he acquired his wealth by hard work and the practical know-how and farsighted vision of a good businessman. Why, then, was he a fool?

ONE

The rich man was a fool because he permitted the ends for which he lived to become confused with the means by which he lived. The economic structure of his life absorbed his destiny. Each of us lives in two realms, the internal and the external. The internal is that realm of spiritual ends expressed in art, literature, morals, and religion. The external is that complex of devices, techniques, mechanisms, and instrumentalities by means of which we live. These include the house we live in, the car we drive, the clothes we wear, the economic resources we acquire—the material stuff we must have to exist. There is always a danger that we will permit the means by which we live to replace the ends for which we live, the internal to become lost in the external. The rich man was a fool because he failed to keep a line of distinction between means and ends, between structure and destiny. His life was submerged in the rolling waters of his livelihood.

This does not mean that the external in our lives is not important. We have both a privilege and a duty to seek the basic material necessities of life. Only an irrelevant religion fails to be concerned about man's economic well-being. Religion at its best realizes that the soul is crushed as long as the body is tortured with hunger pangs and harrowed with the need for shelter. Jesus realized that we need food, clothing, shelter, and economic security. He said in clear and concise terms: "Your Father knoweth what things ye have need of."[30] But Jesus knew that man was more than a dog to be satisfied by a few economic bones. He realized that the internal of a man's life is as significant as the external. So he added, "Seek ye first the kingdom of God, and his righteousness; and all these things shall be added unto you."[31] The tragedy of the rich man was that he sought the means first, and in the process the ends were swallowed in the means.

The richer this man became materially the poorer he became intellectually and spiritually. He may have been married, but he probably could not love his wife. It is possible that he gave her countless material gifts, but he could not give her that which she needed most, love and affection. He may have had children, but he probably did not appreciate them. He may have had the great books of the ages shelved neatly in his library, but he never read them. He may have had access to great music, but he did not listen. His eyes did not behold the majestic splendor of the skies. His ears were not attunded to the melodious sweetness of heavenly music. His mind was closed to the insights of poets, prophets, and philosophers. His title was justly merited—"Thou fool!"

TWO

The rich man was a fool because he failed to realize his dependence on others. His soliloquy contains approximately sixty words, yet "I" and "my" occur twelve times. He had said "I" and "my" so often that he had lost the capacity to say "we" and "our." A victim of the cancerous disease of egotism, he failed to realize that wealth always comes as a result of the commonwealth. He talked as though he could plow the fields and build the barns alone. He failed to realize that he was an heir of a vast treasury of ideas and labor to which both the living and the dead had contributed. When an individual or a nation overlooks this interdependence, we find a tragic foolishness.

We can clearly see the meaning of this parable for the present world crisis. Our nation's productive machinery constantly brings forth such an abundance of food that we must build larger barns and spend more than a million dollars daily to store our surplus. Year after year we ask, "What shall I do, because I have no room where to bestow my fruits?" I have seen an answer in the faces of millions of poverty-stricken men and women in Asia, Africa, and South America. I have seen an answer in the appalling poverty in the Mississippi Delta and the tragic insecurity of the unemployed in large industrial cities of the North. What can we do? The answer is simple: feed the poor, cloth the naked, and heal the sick. Where can we store our goods? Again the answer is simple: We can store our surplus food free of charge in the shriveled stomachs of the millions of God's children who go to bed hungry at night. We can use our vast resources of wealth to wipe poverty from the earth.

All of this tells us something basic about the interdependence of men and nations. Whether we realize it or not, each of us is eternally "in the red." We are everlasting debtors to known and unknown men and women. We do not finish breakfast without being dependent on more than half of the world. When we arise in the morning, we go into the bathroom where we reach for a sponge which is provided for us by a Pacific Islander. We reach for soap that is created for us by a Frenchman. The towel is provided by a Turk. Then at the table we drink coffee which is provided for us by a South American, or tea by a Chinese, or cocoa by a West African. Before we leave for our jobs we are beholden to more than half the world. In a real sense, all life is interrelated. All men are caught in an inescapable network of mutuality, tied in a single garment of destiny. Whatever affects one directly affects all indirectly. I can never be what I ought to be until you are what you ought to be, and you can never be what you ought to be until I am what I ought to be. This is the interrelated structure of reality.

The rich man tragically failed to realize this. He thought that he could live and grow in his little self-centered world. He was an individualist gone wild. Indeed, he was an eternal fool!

THREE

Jesus called the rich man a fool because he failed to realize his dependence on God. He talked as though he unfolded the seasons and provided the fertility of the soil, controlled the rising and the setting of the sun, and regulated the natural processes that produce the rain and the dew. He had an unconscious feeling that he was the Creator, not a creature.

This man-centered foolishness has had a long and ofttimes disastrous reign in the history of mankind. Sometimes it is theoretically expressed in the doctrine of materialism, which contends that reality may be explained in terms of matter in motion, that life is "a physiological process with a physiological meaning," that man is a transient accident of protons and electrons traveling blind, that thought is a temporary product of gray matter, and that the events of history are an interaction of matter and motion operating by the principle of necessity. Having no place for God or for eternal ideas, materialism is opposed to both theism and idealism.

This materialistic philosophy leads inevitably into a dead-end street in an intellectually senseless world. To believe that human personality is the result of the fortuitous interplay of atoms and electrons is as absurd as to believe that a monkey by hitting typewriter keys at random will eventually produce a Shakespearean play. Sheer magic! It is much more sensible to say with Sir James Jeans, the physicist, that "the universe seems to be nearer to a great thought than to a great machine," or with Arthur Balfour, the philosopher, that "we now know too much about matter to be materialists." Materialism is a weak flame that is blown out by the breath of mature thinking.

Another attempt to make God irrelevant is found in nontheistic humanism, a philosophy that deifies man by affirming that humanity is God. Man is the measure of all things. Many modern men who have embraced this philosophy contend, as did Rousseau, that human nature is essentially good. Evil is to be found only in institutions, and if poverty and ignorance were to be removed everything would be all right. The twentieth century opened with such a glowing optimism. Men believed that civilization was evolving toward an earthly paradise. Herbert Spencer skillfully molded the Darwinian theory of evolution into the heady idea of automatic progress. Men became convinced that there is a sociological law of progress which is as valid as the physical law of gravitation.

Possessed of this spirit of optimism, modern man broke into the storehouse of nature and emerged with many scientific insights and technological developments that completely revolutionized the earth. The achievements of science have been marvelous, tangible, and concrete.

Witnessing the amazing advances of science, modern man exclaimed:

Science is my shepherd; I shall not want.
It maketh me to lie down in green pastures:
It leadeth me beside the still waters.
It restoreth my soul. . . .
I will fear no evil: for science is with me;
Its rod and its staff they comfort me.

Man's aspirations no longer turned Godward and heavenward. Rather, man's thoughts were confined to man and earth. And man offered a strange parody on the Lord's Prayer: "Our brethren which art upon the earth, Hallowed be our name. Our kingdom come. Our will be done on earth, for there is no heaven." Those who formerly turned to God to find solutions for their problems turned to science and technology, convinced that they now possessed the instruments needed to usher in the new society.

Then came the explosion of this myth. It climaxed in the horrors of Nagasaki and Hiroshima and in the fierce fury of fifty-megaton bombs. Now we have come to see that science can give us only physical power, which, if not controlled by spiritual power, will lead inevitably to cosmic doom. The words of Alfred the Great are still true: "Power is never a good unless he be good that has it." We need something more spiritually sustaining and morally controlling than science. It is an instrument which, under the power of God's spirit, may lead man to greater heights of physical security, but apart from God's spirit, science is a deadly weapon that will lead only to deeper chaos. Why fool ourselves about automatic progress and the ability of man to save himself? We must lift up our minds and eyes unto the hills from whence cometh our true help. Then, and only then, will the advances of modern science be a blessing rather than a curse.

Without dependence on God our efforts turn to ashes and our sunrises into darkest night. Unless his spirit pervades our lives, we find only what G. K. Chesterton called "cures that don't cure, blessings that don't bless, and solutions that don't solve." "God is our refuge and strength, a very present help in trouble."[32]

Unfortunately, the rich man did not realize this. He, like many men of the twentieth century, became so involved in big affairs and small trivialities that he forgot God. He gave the finite infinite significance and elevated a preliminary concern to ultimate standing.

After the rich man had accumulated his

vast resources of wealth—at the moment when his stocks were accruing the greatest interest and his palatial home was the talk of the town—he came to that experience which is the irreducible common denominator of all men, death. The fact that he died at this particular time adds verve and drama to the story, but the essential truth of the parable would have remained the same had he lived to be as old as Methuselah. Even if he had not died physically, he was already dead spiritually. The cessation of breathing was a belated announcement of an earlier death. He died when he failed to keep a line of distinction between the means by which he lived and the ends for which he lived and when he failed to recognize his dependence on others and on God.

May it not be that the "certain rich man" is Western civilization? Rich in goods and material resources, our standards of success are almost inextricably bound to the lust for acquisition. The means by which we live are marvelous indeed. And yet something is missing. We have learned to fly the air like birds and swim the sea like fish, but we have not learned the simple art of living together as brothers. Our abundance has brought us neither peace of mind nor serenity of spirit. An Oriental writer has portrayed our dilemma in candid terms:

> You call your thousand material devices "labor-saving machinery," yet you are forever "busy." With the multiplying of your machinery you grow increasingly fatigued, anxious, nervous, dissatisfied. Whatever you have, you want more; and wherever you are you want to go somewhere else. You have a machine to dig the raw material for you . . . , a machine to manufacture [it] . . . , a machine to transport [it] . . . , a machine to sweep and dust, one to carry messages, one to write, one to talk, one to sing, one to play at the theater, one to vote, one to sew, . . . and a hundred others to do a hundred other things for you, and still you are the most nervously busy man in the world . . . your devices are neither time-saving nor soul-saving machinery. They are so many sharp spurs which urge you on to invent more machinery and to do more business.[33]

This is poignantly true and tells us something about Western civilization that cannot be cast aside as a prejudiced charge by an Oriental thinker who is jealous of Occidental prosperity. We cannot escape the indictment. The means by which we live have outdistanced the ends for which we live. Our scientific power has outrun our spiritual power. We have guided missiles and misguided men. Like the rich man of old, we have foolishly minimized the internal of our lives and maximized the external. We have absorbed life in livelihood. We will not find peace in our generation until we learn anew that "a man's life consisteth not in the abundance of the things which he possesseth,"[34] but in those inner treasuries of the spirit which "no thief approacheth, neither moth corrupteth."[35]

Our hope for creative living lies in our ability to re-establish the spiritual ends of our lives in personal character and social justice. Without this spiritual and moral reawakening we shall destroy ourselves in the misuse of our own instruments. Our generation cannot escape the question of our Lord: What shall it profit a man, if he gain the whole world of externals—airplanes, electric lights, automobiles, and color televison—and lose the internal—his own soul?

CHAPTER VIII

THE DEATH OF EVIL
UPON THE SEASHORE

*And Moses stretched out his hand over the sea; and the LORD
caused the sea to go back by a strong east wind all that night,
and made the sea dry land, and the waters were divided.*

*And the children of Israel went into the midst of the sea
upon the dry ground: and the waters were a wall unto them
on their right hand, and on their left.*

*And the Egyptians pursued, and went in after them to the midst of the sea,
even all Pharaoh's horses, his chariots, and his horsemen.*

*And it came to pass, that in the morning watch the LORD looked
unto the host of the Egyptians through the pillar of fire and of the cloud,
and troubled the host of the Egyptians.*

*And took off their chariot wheels, that they drave them heavily:
so that the Egyptians said, Let us flee from the face of Israel;
for the LORD fighteth for them against the Egyptians.*

And the LORD said unto Moses, Stretch out thine hand over the sea,

that the waters may come again upon the Egyptians,

upon their chariots, and upon their horsemen.

And Moses stretched forth his hand over the sea,

and the sea returned to his strength when the morning appeared;

and the Egyptians fled against it;

and the LORD overthrew the Egyptians in the midst of the sea.

And the waters returned, and covered the chariots, and the horsemen,

and all the host of Pharaoh that came into the sea after them;

there remained not so much as one of them.

But the children of Israel walked upon dry land in the midst of the sea;

and the waters were a wall unto them on their right hand, and on their left.

Thus the LORD saved Israel that day out of the hand of the Egyptians;

and Israel saw the Egyptians dead upon the sea shore.

Exodus 14

Is ANYTHING MORE OBVIOUS than the presence of evil in the universe? Its nagging, prehensile tentacles project into every level of human existence. We may debate the origin of evil, but only a victim of superficial optimism would debate its reality. Evil is stark, grim, and colossally real.

Affirming the reality of evil in unmistakable terms, the Bible symbolically pictures the conniving work of a serpent which injects discord into the harmonious symphony of life in a garden, prophetically denounces callous injustice and ugly hypocrisy, and dramatically portrays a misguided mob hanging the world's most precious Person on a cross between two thieves. Crystal clear is the biblical perception of evil. Nor was Jesus unmindful of the reality of evil. Although he never offered a theological explanation of the origin of evil, he never attempted to explain it away. In the parable of the tares, Jesus says that tares are tares, not illusions or errors of the mortal mind. Real weeds disrupt the orderly growth of stately wheat. Whether sown by Satan or by man's misuse of his own freedom, the tares are always poisonous and deadly. Concerning the choking weeds, Jesus says in substance, "I do not attempt to explain their origin, but they are the work of an enemy." He recognized that the force of evil was as real as the force of good.

Within the wide arena of everyday life we see evil in all of its ugly dimensions. We see it expressed in tragic lust and inordinate selfishness. We see it in high places where men are willing to sacrifice truth on the altars of their self-interest. We see it in imperialistic nations crushing other people with the battering rams of social injustice. We see it clothed in the garments of calamitous wars which leave men and nations morally and physically bankrupt.

In a sense, the history of man is the story of the struggle between good and evil. All of the great religions have recognized a tension at the very core of the universe. Hinduism, for instance, calls this tension a conflict between illusion and reality; Zoroastrianism, a conflict between the god of light and the god of darkness; and traditional Judaism and Christianity, a conflict between God and Satan. Each realizes that in the midst of the upward thrust of goodness there is the downward pull of evil.

Christianity clearly affirms that in the long struggle between good and evil, good eventually will emerge as victor. Evil is ultimately doomed by the powerful, inexorable forces of good. Good Friday must give way to the triumphant music of Easter. Degrading tares choke the sprouting necks of growing wheat for a season, but when the harvest is gleaned the evil tares will be separated from the good wheat. Caesar occupied a palace and Christ a cross, but the same Christ so split history into A.D. and B.C. that even the reign of Caesar was subsequently dated by his name.

Long ago biblical religion recognized what William Cullen Bryant affirmed, "Truth crushed to earth will rise again,"[36] and what Thomas Carlyle wrote, "No lie you can speak or act but it will come, after longer or shorter circulation, like a bill drawn on Nature's Reality, and be presented there for payment,—with the answer, No effects."[37]

ONE

A graphic example of this truth is found in the early history of the Hebrew people. When the children of Israel were held under the gripping yoke of Egyptian slavery, Egypt symbolized evil in the form of humiliating oppression, ungodly exploitation, and crushing domination, and the Israelites symbolized goodness in the form of devotion and dedication to the God of Abraham, Isaac, and Jacob. Egypt struggled to maintain her oppressive yoke, and Israel struggled to gain freedom. Pharaoh stubbornly refused to respond to the cry of Moses, even when plague after plague threatened his domain. This tells us something about evil that we must never forget, namely, that evil is recalcitrant and determined, and never voluntarily relinquishes its hold short of a persistent, almost fanatical resistance. But there is a checkpoint in the universe: evil cannot permanently organize itself. So after a long and trying struggle, the Israelites, through the providence of God, crossed the Red Sea. But like the old guard that never surrenders, the Egyptians, in a desperate attempt to prevent the Israelites from escaping, had their armies go in the Red

Sea behind them. As soon as the Egyptians got into the dried-up sea the parted waters swept back upon them, and the turbulence and momentum of the tidal waves soon drowned all of them. When the Israelites looked back, all they could see was here and there a poor drowned body beaten upon the seashore. For the Israelites, this was a great moment. It was the end of a frightful period in their history. It was a joyous daybreak that had come to end the long night of their captivity. The meaning of this story is not found in the drowning of Egyptian soldiers, for no one should rejoice at the death or defeat of a human being. Rather, this story symbolizes the death of evil and of inhuman oppression and unjust exploitation.

The death of the Egyptians upon the seashore is a vivid reminder that something in the very nature of the universe assists goodness in its perennial struggle with evil. The New Testament rightly declares: "No chastening for the present seemeth to be joyous, but grievous: *nevertheless afterward* it yieldeth the peaceable fruit of righteousness."[38] Pharaoh exploits the children of Israel—*nevertheless afterward!* Pilate yields to the crowd which crucifies Christ—*nevertheless afterward!* The early Christians are thrown to the lions and carried to the chopping blocks—*nevertheless afterward!* Something in this universe justifies Shakespeare in saying:

There's a divinity that shapes our ends,
Rough-hew them how we will,[39]

and Lowell in saying,

Though the cause of Evil prosper,
Yet 'tis Truth alone is strong,[40]

and Tennyson in saying,

I can but trust that good shall fall,
At last—far off—at last, to all,
And every winter change to spring.[41]

TWO

The truth of this text is revealed in the contemporary struggle between good in the form of freedom and justice, and evil in the form of oppression and colonialism. Of the approximately 3,000,000,000 people in our world, more than 1,900,000,000—a vast majority—live on the continents of Asia and Africa. Less than two decades ago most of the Asian and African peoples were colonial subjects, dominated politically, exploited economically, and segregated and humiliated by foreign powers. For years they protested against these grave injustices. In nearly every territory in Asia and Africa a courageous Moses pleaded passionately for the freedom of his people. For more than twenty years Mahatma Gandhi unrelentingly urged British viceroys, governors general, prime ministers, and kings to let his people go. Like the pharaohs of old, the British leaders turned deaf ears to these agonizing pleas. Even the great Winston Churchill reponded to Gandhi's cry for independence by saying, "I have not become the King's First Minister in order to preside over the liquidation of the British Empire."[42] The conflict between two determined forces, the colonial powers and the Asian and African peoples, has been one of the most momentous and critical struggles of the twentieth century.

But in spite of the resistance and recalcitrance of the colonial powers, the victory of the forces of justice and human dignity is gradually being achieved. Twenty-five years ago there were only three independent countries in the whole continent of Africa, but today thirty-two countries are independent. A short fifteen years ago the British Empire politically dominated more than 650,000,000 people in Asia and Africa, but today the number is less than 60,000,000. The Red Sea has opened. The oppressed masses in Asia and Africa have won their freedom from the Egypt of colonialism and now move toward the promised land of economic and cultural stability. These peoples see the evils of colonialism and imperialism dead upon the seashore.

In our own American struggle for freedom and justice, we are seeing the death of evil. In 1619, the Negro was brought to America from the soils of Africa. For more than two hundred years Africa was raped and plundered, her native kingdoms disorganized, and her people and rulers demoralized. In America, the Negro slave was merely a depersonalized cog in a vast plantation machine.

But there were those who had a nagging conscience and knew that so unjust a system represented a strange paradox in a nation founded on the priniciple that all men are created equal. In 1820, six years before his death, Thomas Jefferson wrote these melancholy words:

> But the momentous question [slavery], like a fire-bell in the night, awakened and filled me with terror. I considered it at once as the knell of the Union. . . . I regret that I am now to die in the belief, that the useless sacrifice of themselves by the generation of 1776, to acquire self-government and happiness to their country, is to be thrown away . . . and my only consolation is to be, that I live not to weep over it.[43]

Numerous abolitionists, like Jefferson, were tortured in their hearts by the question of slavery. With keen perception they saw that the immorality of slavery degraded the white master as well as the Negro.

Then came the day when Abraham Lincoln faced squarely this matter of slavery. His torments and vacillations are well known, yet the conclusion of his search is embodied in these words: "In giving freedom to the slave, we assure freedom to the free,—honourable alike in what we give and what we preserve."[44] On this moral foundation Lincoln drafted the Emancipation Proclamation, an executive order that brought an end to chattel slavery. The significance of the Emancipation Proclamation was colorfully described by a great American, Frederick Douglass, in these words:

> It recognizes and declares the real nature of the contest and places the North on the side of justice and civilization. . . . Unquestionably the first of January, 1863, is to be the most memorable day in American annals. The Fourth of July was great, but the First of January, when we consider it in all its relations and bearings, is incomparably greater. The one had respect to the mere political birth of a nation; the last concerns the national life and character and is to determine whether that life and

character shall be radiantly glorious with all high and noble virtues, or infamously blackened forevermore.[45]

The Emancipation Proclamation did not, however, bring full freedom to the Negro, for although he enjoyed certain political and social opportunities during the Reconstruction, the Negro soon discovered that the pharaohs of the South were determined to keep him in slavery. Certainly the Emancipation Proclamation brought him nearer to the Red Sea, but it did not guarantee his passage through parted waters. Racial segregation, backed by a decision of the United States Supreme Court in 1896, was a new form of slavery disguised by certain niceties of complexity. In the great struggle of the last half century between the forces of justice attempting to end the evil system of segregation and the forces of injustice attempting to maintain it, the pharaohs have employed legal maneuvers, economic reprisals, and even physical violence to hold the Negro in the Egypt of segregation. Despite the patient cry of many a Moses, they refused to let the Negro people go.

Today we are witnessing a massive change. A world-shaking decree by the nine justices of the United States Supreme Court opened the Red Sea and the forces of justice are moving to the other side. The Court decreed an end to the old Plessy decision of 1896 and affirmed that separate facilities are inherently unequal and that to segregate a child on the basis of race is to deny the child an equal legal protection. This decision is a great beacon light of hope to millions of disinherited people. Looking back, we see the forces of segregation gradually dying on the seashore. The problem is far from solved and gigantic mountains of opposition lie ahead, but at least we have left Egypt, and with patient yet firm determination we shall reach the promised land. Evil in the form of injustice and exploitation shall not survive forever. A Red Sea passage in history ultimately brings the forces of goodness to victory, and the closing of the same waters marks the doom and destruction of the forces of evil.

All of this reminds us that evil carries the seed of its own destruction. In the long run right defeated is stronger than evil triumphant. Historian Charles A. Beard, when asked what major lessons he had learned from history, answered:

First, whom the gods would destroy they must first make mad with power. Second, the mills of God grind slowly, yet they grind exceeding small. Third, the bee fertilizes the flower it robs. Fourth, when it is dark enough you can see the stars.

These are the words, not of a preacher, but of a hardheaded historian, whose long and painstaking study of history revealed to him that evil has a self-defeating quality. It can go a long way, but then it reaches its limit. There is something in this universe that Greek mythology referred to as the goddess of Nemesis.

THREE

We must be careful at this point not to engage in a superficial optimism or to conclude that the death of a particular evil means that all evil lies dead upon the seashore. All progress is precarious, and the solution of one problem brings us face to face with another problem. The Kingdom of God as a universal reality is *not yet*. Because sin exists on every level of man's existence, the death of one tyranny is followed by the emergence of another tyranny.

But just as we must avoid a superficial optimism, we must also avoid a crippling pessimism. Even though all progress is precarious, within limits real social progress may be made. Although man's moral pilgrimage may never reach a destination point on earth, his never-ceasing strivings may bring him ever closer to the city of righteousness. And though the Kingdom of God may remain *not yet* as a universal reality in history, in the present it may exist in such isolated forms as in judgment, in personal devotion, and in some group life. "The Kingdom of God is in the midst of you."[46]

Above all, we must be reminded anew that God is at work in his universe. He is not outside the world looking on with a sort of cold indifference. Here on all the roads of life, he is striving in our striving. Like an ever-loving Father, he is working through history for the salvation of his children. As we struggle to defeat the forces of evil, the God of the universe struggles with us. Evil dies on the seashore, not merely because of man's endless struggle against it, but because of God's power to defeat it.

But why is God so slow in conquering the forces of evil? Why did God permit Hitler to kill six million Jews? Why did God permit slavery to continue in America for two hundred and forty-four years? Why does God permit bloodthirsty mobs to lynch Negro men and women at will and drown Negro boys and girls at whim? Why does not God break in and smash the evil schemes of wicked men?

I do not pretend to understand all of the ways of God or his particular timetable for grappling with evil. Perhaps if God dealt with evil in the overbearing way that we wish, he would defeat his ultimate purpose. We are responsible human beings, not blind automatons: persons, not puppets. By endowing us with freedom, God relinquished a measure of his own sovereignty and imposed certain limitations upon himself. If his children are free, they must do his will by a voluntary choice. Therefore, God cannot at the same time impose his will upon his children and also maintain his purpose for man. If through sheer omnipotence God were to defeat his purpose, he would express weakness rather than power. Power is the ability to fulfill purpose; action which defeats purpose is weakness.

God's unwillingness to deal with evil with an overbearing immediacy does not mean that he is doing nothing. We weak and finite human beings are not alone in our quest for the triumph of righteousness. There is, as Matthew Arnold wrote, an "enduring power, not ourselves, which makes for righteousness."[47]

We must also remember that God does not forget his children who are the victims of evil forces. He gives us the interior resources to bear the burdens and tribulations of life. When we are in the darkness of some oppressive Egypt, God is a light unto our path. He imbues us with the strength needed to endure the ordeals of Egypt, and he gives us the courage and power to undertake the journey ahead. When the lamp of hope flickers and the candle of faith runs low, he restoreth our souls, giving us renewed vigor to carry on. He is with us not only in the noontime of fulfillment, but also in the midnight of despair.

In India Mrs. King and I spent a lovely weekend in the State of Karala, the southernmost point of that vast country. While there we visited the beautiful beach on Cape Comorin, which is called "Land's End," because this is actually where the land of India comes to an end. Nothing stretches before you except the broad expanse of rolling waters. This beautiful spot is a point at which meet three great bodies of water, the Indian Ocean, the Arabian Sea, and the Bay of Bengal. Seated on a huge rock that slightly protrudes into the ocean, we were enthralled by the vastness of the ocean and its terrifying immensities. As the waves unfolded in almost rhythmic succession and crashed against the base of the rock on which we were seated, an oceanic music brought sweetness to the ear. To the west we saw the magnificent sun, a great cosmic ball of fire, appear to sink into the very ocean itself. Just as it was almost lost from sight, Mrs. King touched me and said, "Look, Martin, isn't that beautiful!" I looked around and saw the moon, another ball of scintillating beauty. As the sun appeared to be sinking into the ocean, the moon appeared to be rising from the ocean. When the sun finally passed completely beyond sight, darkness engulfed the earth, but in the east the radiant light of the rising moon shone supreme.

To my wife I said, "This is an analogy of what often happens in life." We have experiences when the light of day vanishes, leaving us in some dark and desolate midnight— moments when our highest hopes are turned into shambles of despair or when we are the victims of some tragic injustice and some terrible exploitation. During such moments our spirits are almost overcome by gloom and despair, and we feel that there is no light anywhere. But ever and again, we look toward the east and discover that there is another light which shines even in the darkness, and "the spear of frustration" is transformed "into a shaft of light."

This would be an unbearable world were God to have only a single light, but we may be consoled that God has two lights: a light to guide us in the brightness of the day when hopes are fulfilled and circumstances are favorable, and a light to guide us in the darkness of the midnight when we are thwarted and the slumbering giants of gloom and hopelessness rise in our souls. The testimony of the Psalmist is that we need never walk in darkness:

> Whither shall I go from thy spirit? or whither shall I flee from thy presence? If I ascend up into heaven, thou art there: if I make my bed in hell, behold, thou art there. If I take the wings of the morning, and dwell in the uttermost parts of the sea; even there shall thy hand lead me, and thy right hand shall hold me. If I say, Surely the darkness shall cover me; even the night shall be light about me. Yea, the darkness hideth not from thee; but the night shineth as the day: the darkness and the light are both alike to thee.[48]

This faith will sustain us in our struggle to escape from the bondage of every evil Egypt. This faith will be a lamp unto our weary feet and a light unto our meandering path. Without such faith, man's highest dreams will pass silently to the dust.

THREE DIMENSIONS
OF A COMPLETE LIFE

And there came unto me one of the seven angels . . .
and talked with me, saying, Come hither . . .

And he carried me away in the spirit to a great and high mountain,
and shewed me that great city, the holy Jerusalem,
descending out of heaven from God.

Having the glory of God: and her light was like unto a stone most precious,
even like a jasper stone, clear as crystal;

And had a wall great and high, and had twelve gates,
and at the gates twelve angels, and names written thereon,
which are the names of the twelve tribes of the children of Israel:

On the east three gates; on the north three gates;
on the south three gates; and on the west three gates.

And the wall of the city had twelve foundations,
and in them the names of the twelve apostles of the Lamb.

And he that talked with me had a golden reed to measure the city,
and the gates thereof, and the wall thereof.

And the city lieth foursquare, and the length is as large as the breadth:
and he measured the city with the reed, twelve thousand furlongs.
The length and the breadth and the height of it are equal.

Revelation 21

Jᴏʜɴ ᴛʜᴇ Rᴇᴠᴇʟᴀᴛᴏʀ, imprisoned on a lonely, obscure island called Patmos, was deprived of almost every freedom except the freedom to think. So he thought about many things. He thought about the old political order and its tragic incompleteness and its horrible injustices. He thought about the old Jerusalem and its superficial piety and its perfunctory ritualism. But in the midst of his agonizing vision of the old, John also had a glorious vision of something new and great. He saw a new and holy Jerusalem descending out of heaven from God. The most noble thing about this new heavenly city was its completeness, radiant as daybreak ending the long night of stagnating incompleteness. It would not be partial or one-sided, but complete in all three of its dimensions. In describing the city, John says, "The length and the breadth and the height of it are equal." This new city of God would not be an unbalanced entity with towering virtues on one side and degrading vices on the other; it would be complete on all sides.

For many people the Book of Revelation is a strange book and puzzling to decode. It is often cast aside as an enigma wrapped in mystery. But beneath John's peculiar jargon and his prevailing apocalyptic symbolism, we find many challenging and profound truths. One such truth is set forth in our text. When John describes the new city of God, he is really describing ideal humanity. He is saying, in substance, that life at its best is complete on all sides.

In our individual and collective lives are a disturbing incompleteness and an agonizing partialness. Very seldom are we able to affirm greatness in an unqualified sense. Following almost every affirmation of greatness is the conjunction "but." Naaman "was a great man," says the Old Testament, "but—" That *but* reveals something tragic and disturbing. "But he was a leper."[49] How much of man's life can be so described!

Greece was a great nation, which left for succeeding generations an inexhaustible treasury of knowledge. She gave to the world the poetic insights of Aeschylus, Sophocles, and Euripides, and the philosophical insights of Socrates, Plato, and Aristotle. Because of these great minds, each of us is an heir to a legacy of creative ideas. Greece was a great nation, but— That *but* underscores the tragic fact that Greece was really an aristocracy for *some* of the people and not a democracy for *all* of the people. That *but* stands for the ugly fact that the Greek city-states were built on a foundation of slavery.

Western civilization is a great civilization, bequeathing to the world the magnificent insights of the Renaissance; the glad thunders and the gentle sighings of Handel, the majestic sweetness of Beethoven, and the charming melodies of Bach; the industrial revolution and man's commencement on his marvelous trek toward the city of material abundance. Western civilization is great, but— That *but* reminds us of the injustices and evils of colonialism, and of a civilization that has permitted its material means to outdistance its spiritual ends.

America is a great nation, offering to the world, through the Declaration of Independence, the most eloquent and unequivocal expression of the dignity of man ever set forth in a sociopolitical document. In technology, America has produced mighty bridges to span the seas and skyscraping buildings to kiss the skies. Through the Wright brothers, she has given to the world the airplane and made it possible for man to annihilate distance and circumscribe time. Through medical science, her numerous wonder drugs have cured many dread diseases and greatly prolonged the life of man. America is a great nation, but— That *but* is a commentary on two hundred and more years of chattel slavery and on twenty million Negro men and women deprived of life, liberty, and the pursuit of happiness. That *but* stands for a practical materialism that is often more interested in things than values.

So almost every affirmation of greatness is followed, not by a period symbolizing completeness, but by a comma punctuating its nagging partialness. Many of our greatest civilizations are great only in certain aspects. Many of our greatest men are great only in certain ways and are low and degrading in other regards.

Yet life should be strong and complete on every side. Any complete life has the three dimensions suggested in our text—length, breadth, and height. The length of life is the inward drive to achieve one's personal ends and ambitions, an inward concern for one's own welfare and achievements. The breadth of life is the outward concern for the welfare of others. The height of life is the upward reach for God. Life at its best is a coherent triangle. At one angle is the individual person. At the other angle are other persons. At the tiptop is the Infinite Person, God. Without the due development of each part of the triangle, no life can be complete.

ONE

Let us turn, first, to the length of life or the individual's concern about developing his inner powers. In a sense this is the selfish dimension of life. There is such a thing as rational and healthy self-interest. The late Rabbi Joshua Liebman pointed out in an interesting chapter in his book *Peace of Mind* that we must love ourselves properly before we can adequately love others. Many people are plunged into the abyss of emotional fatalism because they do not love themselves in a wholesome way.

Every person must have a concern for self and feel a responsibility to discover his mission in life. God has given each normal person a capacity to achieve some end. True, some are endowed with more talent than others, but God has left none of us talentless. Potential powers of creativity are within us, and we have the duty to work assiduously to discover these powers.

After one has discovered what he is made for, he should surrender all of the power in his being to the achievement of this. He should seek to do it so well that nobody could do it better. He should do it as though God Almighty called him at this particular moment of history for this reason. No one ever makes a great contribution to humanity without this majestic sense of purpose and this dogged determination. No one ever brings his potentiality into actuality without this powerful inner drive. Longfellow wrote:

The heights by great men reached and kept
 Were not attained by sudden flight,

But they, while their companions slept,
  Were toiling upward in the night.[50]

May I offer a special word to our young people. The dimension of length stands as a unique challenge. Many of you are in college and many more in high school. I cannot over-emphasize the importance of these years of study. You must realize that doors of opportunity are opening now that were not opened to your mothers and fathers. The great challenge you face is to be ready to enter these doors. You must early discover what you are made for, and you must work indefatigably to achieve excellence in your various fields of endeavor. Ralph Waldo Emerson has been quoted as saying, "If a man can write a better book, preach a better sermon, or make a better mousetrap than his neighbour, tho' he build his house in the woods, the world will make a beaten path to his door." This will become increasingly true. You must not wait until the day of full emancipation before you make a creative contribution to the life of this nation. Although you experience a natural dilemma as a result of the legacy of slavery and segregation, inferior schools, and second-class citizenship, you must with determination break through the outer shackles of circumstance. We already have inspiring examples of Negroes who in cloud-filled nights of oppression have become new and blazing stars of achievement. From an old slave cabin in Virginia's hills, Booker T. Washington rose to become one of America's great leaders. From the oppressive red hills of Gordon County, Georgia, and the arms of a mother who could neither read nor write, Roland Hayes emerged as one of the world's foremost singers, whose melodious voice was heard in the palaces of kings and the mansions of queens. Coming from a poverty-stricken environment in Philadelphia, Marian Anderson achieved the distinction of being the world's greatest contralto, and so much so that Toscanini said that a voice like hers comes only once in a century and Sibelius exclaimed that his roof was too low for such a voice. From crippling circumstance, George Washington Carver made for himself an imperishable niche in the annals of science. Ralph J. Bunche, the grandson of a slave preacher, has brought a rare distinction to diplomacy. These are only a few of the numerous examples which remind us that, in spite of our lack of full freedom, we can make a contribution here and now.

We are challenged on every hand to work untiringly to achieve excellence in our life-work. Not all men are called to specialized or professional jobs; even fewer rise to the heights of genius in the arts and sciences; many are called to be laborers in factories, fields, and streets. But no work is insignificant. All labor that uplifts humanity has dignity and importance and should be undertaken with painstaking excellence. If a man is called to be a street sweeper, he should sweep streets even as Michelangelo painted, or Beethoven composed music, or Shakespeare wrote poetry. He should sweep streets so well that all the host of heaven and earth will pause to say, "Here lived a great street sweeper who did his job well." This is what Douglas Mallock meant when he wrote:

If you can't be a pine on the top of the hill
Be a scrub in the valley—but be
The best little scrub by the side of the rill,
Be a bush, if you can't be a tree.

If you can't be a highway, just be a trail
If you can't be the sun, be a star;
It isn't by size, that you win or fail—
Be the best of whatever you are.

Set yourself earnestly to discover what you are made to do, and then give yourself passionately to the doing of it. This clear onward drive toward self-fulfillment is the length of a man's life.

TWO

Some people never get beyond this first dimension. They may be brilliant people who superbly develop their inner powers, but they are shackled by the chains of a paralyzing self-centeredness. They live within the narrow confines of their personal ambitions and desires. What is more tragic than to find an individual who is bogged down in the length of life devoid of breadth?

If life is to be complete, it must include not only the dimension of length but also of breadth by which the individual concerns himself in the welfare of others. No man has learned to live until he can rise above the narrow confines of his individualistic concerns to the broader concerns of all humanity. Length without breadth is like a self-contained tributary having no outward flow to the ocean. Stagnant, still, and stale, it lacks both life and freshness. In order to live creatively and meaningfully, our self-concern must be wedded to other-concern.

When Jesus painted that symbolic picture of the great assize, he made it clear that the norm for determining the division between the sheep and the goats would be deeds done for others. One will not be asked how many academic degrees he obtained or how much money he acquired, but how much he did for others. Did you feed the hungry? Did you give a cup of cold water to the thirsty? Did you clothe the naked? Did you visit the sick

and minister to the imprisoned? These are the questions asked by the Lord of life. In a sense every day is judgment day, and we, through our deeds and words, our silence and speech, are constantly writing in the Book of Life.

Light has come into the world, and every man must decide whether he will walk in the light of creative altruism or the darkness of destructive selfishness. This is the judgment. Life's most persistent and urgent question is, "What are you doing for others?"

God has so structured this universe that things do not quite work out rightly if men are not diligent in their cultivation of the dimension of breadth. "I" cannot reach fulfillment without "thou." The self cannot be self without other selves. Social psychologists tell us that we cannot truly be persons unless we interact with other persons. All life is interrelated, and all men are interdependent. And yet we continue to travel a road paved with the slippery cement of inordinate selfishness. Most of the tragic problems we are confronting in the world today mirror man's failure to add breadth to length.

This is clearly seen in the racial crisis facing our nation. The tension in race relations is a result of the fact that many of our white brothers are inordinately concerned in the length of life—their economically privileged positions, their political power, their social status, their so-called "way of life." If only they would add breadth to length—the other-regarding dimension to the self-regarding dimension—the jangling discords in our nation would be transformed into a beautiful symphony of brotherhood.

This need for adding breadth to length is also to be seen in international relations. No nation can live alone. Mrs. King and I were privileged to make a memorable visit to India. Although there were many high and rewarding moments, there were also many depressing moments during our journey through India. How can one avoid being depressed when he sees with his own eyes millions of people who go to bed hungry? How can one avoid being depressed when he sees with his own eyes millions of people sleeping on the sidewalks? How can one avoid being depressed when he learns that 350,000,000 of India's population of more than 435,000,000 people make an annual income of less than $70 per year, and is told that most of them have never seen a doctor or a dentist?

Can we in America remain unconcerned about these conditions? The answer is emphatically no. Our destiny as a nation is linked to the destiny of India. So long as India, or any other nation, is insecure, we shall never be secure. We must use our vast resources of wealth to aid the undeveloped countries of the world. Have we spent far too much of our national budget in establishing military bases around the world and far too little in establishing bases of genuine concern and understanding?

In the final analysis, all men are interdependent and are thereby involved in a single process. We are inevitably our brother's keeper because of the interrelated structure of reality. No nation or individual can live in isolation. John Donne interpreted this truth in graphic terms when he affirmed:

> No man is an Iland, intire of its selfe; every man is a peece of the Continent, a part of the maine; if a Clod bee washed away by the Sea, Europe is the lesse, as well as if a Promontorie were, as well as if a Mannor of thy friends or of thine owne were; any mans death diminishes me, because I am involved in Mankinde; And therefore never send to know for whom the bell tolls; It tolls for thee.[51]

This recognition of the oneness of humanity and the need of an active brotherly concern for the welfare of others is the breadth of man's life.

THREE

One more dimension of the complete life remains, namely, the height or that upward reach toward something distinctly greater than humanity. We must rise above earth and give our ultimate allegiance to that eternal Being who is the source and ground of all reality. When we add height to length and breadth, we have the complete life.

Just as there are some people who never get beyond length, so there are others who never get beyond the combination of length and breadth. They brilliantly develop their inner powers, and they have a genuine humanitarian concern. But they stop short. They are so earth-bound that they conclude that humanity is God. They seek to live without a sky.

There are probably several reasons why modern man has neglected this third dimension. Some men have honest intellectual doubts. Looking upon the horrors of moral and natural evil, they ask, "If there is a good God who is all-powerful, why does he permit such unmerited pain and suffering to exist?" Their inability adequately to answer this question leads them to agnosticism. And there are those who also find it difficult to square their scientific and rationalistic findings with the sometimes unscientific dogmas of religion and the primitive conceptions of God.

I suspect, however, that a majority of people fit into still another category. They are not theoretical atheists; they are practical atheists. They do not deny the existence of God with their lips, but they are continually denying his existence with their lives. They live as though there is no God. This erasing of God from the agenda of life may well have been an unconscious process. Most men do not say, "Good-by, God, I am going to leave you now." But they become so involved in the things of this world that they are unconsciously carried away by the rushing tide of materialism and are left treading in the confused waters of secularism. Modern man, living in what Professor Sorokin has called "a sensate culture," believes only those things which can be known by the five senses.

But this attempt to substitute a man-centered universe for a God-centered universe leads only to deeper frustration. Reinhold Niebuhr has said, "Since 1914 one tragic event has followed another as if history were designed to refute the vain delusions of modern man." We sail upon the seas of modern history like a ship without a compass. We have neither a guide nor a sense of direction. We doubt our doubts, and wonder whether, after all, there may not in truth be some spiritual force undergirding reality.

In spite of our theoretical denials, we have spiritual experiences that cannot be explained in materialistic terms. In spite of our worship of the natural order, ever and again we feel impinging upon us something that causes us to wonder how the magnificent orderliness of the universe can be the result of a fortuitous interplay of atoms and electrons. In spite of our inordinate reverence for material things, ever and again something reminds us of the reality of the unseen. At night we look up at the stars which bedeck the heavens like swinging lanterns of eternity. For the moment we may think we see all, but something reminds us that we do not see the law of gravitation that holds them there. Enraptured, we gaze at the architectural beauty of some impressive house of God, but soon something reminds us that our eyes cannot

behold that cathedral in its total reality. We have not seen within the mind of the architect who drew the blueprint. We can never see the love and the faith of the individuals whose sacrifices made the construction possible. Looking at each other, we quickly conclude that our perception of the physical body is a vision of all that we are. As you presently gaze at the pulpit and witness me preaching this sermon, you may immediately conclude that you see Martin Luther King. But then you are reminded that you see only my body, which in itself can neither reason nor think. You can never see the *me* that makes me me, and I can never see the *you* that makes you you. That invisible something we call personality is beyond our physical gaze. Plato was right when he said that the visible is a shadow cast by the invisible.

God is still in his universe. Our new technological and scientific developments can neither banish him from the microcosmic compass of the atom nor from the vast, unfathomable ranges of interstellar space. Living in a universe in which the distances of some heavenly bodies must be dated in terms of billions of light years, modern man exclaims with the Psalmist of old, "When I consider thy heavens, the work of thy fingers, the moon and the stars, which thou hast ordained; what is man, that thou are mindful of him? and the son of man, that thou visitest him?"[52]

I would urge you to give priority to the search for God. Allow his spirit to permeate your being. To meet the difficulties and challenges of life you will need him. Before the ship of your life reaches its last harbor, there will be long, drawn-out storms, howling and jostling winds, and tempestuous seas that make the heart stand still. If you do not have a deep and patient faith in God, you will be powerless to face the delays, disappointments, and vicissitudes that inevitably come.

Without God, all our efforts turn to ashes and our sunrises into darkest nights. Without him, life is a meaningless drama in which the decisive scenes are missing. But with him, we are able to rise from tension-packed valleys to the sublime heights of inner peace, and find radiant stars of hope against the nocturnal bosom of life's most depressing nights. St. Augustine was right: "Thou hast created us for thyself, and our heart cannot be quieted till it find repose in thee."[53]

A wise old preacher went to a college to deliver a baccalaureate sermon. After finishing his message, he lingered on the campus to talk with members of the graduating class. He spoke with a brilliant young graduate named Robert. His first question to Robert was: "What are your plans for the future?" "I plan to go immediately to law school," said Robert. "What then, Robert?" inquired the preacher. "Well," responded Robert, "I plan to get married and start a family and then get myself securely established in my law practice." "What then, Robert?" continued the preacher. Robert retorted, "I must frankly say that I plan to make lots of money from my law practice and thereby I hope to retire rather early and spend a great deal of time traveling to various parts of the world—something that I have always wanted to do." "What then, Robert?" added the preacher with an almost annoying inquisitiveness. "Well," said Robert, "these are all of my plans." Looking at Robert with a countenance expressing pity and fatherly concern, the preacher said, "Young man, your plans are far too small. They can extend only seventy-five or a hundred years at the most. You must make your plans big enough to include God and large enough to include eternity."

This is wise advice. I suspect that all too many of us are still dabbling with plans that are big in quantity, but small in quality, plans that move on the horizontal plane of time rather than on the vertical plane of eternity. I, too, would urge you to make your plans so large and broad that they cannot be bound by the chains of time and the manacles of space. Give your life—all you have and are—to the God of the universe whose purpose changeth not.

Where do we find this God? In a test tube? No. Where else except in Jesus Christ, the Lord of our lives? By knowing him we know God. Christ is not only Godlike but God is Christlike. Christ is the word made flesh. He is the language of eternity translated in the words of time. If we are to know what God is like and understand his purposes for mankind, we must turn to Christ. By committing ourselves absolutely to Christ and his way, we will participate in that marvelous act of faith that will bring us to the true knowledge of God.

What then is the conclusion of the matter? Love yourself, if that means rational and healthy self-interest. You are commanded to do that. That is the length of life. Love your neighbor as you love yourself. You are commanded to do that. That is the breadth of life. But never forget that there is a first and even greater commandment: "Love the Lord thy God with all thy heart, and with all thy soul, and with all thy mind."[54] This is the height of life. Only by a painstaking development of all three of these dimensions can you expect to live a complete life.

Thank God for John who, many centuries ago, lifted his vision to high heaven and there saw the new Jerusalem in all of its magnificence. God grant that we, too, will catch the vision and move with unrelenting passion toward that city of complete life in which the length and the breadth and the height are equal. Only by reaching this city can we achieve our true essence. Only by attaining this completeness can we be true sons of God.

SHATTERED DREAMS

But now having no more place in these parts,
and having a great desire these many years to come unto you;

Whensoever I take my journey into Spain, I will come to you:
for I trust to see you in my journey, and to be brought
on my way thitherward by you, if first I be somewhat filled with
your company.

Romans 15

ONE OF THE MOST agonizing problems within our human experience is that few, if any, of us live to see our fondest hopes fulfilled. The hopes of our childhood and the promises of our mature years are unfinished symphonies. In a famous painting, George Frederic Watts portrays Hope as a tranquil figure who, seated atop our planet, her head sadly bowed, plucks a single unbroken harpstring. Is there any one of us who has not faced the agony of blasted hopes and shattered dreams?

In Paul's letter to the Roman Christians we find a potent illustration of this vexing problem of disappointed hopes: "Whensoever I take my journey into Spain, I will come to you." One of his ardent hopes was to travel to Spain where, at the edge of the then known world, he might further proclaim the Christian gospel. On his return he wished to have personal fellowship with that valiant group of Roman Christians. The more he anticipated this privilege, the more his heart quickened with joy. His preparations now centered in carrying the gospel to the capital city of Rome and to Spain at the distant fringe of the empire.

What a glowing hope stirred within Paul's heart! but he never got to Rome according to the pattern of his hopes. Because of his daring faith in Jesus Christ, he was indeed taken there but as a prisoner and was held captive in a little prison cell. Nor did he ever walk the dusty roads of Spain, nor look upon its curvacious slopes, nor watch its busy coastal life. He was put to death, we presume, as a martyr for Christ in Rome. Paul's life is a tragic story of a shattered dream.

Life mirrors many similar experiences. Who has not set out toward some distant Spain, some momentous goal, or some glorious realization, only to learn at last that he must settle for much less? We never walk as free men through the streets of our Rome; instead, circumstances decree that we live within little confining cells. Written across our lives is a fatal flaw and within history runs an irrational and unpredictable vein. Like Abraham, we too sojourn in the land of promise, but so often we do not become "heirs with him of the same promise."[55] Always our reach exceeds our grasp.

After struggling for years to achieve independence, Mahatma Gandhi witnessed a bloody religious war between the Hindus and the Moslems, and the subsequent division of

India and Pakistan shattered his heart's desire for a united nation. Woodrow Wilson died before realizing fulfillment of his consuming vision of a League of Nations. Many Negro slaves in America, having longed passionately for freedom, died before emancipation. After praying in the garden of Gethsemane that the cup might pass, Jesus, nonetheless, drank to the last bitter dregs. And the Apostle Paul repeatedly and fervently prayed that the "thorn" might be removed from his flesh, but the pain and annoyance continued to the end of his days. Shattered dreams are a hallmark of our mortal life.

ONE

Before we determine how to live in a world where our highest hopes are not satisfied, we must ask, What does one do under such circumstances?

One possible reaction is to distill all of our frustrations into a core of bitterness and resentment. The person who pursues this path is likely to develop a callous attitude, a cold heart, and a bitter hatred toward God, toward those with whom he lives, and toward himself. Because he cannot corner God or life, he releases his pent-up vindictiveness in hostility toward other people. He may be extremely cruel to his mate and inhuman to his children. In short, meanness becomes his dominating characteristic. He loves no one and requires love from no one. He trusts no one and does not expect others to trust him. He finds fault in everything and everybody, and he continually complains.

Such a reaction poisons the soul and scars the personality, always harming the person who harbors this feeling more than anyone else. Medical science reveals that such physical ailments as arthritis, gastric ulcer, and asthma have on occasion been encouraged by bitter resentments. Psychosomatic medicine, dealing with bodily sicknesses which come from mental illnesses, shows how deep resentment may result in physical deterioration.

Another common reaction of persons experiencing the blighting of hope is to withdraw completely into themselves and to become absolute introverts. No one is permitted to enter into their lives and they refuse to enter into the lives of others. Such persons give up the struggle of life, lose their zest for living, and attempt to escape by lifting their minds to a transcendent realm of cold indifference. Detachment is the word which best describes them. Too unconcerned to love and too passionless to hate, too detached to be selfish and too lifeless to be unselfish, too indifferent to experience joy and too cold to experience sorrow, they are neither dead nor alive; they merely exist. Their eyes do not see the beauties of nature, their ears are insensitive to the majestic sounds of great music, and their hands are even unresponsive to the touch of a charming little baby. Nothing of the aliveness of life is left in them; only the dull motion of bare existence. Disappointed hopes lead them to a crippling cynicism such as Omar Khayyám described:

The Worldly Hope men set their Hearts upon
Turns Ashes—or it prospers; and anon,
*   Like Snow upon the Desert's dusty Face,*
Lighting a little hour or two—is gone.[56]

This reaction is based on an attempt to escape from life. Psychiatrists say that when individuals attempt to escape from reality their personalities become thinner and thinner until finally they split. This is one of the causal sources of the schizophrenic personality.

A third way by which persons respond to disappointments in life is to adopt a fatalistic philosophy stipulating that whatever happens must happen and that all events are determined by necessity. Fatalism implies that everything is foreordained and inescapable. People who subscribe to this philosophy succumb to an absolute resignation to that which they consider to be their fate and think of themselves as being little more than helpless orphans cast into the terrifying immensities of space. Because they believe that man has no freedom, they seek neither to deliberate nor to make decisions, but rather they wait passively for external forces to decide for them. They never actively seek to change their circumstances, for they believe that all circumstances, as in the Greek tragedies, are controlled by irresistible and foreordained forces. Some fatalists are very religious people who think of God as the determiner and controller of destiny. This view is expressed in a verse of one of our Christian hymns:

Though dark my path and sad my lot,
Let me be still and murmur not,
But breathe the prayer divinely taught,
Thy will be done.

Fatalists, believing that freedom is a myth, surrender to a paralyzing determinism which concludes that we are

But helpless Pieces of the Game He plays
Upon this Chequer-board of Nights and
    Days;[57]

and that we need not trouble about the future, for

The Moving Finger writes; and, having writ,
Moves on: nor all your Piety nor Wit
  Shall lure it back to cancel half a Line,
Nor all your Tears wash out a Word of it.[58]

To sink in the quicksands of fatalism is both intellectually and psychologically stifling. Because freedom is a part of the essence of man, the fatalist, by denying freedom, becomes a puppet, not a person. He is, of course, right in his conviction that there is no absolute freedom and that freedom always operates within the context of predestined structure. Common experience teaches that a man is free to go north from Atlanta to Washington or south from Atlanta to Miami, but not north to Miami nor south to Washington. Freedom is always within the framework of destiny. *But there is freedom.* We are both free and destined. Freedom is the act of deliberating, deciding, and responding within our destined nature. Even though destiny may prevent our going to some attractive Spain, we do have the capacity to accept such a disappointment, to respond to it, and to do something about the disappointment itself. But fatalism stymies the individual, leaving him helplessly inadequate for life.

Fatalism, furthermore, is based on an appalling conception of God, for everything, whether good or evil, is considered to represent the will of God. A healthy religion rises above the idea that God wills evil. Although God permits evil in order to preserve the freedom of man, he does not cause evil. That which is willed is intended, and the thought that God intends for a child to be born blind or for a man to suffer the ravages of insanity is sheer heresy that pictures God as a devil rather than as a loving Father. The embracing of fatalism is as tragic and dangerous a way to meet the problem of unfulfilled dreams as are bitterness and withdrawal.

TWO

What, then, is the answer? The answer lies in

our willing acceptance of unwanted and unfortunate circumstances even as we still cling to a radiant hope, our acceptance of finite disappointment even as we adhere to infinite hope. This is not the grim, bitter acceptance of the fatalist, but the achievement found in Jeremiah's words, "This is a grief, and I must bear it."[59]

You must honestly confront your shattered dream. To follow the escapist method of attempting to put the disappointment out of your mind will lead to a psychologically injurious repression. Place your failure at the forefront of your mind and stare daringly at it. Ask yourself, "How may I transform this liability into an asset? How may I, confined in some narrow Roman cell and unable to reach life's Spain, transmute this dungeon of shame into a haven of redemptive suffering?" Almost anything that happens to us may be woven into the purposes of God. It may lengthen our cords of sympathy. It may break our self-centered pride. The cross, which was willed by wicked men, was woven by God into the tapestry of world redemption.

Many of the world's most influential personalities have exchanged their thorns for crowns. Charles Darwin, suffering from a recurrent physical illness; Robert Louis Stevenson, plagued with tuberculosis; and Helen Keller, inflicted with blindness and deafness, responded not with bitterness or fatalism, but rather by the exercise of a dynamic will transformed negative circumstances into positive assets. Writes the biographer of George Frederick Handel:

> His health and his fortunes had reached the lowest ebb. His right side had become paralyzed, and his money was all gone. His creditors seized him and threatened him with imprisonment. For a brief time he was tempted to give up the fight— but then he rebounded again to compose the greatest of his inspirations, the epic *Messiah*.

The "Hallelujah Chorus" was born, not in a sequestered villa in Spain, but in a narrow, undesirable cell.

How familiar is the experience of longing for Spain and settling for a Roman prison, and how less familiar the transforming of the broken remains of a disappointed expectation into opportunities to serve God's purpose! Yet powerful living always involves such victories over one's own soul and one's situation.

We Negroes have long dreamed of freedom, but still we are confined in an oppressive prison of segregation and discrimination. Must we respond with bitterness and cynicism? Certainly not, for this will destroy and poison our personalities. Must we, by concluding that segregation is within the will of God, resign ourselves to oppression? Of course not, for this blasphemously attributes to God that which is of the devil. To cooperate passively with an unjust system makes the oppressed as evil as the oppressor. Our most fruitful course is to stand firm with courageous determination, move forward nonviolently amid obstacles and setbacks, accept disappointments, and cling to hope. Our determined refusal not to be stopped will eventually open the door of fulfillment. While still in the prison of segregation, we must ask, "How may we turn this liability into an asset?" By recognizing the necessity of suffering in a righteous cause, we may possibly achieve our humanity's full stature. To guard ourselves from bitterness, we need the vision to see in this generation's ordeals the opportunity to transfigure both ourselves and American society. Our present suffering and our nonviolent struggle to be free may well offer to Western civilization the kind of spiritual dynamic so desperately needed for survival.

Some of us, of course, will die without having received the realization of freedom, but we must continue to sail on our charted course. We must accept finite disappointment, but we must never lose infinite hope. Only in this way shall we live without the fatigue of bitterness and the drain of resentment.

This was the secret of the survival of our slave foreparents. Slavery was a low, dirty, and inhuman business. When the slaves were taken from Africa, they were cut off from their family ties and chained to ships like beasts. Nothing is more tragic than to be divorced from family, language, and roots. In many instances, husbands were separated from wives and children from parents. When women were forced to satisfy the biological urges of white masters, slave husbands were powerless to intervene. Yet, in spite of inexpressible cruelties, our foreparents survived. When a new morning offered only the same long rows of cotton, sweltering heat, and the rawhide whip of the overseer, these brave and courageous men and women dreamed of the brighter day. They had no alternative except to accept the fact of slavery, but they clung tenaciously to the hope of freedom. In a seemingly hopeless situation, they fashioned within their souls a creative optimism that strengthened them. Their bottomless vitality transformed the darkness of frustration into the light of hope.

THREE

I first flew from New York to London in the propeller-type aircraft that required nine and a half hours for a flight now made in six hours by jet. When returning from London to the States, I was told that the flying time would be twelve and a half hours. The distance was the same. Why an additional three hours? When the pilot entered the cabin to greet the passengers, I asked him to explain the difference in flight time. "You must understand something about the winds," he said. "When we leave New York, a strong tail wind is in our favor, but when we return, a strong head wind is against us." Then he added, "Don't worry. These four engines are capable of battling the winds." At times in our lives the tail winds of joy, triumph, and fulfillment favor us, and at times the head winds of disappointment, sorrow, and tragedy beat unrelentingly against us. Shall we permit adverse winds to overwhelm us as we journey across life's mighty Atlantic, or will our inner spiritual engines sustain us in spite of the winds? Our refusal to be stopped, our "courage to be," our determination to go on "in spite of," reveal the divine image within us. The man who has made this discovery knows that no burden can overwhelm him and no wind of adversity can blow his hope away. He can stand anything that can happen to him.

Certainly the Apostle Paul possessed this type of "courage to be." His life was a continual round of disappointments. On every side were broken plans and shattered dreams. Planning to visit Spain, he was consigned to a Roman prison. Hoping to go to Bithynia, he was sidetracked to Troas. His gallant mission for Christ was measured "in journeyings often, in perils of waters, in perils of robbers, in perils by mine own countrymen, in perils by the heathen, in perils in the city, in perils in the wilderness, in perils in the sea, in perils among false brethren."[60] Did he permit these conditions to master him? "I have learned," he testified, "in whatsoever state I am, therewith to be content."[61] Not that Paul had learned to be complacent, for nothing in his life characterizes him as a complacent individual. In his *Decline and Fall of the Roman Empire,* Edward Gibbon records, "Paul has done more to promote the idea of freedom and liberty than any man who set foot on western soil." Does this sound like complacency? Nor did he learn resignation to inscrutable fate. By discovering the distinction between spiritual tranquillity and the outward accidents of circumstance, Paul learned to stand tall and without despairing amid the disappointments of life.

Each of us who makes this magnificent discovery will, like Paul, be a recipient of that true peace "which passeth all understanding."[62] Peace as the world commonly understands it comes when the summer sky is clear and the sun shines in scintillating beauty, when the pocketbook is full, when the mind and body are free of ache and pain, and when the shores of Spain have been reached. But this is not true peace. The peace of which Paul spoke is a calmness of soul amid terrors of trouble, inner tranquillity amid the howl and rage of outer storm, the serene quiet at the center of a hurricane amid the howling and jostling winds. We readily understand the meaning of peace when everything is going right and when one is "up and in," but we are baffled when Paul speaks of that true peace which comes when a man is "down and out," when burdens lie heavy upon his shoulders, when pain throbs annoyingly in his body, when he is confined by the stone walls of a prison cell, and when disappointment is inescapably real. True peace, a calm that exceeds all description and all explanation, is peace amid storm and tranquillity amid disaster.

Through faith we may inherit Jesus' legacy, "Peace I leave with you, my peace I give unto you."[63] Paul at Philippi, incarcerated in a dark and desolate dungeon, his body beaten and bloody, his feet chained, and his spirit tired, joyously sang the songs of Zion at midnight. The early Christians, facing hungry lions in the arena and the excruciating pain of the chopping block, rejoiced that they had been deemed worthy to suffer for the sake of Christ. Negro slaves, bone-weary in the sizzling heat and the marks of whip lashes freshly etched on their backs, sang triumphantly, "By and by I'm gwin to lay down this heavy load." These are living examples of peace that passeth all understanding.

Our capacity to deal creatively with shattered dreams is ultimately determined by our faith in God. Genuine faith embues us with the conviction that beyond time is a divine Spirit and beyond life is Life. However dismal and catastrophic may be the present circumstance, we know we are not alone, for God dwells with us in life's most confining and oppressive cells. And even if we die there without having received the earthly promise, he shall lead us down that mysterious road called death and at last to that indescribable city he has prepared for us. His creative power is not exhausted by this earthly life, nor is his majestic love locked within the limited walls of time and space. Would not this be a strangely irrational universe if God did not ultimately join virtue and fulfillment, and an absurdly meaningless universe if death were a blind alley leading the human race into a state of nothingness? God through Christ has taken the sting from death by freeing us from its dominion. Our earthly life is a prelude to a glorious new awakening, and death is an open door that leads us into life eternal.

The Christian faith makes it possible for us nobly to accept that which cannot be changed, to meet disappointments and sorrow with an inner poise, and to absorb the most intense pain without abandoning our sense of hope, for we know, as Paul testified, in life or in death, in Spain or in Rome, "that all things work together for good to them that love God, to them who are the called according to his purpose."[64]

CHAPTER XI

O Lord, our Lord
how majestic is thy name in all the earth!
Thou whose glory above the heavens is chanted
by the mouths of babes and infants—

Thou who hast founded a bulwark
because of thy foes to still the enemy and the avenger.

When I look at thy heavens, the work of thy fingers,
the moon and the stars which thou hast established,

what is man that thou art mindful of him
and the son of man that thou dost care for him?

Yet thou hast made him little less than God
and dost crown him with glory and honor.

Psalm 8 RSV

WHAT IS MAN?

THE WHOLE POLITICAL, social, and economic structure of a society is largely determined by its answer to this vital question. Indeed, the conflict we witness between totalitarianism and democracy is fundamentally centered in this: Is man a person or a pawn? Is he a cog in the wheel of the state or a free, creative being capable of accepting responsibility? This inquiry is as old as ancient man and as new as the morning newspaper. Although there is widespread agreement in asking this question, there is sharp disagreement in answering it.

Those who think of man purely in materialistic terms argue that man is simply an animal, a tiny object in the vast, ever-changing organism called nature, which is wholly unconscious and impersonal. His whole life may be explained in terms of matter in motion. Such a system of thought affirms that the conduct of man is physically determined and that the mind is merely an effect of the brain.

Those who posit the materialistic conception of man are often driven to the dark chambers of pessimism. They often find themselves agreeing with a recent writer that "man is a cosmic accident, a disease on this planet not soon to be cured," or with Jonathan Swift, who wrote, "Man is the most pernicious little race of ominous vermin that nature ever suffered to walk across the face of the earth."[65]

Humanism is another answer frequently given to the question, "What is man?" (See Chapter VII, "The Man Who Was a Fool," for a fuller development of this point.) Believing neither in God nor in the existence of any supernatural power, the humanist affirms that man is the highest form of being which has evolved in the natural universe. Over against the pessimism of materialism, the humanist posits a glowing optimism, exclaiming with Shakespeare's Hamlet:

> What a piece of work is man! How noble in reason! how infinite in faculties! in form, in moving, how express and admirable! in action how like an angel! in apprehension how like a god! the beauty of the world! the paragon of animals![66]

There are those who, seeking to be a little more realistic about man, wish to reconcile the truths of these opposites, while avoiding the extremes of both. They contend that the truth about man is found neither in the thesis of pessimistic materialism nor the antithesis of optimistic humanism, but in a higher synthesis. Man is neither villain nor hero; he is rather both villain and hero. The realist agrees with Carlyle that "there are depths in man which go down to the lowest hell and heights which reach the highest heaven, for are not both heaven and hell made out of him, everlasting miracle and mystery that he is?"

Centuries ago the Psalmist looked to the infinite expanse of the solar system. He gazed at the scintillating beauty of the moon and at the stars, hung like swinging lanterns of eternity. As he beheld this huge pattern and this vast cosmic order, the old familiar question came rushing to his mind, "What is man?" His answer breathes with creative truth: "Thou hast made him little less than God, and dost crown him with glory and honor."

His words serve as a basis for our thinking as we seek a realistic Christian view of man.

ONE

First, the Christian view recognizes that man is a biological being having a physical body. In this sense, he is an animal. So the Psalmist says, "Thou hast made him little less than God." We do not think of God as a being having a body. God is a being of pure spirit, lifted above the categories of time and space; but man, being less than God, is enmeshed in the limitations of time and space. He is in nature and can never disown his kinship with it.

The Psalmist goes on to say that God made man that way. Since this is true, there is nothing essentially wrong with man's created nature, for we read in the Book of Genesis that everything God made is good. There is nothing derogatory in having a body. This assertion is one of the things that distinguish the

Christian doctrine of man from the Greek doctrine. Under the impetus of Plato, the Greeks came to feel that the body is inherently evil and that the soul will never reach its full maturity until it is freed from the prison of the body. Christianity, on the other hand, contends that the will, and not the body, is the principle of evil. The body is both sacred and significant in Christian thought.

In any realistic doctrine of man we must be forever concerned about his physical and material well-being. When Jesus said that man cannot live by bread alone, he did not imply that men can live without bread. As Christians we must think not only about "mansions in the sky," but also about the slums and ghettos that cripple the human soul, not merely about streets in heaven "flowing with milk and honey," but also about the millions of people in this world who go to bed hungry at night. Any religion that professes concern regarding the souls of men and fails to be concerned by social conditions that corrupt and economic conditions that cripple the soul, is a do-nothing religion, in need of new blood. Such a religion fails to realize that man is an animal having physical and material needs.

TWO

But we must not stop here. Some thinkers never get beyond the point of seeing man as an animal. The Marxists, for instance, following a theory of dialectical materialism, contend that man is merely a producing animal who supplies his own needs and whose life is determined largely by economic forces. Others contend that the whole life of man is nothing but a materialistic process with a materialistic meaning.

Can man be explained in such shallow terms? Can we explain the literary genius of Shakespeare, the musical genuis of Beethoven, and the artistic genius of Michelangelo in materialistic terms? Can we explain the spiritual genius of Jesus of Nazareth in materialistic terms? Can we explain the mystery and the magic of the human soul in materialistic terms? Oh, no! There is something within man which cannot be explained in chemical and biological terms, for man is more than a tiny vagary of whirling electrons.

This brings us to a second point that must be included in any Christian doctrine of man. Man is a being of spirit. He moves up "the stairs of his concepts" into a wonder world of thought. Conscience speaks to him, and he is reminded of things divine. This is what the Psalmist means when he says that man has been crowned with glory and honor.

This spiritual quality gives him the unique capacity to live on two levels. He is in nature, yet above nature; he is in space and time, yet above them. He can do creative things that lower animals could never do. Man can think a poem and write it; he can think a symphony and compose it; he can think of a great civilization and produce it. Because of this capacity, he is not bound completely by space and time. He may be a John Bunyan, held within spatial boundaries of Bedford Jail, whose mind transcends the bars and produces *The Pilgrim's Progress*. He may be a Handel, moving into the evening of life, his physical vision almost gone, raising his mental vision to the highest heavens and transcribing the glad thunders and gentle sighings of the great *Messiah*. By his ability to reason, his power of memory, and his gift of imagination, man transcends time and space. As marvelous as are the stars is the mind of man that studies them.

This is what the Bible means when it affirms that man is made in the image of God. The *imago dei* has been interpreted by different thinkers in terms of fellowship, responsiveness, reason, and conscience. An abiding expression of man's higher spiritual nature is his freedom. Man is man because he is free to operate within the framework of his destiny. He is free to deliberate, to make decisions, and to choose between alternatives. He is distinguished from animals by his freedom to do evil or to do good and to walk the high road of beauty or tread the low road of ugly degeneracy.

THREE

To avoid being victimized by an illusion born of superficiality, it should be said that we err when we assume that because man is made in the image of God, man is basically good. Through his all too prevalent inclination for evil, man has terribly scarred God's image.

We hate to be told that man is a sinner. Nothing so insults modern man's pride. We have tried desperately to find other words— error of nature, absence of good, false concept of mind—to explain the sin of man. Turning to depth psychology, we attempt to dismiss sin as the result of inner conflicts, inhibitions, or a battle between the "id" and the "super-ego." These concepts only serve to remind us that engulfing human nature is a tragic, threefold estrangement by which man is separated from himself, his neighbors, and his God. There is a corruption in man's will.

When we lay our lives bare before the scrutiny of God, we admit that though we know truth, yet we lie; we know how to be just, yet we are unjust; we know we should love, yet we hate; we stand at the juncture of the high road, yet we deliberately choose the low road. "All we like sheep have gone astray."[67]

Man's sinfulness sinks to such devastating depths in his collective life that Reinhold Niebuhr could write a book titled *Moral Man and Immoral Society*. Man collectivized in the group, the tribe, the race, and the nation often sinks to levels of barbarity unthinkable even among lower animals. We see the tragic expression of Immoral Society in the doctrine of white supremacy which plunges millions of black men into the abyss of exploitation and in the horrors of two world wars which have left battlefields drenched with blood, national debts higher than mountains of gold, men psychologically deranged and physically handicapped, and nations of widows and orphans. Man is a sinner in need of God's forgiving grace. This is not deadening pessimism; it is Christian realism.

Despite man's tendency to live on low and degrading planes, something reminds him that he is not made for that. As he trails in the dust, something reminds him that he is made for the stars. As he makes folly his bed-fellow, a nagging inner voice tells him that he is born for eternity. God's unbroken hold on us is something that will never permit us to feel right when we do wrong or to feel natural when we do the unnatural.

Jesus told of a young man who left home and wandered into a far country, where in adventure after adventure and sensation after sensation, he sought life. But he never found it; he found only frustration and bewilderment. The farther he moved from his father's house, the closer he came to the house of despair. The more he did what he liked, the less he liked what he did. Instead of leading him to a land flowing with the milk of happiness, the prodigal's journey led him to a pig's trough. This parable is an eternal reminder of the fact that man is made for the Father's house and that every excursion into the far country brings only frustration and homesickness.

Thank God the parable tells us more. The prodigal son was not himself when he left his father's house or when he dreamed that pleasure was the end of life. Only when he made up his mind to go home and be a son again did he really come to himself. There he found a loving father waiting with outstretched arms and a heart filled with unutterable joy. When the soul returns to its true home, there is always joy.

Man has strayed to the far countries of secularism, materialism, sexuality, and racial injustice. His journey has brought a moral and spiritual famine in Western civilization. *But it is not too late to return home.*

The heavenly Father speaks to Western civilization today: "In the far country of co-lonialism more than one billion six hundred million colored brothers have been dominated politically, exploited economically, and deprived of their sense of personal worth. Come to yourself and return to your true home of justice, freedom, and brotherhood, and I will joyously take you in." With an equal urgency God speaks to America: "In the far country of segregation and discrimination, you have oppressed nineteen million of your Negro brothers, binding them economically and driving them into the ghetto, and you have stripped them of their self-respect and self-dignity, making them feel that they are nobodies. Return to your true home of democracy, brotherhood, and fatherhood in God, and I will take you in and give you a new opportunity to be a truly great nation."

As individuals and as a world, may we realize that we are made for that which is high, noble, and good, and that our true home is within the Father's will. Let us choose the road that leads to abundant life.

To every man there openeth
A Way, and Ways, and a Way,
And the High Soul climbs the High Way,
And the Low Soul gropes the Low,
And in between, on the misty flats,
The rest drift to and fro.
But to every man there openeth
A High Way, and a Low,
And every man decideth
The Way his soul shall go.[68]

God grant that we will choose the high way and that everywhere and at all times we shall be known as men who are crowned with glory and honor.

HOW SHOULD

A CHRISTIAN VIEW COMMUNISM?

Though ye offer me burnt offerings and your meat offerings,
I will not accept them:
neither will I regard the peace offerings of your fat beasts.

Take thou away from me the noise of thy songs;
for I will not hear the melody of thy viols.

But let judgment run down as waters, and righteousness as a mighty stream.

Amos 5

CHAPTER XII

Few issues demand a more thorough and sober discussion than that presented by Communism. For at least three reasons every Christian minister should feel obligated to speak to his people on this controversial theme.

The first reason recognizes that the widespread influence of Communism has, like a mighty tidal wave, spread through Russia, China, Eastern Europe, and now even to our hemisphere. Nearly one billion of the peoples of the world believe in its teachings, many of them embracing it as a new religion to which they have surrendered completely. Such a force cannot be ignored.

A second reason is that Communism is the only serious rival to Christianity. Such great world religions as Judaism, Buddhism, Hinduism, and Mohammedanism are possible alternatives to Christianity, but no one conversant with the hard facts of the modern world will deny that Communism is Christianity's most formidable rival.

A third reason is that it is unfair and certainly unscientific to condemn a system before we know what that system teaches and why it is wrong.

Let me state clearly the basic premise of this sermon: Communism and Christianity are fundamentally incompatible. A true Christian cannot be a true Communist, for the two philosophies are antithetical and all the dialectics of the logicians cannot reconcile them. Why is this true?

ONE

First, Communism is based on a materialistic and humanistic view of life and history. According to Communist theory, matter, not mind or spirit, speaks the last word in the universe. Such a philosophy is avowedly secularistic and atheistic. Under it, God is merely a figment of the imagination, religion is a product of fear and ignorance, and the church is an invention of the rulers to control the masses. Moreover, Communism, like humanism, thrives on the grand illusion that man, unaided by any divine power, can save himself and usher in a new society—

> I fight alone, and win or sink,
>   I need no one to make me free;
> I want no Jesus Christ to think,
>   That He could ever die for me.

Cold atheism wrapped in the garments of materialism, Communism provides no place for God or Christ.

At the center of the Christian faith is the affirmation that there is a God in the universe who is the ground and essence of all reality. A Being of infinite love and boundless power, God is the creator, sustainer, and conserver of values. In opposition to Communism's atheistic materialism, Christianity posits a theistic idealism. Reality cannot be explained by matter in motion or the push and pull of economic forces. Christianity affirms that at the heart of reality is a Heart, a loving Father who works through history for the salvation of his children. Man cannot save himself, for man is not the measure of all things and humanity is not God. Bound by the chains of his own sin and finiteness, man needs a Saviour.

Second, Communism is based on ethical relativism and accepts no stable moral absolutes. Right and wrong are relative to the most expedient methods for dealing with class war. Communism exploits the dreadful philosophy that the end justifies the means. It enunciates movingly the theory of a classless society, but alas! its methods for achieving this noble end are all too often ignoble. Lying, violence, murder, and torture are considered to be justifiable means to achieve the millennial end. Is this an unfair indictment? Listen to the words of Lenin, the real tactician of Communist theory: "We must be ready to employ trickery, deceit, lawbreaking, withholding and concealing truth." Modern history has known many tortuous nights and horror-filled days because his followers have taken this statement seriously.

In contrast to the ethical relativism of Communism, Christianity sets forth a system of absolute moral values and affirms that God has placed within the very structure of this universe certain moral principles that are fixed and immutable. The law of love as an imperative is the norm for all of man's actions. Furthermore, Christianity at its best refuses to live by a philosophy of ends justifying means. Destructive means cannot bring constructive ends, because the means represent the-ideal-in-the-making and the-end-in-progress. Immoral means cannot bring moral ends, for the ends are pre-existent in the means.

Third, Communism attributes ultimate value to the state. Man is made for the state and not the state for man. One may object, saying that in Communist theory the state is an "interim reality," which will "wither away" when the classless society emerges. True—in theory; but it is also true that, while it lasts, the state is the end. Man is a means to that end. Man has no inalienable rights. His only rights are derived from, and conferred by, the state. Under such a system, the fountain of freedom runs dry. Restricted are man's liberties of press and assembly, his freedom to vote, and his freedom to listen and to read. Art, religion, education, music, and science come under the gripping yoke of governmental control. Man must be a dutiful servant to the omnipotent state.

All of this is contrary, not only to the Christian doctrine of God, but also to the Christian estimate of man. Christianity insists that man is an end because he is a child of God, made in God's image. Man is more than a producing animal guided by economic forces; he is a being of spirit, crowned with glory and honor, endowed with the gift of freedom. The ultimate weakness of Communism is that it robs man of that quality which makes him man. Man, says Paul Tillich, is man because he is free. This freedom is expressed through man's capacity to deliberate, decide, and respond. Under Communism, the individual soul is shackled by the chains of conformity; his spirit is bound by the manacles of party allegiance. He is stripped of both conscience and reason. The trouble with Communism is that it has neither a theology nor a Christology; therefore it emerges with a mixed-up anthropology. Confused about God, it is also confused about man. In spite of its glowing talk about the welfare of the masses, Communism's methods and philosophy strip man of his dignity and worth, leaving him as little more than a depersonalized cog in the ever-turning wheel of the state.

Clearly, then, all of this is out of harmony with the Christian view of things. We must not fool ourselves. These systems of thought are too contradictory to be reconciled; they represent diametrically opposed ways of looking at the world and of transforming it. We should as Christians pray for the Communist constantly, but never can we, as true Christians, tolerate the philosophy of Communism.

Yet, something in the spirit and threat of Communism challenges us. The late Archbishop of Canterbury, William Temple, referred to Communism as a Christian heresy.

He meant that Communism had laid hold on certain truths which are essential parts of the Christian view of things, although bound to them are theories and practices which no Christian could ever accept.

TWO

The theory, though surely not the practice, of Communism challenges us to be more concerned about social justice. With all of its false assumptions and evil methods, Communism arose as a protest against the injustices and indignities inflicted upon the underprivileged. *The Communist Manifesto* was written by men aflame with a passion for social justice. Karl Marx, born of Jewish parents who both came from rabbinic stock, and trained, as he must have been, in the Hebrew Scriptures, could never forget the words of Amos: "Let judgment roll down as waters, and righteousness as a mighty stream."[69] Marx's parents adopted Christianity when he was a child of six, thus adding to the Old Testament heritage that of the New. In spite of his later atheism and antiecclesiasticism, Marx could not quite forget Jesus' concern for "the least of these." In his writings, he champions the cause of the poor, the exploited, and the disinherited.

Communism in theory emphasizes a classless society. Although the world knows from sad experience that Communism has created new classes and a new lexicon of injustice, in its theoretical formulation it envisages a world society transcending the superficialities of race and color, class and caste. Membership in the Communist party theoretically is not determined by the color of a man's skin or the quality of blood in his veins.

Christians are bound to recognize any passionate concern for social justice. Such concern is basic in the Christian doctrine of the Fatherhood of God and the brotherhood of man. The Gospels abound with expressions of concern for the welfare of the poor. Listen to the words of the Magnificat: "He hath put down the mighty from their seats, and exalted them of low degree. He hath filled the hungry with good things; and the rich he hath sent empty away."[70] No doctrinaire Communist ever expressed a passion for the poor and oppressed such as we find in the Manifesto of Jesus which affirms: "The Spirit of the Lord is upon me, because he hath anointed me to preach the gospel to the poor; he hath sent me to heal the brokenhearted, to preach deliverance to the captives, and recovering of sight to the blind, to set at liberty them that are bruised, to preach the acceptable year of the Lord."[71]

Christians are also bound to recognize the ideal of a world unity in which all barriers of caste and color are abolished. Christianity repudiates racism. The broad universalism standing at the center of the gospel makes both the theory and practice of racial injustice morally unjustifiable. Racial prejudice is a blatant denial of the unity which we have in Christ, for in Christ there is neither Jew nor Gentile, bond nor free, Negro nor white.

In spite of the noble affirmations of Christianity, the church has often lagged in its concern for social justice and too often has been content to mouth pious irrelevances and sanctimonious trivialities. It has often been so absorbed in a future good "over yonder" that it forgets the present evils "down here." Yet the church is challenged to make the gospel of Jesus Christ relevant within the social situation. We must come to see that the Christian gospel is a two-way road. On the one side, it seeks to change the souls of men and thereby unite them with God; on the other, it seeks to change the environmental conditions of men so that the soul will have a chance after it is changed. Any religion that professes to be concerned with the souls of men and yet is not concerned with the economic and social conditions that strangle them and the social conditions that cripple them is the kind the Marxist describes as "an opiate of the people."

Honesty also impels us to admit that the church has not been true to its social mission on the question of racial justice. In this area it has failed Christ miserably. This failure is due, not only to the fact that the church has been appallingly silent and disastrously indifferent in the realm of race relations, but even more to the fact that it has often been an active participant in shaping and crystallizing the patterns of the race-caste system. Colonialism could not have been perpetuated if the Christian Church had really taken a stand against it. One of the chief defenders of the vicious system of apartheid in South Africa today is the Dutch Reformed Protestant Church. In America slavery could not have existed for almost two hundred and fifty years if the church had not sanctioned it, nor could segregation and discrimination exist today if the Christian Church were not a silent and often vocal partner. We must face the shameful fact that the church is the most segregated major institution in American society, and the most segregated hour of the week is, as Professor Liston Pope has pointed out, eleven o'clock on Sunday morning. How often the church has been an echo rather than a voice, a taillight behind the Supreme Court and other secular agencies, rather than a headlight guiding men progressively and decisively to higher levels of understanding.

The judgment of God is upon the church. The church has a schism in its own soul that it must close. It will be one of the tragedies of Christian history if future historians record that at the height of the twentieth century the church was one of the greatest bulwarks of white supremacy.

THREE

In the face of the Communist challenge we must examine honestly the weaknesses of traditional capitalism. In all fairness, we must admit that capitalism has often left a gulf between superfluous wealth and abject poverty, has created conditions permitting necessities to be taken from the many to give luxuries to the few, and has encouraged small-hearted men to become cold and conscienceless so that, like Dives before Lazarus, they are unmoved by suffering, poverty-stricken humanity. Although through social reform American capitalism is doing much to reduce such tendencies, there is much yet to be accomplished. God intends that all of his children shall have the basic necessities for meaningful, healthful life. Surely it is unchristian and unethical for some to wallow in the soft beds of luxury while others sink in the quicksands of poverty.

The profit motive, when it is the sole basis of an economic system, encourages a cutthroat competition and selfish ambition that inspires men to be more concerned about making a living than making a life. It can make men so I-centered that they no longer are Thou-centered. Are we not too prone to judge success by the index of our salaries and the size of the wheel base of our automobiles, and not by the quality of our service and relationship to humanity? Capitalism may lead to a practical materialism that is as pernicious as the theoretical materialism taught by Communism.

We must honestly recognize that truth is not to be found either in traditional capitalism or in Marxism. Each represents a partial truth. Historically, capitalism failed to discern the truth in collective enterprise and Marxism failed to see the truth in individual enterprise. Nineteenth-century capitalism failed to appreciate that life is social, and Marxism failed, and still fails, to see that life is individual and social. The Kingdom of God is neither the thesis of individual enterprise nor the antithesis of collective enterprise, but a synthesis which reconciles the truth of both.

FOUR

Finally, we are challenged to dedicate our lives to the cause of Christ even as the Communists dedicate theirs to Communism. We who cannot accept the creed of the Communists recognize their zeal and commitment to a cause which they believe will create a better world. They have a sense of purpose and destiny, and they work passionately and assiduously to win others to Communism. How many Christians are as concerned to win others to Christ? Often we have neither zeal for Christ nor zest for his kingdom. For so many Christians, Christianity is a Sunday activity having no relevancy for Monday and the church is little more than a secular social club having a thin veneer of religiosity. Jesus is an ancient symbol whom we do the honor of calling Christ, and yet his Lordship is neither affirmed nor acknowledged by our substanceless lives. Would that the Christian fire were burning in the hearts of all Christians with the same intensity as the Communist fire is burning in the hearts of Communists! Is Communism alive in the world today because we have not been Christian enough?

We need to pledge ourselves anew to the cause of Christ. We must recapture the spirit of the early church. Wherever the early Christians went, they made a triumphant witness for Christ. Whether on the village streets or in the city jails, they daringly proclaimed the good news of the gospel. Their reward for this audacious witness was often the excruciating agony of a lion's den or the poignant pain of a chopping block, but they continued in the faith that they had discovered a cause so great and had been transformed by a Saviour so divine that even death was not too great a sacrifice. When they entered a town, the power structure became disturbed. Their new gospel brought the refreshing warmth of spring to men whose lives had been hardened by the long winter of traditionalism. They urged men to revolt against old systems of injustice and old structures of immorality. When the rulers objected, these strange people, intoxicated with the wine of God's grace, continued to proclaim the gospel until even men and women in Caesar's household were convinced, until jailers dropped their keys, and until kings trembled on their thrones. T. R. Glover has written that the early Christians "out-thought, out-lived, and out-died"[72] everyone else.

Where is that kind of fervor today? Where is that kind of daring, revolutionary commitment to Christ today? Is it hidden behind smoke screens and altars? Is it buried in a grave called respectability? Is it inextricably bound with nameless status quos and imprisoned within cells of stagnant mores? This devotion must again be released. Christ must once more be enthroned in our lives.

This is our best defense against Communism. War is not the answer. Communism will never be defeated by the use of atomic bombs or nuclear weapons. Let us not join those who shout war and who through their misguided passions urge the United States to relinquish its participation in the United Nations. These are days when Christians must evince wise restraint and calm reasonableness. We must not call everyone a Communist or an appeaser who recognizes that hate and hysteria are not the final answers to the problems of these turbulent days. We must not engage in a negative anti-Communism, but rather in a positive thrust for democracy, realizing that our greatest defense against Communism is to take offensive action in behalf of justice and righteousness. After our condemnation of the philosophy of Communism has been eloquently expressed, we must with positive action seek to remove those conditions of poverty, insecurity, injustice, and racial discrimination which are the fertile soil in which the seed of Communism grows and develops. Communism thrives only when the doors of opportunity are closed and human aspirations are stifled. Like the early Christians, we must move into a sometimes hostile world armed with the revolutionary gospel of Jesus Christ. With this powerful gospel we shall boldly challenge the status quos and unjust mores and thereby speed the day when "every valley shall be exalted, and every mountain and hill shall be made low: and the crooked shall be made straight, and the rough places plain: and the glory of the Lord shall be revealed."[73]

Our hard challenge and our sublime opportunity is to bear witness to the spirit of Christ in fashioning a truly Christian world. If we accept the challenge with devotion and valor, the bell of history will toll for Communism, and we shall make the world safe for democracy and secure for the people of Christ.

CHAPTER XIII

OUR GOD IS ABLE

Now unto him that is able to keep you from falling,

and to present you faultless

before the presence of his glory with exceeding joy,

To the only wise God our Saviour,

be glory and majesty, dominion and power, both now and ever. Amen.

Jude

AT THE CENTER of the Christian faith is the conviction that in the universe there is a God of power who is able to do exceedingly abundant things in nature and in history. This conviction is stressed over and over in the Old and the New Testaments. Theologically, this affirmation is expressed in the doctrine of the omnipotence of God. The God whom we worship is not a weak and incompetent God. He is able to beat back gigantic waves of opposition and to bring low prodigious mountains of evil. The ringing testimony of the Christian faith is that God is able.

There are those who seek to convince us that only man is able. Their attempt to substitute a man-centered universe for a God-centered universe is not new. It had its modern beginnings in the Renaissance and subsequently in the Age of Reason, when some men gradually came to feel that God was an unnecessary item on the agenda of life. In these periods and later in the industrial revolution in England, others questioned whether God was any longer relevant. The laboratory began to replace the church, and the scientist became a substitute for the prophet. Not a few joined Swinburne in singing a new anthem: "Glory to Man in the highest! for Man is the master of things."[74]

The devotees of the new man-centered religion point to the spectacular advances of modern science as justification for their faith. Science and technology have enlarged man's body. The telescope and television have enlarged his eyes. The telephone, radio, and microphone have strengthened his voice and ears. The automobile and airplane have lengthened his legs. The wonder drugs have prolonged his life. Have not these amazing achievements assured us that man is able?

But alas! something has shaken the faith of those who have made the laboratory "the new cathedral of men's hopes." The instruments which yesterday were worshiped today contain cosmic death, threatening to plunge all of us into the abyss of annihilation. Man is not able to save himself or the world. Unless he is guided by God's spirit, his new-found scientific power will become a devastating Frankenstein monster that will bring to ashes his earthly life.

At times other forces cause us to question

the ableness of God. The stark and colossal reality of evil in the world—what Keats calls "the giant agony of the world"; ruthless floods and tornadoes that wipe away people as though they were weeds in an open field; ills like insanity plaguing some individuals from birth and reducing their days to tragic cycles of meaninglessness; the madness of war and the barbarity of man's inhumanity to man—why, we ask, do these things occur if God is able to prevent them? This problem, namely, the problem of evil, has always plagued the mind of man. I would limit my response to an assertion that much of the evil which we experience is caused by man's folly and ignorance and also by the misuse of his freedom. Beyond this, I can say only that there is and always will be a penumbra of mystery surrounding God. What appears at the moment to be evil may have a purpose that our finite minds are incapable of comprehending. So in spite of the presence of evil and the doubts that lurk in our minds, we shall wish not to surrender the conviction that our God is able.

broader look at the universe. Will we not soon discover that our man-made instruments seem barely to be moving in comparison to the movement of the God-created solar system? Think about the fact, for instance, that the earth is circling the sun so fast that the fastest jet would be left sixty-six thousand miles behind in the first hour of a space race. In the past seven minutes we have been hurtled more than eight thousand miles through space. Or consider the sun which scientists tell us is the center of the solar system. Our earth revolves around this cosmic ball of fire once each year, traveling 584,000,000 miles at the rate of 66,700 miles per hour or 1,600,000 miles per day. By this time tomorrow we shall be 1,600,000 miles from where we are at this hundredth of a second. The sun, which seems to be remarkably near, is 93,000,000 miles from the earth. Six months from now we shall be on the other side of the sun—93,000,000 miles beyond it—and in a year from now we shall have been swung completely around it and back to where we are right now. So when we behold the illimitable expanse of space, in which we are compelled to measure stellar distance in light years and in which heavenly bodies travel at incredible speeds, we are forced to look beyond man and affirm anew that God is able.

ONE

Let us notice, first, that God is able to sustain the vast scope of the physical universe. Here again, we are tempted to feel that man is the true master of the physical universe. Man-made jet planes compress into minutes distances that formerly required weeks of tortuous effort. Man-made space ships carry cosmonauts through outer space at fantastic speeds. Is not God being replaced in the mastery of the cosmic order?

But before we are consumed too greatly by our man-centered arrogance, let us take a

TWO

Let us notice also that God is able to subdue all the powers of evil. In affirming that God is able to conquer evil we admit the reality of evil. Christianity has never dismissed evil as illusory, or an error of the mortal mind. It reckons with evil as a force that has objective reality. But Christianity contends that evil contains the seed of its own destruction. History is the story of evil forces that advance with seemingly irresistible power only to be crushed by the battling rams of the forces of justice. There is a law in the moral world—a silent, invisible imperative, akin to the laws in the physical world—which reminds us that life will work only in a certain way. The Hitlers and the Mussolinis have their day, and for a period they may wield great power, spreading themselves like a green bay tree, but soon they are cut down like the grass and wither as the green herb.

In his graphic account of the Battle of Waterloo in *Les Misérables,* Victor Hugo wrote:

> Was it possible that Napoleon should win this battle? We answer no. Why? Because of Wellington? Because of Blücher? No. Because of God. . . . Napoleon had been impeached before the Infinite, and his fall was decreed. He vexed God. Waterloo is not a battle; it is the change of front of the universe.

In a real sense, Waterloo symbolizes the doom of every Napoleon and is an eternal reminder to a generation drunk with military power that in the long run of history might does not make right and the power of the sword cannot conquer the power of the spirit.

An evil system, known as colonialism, swept across Africa and Asia. But then the quite invisible law began to operate. Prime Minister Macmillan said, "The wind of change began to blow." The powerful colonial empires began to disintegrate like stacks of cards, and new, independent nations began to emerge like refreshing oases in deserts sweltering under the heat of injustice. In less than fifteen years independence has swept through Asia and Africa like an irresistible tidal wave, releasing more than 1,500,000 people from the crippling manacles of colonialism.

In our own nation another unjust and evil system, known as segregation, for nearly one hundred years inflicted the Negro with a sense of inferiority, deprived him of his personhood, and denied him his birthright of life, liberty, and the pursuit of happiness. Segregation has been the Negroes' burden and America's shame. But as on the world scale, so in our nation, the wind of change began to blow. One event has followed another to bring a gradual end to the system of segregation. Today we know with certainty that segregation is dead. The only question remaining is how costly will be the funeral.

These great changes are not mere political and sociological shifts. They represent the passing of systems that were born in injustice, nurtured in inequality, and reared in exploitation. They represent the inevitable decay of any system based on principles that are not in harmony with the moral laws of the universe. When in future generations men look back upon these turbulent, tension-packed days through which we are passing, they will see God working through history for the salvation of man. They will know that God was working through those men who had the vision to perceive that no nation could survive half slave and half free.

God is able to conquer the evils of history. His control is never usurped. If at times we despair because of the relatively slow progress being made in ending racial discrimination and if we become disappointed because of the undue cautiousness of the federal government, let us gain new heart in the fact that God is able. In our sometimes difficult and often lonesome walk up freedom's road, we do not walk alone. God walks with us. He has placed within the very structure of this universe certain absolute moral laws. We can neither defy nor break them. If we disobey them, they will break us. The forces of evil may temporarily conquer truth, but truth will ultimately conquer its conqueror. Our God is able. James Russell Lowell was right:

Truth forever on the scaffold,
Wrong forever on the throne,—
Yet that scaffold sways the future, and,
behind the dim unknown,
Standeth God within the shadow,
keeping watch above his own.[75]

THREE

Let us notice, finally, that God is able to give us interior resources to confront the trials and difficulties of life. Each of us faces circumstances in life which compel us to carry heavy burdens of sorrow. Adversity assails us with hurricane force. Glowing sunrises are transformed into darkest nights. Our highest hopes are blasted and our noblest dreams are shattered.

Christianity has never overlooked these experiences. They come inevitably. Like the rhythmic alternation in the natural order, life has the glittering sunlight of its summers and the piercing chill of its winters. Days of unutterable joy are followed by days of overwhelming sorrow. Life brings periods of flooding and periods of drought. When these dark hours of life emerge, many cry out with Paul Laurence Dunbar:

A crust of bread and a corner to sleep in,
A minute to smile and an hour to weep in,
A pint of joy to a peck of trouble,
And never a laugh but the moans come double;
And that is life![76]

Admitting the weighty problems and staggering disappointments, Christianity affirms that God is able to give us the power to meet them. He is able to give us the inner equilibrium to stand tall amid the trials and burdens of life. He is able to provide inner peace amid outer storms. This inner stability of the man of faith is Christ's chief legacy to his disciples. He offers neither material resources nor a magical formula that exempts us from suffering and persecution, but he brings an imperishable gift: "Peace I leave with thee."[77] This is that peace which passeth all understanding.

At times we may feel that we do not need God, but on the day when the storms of disappointment rage, the winds of disaster blow, and the tidal waves of grief beat against our lives, if we do not have a deep and patient faith our emotional lives will be ripped to shreds. There is so much frustration in the world because we have relied on gods rather than God. We have genuflected before the god of science only to find that it has given us the atomic bomb, producing fears and anxieties that science can never mitigate. We have worshiped the god of pleasure only to discover that thrills play out and sensations are short-lived. We have bowed before the god of money only to learn that there are such things as love and friendship that money cannot buy and that in a world of possible depressions, stock market crashes, and bad business investments, money is a rather uncertain deity. These transitory gods are not able to save us or bring happiness to the human heart.

Only God is able. It is faith in him that we must rediscover. With this faith we can transform bleak and desolate valleys into sunlit paths of joy and bring new light into the dark caverns of pessimism. Is someone here moving toward the twilight of life and fearful of that which we call death? Why be afraid? God is able. Is someone here on the brink of despair because of the death of a loved one, the breaking of a marriage, or the waywardness of a child? Why despair? God is able to give you the power to endure that which cannot be changed. Is someone here anxious because of bad health? Why be anxious? Come what may, God is able.

As I come to the conclusion of my message, I would wish you to permit a personal experience. The first twenty-four years of my life were years packed with fulfillment. I had no basic problems or burdens. Because of concerned and loving parents who provided for my every need, I sallied through high school, college, theological school, and graduate school without interruption. It was not until I became a part of the leadership of the Montgomery bus protest that I was actually confronted with the trials of life. Almost immediately after the protest had been undertaken, we began to receive threatening telephone calls and letters in our home. Sporadic in the beginning, they increased day after day. At first I took them in stride, feeling that they were the work of a few hotheads who would become discouraged after they discovered that we would not fight back. But as the weeks passed, I realized that many of the threats were in earnest. I felt myself faltering and growing in fear.

After a particularly strenuous day, I settled in bed at a late hour. My wife had already fallen asleep and I was about to doze off when the telephone rang. An angry voice said, "Listen, nigger, we've taken all we want from you. Before next week you'll be sorry you ever came to Montgomery." I hung up, but I could not sleep. It seemed that all of my fears had come down on me at once. I had reached the saturation point.

I got out of bed and began to walk the floor. Finally, I went to the kitchen and heated a pot of coffee. I was ready to give up. I tried to think of a way to move out of the picture without appearing to be a coward. In this state of exhaustion, when my courage had almost gone, I determined to take my problem to God. My head in my hands, I bowed over the kitchen table and prayed aloud. The words I spoke to God that midnight are still vivid in my memory. "I am here taking a stand for what I believe is right. But now I am afraid. The people are looking to me for leadership, and if I stand before them without strength and courage, they too will falter. I am at the end of my powers. I have nothing left. I've come to the point where I can't face it alone."

At that moment I experienced the presence of the Divine as I had never before experienced him. It seemed as though I could hear the quiet assurance of an inner voice, saying, "Stand up for righteousness, stand up for truth. God will be at your side forever." Almost at once my fears began to pass from me. My uncertainty disappeared. I was ready to face anything. The outer situation remained the same, but God had given me inner calm.

Three nights later, our home was bombed. Strangely enough, I accepted the word of the bombing calmly. My experience with God had given me a new strength and trust. I knew now that God is able to give us the interior resources to face the storms and problems of life.

Let this affirmation be our ringing cry. It will give us courage to face the uncertainties of the future. It will give our tired feet new strength as we continue our forward stride toward the city of freedom. When our days become dreary with low-hovering clouds and our nights become darker than a thousand midnights, let us remember that there is a great benign Power in the universe whose name is God, and he is able to make a way out of no way, and transform dark yesterdays into bright tomorrows. This is our hope for becoming better men. This is our mandate for seeking to make a better world.

And we have known and believed the love that God hath to us.

God is love;

and he that dwelleth in love dwelleth in God,

and God in him.

Herein is our love made perfect,

that we may have boldness in the day of judgment:

because as he is, so are we in this world.

There is no fear in love;

but perfect love casteth our fear: because fear hath torment.

He that feareth is not made perfect in love.

I John 4

IN THESE DAYS of catastrophic change and calamitous uncertainty, is there any man who does not experience the depression and bewilderment of crippling fear, which, like a nagging hound of hell, pursues our every footstep?

Everywhere men and women are confronted by fears that often appear in strange disguises and a variety of wardrobes. Haunted by the possibility of bad health, we detect in every meaningless symptom an evidence of disease. Troubled by the fact that days and years pass so quickly, we dose ourselves with drugs which promise eternal youth. If we are physically vigorous, we become so concerned by the prospect that our personalities may collapse that we develop an inferiority complex and stumble through life with a feeling of insecurity, a lack of self-confidence, and a sense of impending failure. A fear of what life may bring encourages some persons to wander aimlessly along the frittering road of excessive drink and sexual promiscuity. Almost without being aware of the change, many people have permitted fear to transform the sunrise of love and peace into a sunset of inner depression.

When unchecked, fear spawns a whole brood of phobias—fear of water, high places, closed rooms, darkness, loneliness, among others—and such an accumulation culminates in phobiaphobia or the fear of fear itself.

Especially common in our highly competi-

CHAPTER XIV

ANTIDOTES FOR FEAR

tive society are economic fears, from which, Karen Horney says, come most of the psychological problems of our age. Captains of industry are tormented by the possible failure of their business and the capriciousness of the stock market. Employees are plagued by the prospect of unemployment and the consequences of an ever-increasing automation.

And consider, too, the multiplication in our day of religious and ontological fears, which include the fear of death and racial annihilation. The advent of the atomic age, which should have ushered in an era of plenty and of prosperity, has lifted the fear of death to morbid proportions. The terrifying spectacle of nuclear warfare has put Hamlet's words, "To be or not to be,"[78] on millions of trembling lips. Witness our frenzied efforts to construct fallout shelters. As though even these offer sanctuary from an H-bomb attack! Witness the agonizing desperation of our petitions that our government increase the nuclear stockpile. But our fanatical quest to maintain "a balance of terror" only increases our fear and leaves nations on tiptoes lest some diplomatic *faux pas* ignite a frightful holocaust.

Realizing that fear drains a man's energy and depletes his resources, Emerson wrote, "He has not learned the lesson of life who does not every day surmount a fear."[79]

But I do not mean to suggest that we should seek to eliminate fear altogether from human life. Were this humanly possible, it would be practically undesirable. Fear is the elemental alarm system of the human organism which warns of approaching dangers and without which man could not have survived in either the primitive or modern worlds. Fear, moreover, is a powerfully creative force. Every great invention and intellectual advance represents a desire to escape from some dreaded circumstance or condition. The fear of darkness led to the discovery of the secret of electricity. The fear of pain led to the marvelous advances of medical science. The fear of ignorance was one reason that man built great institutions of learning. The fear of war was one of the forces behind the birth of the United Nations. Angelo Patri has rightly said, "Education consists in being afraid at the right time." If man were to lose his capacity to fear, he would be deprived of his capacity to grow, invent, and create. So in a sense fear is normal, necessary, and creative.

But we must remember that abnormal fears are emotionally ruinous and psychologically destructive. To illustrate the difference between normal and abnormal fear, Sigmund Freud spoke of a person who was quite properly afraid of snakes in the heart of an African jungle and of another person who neurotically feared that snakes were under the carpet in his city apartment. Psychologists say that normal children are born with only two fears—the fear of falling and the fear of loud noises—and that all others are environmentally acquired. Most of these acquired fears are snakes under the carpet.

It is to such fears that we usually refer when we speak of getting rid of fear. But this is only a part of the story. Normal fear protects us; abnormal fear paralyzes us. Normal fear motivates us to improve our individual and collective welfare; abnormal fear constantly poisons and distorts our inner lives. Our problem is not to be rid of fear but rather to harness and master it. How may it be mastered?

ONE

First, we must unflinchingly face our fears and honestly ask ourselves why we are afraid. This confrontation will, to some measure, grant us power. We shall never be cured of fear by escapism or repression, for the more we attempt to ignore and repress our fears, the more we multiply our inner conflicts.

By looking squarely and honestly at our fears we learn that many of them are residues of some childhood need or apprehension. Here, for instance, is a person haunted by a fear of death or the thought of punishment in the afterlife, who discovers that he has unconsciously projected into the whole of reality the childhood experience of being punished by parents, locked in a room, and seemingly deserted. Or here is a man plagued by the fear of inferiority and social rejection, who discovers that rejection in childhood by a self-centered mother and a preoccupied father left him with a self-defeating sense of inadequacy and a repressed bitterness toward life.

By bringing our fears to the forefront of consciousness, we may find them to be more imaginary than real. Some of them will turn out to be snakes under the carpet.

And let us also remember that, more often than not, fear involves the misuse of the imagination. When we get our fears into the open, we may laugh at some of them, and this is good. One psychiatrist said, "Ridicule is the master cure for fear and anxiety."

TWO

Second, we can master fear through one of the supreme virtues known to man: courage. Plato considered courage to be an element of the soul which bridges the cleavage between reason and desire. Aristotle thought of courage as the affirmation of man's essential nature. Thomas Aquinas said that courage is the strength of mind capable of conquering whatever threatens the attainment of the highest good.

Courage, therefore, is the power of the mind to overcome fear. Unlike anxiety, fear has a definite object which may be faced, analyzed, attacked, and, if need be, endured. How often the object of our fear is fear itself! In his *Journal* Henry David Thoreau wrote, "Nothing is so much to be feared as fear." Centuries earlier, Epictetus wrote, "For it is not death or hardship that is a fearful thing, but the fear of hardship and death."[80] Courage takes the fear produced by a definite object into itself and thereby conquers the fear involved. Paul Tillich has written, "Courage is self-affirmation 'in spite of' . . . that which tends to hinder the self from affirming itself." It is self-affirmation in spite of death and nonbeing, and he who is courageous takes the fear of death into his self-affirmation and acts upon it. This courageous self-affirmation, which is surely a remedy for fear, is not selfishness, for self-affirmation includes both a proper self-love and a properly propositioned love of others. Erich Fromm has shown in convincing terms that the right kind of self-love and the right kind of love of others are interdependent.

Courage, the determination not to be over-whelmed by any object, however frightful, enables us to stand up to any fear. Many of our fears are not mere snakes under the carpet. Trouble is a reality in this strange medley of life, dangers lurk within the circumference of every action, accidents do occur, bad health is an ever-threatening possibility, and death is a stark, grim, and inevitable fact of human experience. Evil and pain in this conundrum of life are close to each of us, and we do both ourselves and our neighbors a great disservice when we attempt to prove that there is nothing in this world of which we should be frightened. These forces that threaten to negate life must be challenged by courage, which is the power of life to affirm itself in spite of life's ambiguities. This requires the exercise of a creative will that enables us to hew out a stone of hope from a mountain of despair.

Courage and cowardice are antithetical. Courage is an inner resolution to go forward in spite of obstacles and frightening situations; cowardice is a submissive surrender to circumstance. Courage breeds creative self-affirmation; cowardice produces destructive self-abnegation. Courage faces fear and thereby masters it; cowardice represses fear and is thereby mastered by it. Courageous men never lose the zest for living even though their life situation is zestless; cowardly men, overwhelmed by the uncertainties of life, lose the will to live. We must constantly build dykes of courage to hold back the flood of fear.

THREE

Third, fear is mastered through love. The

New Testament affirms, "There is no fear in love; but perfect love casteth out fear." The kind of love which led Christ to a cross and kept Paul unembittered amid the angry torrents of persecution is not soft, anemic, and sentimental. Such love confronts evil without flinching and shows in our popular parlance an infinite capacity "to take it." Such love overcomes the world even from a rough-hewn cross against the skyline.

But does love have a relationship to our modern fear of war, economic displacement, and racial injustice? Hate is rooted in fear, and the only cure for fear-hate is love. Our deteriorating international situation is shot through with the lethal darts of fear. Russia fears America, and America fears Russia. Likewise China and India, and the Israelis and the Arabs. These fears include another nation's aggression, scientific and technological supremacy, and economic power, and our own loss of status and power. Is not fear one of the major causes of war? We say that war is a consequence of hate, but close scrutiny reveals this sequence: first fear, then hate, then war, and finally deeper hatred. Were a nightmarish nuclear war to engulf our world, the cause would be not so much that one nation hated another, but that both nations feared each other.

What method has the sophisticated ingenuity of modern man employed to deal with the fear of war? We have armed ourselves to the nth degree. The West and the East have engaged in a fever-pitched arms race. Expenditures for defense have risen to mountainous proportions, and weapons of destruction have been assigned priority over all other human endeavors. The nations have believed that greater armaments will cast out fear. But alas! they have produced greater fear. In these turbulent, panic-stricken days we are once more reminded of the judicious words of old, "Perfect love casteth out fear." Not arms, but love, understanding, and organized goodwill can cast out fear. Only disarmament, based on good faith, will make mutual trust a living reality.

Our own problem of racial injustice must be solved by the same formula. Racial segregation is buttressed by such irrational fears as loss of preferred economic privilege, altered social status, intermarriage, and adjustment to new situations. Through sleepless nights and haggard days numerous white people attempt to combat these corroding fears by diverse methods. By following the path of escape, some seek to ignore the question of race relations and to close their mind to the issues involved. Others placing their faith in such legal maneuvers as interposition and nullification, counsel massive resistance. Still others hope to drown their fear by engaging in acts of violence and meanness toward their Negro brethren. But how futile are all these remedies! Instead of eliminating fear, they instill deeper and more pathological fears that leave the victims inflicted with strange psychoses and peculiar cases of paranoia. Neither repression, massive resistance, nor aggressive violence will cast out the fear of integration; only love and goodwill can do that.

If our white brothers are to master fear, they must depend not only on their commitment to Christian love but also on the Christlike love which the Negro generates toward them. Only through our adherence to love and nonviolence will the fear in the white community be mitigated. A guilt-ridden white minority fears that if the Negro attains power, he will without restraint or pity act to revenge the accumulated injustices and brutality of the years. A parent, who has continually mistreated his son, suddenly realizes that he is now taller than the parent. Will the son use his new physical power to repay for all of the blows of the past?

Once a helpless child, the Negro has now grown politically, culturally, and economically. Many white men fear retaliation. The Negro must show them that they have nothing to fear, for the Negro forgives and is willing to forget the past. *The Negro must convince the white man that he seeks justice for both himself and the white man.* A mass movement exercising love and nonviolence and demonstrating power under discipline should convince the white community that were such a movement to attain strength its power would be used creatively and not vengefully.

What then is the cure of this morbid fear of integration? We know the cure. God help us to achieve it! Love casts out fear.

This truth is not without a bearing on our personal anxieties. We are afraid of the superiority of other people, of failure, and of the scorn or disapproval of those whose opinions we most value. Envy, jealousy, a lack of self-confidence, a feeling of insecurity, and a haunting sense of inferiority are all rooted in fear. We do not envy people and then fear them; first we fear them and subsequently we become jealous of them. Is there a cure for these annoying fears that pervert our personal lives? Yes, a deep and abiding commitment to the way of love. "Perfect love casteth out fear."

Hatred and bitterness can never cure the disease of fear; only love can do that. Hatred paralyzes life; love releases it. Hatred confuses life; love harmonizes it. Hatred darkens life; love illumines it.

FOUR

Fourth, fear is mastered through faith. A common source of fear is an awareness of deficient resources and of a consequent inadequacy for life. All too many people attempt to fade the tensions of life with inadequate spiritual resources. When vacationing in Mexico, Mrs. King and I wished to go deep-sea fishing. For reasons of economy, we rented an old and poorly equipped boat. We gave this little thought until, ten miles from shore, the clouds lowered and howling winds blew. Then we became paralyzed with fear, for we knew our boat was deficient. Multitudes of people are in a similar situation. Heavy winds and weak boats explain their fear.

Many of our abnormal fears can be dealt with by the skills of psychiatry, a relatively new discipline pioneered by Sigmund Freud, which investigates the subconscious drives of men and seeks to discover how and why fundamental energies are diverted into neurotic channels. Psychiatry helps us to look candidly at our inner selves and to search out the causes of our failures and fears. But much of our fearful living encompasses a realm where the service of psychiatry is ineffectual unless the psychiatrist is a man of religious faith. For our trouble is simply that we attempt to confront fear without faith; we sail through the stormy seas of life without adequate spiritual boats. One of the leading physicians and psychiatrists in America has said, "The only known cure for fear is faith."

Abnormal fears and phobias that are expressed in neurotic anxiety may be cured by psychiatry; but the fear of death, nonbeing, and nothingness, expressed in existential anxiety, may be cured only by a positive religious faith.

A positive religious faith does not offer an illusion that we shall be exempt from pain and suffering, nor does it imbue us with the idea that life is a drama of unalloyed comfort and untroubled ease. Rather, it instills us with the inner equilibrium needed to face strains, burdens, and fears that inevitably come, and assures us that the universe is trustworthy and that God is concerned.

Irreligion, on the other hand, would have us believe that we are orphans cast into the terrifying immensities of space in a universe that is without purpose or intelligence. Such a view drains courage and exhausts the energies of men. In his *Confession* Tolstoi wrote concerning the aloneness and emptiness he felt before his conversion:

> There was a period in my life when everything seemed to be crumbling, the very foundations of my convictions were beginning to give way, and I felt myself going to pieces. There was no sustaining influence in my life and there was no God there, and so every night before I went to sleep, I made sure that there was no rope in my room lest I be tempted during the night to hang myself from the rafters of my room; and I stopped from going out shooting lest I be tempted to put a quick end to my life and to my misery.

Like so many people, Tolstoi at that stage of his life lacked the sustaining influence which comes from the conviction that this universe is guided by a benign Intelligence whose infinite love embraces all mankind.

Religion endows us with the conviction that we are not alone in this vast, uncertain universe. Beneath and above the shifting sands of time, the uncertainties that darken our days, and the vicissitudes that cloud our nights is a wise and loving God. This universe is not a tragic expression of meaningless chaos but a marvelous display of orderly cosmos—"The Lord by wisdom hath founded the earth; by understanding hath he established the heavens."[81] Man is not a wisp of smoke from a limitless smoldering, but a child of God created "a little lower than the angels."[82] Above the manyness of time stands the one eternal God, with wisdom to guide us, strength to protect us, and love to keep us. His boundless love supports and contains us as a mighty ocean contains and supports the tiny drops of every wave. With a surging fullness he is forever moving toward us, seeking to fill the little creeks and bays of our lives with unlimited resources. This is religion's everlasting diapason, its eternal answer to the enigma of existence. Any man who finds this cosmic sustenance can walk the highways of life without the fatigue of pessimism and the weight of morbid fears.

Herein lies the answer to the neurotic fear of death that plagues so many of our lives. Let us face the fear that the atomic bomb has aroused with the faith that we can never travel beyond the arms of the Divine. Death is inevitable. It is a democracy for all of the people, not an aristocracy for some of the people—kings die and beggars die; young men die and old men die; learned men die and ignorant men die. We need not fear it. The God who brought our whirling planet from primal vapor and has led the human pilgrimage for lo these many centuries can most assuredly lead us through death's dark night into the bright daybreak of eternal life. His will is too perfect and his purposes are too extensive to be contained in the limited receptacle of time and the narrow walls of earth. Death is not the ultimate evil; the ultimate evil is to be outside God's love. We need not join the mad rush to purchase an earthly fallout shelter. God is our eternal fallout shelter.

Jesus knew that nothing could separate man from the love of God. Listen to his majestic words:

> Fear them not therefore: for there is nothing covered, that shall

not be revealed; and hid, that shall not be known. . . . And fear not them which kill the body, but are not able to kill the soul: but rather fear him which is able to destroy both soul and body in hell. Are not two sparrows sold for a farthing? and one of them shall not fall on the ground without your Father. But the very hairs of your head are all numbered. Fear ye not therefore, ye are of more value than many sparrows.[83]

Man, for Jesus, is not mere flotsam and jetsam in the river of life, but he is a child of God. Is it not unreasonable to assume that God, whose creative activity is expressed in an awareness of a sparrow's fall and the number of hairs on a man's head, excludes from his encompassing love the life of man itself? The confidence that God is mindful of the individual is of tremendous value in dealing with the disease of fear, for it gives us a sense of worth, of belonging, and of at-homeness in the universe.

One of the most dedicated participants in the bus protest in Montgomery, Alabama, was an elderly Negro whom we affectionately called Mother Pollard. Although poverty-stricken and uneducated, she was amazingly intelligent and possessed a deep understanding of the meaning of the movement. After having walked for several weeks, she was asked if she were tired. With ungrammatical profundity, she answered, "My feets is tired, but my soul is rested."

On a particular Monday evening, following a tension-packed week which included being arrested and receiving numerous threatening telephone calls, I spoke at a mass meeting. I attempted to convey an overt impression of strength and courage, although I was inwardly depressed and fear-stricken. At the end of the meeting, Mother Pollard came to the front of the church and said, "Come here, son." I immediately went to her and hugged her affectionately. "Something is wrong with you," she said. "You didn't talk strong tonight." Seeking further to disguise my fears, I retorted, "Oh no, Mother Pollard, nothing is wrong. I am feeling as fine as ever." But her insight was discerning. "Now you can't fool me," she said. "I knows something is wrong. Is it that we ain't doing things to please you? Or is it that the white folks is bothering you?" Before I could respond, she looked directly into my eyes and said, "I don told you we is with you all the way." Then her face became radiant and she said in words of quiet certainty, "But even if we ain't with you, God's gonna take care of you." As she spoke these consoling words, everything in me quivered and quickened with the pulsing tremor of raw energy.

Since that dreary night in 1956, Mother Pollard has passed on to glory and I have known very few quiet days. I have been tortured without and tormented within by the raging fires of tribulation. I have been forced to muster what strength and courage I have to withstand howling winds of pain and jostling storms of adversity. But as the years have unfolded the eloquently simple words of Mother Pollard have come back again and again to give light and peace and guidance to my troubled soul. "God's gonna take care of you."

This faith transforms the whirlwind of despair into a warm and reviving breeze of hope. The words of a motto which a generation ago were commonly found on the wall in the homes of devout persons need to be etched on our hearts:

> Fear knocked at the door.
> Faith answered.
> There was no one there.

CHAPTER XV

THE ANSWER TO A

And when they were come to the multitude,
there came to him a certain man, kneeling down to him, and saying,

Lord, have mercy on my son: for he is lunatick, and sore vexed:
for ofttimes he falleth into the fire, and oft into the water.

And I brought him to thy disciples, and they could not cure him.

Then Jesus answered and said,
O faithless and perverse generation, how long shall I be with you?
how long shall I suffer you? bring him hither to me.

And Jesus rebuked the devil; and he departed out of him:
and the child was cured from that very hour.

Then came the disciples to Jesus apart, and said,
Why could not we cast him out?

And Jesus said unto them,
Because of your unbelief:
for verily I say unto you, If ye have faith as a grain of mustard seed,
ye shall say unto this mountain, Remove hence to yonder place;
and it shall remove; and nothing shall be impossible unto you.

Matthew 17

PERPLEXING QUESTION

HUMAN LIFE through the centuries has been characterized by man's persistent efforts to remove evil from the earth. Seldom has man thoroughly adjusted himself to evil, for in spite of his rationalizations, compromises, and alibis, he knows the "is" is not the "ought" and the actual is not the possible. Though the evils of sensuality, selfishness, and cruelty often rise aggressively in his soul, something within tells him that they are intruders and reminds him of his higher destiny and more noble allegiance. Man's hankering after the demonic is always disturbed by his longing for the divine. As he seeks to adjust to the demands of time, he knows that eternity is his ultimate habitat. When man comes to himself, he knows that evil is a foreign invader that must be driven from the native soils of his soul before he can achieve moral and spiritual dignity.

But the problem that has always hampered man has been his inability to conquer evil by his own power. In pathetic amazement, he asks, "Why can I not cast it out? Why can I not remove this evil from my life?"

This agonizing, perplexing question recalls an event that occurred immediately after Christ's transfiguration. Coming down from the mountain, Jesus found a small boy who was in wild convulsions. His disciples had tried desperately to cure the unhappy child, but the more they labored to heal him the more they realized their own inadequacies and the pathetic limitations of their power. When they were about to give up in despair, their Lord appeared on the scene. After the father of the child told Jesus of the failure of the disciples, Jesus "rebuked the devil; and he departed out of him: and the child was cured from that very hour." When the disciples were later alone with their Master, they asked, "Why could not we cast him out?" They wanted an explanation for their obvious limitations. Jesus said their failure was caused by their unbelief: "If ye have faith as a grain of mustard seed, ye shall say unto this mountain, Remove hence to yonder place; and it shall remove; and nothing shall be impossible unto you." They had tried to do by themselves what could be done only after they had so surrendered their natures to God that his strength flowed freely through them.

ONE

How can evil be cast out? Men have usually pursued two paths to eliminate evil and thereby save the world. The first calls upon man to remove evil through his own power and ingenuity in the strange conviction that by thinking, inventing, and governing, he will at last conquer the nagging forces of evil. Give people a fair chance and a decent education, and they will save themselves. This idea, sweeping across the modern world like a plague, has ushered God out and escorted man in and has substituted human ingenuity for divine guidance. Some people suggest that this concept was introduced during the Renaissance when reason dethroned religion, or later when Darwin's *Origin of Species* replaced belief in creation by the theory of evolution, or when the industrial revolution turned the hearts of men to material comforts and physical conveniences. At any rate, the idea of the adequacy of man to solve the evils of history captured the minds of people, giving rise to the easy optimism of the nineteenth century, the doctrine of inevitable progress, Rousseau's maxim of "the original goodness of human nature," and Condorcet's conviction that by reason alone the whole world would soon be cleansed of crime, poverty, and war.

Armed with this growing faith in the capability of reason and science, modern man set out to change the world. He turned his attention from God and the human soul to the outer world and its possibilities. He observed, analyzed, and explored. The laboratory became man's sanctuary and scientists his priests and prophets. A modern humanist confidently affirmed:

> The future is not with the churches but with the laboratories, not with prophets but with scientists, not with piety but with efficiency. Man is at last becoming aware that he alone is responsible for the realization of the world of his dreams, that he has within himself the power for its achievement.

Man has subpoenaed nature to appear before the judgment seat of scientific investigation. None doubt that man's work in the scientific laboratories has brought unbelievable advances in power and comfort, producing machines that think and gadgets that soar majestically through the skies, stand impressively on the land, and move with stately dignity on the seas.

But in spite of these astounding new scientific developments, the old evils continue and the age of reason has been transformed into an age of terror. Selfishness and hatred have not vanished with an enlargement of our educational system and an extension of our legislative policies. A once optimistic generation now asks in utter bewilderment, "Why could not we cast it out?"

The answer is rather simple: Man by his own power can never cast evil from the world. The humanist's hope is an illusion, based on too great an optimism concerning the inherent goodness of human nature.

I would be the last to condemn the thousands of sincere and dedicated people outside the churches who have labored unselfishly through various humanitarian movements to cure the world of social evils, for I would rather a man be a committed humanist than an uncommitted Christian. But so many of these dedicated persons, seeking salvation within the human context, have become understandably pessimistic and disillusioned, because their efforts are based on a kind of self-delusion which ignores fundamental facts about our mortal nature.

Nor would I minimize the importance of science and the great contributions which have come in the wake of the Renaissance. These have lifted us from the stagnating valleys of superstition and half-truth to the sunlit mountains of creative analysis and objective appraisal. The unquestioned authority of the church in scientific matters needed to be freed from paralyzing obscurantism, antiquated notions, and shameful inquisitions. But the exalted Renaissance optimism, while attempting to free the mind of man, forgot about man's capacity for sin.

TWO

The second idea for removing evil from the world stipulates that if man waits submissively upon the Lord, in his own good time God alone will redeem the world. Rooted in a pessimistic doctrine of human nature, this idea, which eliminates completely the capability of sinful man to do anything, was prominent in the Reformation, that great spiritual movement which gave birth to the Protestant concern for moral and spiritual freedom and served as a necessary corrective for a corrupt and stagnant medieval church. The doctrines of justification by faith and the priesthood of all believers are towering principles which we as Protestants must forever affirm, but the Reformation doctrine of human nature overstressed the corruption of man. The Renaissance was too optimistic, and the Reformation too pessimistic. The former so concentrated on the goodness of man that it overlooked his capacity for evil; the latter so concentrated on the wickedness of man that it overlooked his capacity for goodness. While rightly affirming the sinfulness of human nature and man's incapacity to save himself, the Reformation wrongly affirmed that the image of God had been completely erased from man.

This led to the Calvinistic concept of the total depravity of man and to a resurrection of the terrible idea of infant damnation. So depraved is human nature, said the doctrinaire Calvinist, that if a baby dies without baptism he will burn forever in hell. Certainly this carries the idea of man's sinfulness too far.

This lopsided Reformation theology has often emphasized a purely otherworldly religion, which stresses the utter hopelessness of this world and calls upon the individual to concentrate on preparing his soul for the world to come. By ignoring the need for social reform, religion is divorced from the mainstream of human life. A pulpit committee listed as the first essential qualification for a new minister: "He must preach the true gospel and not talk about social issues." This is a blueprint for a dangerously irrelevant church where people assemble to hear only pious platitudes.

By disregarding the fact that the gospel deals with man's body as well as with his soul, such a one-sided emphasis creates a tragic dichotomy between the sacred and the secular. To be worthy of its New Testament origin, the church must seek to transform both individual lives and the social situation that brings to many people anguish of spirit and cruel bondage.

The idea that man expects God to do everything leads inevitably to a callous misuse of prayer. For if God does everything, man then asks him for anything, and God becomes little more than a "cosmic bellhop" who is summoned for every trivial need. Or God is considered so omnipotent and man so powerless that prayer is a substitute for work and intelligence. A man said to me, "I believe in integration, but I know it will not come until God wants it to come. You Negroes should stop protesting and start praying." I am certain we need to pray for God's help and guidance in this integration struggle, but we are gravely misled if we think the struggle will be won only by prayer. God, who gave us minds for thinking and bodies for working, would defeat his own purpose if he permitted us to obtain through prayer what may come through work and intelligence. Prayer is a marvelous and necessary supplement of our feeble efforts, but it is a dangerous substitute. When Moses strove to lead the Israelites to the Promised Land, God made it clear that he would not do for them what they could do for themselves. "And the Lord said unto Moses, Wherefore criest thou unto me? speak unto the children of Israel, that they go forward."[84]

We must pray earnestly for peace, but we must also work vigorously for disarmament and the suspension of weapon testing. We must use our minds as rigorously to plan for peace as we have used them to plan for war. We must pray with unceasing passion for racial justice, but we must also use our minds to develop a program, organize ourselves into mass nonviolent action, and employ every resource of our bodies and souls to bring an end to racial injustice. We must pray unrelentingly for economic justice, but we must also work diligently to bring into being those social changes that make for a better distribution of wealth within our nation and in the undeveloped countries of the world.

Does not all of this reveal the fallacy of thinking that God will cast evil from the earth, even if man does nothing except to sit complacently by the wayside? No prodigious thunderbolt from heaven will blast away evil. No mighty army of angels will descend to force men to do what their wills resist. The Bible portrays God, not as an omnipotent czar who makes all decisions for his subjects nor as a cosmic tyrant who with gestapo-like methods invades the inner lives of men, but rather as a loving Father who gives to his children such abundant blessings as they may be willing to receive. Always man must do something. "Stand upon thy feet," says God to Ezekiel, "and I will speak unto you."[85] Man is no helpless invalid left in a valley of total depravity until God pulls him out. Man is rather an upstanding human being whose vision has been impaired by the cataracts of sin and whose soul has been weakened by the virus of pride, but there is sufficient vision left for him to lift his eyes unto the hills, and there remains enough of God's image for him to turn his weak and sin-battered life toward the Great Physician, the curer of the ravages of sin.

The real weakness of the idea that God will do everything is its false conception of both God and man. It makes God so absolutely sovereign that man is absolutely helpless. It makes man so absolutely depraved that he can do nothing but wait on God. It sees the world as so contaminated with sin that God totally transcends it and touches it only here and there through a mighty invasion. This view ends up with a God who is a despot and not a Father. It ends up with such a pessimism concerning human nature that it leaves man little more than a helpless worm crawling through the morass of an evil world. But man is neither totally depraved, nor is God an almighty dictator. We must surely affirm the majesty and sovereignty of God, but this should not lead us to believe that God is an Almighty Monarch who will impose his will upon us and deprive us of the freedom to choose what is good or what is not good. He will not thrust himself upon us nor force us to stay home when our minds are bent on journeying to some degrading far country. But he follows us in love, and when we come to ourselves and turn our tired feet back to the Father's house, he stands waiting with outstretched arms of forgiveness.

Therefore we must never feel that God will, through some breathtaking miracle or a wave of the hand, cast evil out of the world. As long as we believe this we will pray unanswerable prayers and ask God to do things that he will never do. The belief that God will do everything for man is as untenable as the belief that man can do everything for himself. It, too, is based on a lack of faith. We must learn that to expect God to do everything while we do nothing is not faith, but superstition.

THREE

What, then, is the answer to life's perplexing question, "How can evil be cast out of our individual and collective lives?" If the world is not to be purified by God alone nor by man alone, who will do it?

The answer is found in an idea which is distinctly different from the two we have discussed, for neither God nor man will individually bring the world's salvation. Rather, both man and God, made one in a marvelous unity of purpose through an overflowing love as the free gift of himself on the part of God and by perfect obedience and receptivity on the part of man, can transform the old into the new and drive out the deadly cancer of sin.

The principle which opens the door for God to work through man is faith. This is what the disciples lacked when they desperately tried to remove the nagging evil from the body of the sick child. Jesus reminded them that they had been attempting to do by themselves what could be done only when their lives were open receptacles, as it were, into which God's strength could be freely poured.

Two types of faith in God are clearly set forth in the Scriptures. One may be called the mind's faith, wherein the intellect assents to a belief that God exists. The other may be referred to as the heart's faith, whereby the whole man is involved in a trusting act of self-surrender. To know God, a man must possess this latter type of faith, for the mind's faith is directed toward a theory, but the heart's faith is centered in a Person. Gabriel Marcel claims that faith is *believing in,* not *believing that.* It is "opening a credit; which puts me at the disposal of the one in whom I believe." When I believe, he says, "I rally to with that sort of interior gathering of oneself which the act of rallying implies." Faith is the opening of all sides and at every level of one's life to the divine inflow.

This is what the Apostle Paul emphasized in his doctrine of salvation by faith. For him, faith is man's capacity to accept God's willingness through Christ to rescue us from the bondage of sin. In his magnanimous love, God freely offers to do for us what we cannot do for ourselves. Our humble and open-hearted acceptance is faith. So by faith we are saved. Man filled with God and God operating through man bring unbelievable changes in our individual and social lives.

Social evils have trapped multitudes of men in a dark and murky corridor where there is no exit sign and plunged others into a dark abyss of psychological fatalism. These deadly, paralyzing evils can be removed by a humanity perfectly united through obedience with God. Moral victory will come as God fills man and man opens his life by faith to God, even as the gulf opens to the overflowing waters of the river. Racial justice, a genuine possibility in our nation and in the world, will come neither by our frail and often misguided efforts nor by God imposing his will on wayward men, but when enough people open their lives to God and allow him to pour his triumphant, divine energy into their souls. Our age-old and noble dream of a world of peace may yet become a reality, but it will come neither by man working alone nor by God destroying the wicked schemes of men, but when men so open their lives to God that he may fill them with love, mutual respect, understanding, and goodwill. Social salvation will come only through man's willing acceptance of God's mighty gift.

Let me apply what I have been saying to our personal lives. Many of you know what it means to struggle with sin. Year by year you were aware that a terrible sin—slavery to drink, perhaps, or untruthfulness, impurity, selfishness—was taking possession of your life. As the years unfolded and the vice widened its landmarks on your soul, you knew that it was an unnatural intruder. You may have thought, "One day I shall drive this evil out. I know it is destroying my character and embarrassing my family." At last you determined to purge yourself of the evil by making a New Year's resolution. Do you remember your surprise and disappointment when you discovered, three hundred and sixty-five days later, that your most sincere efforts had not banished the old habit from your life? In complete amazement you asked, "Why could not I cast it out?"

In despair you decided to take your problem to God, but instead of asking him to work through you, you said, "God, you must solve this problem for me. I can't do anything about it." But days and months later the evil was still with you. God would not cast it out, for he never removes sin without the cordial co-operation of the sinner. No problem is solved when we idly wait for God to undertake full responsibility.

One cannot remove an evil habit by mere resolution nor by simply calling on God to do the job, but only as he surrenders himself and becomes an instrument of God. We shall be delivered from the accumulated weight of evil only when we permit the energy of God to come into our souls.

God has promised to co-operate with us when we seek to cast evil from our lives and become true children of his divine will. "If any one is in Christ," says Paul, "he is a new creation; the old has passed away, behold, the new has come."[86] If any man is in Christ, he is a new person, his old self has gone, and he becomes a divinely transformed son of God.

One of the great glories of the gospel is that Christ has transformed nameless prodigals. He turned a Simon of sand into a Peter of rock. He changed a persecuting Saul into an Apostle Paul. He converted a lust-feasted Augustine into a St. Augustine. The measured words of Leo Tolstoi's confession in *My Religion* reflect an experience many have shared:

> Five years ago faith came to me; I believed in the doctrine of Jesus, and my whole life underwent a sudden transformation. What I had once wished for I wished for no longer, and I began to desire what I had never desired before. What had once appeared to me right now became wrong, and the wrong of the past I beheld as right. . . . My life and my desires were completely changed; good and evil interchanged meanings.

Herein we find the answer to a perplexing question. Evil can be cast out, not by man alone nor by a dictatorial God who invades our lives, but when we open the door and invite God through Christ to enter. "Behold, I stand at the door, and knock: if any man hear my voice, and open the door, I will come in to him, and will sup with him, and he with me."[87] God is too courteous to break open the door, but when we open it in faith believing, a divine and human confrontation will transform our sin-ruined lives into radiant personalities.

CHAPTER XVI

PAUL'S LETTER TO AMERICAN CHRISTIANS

I would like to share with you an imaginary letter from the pen of the Apostle Paul. The postmark reveals that it comes from the port city of Troas. On opening the letter I discovered that it was written in Greek rather than in English. After working assiduously with the translation for several weeks, I think I have now deciphered its true meaning. If the content of this epistle sounds strangely Kingian instead of Paulinian, attribute it to my lack of complete objectivity rather than Paul's lack of clarity. Here is the letter as it stands before me.

PAUL, CALLED TO BE an apostle of Jesus Christ by the will of God, to you who are in America, grace be unto you, and peace, from God our Father, through our Lord and Savior, Jesus Christ. For many years I have longed to see you. I have heard so much about you and of what you are doing. News has come to me regarding the fascinating and astounding advances that you have made in the scientific realm. I have learned of your dashing subways and flashing airplanes. Through your scientific genius you have dwarfed distance and placed time in chains. You have made it possible to eat breakfast in Paris, France, and lunch in New York City.

I have also heard of your skyscraping buildings with their prodigious towers rising heavenward. I am told of your great medical advances and the curing of many dread plagues and diseases, thereby prolonging your lives and offering greater security and physical well-being. All of that is marvelous. You can do so many things in your day that I could not do in the Greco-Roman world of my day. You travel distances in a single day that in my generation required three months. That is wonderful. What tremendous strides in the areas of scientific and technological development you have made!

But, America, I wonder whether your moral and spiritual progress has been commensurate with your scientific progress. It appears to me that your moral progress lags behind your scientific progress, your mentality outdistances your morality, and your civilization outshines your culture. How much of your modern life can be summarized in the words of your poet Thoreau: "Improved means to an unimproved end." Through your scientific genius you have made of the world a neighborhood, but you have failed to employ your moral and spiritual genius to make of it a brotherhood. So, America, the atomic bomb you have to fear today is not merely that deadly weapon which can be dropped from an airplane on the heads of millions of people, but that atomic bomb which lies in the hearts of men, capable of exploding into the most staggering hate and the most devastating selfishness. Therefore I would urge you to keep your moral advances abreast of your scientific advances.

I find it necessary to remind you of the responsibility laid upon you to represent the ethical principles of Christianity amid a time that popularly disregards them. That was a task laid on me. I understand that there are many Christians in America who give their ultimate allegiance to man-made systems and customs. They are afraid to be different. Their great concern is to be accepted socially. They live by some such principle as this: "Everybody is doing it, so it must be all right." For so many of you morality merely reflects group consensus. In your modern sociological lingo, the mores are accepted as the right ways. You have unconsciously come to believe that what is right is determined by Gallup polls.

American Christians, I must say to you what I wrote to the Roman Christians years ago: "Be not conformed to this world: but be ye transformed by the renewing of your mind."[88] You have a dual citizenry. You live both in time and eternity. Your highest loyalty is to God, and not to the mores or the folkways, the state or the nation, or any man-made institution. If any earthly institution or custom conflicts with God's will, it is your Christian duty to oppose it. You must never allow the transitory, evanescent demands of man-made institutions to take precedence over the eternal demands of the Almighty God. In a time when men are surrendering the high values of the faith you must cling to them, and despite the pressure of an alien generation preserve them for children yet unborn. You must be willing to challenge unjust mores, to champion unpopular causes, and to buck the status quo. You are called to be the salt of the earth. You are to be the light of the world. You are to be that vitally active leaven in the lump of the nation.

I understand that you have an economic system in America known as capitalism, through which you have accomplished wonders. You have become the richest nation in the world, and you have built the greatest system of production that history has ever known. All of this is marvelous. But, Americans, there is the danger that you will misuse your capitalism. I still contend that the love of money is the root of much evil and may cause a man to become a gross materialist. I am afraid that many among you are more concerned in making money than in accumulating spiritual treasures.

The misuse of capitalism may also lead to tragic exploitation. This has so often happened in your nation. I am told that one-tenth of 1 per cent of the population controls more than 40 per cent of the wealth. America, how often have you taken necessities from the masses and given luxuries to the classes. If you are to be a truly Christian nation, you must solve this problem. You cannot solve it by turning to Communism, for Communism is based on an ethical relativism, a metaphysical materialism, a crippling totalitarianism, and a withdrawal of basic freedom that no Christian can accept. But you can work within the framework of democracy to bring about a better distribution of wealth. You must use your powerful economic resources to eliminate poverty from the earth. God never intended one people to live in superfluous and inordinate wealth, while others know only deadening poverty. God wants all of his children to have the basic necessities of life, and he has left in this universe "enough and to spare" for that purpose.

I would that I might be with you in person, so that I could say to you face to face what I am forced to put down in writing. Oh, how I long to share your fellowship!

Let me say something about the church. Americans, I must remind you, as I have told so many others, that the church is the Body of Christ. When the church is true to its nature, it knows neither division nor disunity. I am told that within American Protestantism there are more than two hundred and fifty denominations. The tragedy is not merely that you have such a multiplicity of denominations, but that many groups claim to possess absolute truth. Such narrow sectarianism destroys the unity of the Body of Christ. God is neither Baptist, Methodist, Presbyterian, nor Episcopalian. God transcends our denominations. If you are to be true witnesses for Christ, you must come to know this, America.

I am happy to hear that there is a growing concern for church unity and ecumenicity in America. I have word that you have organized a National Council of Churches and that most of your major denominations are affiliated with the World Council of Churches. All of this is marvelous. Continue to follow this creative path. Keep these church councils alive and continue to give them your unstinted support. I have the encouraging news that there has been some recent dialogue between Roman Catholics and Protestants. I am told that several Protestant churchmen from your nation accepted Pope John's invitation to be observers at a recent ecumenical council in Rome. This is both a significant and healthy sign. I hope it is the beginning of a development that will bring all Christians closer and closer together.

Another thing that disturbs me about the American church is that you have a white church and a Negro church. How can segregation exist in the true Body of Christ? I am told that there is more integration within the entertaining world and other secular agencies than there is in the Christian church. How appalling this is!

I understand that there are Christians among you who try to find biblical bases to justify segregation and argue that the Negro is inferior by nature. Oh, my friends, this is blasphemy and against everything that the Christian religions stands for. I must repeat what I have said to many Christians before, that in Christ "there is neither Jew nor Greek, there is neither bond nor free, there is neither male nor female: for ye are all one in Christ Jesus."[89] Moreover, I must reiterate the words I uttered on Mars Hill: "God that made the world and all things therein . . . hath made of one blood all nations of men for to dwell on all the face of the earth."[90]

So, Americans, I must urge you to be rid of every aspect of segregation. Segregation is a blatant denial of the unity which we have in Christ. It substitutes an "I-it" relationship for the "I-thou" relationship, and relegates persons to the status of things. It scars the soul and degrades the personality. It inflicts the segregated with a false sense of inferiority, while confirming the segregator in a false estimate of his own superiority. It destroys community and makes brotherhood impossible. The underlying philosophy of Christianity is diametrically opposed to the underlying philosophy of racial segregation.

I praise your Supreme Court for rendering a historic desegregation decision and also persons of goodwill who have accepted this as a great moral victory, but I understand that some brothers have risen up in open defiance and that their legislative halls ring loud with such words as "nullification" and "interposition." Because these brothers have lost the true meaning of democracy and Christianity, I urge each of you to plead patiently with them. With understanding and goodwill, you are obligated to seek to change their attitudes. Let them know that in standing against integration, they are not only opposing the noble precepts of your democracy, but also the eternal edicts of God himself.

I hope the churches of America will play a significant role in conquering segregation. It has always been the responsibility of the church to broaden horizons and challenge the status quo. The church must move out into the arena of social action. First, you must see that the church removes the yoke of segregation from its own body. Then you must seek to make the church increasingly active in social action outside its doors. It must seek to keep channels of communication open between the races. It must take an active stand against the injustices which Negroes confront in housing, education, police protection, and in city and state courts. It must exert its influence in the area of economic justice. As guardian of the moral and spiritual life of the community the church cannot look with indifference upon these glaring evils. If you as Christians will accept the challenge with devotion and valor, you will lead the misguided men of your nation from the darkness of falsehood and fear to the light of truth and love.

May I say just a word to those of you who are the victims of the evil system of segregation. You must continue to work passionately and vigorously for your God-given and constitutional rights. It would be both cowardly and immoral for you patiently to accept injustice. You cannot in good conscience sell your birthright of freedom for a mess of segregated pottage. But as you continue your righteous protest always be sure that you struggle with Christian methods and Christian weapons. Be sure that the means you employ are as pure as the end you seek. Never succumb to the temptation of becoming bitter. As you press on for justice, be sure to move with dignity and discipline, using love as your chief weapon. Let no man pull you so low that you hate him. Always avoid violence. If you sow the seeds of violence in your struggle, unborn generations will reap the whirlwind of social disintegration.

In your struggle for justice, let your oppressor know that you have neither a desire to defeat him nor a desire to get even with him for injustices that he has heaped upon you. Let him know that the festering sore of segregation debilitates the white man as well as the Negro. By having this attitude, you will keep your struggle on high Christian levels.

Many persons realize the urgency of eradicating the evil of segregation. Many Negroes will devote their lives to the cause of freedom, and many white persons of goodwill and strong moral sensitivity will dare to speak for justice. Honesty impels me to admit that such a stand requires a willingness to suffer and sacrifice. Do not despair if you are condemned and persecuted for righteousness' sake. When you testify for truth and justice, you are liable to scorn. Often you will be called an impractical idealist or a dangerous radical. You may even be called a Communist merely because you believe in the brotherhood of man. Sometimes you may be put in jail. If such is the case, you must honorably grace the jail with your presence. It may mean losing a job or social standing with your particular group. Even if physical death is the price that some must pay to free their children from psychological death, then nothing could be more Christian. Do not worry about persecution, American Christians; you must accept this when you stand up for a great principle. I speak with some authority, for my life was a continual round of persecutions. After my conversion I was rejected by the disciples of Jerusalem. Later I was tried for heresy at Jerusalem. I was jailed at Philippi, beaten at Thessalonica, mobbed at Ephesus, and depressed at Athens. I came away from each of these experiences more persuaded than ever that "neither death, nor life, nor angels, nor principalities, nor things present, nor things to come . . . shall . . . separate us from the love of God, which is in Christ Jesus our Lord."[91] The end of life is not to be happy nor to achieve pleasure and avoid pain, but to do the will of God, come what may. I have nothing but praise for those of you who have already stood unflinchingly before threats and intimidation, inconvenience, and unpopularity, arrest and physical violence, to declare the doctrine of the Fatherhood of God and the brotherhood of man. For such noble servants of God there is the consolation of the words of Jesus: "Blessed are ye, when men shall revile you, and persecute you, and shall say all manner of evil against you falsely, for my sake. Rejoice, and be exceeding glad, for great is your reward in heaven: for so persecuted they the prophets which were before you."[92]

I must bring my writing to a close. Silas is waiting to deliver this letter, and I must take leave for Macedonia, from which an urgent plea has come requesting help. But before leaving, I must say to you, as I said to the Church of Corinth, that love is the most durable power in the world. Throughout the centuries men have sought to discover the highest good. This has been the chief quest of ethical philosophy. This was one of the big questions of Greek philosophy. The Epicureans and the Stoics sought to answer it; Plato and Aristotle sought to answer it. What is the *summum bonum* of life? I think I have found the answer, America. I have discovered that the highest good is love. This principle is at the center of the cosmos. It is the great unifying force of life. God is love. He who loves has discovered the clue to the meaning of ultimate reality; he who hates stands in immediate candidacy for nonbeing.

American Christians, you may master the intricacies of the English language and you may possess the eloquence of articulate speech; but even though you speak with the tongues of men and of angels, and have not love, you are like sounding brass or a tinkling cymbal.

You may have the gift of scientific prediction and understand the behavior of molecules, you may break into the storehouse of nature and bring forth many new insights, you may ascend to the heights of academic achievement, so that you have all knowledge, and you may boast of your great institutions of learning and the boundless extent of your degrees; but, devoid of love, all of these mean absolutely nothing.

But even more, Americans, you may give your goods to feed the poor, you may bestow great gifts to charity, and you may tower high in philanthropy, but if you have not love, your charity means nothing. You may even give your body to be burned, and die the death of a martyr, and your spilled blood may be a symbol of honor for generations yet unborn, and thousands may praise you as one of history's supreme heroes; and but even so, if you have not love, your blood is spilled in vain. You must come to see that a man may be self-centered in his self-denial and self-righteous in his self-sacrifice. His generosity may feed his ego and his piety his pride. Without love, benevolence becomes egotism and martyrdom becomes spiritual pride.

The greatest of all virtues is love. Here we find the true meaning of the Christian faith and of the cross. Calvary is a telescope through which we look into the long vista of eternity and see the love of God breaking into time. Out of the hugeness of his generosity God allowed his only-begotten Son to die that we may live. By uniting yourselves with Christ and your brothers through love you will be able to matriculate in the university of eternal life. In a world depending on force, coercive tyranny, and bloody violence, you are challenged to follow the way of love. You will then discover that unarmed love is the most powerful force in all the world.

I must say good-by. Extend my warmest greeting to all the saints in the household of Christ. Be of good comfort; be of one mind; and live in peace.

It is improbable that I will see you in America, but I will meet you in God's eternity. And now unto him who is able to keep us from falling, and lift us from the dark valley of despair to the bright mountain of hope, from the midnight of desperation to the daybreak of joy, to him be power and authority, forever and ever. Amen.

PILGRIMAGE TO NONVIOLENCE

IN MY SENIOR YEAR in theological seminary, I engaged in the exciting reading of various theological theories. Having been raised in a rather strict fundamentalist tradition, I was occasionally shocked when my intellectual journey carried me through new and sometimes complex doctrinal lands, but the pilgrimage was always stimulating, gave me a new appreciation for objective appraisal, and critical analysis, and knocked me out of my dogmatic slumber.

Liberalism provided me with an intellectual satisfaction that I had never found in fundamentalism. I became so enamored of the insights of liberalism that I almost fell into the trap of accepting uncritically everything it encompassed. I was absolutely convinced of the natural goodness of man and the natural power of human reason.

ONE

A basic change in my thinking came when I began to question some of the theories that had been associated with so-called liberal theology. Of course, there are aspects of liberalism that I hope to cherish always: its devotion to the search for truth, its insistence on an open and analytical mind, and its refusal to abandon the best lights of reason. The contribution of liberalism to the philological-historical criticism of biblical literature has been of immeasurable value and should be defended with religious and scientific passion.

But I began to question the liberal doctrine of man. The more I observed the tragedies of history and man's shameful inclination to choose the low road, the more I came to see the depths and strength of sin. My reading of the works of Reinhold Niebuhr made me aware of the complexity of human motives and the reality of sin on every level of man's existence. Moreover, I came to recognize the complexity of man's social involvement and the glaring reality of collective evil. I realized that liberalism had been all too sentimental concerning human nature and that it leaned toward a false idealism.

I also came to see that the superficial optimism of liberalism concerning human nature overlooked the fact that reason is darkened by sin. The more I thought about human nature, the more I saw how our tragic inclination for sin encourages us to rationalize our actions. Liberalism failed to show that reason by itself is little more than an instrument to justify man's defensive ways of thinking. Reason, devoid of the purifying power of faith, can never free itself from distortions and rationalizations.

Although I rejected some aspects of liberalism, I never came to an all-out acceptance of neo-orthodoxy. While I saw neo-orthodoxy as a helpful corrective for a sentimental liberalism, I felt that it did not provide an adequate answer to basic questions. If liberalism was too optimistic concerning human nature, neo-orthodoxy was too pessimistic. Not only on the question of man, but also on other vital issues, the revolt of neo-orthodoxy went too far. In its attempt to preserve the transcendence of God, which had been neglected by an overstress of his immanence in liberalism, neo-orthodoxy went to the extreme of stressing a God who was hidden, unknown, and "wholly other." In its revolt against overemphasis on the power of reason in liberalism, neo-orthodoxy fell into a mood of antirationalism and semifundamentalism, stressing a narrow uncritical biblicism. This approach, I felt, was inadequate both for the church and for personal life.

So although liberalism left me unsatisfied on the question of the nature of man, I found no refuge in neo-orthodoxy. I am now convinced that the truth about man is found neither in liberalism nor in neo-orthodoxy. Each represents a partial truth. A large segment of Protestant liberalism defined man only in terms of his essential nature, his capacity for good; neo-orthodoxy tended to define man only in terms of his existential nature, his capacity for evil. An adequate understanding of man is found neither in the thesis of liberalism nor in the antithesis of neo-orthodoxy, but in a synthesis which reconciles the truths of both.

During the intervening years I have gained a new appreciation for the philosophy of existentialism. My first contact with this philosophy came through my reading of Kierkegaard and Nietzsche. Later I turned to a study of Jaspers, Heidegger, and Sartre. These thinkers stimulated my thinking; while questioning each, I nevertheless learned a great deal through a study of them. When I finally engaged in a serious study of the writings of Paul Tillich, I became convinced that existentialism, in spite of the fact that it had become all too fashionable, had grasped certain basic truths about man and his condition that could not be permanently overlooked.

An understanding of the "finite freedom" of man is one of the permanent contributions of existentialism, and its perception of the anxiety and conflict produced in man's personal and social life by the perilous and ambiguous structure of existence is especially meaningful for our time. A common denominator in atheistic or theistic existentialism is

that man's existential situation is estranged from his essential nature. In their revolt against Hegel's essentialism, all existentialists contend that the world is fragmented. History is a series of unreconciled conflicts, and man's existence is filled with anxiety and threatened with meaninglessness. While the ultimate Christian answer is not found in any of these existential assertions, there is much here by which the theologian may describe the true state of man's existence.

Although most of my formal study has been in systematic theology and philosophy, I have become more and more interested in social ethics. During my early teens I was deeply concerned by the problem of racial injustice. I considered segregation both rationally inexplicable and morally unjustifiable. I could never accept my having to sit in the back of a bus or in the segregated section of a train. The first time that I was seated behind a curtain in a dining car I felt as though the curtain had been dropped on my selfhood. I also learned that the inseparable twin of racial unjustice is economic injustice. I saw how the systems of segregation exploited both the Negro and the poor whites. These early experiences made me deeply conscious of the varieties of injustice in our society.

TWO

Not until I entered theological seminary, however, did I begin a serious intellectual quest for a method that would eliminate social evil. I was immediately influenced by the social gospel. In the early 1950s I read Walter Rauschenbusch's *Christianity and the Social Crisis,* a book which left an indelible imprint on my thinking. Of course, there were points at which I differed with Rauschenbusch. I felt that he was a victim of the nineteenth-century "cult of inevitable progress," which led him to an unwarranted optimism concerning human nature. Moreover, he came perilously close to identifying the Kingdom of God with a particular social and economic system, a temptation to which the church must never surrender. But in spite of these shortcomings, Rauschenbusch gave to American Protestantism a sense of social responsibility that it should never lose. The gospel at its best deals with the whole man, not only his soul but also his body, not only his spiritual well-being but also his material well-being. A religion that professes a concern for the souls of men and is not equally concerned about the slums that damn them, the economic conditions that strangle them, and the social conditions that cripple them, is a spiritually moribund religion.

After reading Rauschenbusch, I turned to a serious study of the social and ethical theories of the great philosophers. During this period I had almost despaired of the power of love to solve social problems. The turn-the-other-cheek and the love-your-enemies philosophies are valid, I felt, only when individuals are in conflict with other individuals; when racial groups and nations are in conflict, a more realistic approach is necessary.

Then I was introduced to the life and teachings of Mahatma Gandhi. As I read his works I became deeply fascinated by his campaigns of nonviolent resistance. The whole Gandhian concept of *satyagraha* (*satya* is truth which equals love and *graha* is force; *satyagraha* thus means truth-force or love-force) was profoundly significant to me. As I delved deeper into the philosophy of Gandhi, my skepticism concerning the power of love gradually diminished, and I came to see for the first time that the Christian doctrine of love, operating through the Gandhian method of nonviolence, is one of the most potent weapons available to an oppressed people in their struggle for freedom. At that time, however, I acquired only an intellectual understanding and appreciation of the position, and I had no firm determination to organize it in a socially effective situation.

When I went to Montgomery, Alabama, as a pastor in 1954, I had not the slightest idea that I would later become involved in a crisis in which nonviolent resistance would be applicable. After I had lived in the community about a year, the bus boycott began. The Negro people of Montgomery, exhausted by the humiliating experiences that they had constantly faced on the buses, expressed in a massive act of nonco-operation their determination to be free. They came to see that it was ultimately more honorable to walk the streets in dignity than to ride the buses in humiliation. At the beginning of the protest, the people called on me to serve as their spokesman. In accepting this responsibility, my mind, consciously or unconsciously, was driven back to the Sermon on the Mount and the Gandhian method of non-violent resistance. This principle became the guiding light of our movement. Christ furnished the spirit and motivation and Gandhi furnished the method.

The experience in Montgomery did more to clarify my thinking in regard to the question of nonviolence than all of the books that I had read. As the days unfolded, I became more and more convinced of the power of nonviolence. Nonviolence became more than a method to which I gave intellectual assent; it became a commitment to a way of life. Many issues I had not cleared up intellectually concerning nonviolence were now resolved within the sphere of practical action.

My privilege of traveling to India had a great impact on me personally, for it was invigorating to see firsthand the amazing results of a nonviolent struggle to achieve independence. The aftermath of hatred and bitterness that usually follows a violent campaign was found nowhere in India, and a mutual friendship, based on complete equality, existed between the Indian and British people within the Commonwealth.

I would not wish to give the impression that nonviolence will accomplish miracles overnight. Men are not easily moved from their mental ruts or purged of their prejudiced and irrational feelings. When the underprivileged demand freedom, the privileged at first react with bitterness and resistance. Even when the demands are couched in nonviolent terms, the initial response is substantially the same. I am sure that many of our white brothers in Montgomery and throughout the South are still bitter toward the Negro leaders, even though these leaders have sought to follow a way of love and nonviolence. But the nonviolent approach does something to the hearts and souls of those committed to it. It gives them new self-respect. It calls up resources of strength and courage that they did not know they had. Finally, it so stirs the conscience of the opponent that reconciliation becomes a reality.

THREE

More recently I have come to see the need for the method of nonviolence in international relations. Although I was not yet convinced of its efficacy in conflicts between nations, I felt that while war could never be a positive good, it could serve as a negative good by preventing the spread and growth of an evil force. War, horrible as it is, might be preferable to surrender to a totalitarian system. But I now believe that the potential destructiveness of modern weapons totally rules out the possibility of war ever again achieving a negative good. If we assume that mankind has a right to survive, then we must find an alternative to war and destruction. In our day of space vehicles and guided ballistic missiles, the choice is either nonviolence or nonexistence.

I am no doctrinaire pacifist, but I have tried to embrace a realistic pacifism which finds the pacifist position as the lesser evil in the circumstances. I do not claim to be free from the moral dilemmas that the Christian nonpacifist confronts, but I am convinced that the church cannot be silent while mankind faces the threat of nuclear annihilation. If the church is true to her mission, she must call for an end to the arms race.

Some of my personal sufferings over the last few years have also served to shape my thinking. I always hesitate to mention these experiences for fear of conveying the wrong impression. A person who constantly calls attention to his trials and sufferings is in danger of developing a martyr complex and impressing others that he is consciously seeking sympathy. It is possible for one to be self-centered in his self-sacrifice. So I am always reluctant to refer to my personal sacrifices. But I feel somewhat justified in mentioning them in this essay because of the influence they have had upon my thought.

Due to my involvement in the struggle for the freedom of my people, I have known very few quiet days in the last few years. I have been imprisoned in Alabama and Georgia jails twelve times. My home has been bombed twice. A day seldom passes that my family and I are not the recipients of threats of death. I have been the victim of a near-fatal stabbing. So in a real sense I have been battered by the storms of persecution. I must admit that at times I have felt that I could no longer bear such a heavy burden, and have been tempted to retreat to a more quiet and serene life. But every time such a temptation appeared, something came to strengthen and sustain my determination. I have learned now that the Master's burden is light precisely when we take his yoke upon us.

My personal trials have also taught me the value of unmerited suffering. As my sufferings mounted I soon realized that there were two ways in which I could respond to my situation—either to react with bitterness or seek to transform the suffering into a creative force. I decided to follow the latter course. Recognizing the necessity for suffering, I have tried to make of it a virtue. If only to save myself from bitterness, I have attempted to see my personal ordeals as an opportunity to transfigure myself and heal the people involved in the tragic situation which now obtains. I have lived these last few years with the conviction that unearned suffering is redemptive. There are some who still find the Cross a stumbling block, others consider it foolishness, but I am more convinced than ever before that it is the power of God unto social and individual salvation. So like the Apostle Paul I can now humbly, yet proudly, say, "I bear in my body the marks of the Lord Jesus."

The agonizing moments through which I have passed during the last few years have also drawn me closer to God. More than ever before I am convinced of the reality of a personal God. True, I have always believed in the personality of God. But in the past the idea of a personal God was little more than a metaphysical category that I found theologically and philosophically satisfying. Now it is a living reality that has been validated in the experiences of everyday life. God has been profoundly real to me in recent years. In the midst of outer dangers I have felt an inner calm. In the midst of lonely days and dreary nights I have heard an inner voice saying, "Lo, I will be with you." When the chains of fear and the manacles of frustration have all but stymied my efforts, I have felt the power of God transforming the fatigue of despair into the buoyancy of hope. I am convinced that the universe is under the control of a loving purpose, and that in the struggle for righteousness man has cosmic companionship. Behind the harsh appearances of the world there is a benign power. To say that this God is personal is not to make him a finite object besides other objects or attribute to him the limitations of human personality; it is to take what is finest and noblest in our consciousness and affirm its perfect existence in him. It is certainly true that human personality is limited, but personality as such involves no necessary limitations. It means simply self-consciousness and self-direction. So in the truest sense of the word, God is a living God. In him there is feeling and will, responsive to the deepest yearnings of the human heart: *this* God both evokes and answers prayer.

The past decade has been a most exciting one. In spite of the tensions and uncertainties of this period something profoundly meaningful is taking place. Old systems of exploitation and oppression are passing away; new systems of justice and equality are being born. In a real sense this is a great time to be alive. Therefore, I am not yet discouraged about the future. Granted that the easygoing optimism of yesterday is impossible. Granted that we face a world crisis which leaves us standing so often amid the surging murmur of life's restless sea. But every crisis has both its dangers and its opportunities. It can spell either salvation or doom. In a dark, confused world the Kingdom of God may yet reign in the hearts of men.

The Days of Martin Luther King, Jr.

A PHOTOGRAPHIC DIARY

". . . Life should be strong and complete on every side. Any complete life has . . . three dimensions . . . —length, breadth, and height.

The length of life is the inward *drive to achieve one's personal ends and ambitions, an inward concern for one's own welfare and achievements.*

The breadth of life is the outward *concern for the welfare of others.*

The height of life is the upward *reach for God.*

Only by a painstaking development of all three of these dimensions can you expect to live a complete life."

A view of the Ebenezer Baptist Church, Auburn
Avenue, N.E., and Jackson Street, Atlanta, Georgia.

WORSHIP

"As the physical body needs renewal, so must the spiritual body be renewed. Worship provides the spiritual renewal necessary for a healthy spiritual life. . . ."

The main entrance to Ebenezer Church. The church's slogan is: *"Hitherto hath the Lord helped us."*

The rostrum and the pulpit await occupancy by the co-pastors, the Reverends Martin Luther King—father and son. The prominent placement of the "tithing box" indicates the compliance with the scriptural admonition: *"Bring ye all the tithes into the storehouse."*

TITHES

"Tithing is one of the best methods that we have to symbolize our dedication to God and the work of His kingdom. True tithing is deeper than the mere giving of ten percent of our income; it also means giving of our time and service to the church and its various ministries. . . ."

The weekly church bulletin guides the worshiper in the services and keeps the congregation informed of church activities.

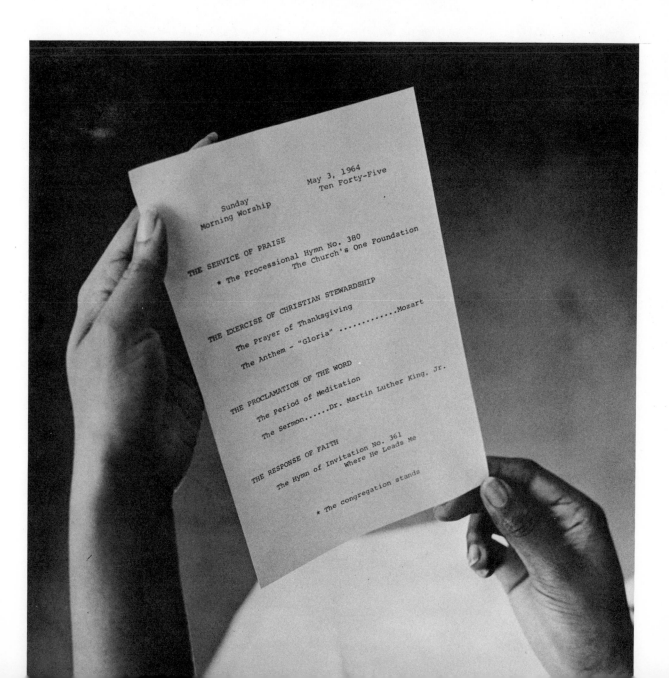

In the busy moments before the services begin, ushers
direct the gathering worshipers to their seats, carefully maintaining the solemn hush of the sanctuary.

THE MINISTRY

"My call to the ministry was not dramatic. . . . It was my

final realization of an inner urge to serve God and humanity.

It was a response to an inescapable challenge. . . ."

Their voices soaring with the organ, the clergy, choir and congregation join
in the spirited singing of the opening hymn:
"The church's one foundation Is Jesus Christ her Lord. . ."

The choir sings an anthem, and Dr. King, a music lover, pays close attention. His wife Coretta, who once trained for a concert career, is a member of the choir.

The Reverend Martin Luther King, Sr. (affectionately called "Daddy King"), presides over the worship service and makes special announcements. Father and son preach on alternate Sundays. *"My father . . . this stern and courageous man . . . led the fight in Atlanta to equalize teachers' salaries, and had been instrumental in the elimination of Jim Crow elevators in the courthouse."*

Dr. King preaches the morning sermon. The message is built according to his own recipe for a good sermon.

THE SERMON

"A good sermon is characterized by the presence of three "P's:

Proving   —an appeal to the intellect.

Painting   —an appeal to the imagination.

Persuading—an appeal to the emotions.

All are necessary ingredients of the well-balanced sermon."

With the singing of the hymn of invitation, the co-pastors "open the doors of the church," a symbolic calling of the un-churched into church membership. (The Ebenezer Church membership numbers more than four thousand.)

SUNDAY AFTERNOON AT HOME

The car, the street and the house all bespeak
the quiet simplicity of the family's way of life.

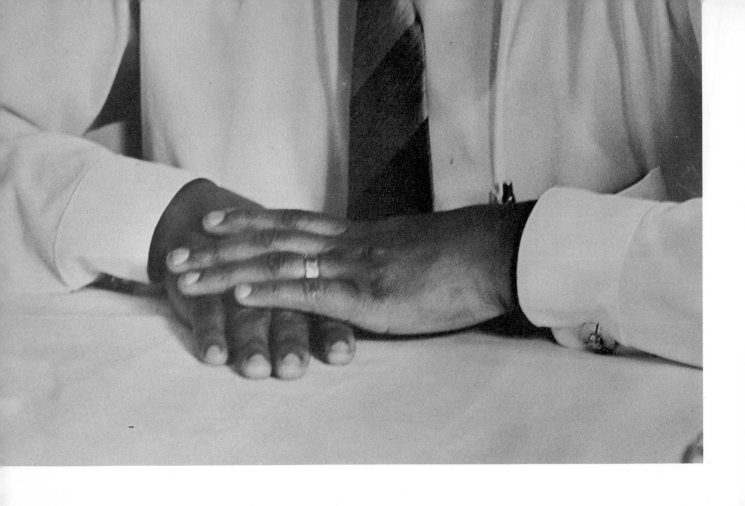

(*Right*) Sunday dinner guests include (counter-clockwise) Mrs. Dorothy Cotton, Mr. and Mrs. Randolph Blackwell, and Mr. and Mrs. Andy Young and their daughter. Dr. and Mrs. King are seated at opposite ends of the table.

Grace is said before dinner.

"Often we sing the prayer that precedes all meals.
Usually it is:

> *'God is great and God is good;*
> *And we thank Him for this food.*
> *By Thy hands must all be fed,*
> *Give us, Lord, our daily bread.'*

or:

> *'We thank Thee, Lord, for this our food,*
> *For health and strength and every good.*
> *Let manna to our souls be given—*
> *The bread of life sent down from heaven!*

but I am especially fond of this one which I learned
from my sister-in-law:

> *'And now transform this food into life, O Lord,*
> *And our lives into service for Thee.'"*

Inevitably, the meal is interrupted by a telephone call. His joint responsibilities as pastor and civil rights leader require that Dr. King be on duty almost twenty-four hours a day.

Mrs. King clears the table and exchanges small talk with the women guests. ". . . *my wife Coretta, without whose love, sacrifices and loyalty neither life nor work would bring fulfillment. She has given me . . . a well-ordered home where Christian love is a reality.*"

THE CHILDREN

"I expect that this generation of Negro children throughout the United States will grow up stronger and better because of the courage and dignity and suffering of the nine children of Little Rock and their counterparts in Nashville, Clinton and Sturges. . . ."

(*Right*) Youthful churchgoers talk with Dr. King at the coffee hour which follows the morning worship at Ebenezer Church. (*Below*) The King children examine a new pet, a pup of unregistered breed.

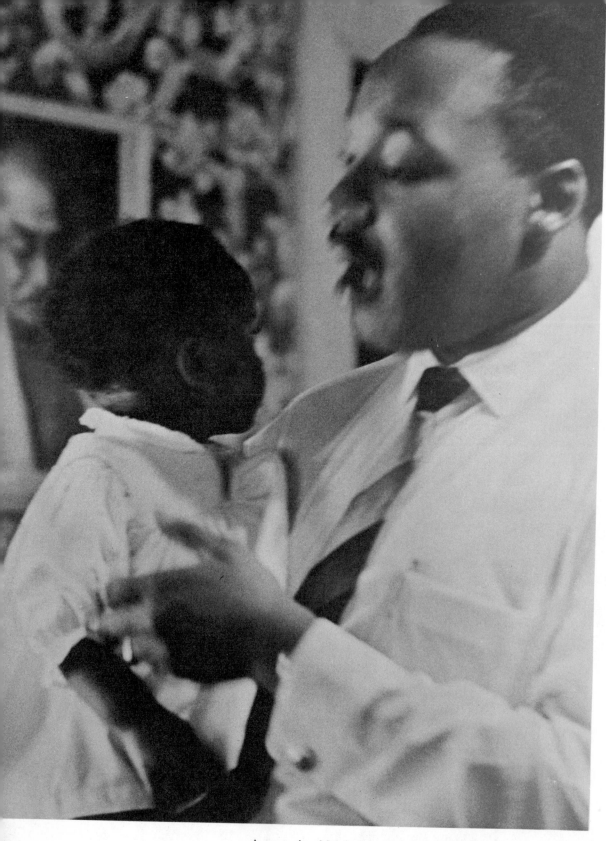

A portrait of Mahatma Gandhi, one of the major influences in Dr. King's life, looks down upon the scene of an adoring father cuddling his daughter, Bernice. *"Negro parents must . . . give their children the love, attention and sense of belonging that a segregated society deprives them of. . . ."*

The "leader" follows the children as they head for bed and the ritual of imploring their father to tell them "just one more" story.

AT SCLC HEADQUARTERS

"This then must be our present program: Nonviolent resistance in all forms of racial injustice, including state and local laws and practices, even when this means going to jail; and imaginative, bold, constructive action to end the demoralization caused by the legacy of slavery and segregation, inferior schools, slums, and second-class citizenship. . . .

"In short, we must work on two fronts. On the one hand, we must continue to resist the system of segregation which is the basic cause of our lagging standards; on the other hand, we must work constructively to improve the standards themselves. There must be a rhythmic alternation between attacking the causes and healing the effects.

"This is a great hour for the Negro."

The sign above SCLC's national office seems to dominate the jungle of markers on a busy street in downtown Atlanta.

Miss Dora McDonald, Dr. King's secretary, opens the mail which runs to several hundreds of letters weekly.

At SCLC Headquarters □ 277

A young correspondent writes for advice from Dr. King, and touchingly confides: *"I have no brother. . . ."*

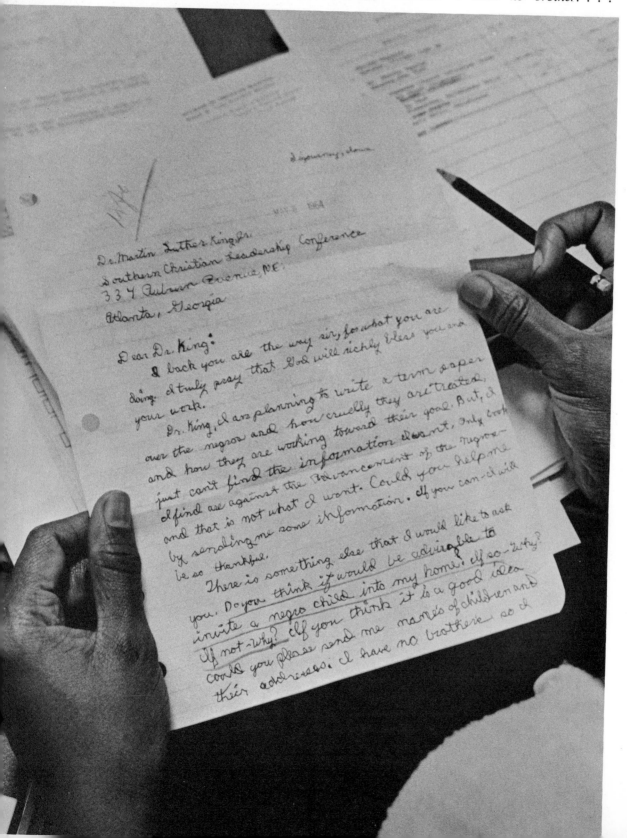

Dr. King and Miss McDonald review the mail and
other urgent business at the start of the work-day.

Dr. King and his top assistant, Wyatt Tee Walker, hold a hurried conference before attending a staff meeting. *"Wyatt Tee Walker is one of the keenest minds of the nonviolent revolution. He has made a tremendous contribution to the life and growth of SCLC and the South as a whole."*

Before the meeting is called to order, staff members catch up on the news, including sports.

The meeting gets under way, and Dr. King presents the
agenda. These meetings usually last several hours.

In a momentary break from the seriousness of their deliberations, Dr. King and Wyatt Tee Walker enjoy a quick jest.

Later that evening Dr. King returns to his office and tackles the mountain of correspondence that requires his personal attention.

Late in the evening, an unexpected caller prevails upon
Dr. King to give him "just a minute" of his time.

The expressive face of Martin Luther King...

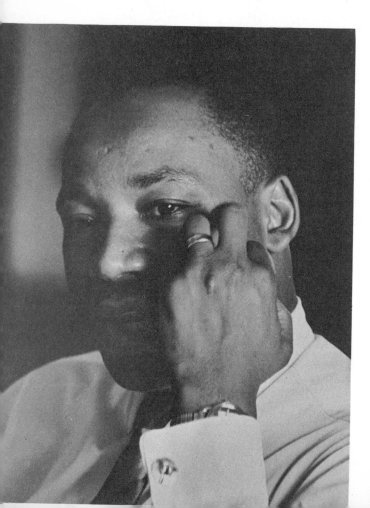

In a series of rare informal photographs the intense and animated face of Dr. King is shown as he considers a provocative statement. Then he replies—becoming more impassioned as he speaks. His point made, he sits back, relaxes, smiles, chuckles and finally laughs heartily.

BOOK THREE

AN APPEAL

TO THE PRESIDENT OF THE UNITED STATES

For

National Rededication

to the Principles

of the Emancipation Proclamation

AN APPEAL

TO THE HONORABLE JOHN F. KENNEDY

PRESIDENT OF THE UNITED STATES

FOR NATIONAL REDEDICATION

TO THE PRINCIPLES OF THE EMANCIPATION PROCLAMATION

AND FOR AN EXECUTIVE ORDER

PROHIBITING SEGREGATION IN THE UNITED STATES OF AMERICA

Submitted May 17, 1962

By the Reverend Dr. Martin Luther King, Jr., President,

Southern Christian Leadership Conference, Atlanta, Georgia

THE APPEAL IS BEING PRESENTED TO THE PRESIDENT OF THE UNITED STATES BY REVEREND DR. MARTIN LUTHER KING, JR. OF ATLANTA GEORGIA ON BEHALF OF THE NEGRO CITIZENRY OF THE UNITED STATES OF AMERICA IN COMMEMORATION OF THE CENTENNIAL OF THE PROCLAMATION OF EMANCIPATION

SECTION I

PREAMBLE

MR. PRESIDENT, the history of any nation is in many respects a record of the decisions taken by its people and its leaders in response to certain crucial challenges. We believe that America today, in the field of race relations, is faced with just such a challenge. Consequently, we would like to discuss with you, as one of our fellow Americans, and as President of these United States, the crossroads at which America stands on the issue of civil rights.

Like you, Mr. President, we are profoundly proud of the democratic heritage of our country. We know that freedom is, indeed, a most precious thing. We know that "this land is our land, from California to the New York island; from the Redwood forests to the Gulfstream waters"; we know that this land exists for *all Americans,* white and Negro. However, we also know that to millions of Negroes throughout these United States, freedom is not yet a "living reality." State enforced segregation and discrimination based on race or color continue in many parts of our country. Thus, as we approach the 100th anniversary of the Emancipation Proclamation, eight years after the unanimous United States Supreme Court desegregation decision in *Brown* v. *Board of Education,* we want to present for your consideration our thoughts on the ways in which the legal and moral responsibility to end state enforced segregation and discrimination can be met.

The wellsprings of equality lie deep within our past. We believe the Centennial of the Emancipation Proclamation is a particularly appropriate time for all our citizens to rededicate themselves to those early precepts and principles of equality before the law. Mr. President, we believe that like Thomas Jefferson before you, you "hold these truths to be self-evident, that all men are created equal, that they are endowed by their Creator with certain unalienable rights. . . ."

The Declaration of Independence gave hope to all the world because it spoke for all men, not just the privileged few.[1]

"And in every succeeding statement of American purpose—The Gettysburg Address, Wilson's

'Fourteen Points,' the 'Four Freedoms,'—that same emphasis on the rights and needs of 'all men' has been present. In different contexts we gave these testaments of national faith and purpose a specific meaning which led a grateful humanity everywhere to raise monuments in their hearts where they honored the very word 'American.' *Yet we cannot rest on those monuments today.*"[2] (emphasis added)

One hundred years ago this September, Mr. President, General Robert E. Lee's gray-clad Army of Northern Virginia crossed the Potomac singing "Maryland, My Maryland." The Civil War was in its second year. A triumphant South was invading the North.

History tells us that the outcome of Lee's invasion was determined on the 17th of September, 1862, at Antietam Creek, fifty miles up the Potomac from Washington.

"In the early hours of the morning it was a battle for two woodlots, a cornfield and a small white church, defended by Confederate divisions under Stonewall Jackson. Toward noon it was a battle for a sunken lane, quickly named 'Bloody Lane' by the Northern attackers, and in the afternoon it was an uphill battle for ridges.

"When night fell, the young men from the cities, towns and farms of the North had won the most important points, but thousands of them were dead and every house and barn for many miles around soon filled with wounded."[3]

September 17th, 1862, according to the historian Bruce Catton, was "the most murderous single day of the entire war."

Abraham Lincoln was profoundly aware of the deep wounds which had been inflicted upon the Union when he spoke those prophetic words on November 19, 1863, to those thousands who had gathered on Cemetery Hill in Gettysburg, Pennsylvania, for the dedication exercises of a National Soldiers' Cemetery.

"It is for us, the living, rather, to be dedicated, here, to the unfinished work which they who fought here have thus far so nobly advanced. It is rather for us to be here dedicated to the great task remaining before us; *that from these honored dead we take increased devotion to that cause for which they gave the last full measure of devotion; that we here highly resolve that these dead shall not have died in vain;* that this nation, under God, shall have a new birth of freedom, and that government of the people, by the people, for the people, shall not perish from the earth." (emphasis added)

Only ten months earlier, shortly after the Battle of Antietam, Lincoln had, on September 22, 1862, summoned his Cabinet and issued an Executive Proclamation, effective as of January 1, 1863, freeing the slaves in the rebellious states. Slavery in America was thus brought to an end.[4]

It is precisely because race relations in America today are so deeply rooted, historically, in the socio-political conditions of Slavery, the Civil War, Reconstruction, the "Black Codes," and their aftermath that we believe the time has come for Presidential leadership to be vigorously exerted to remove from American society, once and for all time, the festering cancer of segregation and discrimination.

The struggle for freedom, Mr. President, of which our Civil War was but a bloody chapter, continues throughout our land today. The courage and heroism of Negro citizens at Montgomery, Little Rock, New Orleans, Prince Edward County, and Jackson, Mississippi, is only a further effort to affirm that democratic heritage so painfully won, in part, upon the grassy battlefields of Antietam, Lookout Mountain, and Gettysburg.[5]

We believe, Mr. President, that you have a unique opportunity to initiate a dramatic and historic step forward in the area of race relations. The exigencies of segregation and the inequities and injustices of discrimination against twenty million Negroes in America demand creative and firm Executive action on behalf of civil rights.

On several occasions you have said the times we live in demand bold, imaginative and courageous action by all our people. We, like you, Mr. President, believe that the time we live in is a time for greatness. The achievement of civil and human rights in America, therefore, can no longer rest solely, or even primarily, on judicial or legislative declaration alone. The conscience of America looks now, again, some one hundred years after the abolition of chattel slavery, to the President of the United States.[6]

We submit that the present state of the law with respect to state enforced segregation and discrimination based on race or color requires, at this juncture in history, catalytic enforcement of civil rights by a strong and morally committed Executive. The time has come, Mr. President, to let those dawn-like rays of freedom, first glimpsed in 1863, fill the heavens with the noonday sunlight of complete human dignity. Morality, and Man's dignity before Man and his God, demand this in this year Nineteen Hundred and Sixty-two.

Sixty-six years ago, some thirty-three years after chattel slavery had ended, Judge Albion Tourgee foresaw that the longer the appurtenances and indicia of slavery continued, the more impatient the Negro would become. Judge Tourgee's argument before the Court in *Plessy* v. *Ferguson*[7] was ultimately vindicated in *Brown* v. *Board of Education.*[8] Today his words serve as a reminder of the wrongs of the past and cry out to the conscience of America to eliminate the injustices of the present:

"It is easy for us to excuse ourselves for the wrongs of slavery, but day by day, it is growing harder for the colored man to do so; and it is simply to state a universal fact of human nature to declare that a great and lasting wrong like slavery done to a whole people grows blacker and darker for generations and ages as they go away from it. The educated grandchild of a slave who looks back into the black pit of slavery will find little excuse for the white Christian civilization which forbade marriage, crushed aspiration, and after two centuries and a half offered the world as the fruits of Christian endeavor five millions of (illegitimate) sons and daughters—the product of a promiscuity enforced by law and upheld by Christian teachings. Slavery will be a more terrible thing to the Negro a hundred years hence than it was to the calloused consciousness of his nameless father, and a more shameful horror to your grandchild's soul than it was to the aching heart of Garrison."[9]

We are confident that with your help, Mr. President, the discontinuance of segregation and state imposed discrimination shall come to pass. We therefore respectfully propose that in glorious commemoration of the Centennial of the Emancipation Proclamation, you as President of these United States, by Executive Order, proclaim:

1. That the full powers of your office will be used to eliminate all forms of statutory-imposed segregation and discrimination from and throughout the respective states of this nation.

2. That effective January 1, 1963 that as of the school year, September 1963, all school districts presently segregated must desegregate.

Such a Proclamation should be accompanied by a Directive authorizing the Department of Health, Education and Welfare to immediately prepare, in consultation with local school officials, a program of integration in compliance with the mandate of *Brown* v. *Board of Education.*

3. That racial segregation in Federally assisted housing is henceforth prohibited and unlawful.

4. That any and all laws within the United States requiring segregation or discrimination because of race or color are contrary to the national policy of the Government of the United States and are detrimental and inimical to the best interests of the United States at home and abroad.

In the pages to follow we will briefly survey the many judicial decisions precluding the application and imposition of laws requiring discrimination and segregation against Negro Americans. These decisions, in conjunction with the Constitutional and statutory provisions cited therewith, demonstrate that in many areas of American life the Negro is entitled to those civil and Constitutional rights for which we now ask Executive support.

SECTION II

RESUME OF THE STATE OF THE LAW WITH RESPECT TO STATE ENFORCED SEGREGATION AND DISCRIMINATION BASED ON RACE OR COLOR

MR. PRESIDENT, in your Proclamation establishing May 1, 1961 as Law Day, you stated:

". . . no nation can remain free unless its people cherish their freedoms, understand the responsibilities they entail, and nurture the will to preserve them. . . .

". . . law is the strongest link between men and freedom, and *by strengthening the rule of law we strengthen freedom and justice in our own country and contribute by example to the goal of justice under law for all mankind.*" (emphasis added)

What greater contribution, "by example," can we make, as a nation, than for the President of the United States to declare that: the retention, continuance and enforcement of any and all laws within the United States requiring segregation or discrimination because of race or color are contrary to the national policy of the Government of the United States and inimical to our best interests at home and abroad.

Enforced segregation is but a new form of slavery—an enslavement of the human spirit and dignity rather than of the body. The enacted legislation and judicially developed case law with respect to equal rights in America today requires the fulfillment of the promise of Emancipation. This law, while admittedly subject to degrees of interpretation, is, nevertheless, in general weighted toward the elimination of any and all forms of state enforced segregation or discrimination. Consequently, we believe that a responsible Executive, nearly 100 years removed from the abolition of chattel slavery, should not remain silent and acquiesce in the persistent enforcement of state laws requiring segregation and discrimination because of race or color.

Article VI, section 2, of our Constitution states:

"This Constitution, and the Laws of the United States which shall be made in Pursuance thereof; and all Treaties made, or which shall be made, under the Authority of the United States, shall be the supreme Law of the Land; and the Judges in every State shall be bound thereby, any Thing in the Constitution or Laws of any State to the Contrary notwithstanding."

The supremacy clause is thus binding on private citizens as well as public officials.

Ours is a federal government under a written Constitution. The United States Supreme Court stands as the final arbiter in the federal system. Its decisions under our form of government are continual additions to the "supreme law" of the land.

During the past eight years the Federal Judiciary has charted historic new roads to the achievement of human dignity in the United States. The law as judicially developed suggests that the country as a whole—North, South, East and West—should be informed by an Executive Proclamation that the national policy of the Government of the United States is forthwith compliance with the numerous decisions of the United States Supreme Court in the area of equal protection of the law.

Mr. President, to millions of your fellow Americans, discrimination because of race and color is a very real and chilling thing in these United States. The realities of second-class citizenship, therefore, naturally cause us to ask whether the achievement of equality in America is so difficult and so complex that, as far as the daily lives of Negroes are concerned, it must still remain only a "dream deferred"? We think not.

The requirements of the equal protection clause are simple and unequivocal. The Supreme Law of the Land forbids any state to enact separation of the races. The simplicity of this Constitutional command pierces through the complexities and legalisms surrounding human rights. Direct and open state action to compel segregation is forbidden. What a state cannot do directly it cannot do indirectly. There is no device, no legal technique, which is permissible to a state if the underlying reality is that the state by its action is recognizing, encouraging, or perpetuating segregation.

The law with respect to equality of treat-ment under the Fourteenth Amendment has undergone significant changes since the case of *Plessy* v. *Ferguson,* 163 U.S. 537 (1896). In that case the Court upheld the constitutionality of a Louisiana travel statute which required racial segregation and imposed penalties on those persons who disobeyed the statute. The Fourteenth Amendment, the Court stated, did not prohibit the states from enacting legislation based on race and color.

EDUCATION

In 1954, some 60 years later, the U.S. Supreme Court reached an opposite interpretation of the requirements of the Fourteenth Amendment.[10] In a unanimous decision, the Court declared:

> "We conclude that in the field of public education the doctrine of 'separate but equal' has no place. Separate educational facilities are inherently unequal. Therefore, we hold that the plaintiffs and others similarly situated for whom the actions have been brought are, *by reason of the segregation* complained of, deprived of the equal protection of the laws guaranteed by the Fourteenth Amendment."[11]

Thus, where the State has undertaken the responsibility of public education, the Fourteenth Amendment requires it to provide an equal opportunity to all for an education. Separate, segregated facilities cannot, by their very nature, be equal.

Shortly after the 1954 *Brown* decision, the Supreme Court of Delaware concluded that the effect of that decision was to nullify all

State constitutional and statutory provisions requiring separate schools for the two races.[12]

The U.S. Supreme Court, in its second decision in the *Brown* case, specifically stated that "All provisions of federal, state, or local law requiring or permitting such discrimination must yield to this principle." (i.e., that racial discrimination in public education is unconstitutional.)

In a companion case to the first *Brown* decision, *Bolling* v. *Sharpe*,[13] the question of school segregation in the District of Columbia was raised. School segregation was also held to violate the Fifth Amendment which states that no person shall be deprived of life, liberty, or property, without due process of law:

> "Liberty under law extends to the full range of conduct which the individual is free to pursue, and it cannot be restricted except for a proper governmental objective. Segregation in public education is not reasonably related to any proper governmental objective."[14]

Realizing that its decision would affect three million Negro children and seven million white children attending compulsorily segregated public schools in almost 3,000 school districts in 17 Southern states, the United States Supreme Court left the implementation of these constitutional principles to the Federal district courts with the safeguard that "it should go without saying that the vitality of these constitutional principles cannot be allowed to yield simply because of disagreement with them."[15]

In *Cooper* v. *Aaron*[16] (the Little Rock case), the Federal district court, pursuant to a request from state officials, granted a 2½ year delay in the integration of the Little Rock, Arkansas, high schools. The U.S. Supreme Court upheld the U.S. Court of Appeals' rejection of this delay. The court said the constitutional principle established in *Brown* "forbids States to use their governmental powers to bar children on racial grounds from attending schools where there is State participation through any arrangement, management, funds, or property."[17] Constitutional rights of school children "can neither be nullified openly and directly by State legislators or State executive or judicial officers, nor nullified indirectly by them through evasive schemes for segregation whether attempted 'ingeniously or ingenuously.' "[18] The duty of state authorities (including local school boards and superintendents of schools) to end segregation was reaffirmed. State authorities, in the words of the Court, are "duty bound to devote every effort toward initiating desegregation and bringing about the elimination of racial discrimination in the public school system."[19]

The last significant decision by the U.S. Supreme Court in the area of public education was *Pennsylvania* v. *Board of Directors of City Trusts*.[20] The Court said:

> "The Board which operates Girard College is an agency of the State of Pennsylvania. Therefore, even though the Board was acting as trustee, its refusal to admit [the Negro applicants] because they were Negroes was discrimination by the State. Such discrimination is forbidden by the Fourteenth Amendment."[21]

Mr. President, despite these numerous signposts designated by our highest court along the road to full equality and equal opportunity in the field of public education, state enforced segregation and discrimination against Negro citizens continues. Some of the most flagrant forms of disregard for the Constitution and the laws of the United States have been curtailed. However, there still remains, overall, state sanctioned and enforced resistance to the decisions of the Court in public education. We cite you only a few examples of the more sophisticated statutory impediments erected by various Southern states in an effort to frustrate any practical implementation of the mandate of *Brown* v. *Board of Education.*[22]

It is well known that following the May 17, 1954 desegregation decision, the legislatures of several Southern states passed measures known as "pupil placement, enrollment or assignment" laws. These enactments were expressly designed to give local school boards the power to designate the schools children are to attend. The process of designation is based on a series of criteria ostensibly and apparently other than race. In reality, Mr. President, most of the pupil placement enrollment or assignment laws are predicated upon race and color as underlying criteria. It is significant to note that in few instances, if any, are these criteria ever used to measure the suitability of *white* children for school enrollment. The practical effect of these state statutes, therefore, permits us to say with a reasonable degree of certainty that they were not enacted to implement desegregation "with all deliberate speed." Indeed, to the millions of Negroes throughout the South in particular and our nation in general, "pupil placement" has in fact become the main bulwark of "token integration," and so-called "marginal desegregation."

Recent decisions indicate that the Federal District Courts are growing more and more impatient with methods applying apparently legitimate criteria, but which in fact are designed to halt or retard desegregation in education. The U.S. Court of Appeals for the 6th Circuit, for example, ruled on March 23, 1962, that the Tennessee Pupil Assignment Law enacted by the Tennessee Legislature in 1957 may not serve as a plan to convert a segregated school system into a non-racial system. At the time the suit was filed in this case (*Northcross et al.* v. *City of Memphis Board of Education*), no Negro child had ever been transferred to a white school, and no white child had ever been transferred to a Negro school under the operation of the Assignment Law. Hence, the court concluded:

> "The practice over a long period of time of separate schools in certain geographical areas of our nation has become a way of life in those areas, and we realize that a change is not easy to accomplish. But as this court must follow the supreme law of the land, as interpreted by the Supreme Court, so must boards of education follow it."[23]

You can be sure, Mr. President, that the impatience of Negro Americans with the delaying tactics of many of our Southern states to desegregate their public education *is no less* than that of the lower federal courts.

It is our growing impatience with the "one (1) percent (%) a year rate of desegregation" in the South which causes us to feel, with great conviction, that what is sorely needed is forceful Executive leadership in behalf of civil rights. This is why we say, Mr. President, *that a glorious new stage in the history of human rights in America would commence if you, via Executive Order, proclaimed: that the continued enforcement of State laws requiring segregation and discrimination, in your best judgment, is contrary to the Constitution and laws of the United States; and that the existence of State laws requiring discrimination because of race or color is inimical to the best interests of the United States at home and abroad; and that, consequently, the full powers of your office will be employed to bring about forthwith compliance with the Constitution and laws of the United States.*

The major social transformation in the mores and customs of a substantial part of our American community provides you, Mr. President, with many opportunities for creative imaginative action. We respectfully submit that it is incumbent upon you personally to exert Executive leadership in the desegregation of public education in the Southern states of this nation. If this is not done, the "peaceful revolution in human rights" taking place in our midst will, to use your own words from another occasion, continue to strain at "the leashes imposed by timid Executive leadership."[24]

We are not unaware that the Department of Justice intervened as a friend of the Court in resisting the attempt by the State of Louisiana to stifle desegregation. Nor are we unmindful that the Justice Department sought to intervene as plaintiff in Prince Edward County, Virginia.

We are similarly not unaware of the March 30, 1962 announcement of Secretary of Health, Education and Welfare Abraham A. Ribicoff, before the Special House Education Subcommittee on integration in federally assisted areas.[25]

But all these actions, Mr. President, though commendatory and needed, are not a satisfactory substitute for the clarion voice of dynamic, forceful Presidential leadership. The parents and children of Negro Americans had to wait sixty-six years, a painfully long time, to be declared constitutionally entitled to the full fruits of public education that had been limited and restricted under the *Plessy* v. *Ferguson* doctrine of separate-but-equal. One hundred years after the abolition of chattel slavery is an even longer time. The extent to which the *Brown* decision will be complied with in "all deliberate speed" rests on your shoulders, Mr. President. The "righteousness which exalteth a nation" on the Centennial of the Emancipation Proc-

lamation demands that the President of the United States, in the name of all the people of the United States, proclaim that as of the school year, September 1963, all school districts presently segregated must desegregate. This could be accomplished by authorizing the Department of Health, Education and Welfare to immediately prepare a program of integration for each school district pursuant to the mandate of *Brown.* Such programs should be worked out now in consultation with local school officials, but in each case the Department of HEW should be mindful of its national duty.

In addition, we think that the proposals advanced by the Southern Regional Council in its report, *The Federal Executive and Civil Rights,* that the President of the United States:

> 1. "—publicly affirm his full support of the Supreme Court's 1954 decision and his intention to employ his executive powers as needed to assure orderly compliance with it;
>
> 2. "—publicly affirm his administration's belief that segregation is an intolerable hindrance to the national goal of higher educational standards"

should be the basis of a formal Executive Proclamation effective January 1, 1963.

The constitutional principles developed in the school segregation cases have been extended to other public facilities and institutions.[26]

HOUSING

A modest but significant step was taken in

the judicial development of the national law in regard to discrimination and segregation in private and public housing in the case of *Buchanan* v. *Warley.*[27]

The U.S. Supreme Court, in a unanimous opinion, found that a racially restrictive zoning ordinance of Louisville, Ky. was not a legitimate exercise of the police power of the state. The enforcement of the ordinance constituted state action in violation of the Fourteenth Amendment in that it deprived persons of property rights without due process of law:

> "But for the ordinance, the state courts would have enforced the contract, and the defendant would have been compelled to pay the purchase price and take a conveyance of the premises. The right of the plaintiff in error to sell his property was directly involved and necessarily impaired because it was held in effect that he could not sell the lot to a person of color who was willing and ready to acquire the property and had obliged himself to take it."[28]

The Court stated that the social purpose behind the ordinance, i.e., to prevent race conflict, miscegenation, and deterioration in the value of property was not sufficient to obviate the objection that it deprived one of property without due process of law.

Between the *Buchanan* case and the landmark decision in *Shelley* v. *Kraemer,* 334 U.S. 1 (1948), the Supreme Court made two other significant contributions toward the achievement of equal rights in public and private housing. Both were predicated upon the reasoning in *Buchanan*. The first, *Harmon* v. *Taylor,*[29] declared unconstitutional a city ordinance forbidding Negroes to establish a home on property in a white community. The

issue was the right of a white seller to dispose of his property free from restrictions as to potential purchasers. The second, *Richmond* v. *Deans,*[30] invalidated a similar city ordinance.

Thus, the legislative trend initially established in Baltimore in 1910 of limiting, by local ordinances, the areas in which whites and Negroes could reside, was judicially terminated by the U.S. Supreme Court. State or city racial zoning laws were declared unconstitutional.

In 1948 in the case of *Shelley* v. *Kraemer,* mentioned above, judicial enforcement of racially restrictive covenants was declared state action in contravention of the equal protection clause of the Fourteenth Amendment. The Court held in effect that a state may not enforce private rights based on contractual agreements between private individuals where to do so would result in the infringement of those constitutional rights guaranteed by the Constitution.[31]

Later, in 1953, in *Barrows* v. *Jackson,*[32] the question arose as to whether or not a restrictive covenant could be enforced at law by a suit for damages against a co-covenantor who had allegedly broken the covenant. The Supreme Court replied that to award damages for the breach of a covenant would be to sanction the validity thereof and as such would also constitute state action violative of the Fourteenth Amendment "as surely as it was state action to enforce such covenants in equity, as in *Shelley* v. *Kraemer.*"[33]

The lower federal courts and state courts have followed the historic lead established by the Supreme Court. There have been numerous cases in which these courts have held that local authorities operating public housing projects are barred by the equal protection and due process clauses of the Fourteenth Amendment to the U.S. Constitution from denying applications for housing facilities because of an applicant's race. Neither may local public housing authorities set up racially segregated housing.[34]

In the *Banks* case, the Appellate Court of the State of California ruled in August 1953 that the San Francisco Housing Authority must abandon its "neighborhood pattern" of resident selection, and admit applicants without discrimination. The U.S. Supreme Court rejected this appeal in May 1954.

Between 1953 and 1958, Federal District Courts in Evansville, Indiana; Louisville, Kentucky; Benton Harbor, Michigan; St. Louis, Missouri; and Columbus and Toledo, Ohio, barred racial segregation in public housing. These federal courts acted within the framework of the Supreme Court's interpretation of the Fourteenth Amendment, which forbids the practice of racial discrimination by any public officials, whether under authority of state statutes and ordinances or in deference to the custom and usage of a community.

In the Housing Act of 1949, Congress stated for the first time an overall national goal in housing:

> "The Congress hereby declares that the general welfare and security of the Nation and the health and living standards of its people require housing production and related community development sufficient to remedy the serious housing shortage, the elimination of substandard and other inadequate housing through the clearance of slums and blighted areas, and the realization as soon as feasible of the goal of a decent home and a suitable living environment for every American family, thus contributing to the development and redevelopment of communities and to the advancement of the growth, wealth, and security of the Na-

tion."[35]

At the time that this legislation was passed, the Federal government had still been following an unbroken policy of providing federal funds for housing without seriously looking to determine whether racial discrimination was in fact being practiced. Shortly after the *Shelley* case, in 1948, the Federal Housing Administration held that it would not provide mortgage insurance money for property on which restrictive covenants were recorded after February 15, 1950.[36] Later, in 1951, the FHA announced that all repossessed FHA-insured housing would be administered and sold on a non-segregated basis.[37] The following year, in connection with the program of housing for non-white defense workers during the Korean War, its field offices were directed to give "some preference" to proposals for open-occupancy developments as against all-minority projects.[38] By 1954 the declared national policy of the FHA was to encourage the development of demonstration open-occupancy projects in certain areas.

The Veterans Administration has taken steps similar to the FHA in regard to restrictive covenants. Its regulations prevent the use of racially restrictive covenants on property financed under a VA guarantee. The Report of the United States Civil Rights Commission states:

> "These regulations apply to property encumbered by racial restrictions created and recorded after February 15, 1950. Unlike FHA, VA does not refuse to issue a guarantee on a loan covering property subject to such a restriction. But the lender is deprived of the very valuable right of conveying the property to VA in the event of default and foreclosure. . . . With respect to the direct loan program,

VA will make no loan on property encumbered by a racial restrictive covenant created and filed after February 15, 1950. A subsequent filing of such a restriction by the borrower subjects the loan to optional acceleration by VA." p. 69.

In view of the numerous decisions and statutory provisions on housing, we are perplexed as to how there can be so much "law" entitling the Negro to equal opportunity and equality of treatment in housing, yet so little equality of treatment in fact. Mr. President, the stated purpose of the National Housing Act of 1949 was to achieve the "goal of a decent home and a suitable environment for every American family"; that of the Housing Act of 1954 was to provide "adequate housing for all people."[39] Though eloquently stated national goals, they remain today harshly unfulfilled for 20 million Negro Americans.

Mr. President, you yourself spoke so eloquently about how an Executive Order in the area of federally assisted housing could be issued by the President of the United States with "the stroke of a pen."

On January 16, 1962, in response to a question posed to you during the course of your press conference on that date as to when you would issue an Executive Order prohibiting racial segregation in federally assisted housing, you said the following:

> "Well, I think that—I stated that I would issue that order when I considered it would be in the public interest and when I considered it to make an important contribution to advancing the rights of our citizens . . . we are proceeding ahead in a way which will maintain a consensus, and which will advance this cause."[40]

We submit that the majority of the people of the United States would welcome an expression of Executive leadership on the question of democracy in housing. The "national consensus" of America is not an impediment to the issuance of an Executive Order in federally assisted housing.[41] In any event, "the President speaks the moral tone of America" and as such has "an incomparable position from which to define the problems of our policy and to indicate by word and example what needs to be done."[42]

TRANSPORTATION

Until recently, the Commerce Clause of the U.S. Constitution had been the primary vehicle used to invalidate state laws requiring racial segregation in interstate travel.[43] In *Southern Pacific Ry.* v. *Arizona,*[44] the Supreme Court held that where uniformity was essential for the functioning of commerce, a state may not impose its own regulations. This same criterion of uniformity was applied by the Court in *Morgan* v. *Virginia,*[45] when it invalidated a Virginia law requiring racial segregation of vehicles traveling through the state.[46]

Two years later, the U.S. Supreme Court sustained the validity of a Michigan antidiscrimination statute as applied to steamboats operating between Detroit, Michigan, and Canada. Conflict with Canada on the issue of discrimination was not to be anticipated. Jack Greenberg, in *Race Relations and American Law,*[47] concludes from these two cases that "the Court places a low value on the state's interest in segregation when balancing it against national uniformity, while placing a high value on nonsegregation in a similar equation.[48]

The Interstate Commerce Act, section 3(1), makes it unlawful for a rail carrier to "subject any particular person . . . to any undue or unreasonable prejudice or disadvantage in any respect whatsoever."[49] The Court has interpreted this section as imposing the same standards as those of the Fourteenth Amendment. Until the U.S. Supreme Court decision in *Brown,* this meant that if railroads could provide "separate but equal" accommodations, they were fulfilling the requirements of the statute. The first major departure from this doctrine, in transportation, occurred in *Mitchell* v. *U.S.,*[50] when the Court ruled that "separate but equal" could not constitutionally apply to Pullmans.

Shortly thereafter, in *Henderson* v. *U.S.,*[51] dining car segregation was set aside not by attacking segregation, per se, as unconstitutional but by stating that Negroes may not be excluded from any empty seats in a diner even if this meant violating a segregation rule.[52] Recently in *Boynton* v. *Virginia,*[53] the I.C.A. was interpreted as guaranteeing to an interstate passenger the right to be served without discrimination in terminal and restaurant facilities operated as an integral part of the carrier's transportation service, even though the carrier does not own, actively operate, or directly control the terminal or restaurant.

As you so well know, Mr. President, *even with these numerous court decisions requiring desegregation* in interstate transportation, discrimination and segregation against Negroes continued. It was not until after the now famous "Freedom Rides" that any significant equality of treatment was accorded Negroes in interstate travel.[54]

Insofar as bus terminals are concerned, it was also not until following the "Freedom Rides" in May 1961 that the Attorney General of the United States petitioned the Interstate Commerce Commission to issue a regulation prohibiting discrimination on interstate buses and in bus terminals.[55]

While there are no state laws requiring segregation aboard airplanes,[56] segregation still exists in the airline terminals of some Southern cities.[57]

In the area of *intrastate* travel, state-imposed segregation is forbidden by the Fourteenth Amendment. In *Browder* v. *Gayle,*[58] the District Court held that state-imposed bus segregation in Montgomery, Alabama, was unconstitutional. Segregation in intrastate travel cannot constitutionally be imposed by state statute, local ordinance, or public officials. In 1958, *Evers* v. *Dwyer*[59] declared that Memphis, Tennessee's continued enforcement of bus segregation was unconstitutional under the Fourteenth Amendment.

You may wonder why, Mr. President, we mention so many court decisions. We do this only because we want to emphasize the fact that in transportation, as in housing and public education, *there is a plethora of law* entitling Negroes to protection against discriminatory treatment because of their race and color. These decisions, in conjunction with the legislation enacted over the years, make it amply clear that Negroes are legally and constitutionally entitled to exercise these very rights we *now* seek to have secured by Presidential leadership.

On the one hand, Mr. President, nearly twenty million citizens find themselves *constitutionally, legislatively* and *judicially* entitled to the immediate discontinuance of the inequities and injustices of racial segregation and discrimination. On the other hand, however, these same persons find that practically, in real life, statutory-imposed racial segregation and discrimination is still enforced by many of the states in this country. This is the dilemma in which Negro Americans find themselves. We thus appeal to you to exert the full powers of your office to end the frustrations and indignities of this dilemma; and the unlawful conditions which give rise to it.

SECTION III

RESUME OF NON-COMPLIANCE WITH THE JUDICIALLY DEVELOPED AND STATUTORY LAW OUTLAWING STATE ENFORCED SEGREGATION IN AMERICAN SOCIETY

ALL THE JUDICIAL and legislative declarations of the rights of Negroes have not discouraged or prevented the nullification and frustration of the patiently won guarantees of human decency and fair play by many of the states of these United States. Public officials in the Southern states of our country have willfully disregarded, disobeyed, and flaunted the Constitution and statutes of the United States and the decisions of our highest court. We suggest, Mr. President, that there is a direct relationship between the hardened resistance of these state officials to the judicial and legislative declarations of our civil and constitutional rights and the absence of forceful Presidential leadership publicly committed to a policy of forthwith compliance.

One of the basic premises on which our Government was organized and on which it continues to exist is a respect for and a belief in the rule of law. A truly democratic society does not close its eyes when a large number of states are consciously and deliberately pursuing a policy of defiance of its national laws. The statute books of the states of the deep South and border areas are filled with legislation which require racial segregation or separation of the races, and which impose criminal penalties for persons who pursue a nondiscriminatory course of conduct in their daily lives.

Following the *Brown* decision, the state legislatures of fifteen Southern and border states enacted over 340 new laws and resolutions to prevent, restrict, or control desegregation.[60] Alabama, Arkansas, Georgia, Louisiana, North Carolina and Virginia have adopted tuition grant laws;[61] Alabama, Arkansas, Florida, Louisiana, Mississippi, North Carolina, Tennessee, Texas and Virginia have set up pupil placement plans.[62] Alabama, Arkansas, Florida, Georgia, Louisiana, Mississippi, South Carolina and Virginia legislators have approved interposition resolutions.[63] Alabama, Florida, Georgia, Mississippi, North Carolina and Texas have local option provisions for closing schools in the event of desegregation.[64]

Much of this legislation has been the subject of litigation. The interposition resolutions have been declared unconstitutional; the pupil placement laws, while not declared unconstitutional per se, have been challenged as to their unconstitutional method of application. Tuition grant laws and local option laws have also been challenged as to their purpose. A total of 226 court cases have been filed in state and federal courts on school segregation, desegregation, and related issues. The outcome of the litigation has been a slow process of desegregation, school by school, child by child, case by case. Only 7.3% of Negro schoolchildren in the South and border areas are presently attending schools with white children; this means that of the region's 3,210,724 Negro children, 233,509 are in schools with white children.[65]

While the above statistics indicate *some* progress, there are still, however, states and state officials, from the governor on down, who are in complete defiance of the laws of the United States and who have been permitted to court lawlessness.

Complete school segregation is maintained in the public school systems in Alabama, Mississippi, and South Carolina. Segregation is maintained on all grade levels in Georgia except in the Atlanta system.[66]

Mr. President, perhaps you can understand why, to some degree, Negro citizens in our Southern states look to you for leadership in securing and protecting their constitutionally and judicially declared civil rights. We cannot in good faith repose our confidence in state officials who enforce segregation and discrimination in flagrant defiance of elementary rights.

In January 1961, *Southern School News,* Vol. 7, No. 7, in reporting on state sanctioned resistance to integration in Alabama reported:

> "Governor John Patterson, noting school desegregation troubles in New Orleans said this was nothing compared to what would happen in Alabama if integration were attempted in this state.

> " 'If you think they've had trouble in New Orleans,' he said Dec. 7 at a news conference, 'just wait until they try integration here. There'll be hell to pay.'

> "He said the ultimate choice facing Alabamians would be private schools or no schools at all. He has previously warned the state that such measures as the placement law are not perfect barriers against integration. And even token integration is intolerable, he said, repeating his absolute opposition to integration in any degree:

> " 'There is no such thing as token integration or planned desegregation. Once you let the bars down, it's all over!

> Closed Schools
> "The governor has said that he would not permit the operation of any mixed schools in Alabama. 'If the federal government continues its present course,' he repeated, 'the only solution will be to close the schools.'

> "While asserting his opposition to mob violence, Patterson warned that when a showdown comes, 'I'll be one of the first ones stirring up trouble, any way I can.' By that he said he meant anything to harass or thwart the Federal Government."

The Governor of Mississippi, Ross R. Barnett, indicated similar defiance in his inaugural message on January 19, 1960:

> "Our people, both white and colored, throughout generations, have successfully operated a dual system of education because we

know it is best for both races. I know that this is the best and only system and I believe that the thinking people of both races feel the same way about it. Regardless, our schools at all levels must be kept segregated at all costs."

Olin D. Johnston, United States Senator from the State of South Carolina, has made the following statement which reflects the official attitude of that state:

"Our dual system of schools is the best in the Nation and the relationship we have between the races is the envy of those upon whom integration has been forced. . . . In the face of much unreality and great danger, there are those in our country who favor integration in schools. . . . It is not good for the white children or the colored children. Both will lose if integration is forced upon us. . . ."[67]

Statements such as those above, when made by the highest officials of many of our Southern states, engender a climate of opinion which sanctions a total disregard of the constitutional rights of Negroes. This, in and of itself, Mr. President, is a serious degenerative social phenomenon in a society which seeks to inspire and imbue its citizens with a respect for law. In addition, such declarations when not countered by a firm *unequivocal* statement of national policy by the Chief Executive of the Government of the United States serve only to encourage and embolden those among us who seek to turn back the clock of history to slavery, the Black Codes, and *Plessy* v. *Ferguson*.

Admittedly, Mr. President, the elimination of segregation and state-imposed discrimination against Negroes involves a substantial change in the customs and mores of a significant section of our country. But customs and usages, to the contrary notwithstanding, cannot be invoked as the rationale for a program of "caution" in eliminating the immoral and unconstitutional practices of segregation and discrimination.

It is too often overlooked and/or forgotten that the South is not the only culture in the world that has had to radically change its customs and mores in the past fifteen, thirty, or fifty years.

"Since World War II, Great Britain, France and other powers have been stripped of colonies purchased with blood and treasure. The Japanese God-Emperor, whose deity had not been questioned for centuries, was made mortal with the stroke of a pen. In all the history of the human race has there been a more rapid and total rejiggering of human attitudes than that which, within a decade, stilled the fanatic hatreds of the West Germans and the Japanese and brought them back into the family of civilized peoples? These epic upheavals, which likewise 'profoundly and personally (touched) the lives of so many millions of individuals,' were accomplished with far less warning, in point of time, than the notice which the South enjoyed, long before 1954, of the ultimate doom of its 'separate but equal' subterfuges; and, generally speaking, they were accomplished with far less sound and fury *per capita* than was recently generated in Mississippi and Alabama by the sight, or thought, of white and Negro students seeking to walk together into a bus station.

"The Supreme Court of the United States, the NAACP, the Freedom Riders and assorted other demons in the new Southern Theology have not demanded that white Southerners cast out their God, dam up their economic lifestreams, or even that they suppress the ancient rancors and hatreds which are their badge, their shield and their sword. Southerners are being asked to do only what 125 million other Americans . . . have done for decades without foaming at the mouth, namely, to assure each citizen the right of public as well as private association with anyone who is disposed to associate with him; to guarantee everyone equal access to facilities which have been paid for with public funds, which operate under governmental license, or which are held out for public use; and, through their elected officials, to preserve the peace when their more depraved fellows take the law into their own hands in defiance of the New Order. Is this really asking too much?"[68]

SECTION IV

THE DUTY AND POWER OF THE PRESIDENT TO SECURE CONSTITUTIONAL AND CIVIL RIGHTS IN AMERICA

THIS ADMINISTRATION HAS, perhaps more than any other recent administration, recognized the importance of those cherished rights generically described as the "Rights of Man." The 1960 platform of the Democratic Party, in referring to the "Rights of Man" and to civil rights in particular, stated that:

"It is the duty of the President to see that these rights are respected and the Constitution and laws as interpreted by the Supreme Court are faithfully executed."[69]

This duty today, some two years later, is of no less importance. Indeed, within the historical context of the Centennial of the Emancipation Proclamation, Presidential responsibility for the securing of civil rights is ever more important and meaningful.

The 1960 Democratic Party platform noted specifically the peculiar role and special responsibility the Chief Executive has for the implementation and achievement of human rights for all citizens. It appropriately said:

"What is now required is effective moral and political leadership by the whole Executive Branch of our government to make equal opportunity a living reality for all Americans."[70]

1963, in the United States of America, Mr. President, must be the year of living reality, not only for some twenty million Negroes, but for all America. To accomplish this goal, the party platform of your Administration recognized that significant executive orders and/or legal actions by the Attorney General would be necessary. Above all, however, it stated that the achievement of full human dignity would require the

> *"strong, active, persuasive and incentive leadership of the President of the United States."*[71] (emphasis added)

Mr. President, as President-elect you displayed an understanding of the consequences of ineffective and "timid executive leadership." In your speech formally accepting your Party's selection of you as their candidate for President of the United States you said, before thousands of Americans who had come to hear you and extend their support:

> "A peaceful revolution for human rights—demanding an end to racial discrimination in all parts of our community life—*has strained at the leashes imposed by timid executive leadership.*"[72] (emphasis added)

Two months later, on September 9, 1960, on your return to Los Angeles, California, you spoke in a way which reflected a keen understanding of the importance of Presidential leadership on behalf of civil rights. You noted that:

> "If the President does not himself wage the struggle for equal rights—if he stands above the battle—then the battle will inevitably be lost . . . He cannot wait for others to act . . . He himself must draft the programs, transmit them to Congress and *fight for their enactment, taking his case to the people if Congress is slow.*"[73] (emphasis added)

It is difficult for us to understand how you

are now more hesitant to exert that bold Executive leadership so persuasively spoken of by you as a candidate. Surely, it must be clear that if the President "does not himself wage the battle for equal rights" the battle will be lost! A President who "waits for others to act" on civil rights is not offering the kind of leadership consistent and commensurate with the invigorating spirit of the "New Frontier."

We believe that you, like Abraham Lincoln before you, stand at a historic crossroads in the life and conscience of our nation. The Centennial of the Emancipation Proclamation must be honored by the complete elimination of all forms of state-imposed segregation and discrimination.

The Proclamation of Emancipation in 1863 was a historic milestone along the high road to freedom and human dignity. Since 1863, however, there have been many "roadblocks." Shortly after 1877 a new *form* of slavery arose to replace the old. In the form of legislation, euphemistically called the "Black Codes," segregation was introduced for the purpose of reinstituting the essence of slavery.[74]

We know, Mr. President, that the Thirteenth Amendment to the United States Constitution was enacted to vindicate "those fundamental rights which appertain to the existence of citizenship and the enjoyment of deprivation of which constitutes the essential distinction between freedom and slavery."[75] Segregation and state enforced discrimination is inconsistent with the letter and spirit of the Proclamation of Emancipation and contrary to the legislative purpose of the Thirteenth Amendment. The continued enforcement of state laws imposing racial discrimination and segregation constitutes a direct violation of those "fundamental rights which appertain to the existence of citizenship."[76]

On September 22, 1862, Lincoln sought to chart a new and high road for America. We believe that you, too, Mr. President, have been seeking to chart a high road for our country.

> "Our overriding obligation in the months ahead is to fulfill the world's hope by fulfilling our own faith."[77]

We welcomed this declaration of policy, however general, in the area of human rights. We noted, with particular attention, some of the statements in your State of the Union message of January 11, 1962:

> ". . . (T)he policy of this Administration is to give to the individual the opportunity to realize his own highest possibilities.

> "Our program is to open to *all* the opportunity to steady and productive employment, to remove from *all* the handicap of arbitrary or irrational exclusion, to offer to *all* the facilities for education and health and welfare, to make society the servant of the individual and the individual the source of progress, and thus to realize for *all* the full promise of America."[78] (emphasis added)

> ". . . *America stands for progress in human rights as well as economic affairs, and a strong America requires the assurance of full and equal rights to all its citizens of any race or of color.*"[79] (emphasis added)

> "*As we approach the 100th anniversary next January of the Emancipation Proclamation, let the acts of every branch of the Gov-*

ernment—and every citizen—portray that 'righteousness that exalteth a nation.' "[80] (emphasis added)

These *statements* are excellent, Mr. President, but the world and the nation wait for that 'righteousness that exalteth' America. The issuance of an Executive Proclamation requesting all states which continue to operate under a segregated system of education to submit plans for immediate desegregation by the school year of September 1963 would exalt the hearts of millions at home and abroad on the 100th anniversary of the Emancipation Proclamation.

The New York Times, editorially, the day after your State of the Union message, said in part:

> "The President linked the approaching centennial of the Emancipation Proclamation with a plea for fuller guarantees of racial equality, *then made it plain he had nothing original to put forward in this regard.*"[81] (emphasis added)

We respectfully suggest that the exigencies of segregation and racial discrimination provide you with a veritable storehouse of materials from which proposals for Executive action can be fashioned. Mr. President, no other office, like the Presidency, within our three branches of Government offers or possesses such inherent capabilities for the exertion of national leadership on the critical issues of our time. When the President of the United States speaks he speaks with the voice of the American people. Woodrow Wilson, writing in his Blumenthal Lectures given at Columbia University in 1907, said:

> "He (the President) cannot escape being the leader of his party except by incapacity and lack of

personal force, because he is at once the choice of the party and of the nation.

> "He can dominate his party by being *spokesman for the real sentiment and purpose of the country, by giving direction to opinion, by giving the country at once the information and the statements of policy which will enable it to form its judgments alike of parties and of men.*

> "His is the only national voice in affairs. Let him once win the admiration and confidence of the country, and no other single force can withstand him, no combination of forces will easily overpower him. His position takes the imagination of the country. He is the representative of no constituency, but of the whole people.

> "He may be both the leader of his party and the leader of the nation, or he may be one or the other. If he lead the nation, his party can hardly resist him. His office is anything he has the sagacity and force to make it.

> "Some of our Presidents have deliberately held themselves off from using the full power they might legitimately have used, because of conscientious scruples, because they were more theorists than statesmen. . . . The President is at liberty, both in law and conscience, to be as big a man as he can.

> "*His is the vital place of action*

in the system, whether he accept it as such or not, and the office is the measure of the man—of his wisdom as well as of his force." (emphasis added)[82]

Segregation and discrimination against millions of American citizens because of their race and skin color is a domestic problem with ramifications throughout the world, the majority of whose people are non-white. What the President of the United States says and does on this crucial issue is observed and heard around the world.

The recent exertion of Executive power in behalf of the public interest to maintain price stability in the Steel Industry revealed to us the tremendous influence which the President of the United States can exert. *You can, Mr. President, if you so choose, creatively utilize this same power in behalf of civil and constitutional rights.* We, respectfully, submit that *human dignity and the immediate discontinuance of state enforced discrimination and discrimination against Negro citizens is as much in the public interest as stabilization of prices and wages.*[83]

As Chief Executive, you have the unique opportunity to activate and direct the moral and democratic conscience of America in the field of race relations. The President of the United States

> "can draw upon his authority as spokesman for the nation in such a way as to inspire those who are working for a more democratic America and to rebuff those who would drag us backward into the swamps of primitivism and oppression—or, still better, to educate all of us in the ways of brotherhood. The moral force of this great office is never so apparent as when he lashes out at the vigilants who spoil

the vines of the First Amendment, its prestige never so imposing as when he set out quietly to persuade the leaders of Southern opinion that a new day has dawned. One thing is certain about our attempt to solve the crisis of desegregation in the schools: a key factor in the equation of success *will be a succession of Presidents determined to use all the resources of this great office."*[84] (emphasis added)

The Constitution of the United States places responsibility for the implementation of the laws directly upon the office of the Presidency. Before the President enters on the execution of this office, he is required to take the following oath:

> "I do solemnly swear (or affirm) that I will faithfully execute the Office of President of the United States, and will to the best of my ability, preserve, protect, and defend the Constitution of the United States."[85]

This solemn oath, which Lincoln characterized as "recorded in Heaven," requires that all the provisions of the Constitution be enforced by the President for the protection of all the citizens of the country regardless of the particular state in which they happen to reside.

This duty to "preserve, protect, and defend" the Constitution is of an entirely different nature than the duties of office prescribed in the oaths of office taken by members of Congress and the Judiciary. Their oath is simply to "support" the Constitution.[86]

The Constitution further requires the President as the Chief Executive to "take care that the Laws be faithfully executed."[87]

"Under Article VI of the Constitution, the Constitution and Acts of Congress are the supreme law of the land. Thus 'Laws,' within the meaning of Article II, Section 3, include the Constitution and the interpretation given it in judicial proceedings."[88]

The question before the Supreme Court in *In Re Neagle*[89] was whether the Presidential duty was limited to enforcement of Acts of Congress or treaties according to the *express terms,* or whether it included the "rights, duties and obligations growing out of the Constitution itself. . . ." The Court reached the latter view:

"In the view we take of the Constitution of the United States, any obligation fairly and properly inferable from that instrument, or any duty . . . is 'a law' within the meaning of this phrase."[90]

and consequently enforceable by the President under his constitutional powers.

Mr. President, a time of greatness calls for acts of greatness. The full panoply of Presidential power must now again, as in 1863, be exerted in behalf of civil rights. A former President of the United States once said, in describing the importance of creatively using the executive power to enforce the Constitution and laws of the United States:

"The most important factor in getting the right spirit in my Administration, next to the insistence upon courage, honesty, and a genuine democracy of desire to serve the plain people, was my insistence upon the theory that the executive power was limited only by specific restrictions and prohibitions ap-pearing in the Constitution or imposed by the Congress under its Constitutional powers. My view was that every executive officer, and above all every executive officer in high position, was a steward of the people, and not to content himself with the negative merit of keeping his talents undamaged in a napkin. I declined to adopt the view that what was imperatively necessary for the Nation could not be done by the President unless he could find some specific authorization to do it. My belief was that it was not only high right but his duty to do anything that the needs of the Nation demanded unless such action was forbidden by the Constitution or by the laws. Under this interpretation of executive power I did and caused to be done many things not previously done by the President and the heads of the Departments. I did not usurp power, but I did greatly broaden the use of executive power. In other words, I acted for the public welfare, I acted for the common well-being of all our people, whenever and in whatever manner was necessary, unless prevented by direct constitutional or legislative prohibition. I did not care a rap for the mere form and show of power; I cared immensely for the use that could be made of the substance."[91]

Candor and frankness require us to remind you again, Mr. President, of *your own* words, quoted earlier in this appeal:

"If the *President* does not himself wage the struggle for equal rights—if he stands above the battle—then the battle will inevitably be lost. . . . He cannot wait for others to act. . . . He himself must draft the program, transmit them to Congress and *fight for their enactment, taking his case to the people if Congress is slow.*"[92] (emphasis added)

Millions of your fellow Americans need, and the moral conscience of our country demands, "your stewardship" of the nation toward the goal of human dignity and equal rights.

We repeated these words from your September 9, 1960, Los Angeles campaign speech only because we firmly believe that there is broad statutory authority for the President of the United States to initiate action to enforce the judicially declared civil and constitutional rights of nearly twenty million Negro Americans.

As is well known, Mr. President, we are morally, spiritually and practically committed to the principles and precepts of non-violence. We are confident that our peaceful resistance to unlawfully imposed segregation and discrimination will awaken the conscience and morality of those who, in ignorance and without love and respect for the dignity of man, seek to impose second-class citizenship upon us.

We believe we need not and should not struggle unaided. Our efforts to achieve human decency and human rights by eliminating the unlawful restrictions upon the exercise of our civil and constitutional rights seek to uplift and enrich our entire country.

Much of the presidential sources of authority and power for executive enforcement of civil rights in the United States arises from Title 10, Sections 332 and 333. These statutory provisions concern the possible exertion of force against some of our fellow citizens. We want to make it unmistakably clear that our present appeal for the exertion of Presidential power on behalf of civil rights is expressly intended to remove these conditions, the continued existence of which decreases the possibility of a peaceful nonviolent achievement of first-class citizenship. We hope and pray that some of the power for Presidential action concerning the use of military force will never become necessary to secure civil and constitutional rights in these United States. Title 10, Section 333 of the United States Code provides:

"The President, by using the militia or the armed forces, or both, or by any other means, shall take such measures as he considers necessary to suppress in a State, any insurrection, domestic violence, unlawful combination, or conspiracy, if it

"(1) So hinders the execution of the laws of that State, and of the United States within the State, that any part or class of its people is deprived of a right, privilege, immunity or protection named in the Constitution and secured by law, and the constituted authorities of that State are unable, fail, or refuse to protect that right, privilege, or immunity, or to give that protection: or

"(2) Opposes or obstructs the execution of the laws of the United States or impedes the course of justice under those laws.

"In any situation covered by clause (1), the State shall be considered to have denied the equal protection of the laws secured by the Constitution."

Section 333 of Title 10 has its origin in the Act of April 20, 1871, which extended Presidential power far beyond the limitations of present section 333. The intent of the enacting Congress was to enable the President to act whenever the state denied the equal protection of the laws to its citizens. It was to be "an Act to enforce the Provisions of the Fourteenth Amendment to the Constitution of the United States, and for other purposes." 17 Stat. 13. The only significant change from the 1871 Act to the present section 333 was the elimination of the following sentence at the end:

> " . . . and any persons who shall be arrested under the provisions of this and the preceding section shall be delivered to the marshal of the proper district to be dealt with according to law."

The mandate from Congress is clear. The President has statutory authority to use the militia, armed forces, or *"ANY OTHER MEANS"* to suppress a conspiracy or unlawful combination if it deprives a class of person of the equal protection of the laws of the United States.

10 U.S.C. 332 relates to the problem of Presidential enforcement of judicial decrees. It provides:

> "Whenever the President considers that unlawful obstructions, combinations, or assemblages, or rebellion against the authority of the United States, make it impracticable to enforce the laws of the United States in any State or Territory by the ordinary course of judicial proceedings, he may call into Federal Service such of the militia of any State, and use such of the armed forces, as he considers necessary to enforce those laws or to suppress the rebellion."[93]

Mr. President, our citation of the constitutional and statutory sources of Presidential power is not done for the purpose of advocating or rationalizing the use of military force to enforce civil rights. On the contrary, we are so urging bold imaginative Executive leadership precisely because we are too deeply committed to a firm but peaceful non-violent achievement of human dignity for 20 million Americans.

The Civil Rights Acts Amendment of 1957 repealed that portion of 10 U.S.C. 332 which authorized the President to employ the armed forces to "aid in the execution of judicial process issued under" the Civil Rights Act. However, the Senate debate on the amendment indicated that the Senate did not intend to deprive the President of the power given him by the George Washington Act of 1795.[94]

In short, Mr. President, we are firmly convinced that there exist sufficient constitutional and statutory sources of power to enable you to use creatively the authority and moral prestige of your office to dramatically advance human rights in America. As the 100th anniversary of the Proclamation of Emancipation draws near, we, along with millions of our fellow citizens and the peoples throughout the world, are watching and waiting to see whether America has at long last fulfilled the hopes and dreams arising from the abolition of slavery. We appeal to you in order that we may now have to wait no longer. We appeal to you because we love so dearly this great land of ours. We appeal to you because we yearn for the time when we can stand in the full sunlight of human decency and join hands with our white brethren, north and south, east and west, and sing in joyous hallelujah,

> *"Sound the loud timbree*
> *O'er Egypt's dark sea,*
> *Jehovah hath triumphed—*
> *His people are free!"*

APPENDIX A

PRESIDENTIAL POWER TO ENFORCE JUDICIAL DECREES AND THE CIVIL RIGHTS ACT OF 1957

ISSUE:
Did the Civil Rights Act of 1957 limit in any way executive power to enforce judicial decrees dealing with civil rights:

CONCLUSION:
No.

FACTS:
The precise question of this memorandum is the effect on executive power of the passage of the Knowland-Humphrey amendment during the course of the debate on the Civil Rights Act of 1957 in the 85th Congress.

The Knowland-Humphrey amendment repealed 42 U.S.C. 1993. That section was originally passed on the Civil Rights Act of 1866. Acts Apr. 9, 1866, c. 31 sec. 9, 14 Stat. 29. It was re-enacted in the Civil Rights Act of 1870 with no substantive changes. May 31, 1870, c. 114, sec. 13, 16 Stat. 143. Entitled "Aid of Military and Naval Forces," sec. 1993 provided:

It shall be lawful for the President of the United States, or such person as he may empower for that purpose, to employ such part of the land or naval forces of the United States or of the militia, as may be necessary to aid in the execution of judicial process issued under Sections 1981–1983 or 1985–1994 of this title.

The events leading to the repeal of sec. 1993 are as follows: In 1957 the Justice Dept. had drafted a civil rights bill which was introduced in both houses as the "Eisenhower administration bill." It consisted of four parts. Part I provided for the establishment of a Commission on Civil Rights. Part II provided for an Assistant Attorney General for Civil Rights. Part III provided that the Attorney General would have standing to sue for an injunction on behalf of those deprived of rights under sec. 1985.[95] This third part was to be an amendment to sec. 1985. Part IV provided that the Attorney General would have standing to sue in his own name for the denial of voting rights.

Identical bills were considered by both Houses. Hearings were held in the Senate. Hearings Before the Subcommitte on Constitutional Rights of the Senate Committee on the Judiciary, 85th Congress, 1st Session. But no Senate reports on the bill were issued, since the Senate placed the House Bill, H.R. 6127, directly on the Senate calendar before the Senate bill was reported out of committee.

Part III amended sec. 1985; it thereby became interrelated to sec. 1993. Sec. 1993 was a general enforcement section for most of the civil rights sections, and so in retrospect it does not seem strange that the amendment did not mention specifically the interrelation. But it was this unmentioned interrelation which provoked the Southern attack that culminated in the repeal of sec. 1993.

Opponents to the bill, both in the House and the Senate, focused their attack on Part III. Three major arguments were developed:

(1) Use of the injunctive remedy by the Attorney General, when he already had power to prosecute criminally, would mean that he would elect the injunctive procedure so as to deny jury trial to those who would be accused of violating sec. 1985 rights.

(2) Granting the Attorney General standing to sue on the behalf of others for denial of sec. 1985 rights would make him an oppressive power wielder.

(3) The administration had represented the bill as one dealing with voting rights. In fact, sec. 1985 rights comprehended many more rights. To pass Part III would go beyond the necessities of the time and would be a fraud on the Congress as well as the American people.

A fourth argument emerged in the Senate debate. It was that by means of the interrelation of the amendments of sec. 1985 (i.e., Part III) to the enforcement provision of sec. 1993, integration in the South would be accomplished by military force. It was to this last argument that the Knowland-Humphrey amendment was addressed.

The House Judiciary Committee report indicates that the "military force" argument was not considered in that body. The majority report speaks in terms of the "injunctive remedy": "The effect . . . of the proposed bill on . . . sec. 1985 is not to expand the rights presently protected but merely to provide the Attorney General . . . with a new remedy." H.R. Rep. No. 291, 85th Cong., 1st Sess. 10 (1957). The minority report also does not mention the military force argument.

Id. at 45.

The first mention of this argument appeared during the course of the Senate hearings. The subject came up during the testimony of Attorney General Brownell. The testimony was:

Mr. Young. [staff] I would like to have an expression from you now as to whether this statute is intended . . . [to be] used for the enforcement of these decrees?

Mr. Brownell. I am rather disturbed by you even raising these points, because, as I said so many times, public statements made by persons who intimate that there is any such thought in the minds of anyone here in Washington to use the military in these cases does not represent the true state of facts, and I frankly think that the only reason it can be brought into the discussion at all is to confuse the issue.

❋❋❋❋❋❋❋❋❋❋❋❋

Mr. Young. It is possible to do it under that statute, however, is it not, General?

Mr. Brownell. There are other statutes that would have to be considered in connection with that, and I think you will find the general rule is that the Governor of the State must request the President.

We do not want to take away any supplementary aid which the Governor of a State may want.

❋❋❋❋❋❋❋❋❋❋❋❋

No one has had in mind any use of the militia in this situation, and I don't think that there should be any implication that they do.

Mr. Young. . . . the power resides in the President to do this, does it not?

Mr. Brownell. The President is presumed to act in a constitutional way and I do not think that there is any indication that he is not going to.

❋❋❋❋❋❋❋❋❋❋❋❋

I frankly don't think it would be appropriate to have an exercise in the interpretation of that statute. [Sec. 1993]

❋❋❋❋❋❋❋❋❋❋❋❋

Since there is not the slightest suggestion on the part of any responsible public official of bringing in matters of the militia into the civil rights area, I think it would be quite misleading really to continue. . . .

❋❋❋❋❋❋❋❋❋❋❋❋

[T]his program does not extend the jurisdiction of the Federal Government. Whatever power is there now, the constitutional power of the President remains exactly the same. We are not extending Federal jurisdiction one bit.[96]

There was no other testimony on this point by Mr. Brownell. But it was at this point that Senator Ervin pointed out the interrelation of sec. 1985 to sec. 1993. He also noted that sec. 1993 was an existing statute, a point sometimes lost sight of in the later debate.

Then on July 2nd Senator Russell took to the floor with a prepared speech. Reveling in the full flower of Southern oratory he declaimed:

[The] bill is cunningly designed to vest in the Attorney General unprecedented power to bring to bear the whole might of the Federal government, including the armed forces, if necessary, to force a commingling of white and Negro children in the State supported public schools of the South.

[Its aim] is to force the white people of the South at the point of a Federal bayonet to conform to almost any conceivable edict directed at the destruction of any of the local customs, laws. . . . 103 Cong. Rec. 10771 (1957).

Voting rights is a smokescreen to obscure the unlimited grant of powers to the Attorney General of the United States to govern by injunction and Federal bayonet. *Id.* at 10772.

If it is proposed to move into the South in this fashion, the concentration camps may as well be prepared now, because there will not be enough jails to hold the people of the South who will oppose the use of raw Federal power forcibly to commingle white and Negro children in the same schools. . . . *Id.* at 10774.

That same day Senator Douglas took the floor and answered:

So far as the use of Federal troops by the President is concerned . . . that power has existed in the United States since the time of the Whiskey Rebellion, and since 1870 when the Force Act was passed. But that power has never been exercised by this Government since 1877, and we pray God it never will be exercised. *Id.* at 10779.

As later insertions into the Congressional Record demonstrate, the opponents of Part III were on the offensive. Playing to the national audience they elaborated these arguments:

(1) The sponsors of the act really wanted to enforce school integration at a bayonet point under the guise of a voting rights bill.

(2) The amendment to sec. 1985, when 1985 by its own terms did not refer to sec. 1993 (the enforcement provision), was a hidden cross reference demonstrating the epitome of legislative trickery.

(3) The invocation of sec. 1993 was pouring salt into old wounds.

(4) The Congressional sponsors were unwitting dupes of the faceless, nameless legislative draftsmen in the Attorney General's office.

(5) The President himself was against it. Or at best, he did not fully realize what he was asking for.

Utilizing TV programs, and capitalizing on newspaper editorials and an article in *Newsweek*, the opponents' campaign was built up.

The Senate sponsors, facing substantial difficulties in attempting to pass the injunctive provisions of Part III, and hoping to save votes which might otherwise be alienated by the interrelation aspect of sec. 1993, chose to propose an amendment which would repeal sec. 1993 in toto. This was the Knowland-Humphrey amendment.

In the subsequent two weeks the debate on the Senate floor turned to other aspects of Part III. As the debate on this section neared to its close, the Administration made its position known in two ways. One was by a press release distributed on July 16 by the White House which was entitled "Statement by the President." It said:

> This legislation seeks to accomplish these four single objectives:
>
> 1. To protect the constitutional right of all citizens to vote regardless of race or color. In this connection we seek to uphold the traditional authority of the Federal courts to enforce their orders. This means that a jury trial should not be interposed in contempt of court cases. . . .
>
> 2. To provide a reasonable program of assistance in efforts to protect other constitutional rights of our citizens.

The second was through the Presidential press conference of the following day, July 17, 1957. The relevant portion of it reads:

> [A]re you aware . . . you now have the authority to use military force to put through the school integration in the South. . . . ?

Well, first of all, lawyers have differed about some of the authorities of which you speak, but I have been informed by various lawyers that that power does exist.

> But I want to say this:
>
> I can't imagine any set of circumstances that would ever induce me to send Federal troops into a Federal Court [sic] and into any area to enforce the orders of a Federal court, because I believe that common sense of America will never require it.
>
> Now, there may be that kind of authority resting somewhere, but certainly I am not seeking any additional authority of that kind, and I would never believe that it would be a wise thing to do in this country. 103 Cong. Rec. 12055 (1957) (official transcript, as reported in The New York Times, inserted).

On July 18th the Senate began discussion of the amendment. And on the next day of the debate, July 22nd, a full discussion of the amendment occurred. The Senate then voted to pass it unanimously. *Id.* at 12310 (90 ayes and 0 nays).

With no substantive discussion of the Senate amendments, the House Rules Committee recommended adoption of the Senate amendments, H.R. Rep. No. 1243, 85th Cong., 1st Sess. 1 (1957).

ANALYSIS: An understanding of the appropriate scope to be attributed to the repeal of sec. 1993 necessarily involves an understanding of the basis of executive power under other statutory and constitutional provisions. Some of these provisions are:

> U.S. Const. art. II, sec. 1. The executive power shall be vested in a President of the United States.

> U.S. Const. art. II, sec. 2. The President shall be Commander in Chief of the Army and Navy of the United States, and of the Militia of the several states, when called into the actual service of the United States.

> U.S. Const. art. II, sec. 3. [H]e shall take Care that the Laws be faithfully executed. . . .

> U.S. Const. art. II, sec. 1. Before he enter on the Execution of his Office, he shall take the following Oath or Affirmation;—"I do solemnly swear (or affirm) that I will faithfully execute the Office of President of the United States, and will to the best of my Ability, preserve, protect and defend the Constitution of the United States."

> U.S. Const. art. VI. [A]nd all executive and judicial officers, both of the United States and of the several States, shall be bound by Oath or Affirmation, to support this Constitution. . . .

Congress has provided the President with

other statutory authority[97] in Title 10 (Armed Forces), Chapter 15 (Insurrection), sec. 331–334, and in Title 50 (War and National Defense), Chapter 13 (Insurrection), secs. 205–226.[98]

The proponents of the thesis, that the appropriate scope to be attributed to the repeal of sec. 1993 is a wide one, necessarily have two contentions.

These are:

(1) The legislative purpose implicit in the repeal of Sec. 1993 was to deny the President the authority to use the armed forces to execute judicial decrees in cases under the civil rights acts.

(2) Without such specific statutory authority as existed under sec. 1993, the President is without authority to implement such decrees.

The legislative purpose

(a) Pollitt

Pollitt's analysis of the repeal of sec. 1993 is as follows:

Congress recognized and sustained the power of the President under the George Washington Act of 1795 to use the armed forces to enforce judicial decrees arising under the civil rights act and other acts of Congress and believed that the supplementary power given him in the civil rights act should be repealed so as to narrow the area of controversy of the then pending business. Pollitt, *Presidential Use of Troops to Execute the Laws: A Brief History,* 36 N.C.L. Rev. 117, 135 (1957).

The Senate debate makes it clear that the 1957 amendment was not intended to deprive the President of what Congress believed to be the identical authority given to him by the George Washington Act of 1795. *Id.* at 137.

The Senate approved the Knowland-Humphrey amendment by. unanimous vote, which fact, when viewed in light of the background of the section eliminated from the announced purposes of the sponsors of the amendment, and the unanimous view of those who spoke on the amendment, leads to but one conclusion: that the Congress that met in 1957 believed that all apart from the express provision in the existing civil rights act, the President had authority under the Constitution and the George Washington Act of 1795 to use federal troops to enforce the execution of judicial decrees issued in civil rights and other judicial cases. *Id.* at 138.

Some of Pollitt's analysis is incorrect, but otherwise his conclusion on the effect of the repealing amendment is a sound one.

(b) Background

First it is necessary to recall the circumstances which surrounded the debate on the repealing amendment. Those were the pre-Little Rock days, and as Senator Douglas had stated, there had been little occasion to invoke sec. 1993 during all the time it had been on the statute books. No doubt the use of military force was never in the minds of those sponsoring the main bill. The President himself had indicated his distaste towards such use. The Attorney General had been evasive on this point. And the opponents of any civil rights legislation were making great capital out of their "discovered" interrelation of sec. 1985 to sec. 1993.

It was in this context that the sponsors of the main bill were faced with several alternatives. They could have directly justified the interrelation, saying that Part III was in no way adding to the enforcement provisions of sec. 1993; that that section already existed, and if there should be a repeal of that section, then the burden of showing a need for its repeal should be on those who wanted it repealed. Or sec. 1993 could have been amended so as to delete any reference to either the whole of sec. 1985, or more narrowly, to the Part III amendments to sec. 1985. Or outright repeal of sec. 1993 could be advanced. Whether or not other alternatives were considered, it was outright repeal which was selected. And it is this last alternative which, when compared to the other alternatives, prevents the strongest argument for the negative implication that by repeal the President is denied the power to enforce judicial decrees under the civil rights act.

In turning to the content of the debate it should be noted that whatever legislative history there is, it is contained in the Senate debate. The House neither in its report, nor on the floor, considered the interrelation aspect of Part III. The Senate had no explanatory reports. The debate then is the legislative record, and whether judicially significant or not, the Senate was highly conscious that it was making a record which would be used in the interpretation of the bill. Not only was there considerable discussion on the importance of making a legislative history for purposes of construing the act, but it was also recognized that there was special probative value that

would be attributed to the remarks of sponsors of amendments. 103 Cong. Rec. 11987 88 (1957).

(c) Debate positions

What emerges from the debate is a slight medley of confusion. The sponsors were not always clear as to the purpose and effect of the repealing amendment. Their opponents were divided. One recognized that the President would still have the power to enforce judicial decrees, and another did not. Other Senators indicated that they did not know what was the real issue involved in the repeal. One thing is certain: the unanimity of views which Pollitt says occurred did not exist.

(d) Sponsors' position

From the sponsors' side, and from those advocates of the entire bill, three positions were taken with regard to the repeal amendment. They were:

(1) It would serve the immediate purpose of narrowing the debate to the real issue of the injunctive power of the Attorney General under Part III, as well as saving votes which otherwise might be alienated by this sec. 1993 "military force" provision.

(2) As a policy matter, a program of integration should not be implemented by military force.

(3) Nonetheless, the power of the President to enforce judicial decrees, despite the repeal of sec. 1993, remained. Therefore nothing would be lost by enacting the repealing amendment.

Senator Humphrey's remarks reflect these somewhat inconsistent positions:

The reference to section 1993 is unfortunate. I think the Attorney General made a very unfortunate mistake in making that kind of reference, because there is plenty of other law to utilize, without rubbing salt into an old wound. 103 Cong. Rec. 11980 (1957) (July 17).

It is the belief of those of us who offered the amendment . . . that provisions relating to the use of military force had no place in the bill, and therefore ought to be eliminated. 103 Cong. Rec. 12074 (July 18).

It is most regrettable and unfortunate that . . . this bill should have been clouded by, and, in fact, distorted by, reference to the use of the Armed Forces of the United States as an instrumentality of law enforcement in civil rights matters. . . . I have felt that the reference was . . . unwise and psychologically unfortunate.

❈❈❈❈❈❈❈❈❈❈

Civil rights, to be meaningful, must be essentially secured by observance of the law. To be sure, enforcement has its role in the fulfillment of any law, or in the fulfillment of the objectives of the law, but . . . when we are dealing with human rights . . . we must seek to obtain compliance . . . through respect for the law. . . . Therefore any reference in this proposed public statute to the use of military forces has an unfortunate connotation, and I must say our opponents found in this particular reference to the use of military power a dramatic incident, putting out of focus the whole purpose of the proposals which are before the Senate in the field of civil rights. 103 Cong. Rec. 12304 (1957) (July 22).

Senator Knowland's statement also indicated a purpose to narrow the issues on the floor, and a purpose to have a civil rights program which would not necessitate the use of military force. But he only intimated that the repeal of sec. 1993 would not affect other Presidential powers. He said:

Although it was not stated in so many words, the inference was that it would be the intention of the sponsors of the bill and those who propose its enactment, that the full weight of the Armed Forces of the United States . . . might be brought to bear upon a school district or locality in the enforcement of certain court orders. . . . [T]hat was not the intent of the President . . . of the House of Representatives . . . and . . . it certainly was not the intent or policy of any member of this body.

❈❈❈❈❈❈❈❈❈❈

At least we should eliminate that argument from the bill.

❈❈❈❈❈❈❈❈❈❈

As I stated, it was for the clarification of the debate that the amendment was offered, and the amendment is only to repeal that particular section of the code which dates from Reconstruction days.

103 Cong. Rec. 12304 (1957)
(July) 22).

The Senators who most consistently and clearly maintained that the repeal of sec. 1993 would have no effect on Presidential powers were Senators Clark and Javits. And their position was clearly understood and acknowledged by one of the prime opponents of the bill, Senator Long.

During his presentation of the whole of Part III, Senator Javits said:

On that point [the Knowland-Humphrey amendment] I see no particular reason why that part of the bill should be stricken out; neither do I see any particular reason why it should be retained. If in connection with the passage of the bill, the Senate wishes to strike out something which is a vestige of the past, and does not belong in the law, that will be perfectly all right. There are many parts of the law that fall into that category. . . .

So in this case, if more Senators will vote for the bill if that part is eliminated, and if Senators will be made happy by its elimination,—that is to say, by striking out provisions which are obsolescent; indeed, provisions which were replaced a year ago by the Armed Forces bill,[99] which gives the President all the power he needs in order to keep order—I would not think of taking the position that I should insist on the retention of that particular part, and that not one word of it should be changed.

Senator Aiken, Is it the opinion of the Senator from New York that if the Knowland-Humphrey amendment is agreed to, the President still will have authority to use troops where necessary?

In the event of some large scale breach of public order, the other statutes which are more specific, in my opinion give the President all the power he needs or all the power he ought to have, regardless of this particular provision of the bill.

❀❀❀❀❀❀❀❀❀❀❀❀

I say the President would not thereby be deprived of any power he needs or any power he ought to have. 103 Cong. Rec. 12098 (1957) (July 18).

Senator Clark's statements, during the main debate on the repealing amendment, was as follows:

Under Article 1, section 3 of the Constitution, the President of the United States is required to see to the faithful execution of the laws. Since 1795 the President has had full power to use the military forces of the United States to execute the laws if wholesale resistance is encountered . . . the 1795 act was the result of the Whiskey Rebellion.

In view of the fact that these laws have been on the books since 1795, and that the President has the constitutional duty to enforce the laws in any event, I am in accord with . . . [the sponsors] that it would be psychologically unsound and unwise further to embitter the civil rights controversy by referring, in the bill under consideration, to an old section of the Ku Klux Klan Act, which inevitably would arouse age-old passions which were better left to die on the ashes of their age.

So I shall support the pending amendment, knowing full well that after the amendment is agreed to, the President will still have, as he has always had, adequate authority to enforce the laws of the United States. 103 Cong. Rec. 12306 (1957) (July 22).

Senator Clark then inserted in the Congressional Record a memorandum prepared by the American Law Division of the Library of Congress which in substance justified his statement.[100]

(e) An opponent's recognition

Senator Long indicated that he fully understood the thrust of statements such as those of Senator Clark, and one is tempted to say, attributed a greater clarity of purpose to the sponsors of the amendment than they deserved when he said:

I believe certain things should be made clear. One of them is that the Senators who are proposing that this provision of the bill be stricken out are not doing so because they do not envision the use of Federal troops to support integration in the South. They are moving to have the provisions stricken out because, as they have explained, they believe that under the Constitution, and other sections of the law, the use of

Federal troops, including the use of bayonets, to enforce such measures will still be available. *Id.* at 12310.

(f) The ambiguous Senators

Other Senators advanced the position of being adamantly against the use of "military force" to implement court orders, and yet recognized the existence of such power in the executive. Senator Lausche was against Part III without the Knowland-Humphrey amendment since:

It is set forth pointedly, harshly, and severely that the Army, the Navy and the militia shall be called out to put the law into effect.

I shudder to think that in America, in connection with a problem of this type, that someone possessed the audacity to sponsor such a provision, notwithstanding the provision of the Constitution which gives the President the power to enforce judicial decrees when they are resisted by armed revolution or otherwise.

✼✼✼✼✼✼✼✼✼✼✼

There was no need for that provision, Mr. President. The Constitution . . . already gave ample powers to the President. *Id.* at 12307.

Senator Carroll thought the amendment was designed "to quiet the fears that have been aroused." *Id.* at 12309. He added: "If I believed that the enactment of the bill would result in the imposition of a police force on

the Southland, I would vote against the bill."
Yet in referring to the Library of Congress
memorandum he said: "Its statement on the
matter is clear. The President has always
had the power to use force to insure the functioning of the United States laws." *Id.* at
12309–10.

Senator Cooper also presented the position
that though it was bad policy to use military
force, yet the President would continue to
have such power. He said:

> A few minutes ago the Senate
> voted to repeal the archaic recon-
> struction statute which gave to the
> President of the United States, pre-
> sumably, the power to enforce the
> orders of the courts by the use of
> military force. It was wise to repeal
> it because it is old and archaic and
> because it would not be enforced.

> Yet everyone who is familiar
> with the Constitution and who
> knows the law is aware that the
> President has such power, without
> that statute. The United States can-
> not permit the Federal system and
> the judicial system to collapse, if
> local law enforcement should col-
> lapse. 103 Cong. Rec. 12317
> (1957).

Other Senators were even less clear about
their positions on the effect and purpose
of the repeal of sec. 1933. Senator Sal-
tonstall wanted no Federal dictation, and
thought the "government should be close to
the people." *Id.* at 12283. Senator Anderson
thought the amendment dealt with "a subject
which might have been handled by separate
legislation." *Id.* at 12284. Senator Aiken
thought it would repeal "an obsolete law

which is unnecessary and which ought not to
remain in the statutes." *Id.* at 12284.

(g) Recapitulation and sole opposing interpretation

Aside from the immediate tactical purpose of
"narrowing the issues," there were only few
statements to the effect that the repeal of sec.
1993 would have absolutely no effect on extant Presidential powers. The majority of the
statements fell in that ambiguous pose that
decried the use of military force but which
nonetheless recognized the existence of a
duplicatory and residual Presidential power
to use military force. Some of these statements
may not have recognized explicitly the existence of such power, but no Senator denied it,
—save one, and that was Senator Russell. He
said:

> Senators may differ as to the gen-
> eral authority of the President of
> the United States to employ the
> military forces, but I assert that the
> adoption of the amendment will
> eliminate from our law the specific
> power of the President to delegate
> the authority to employ troops to
> execute judicial process in specific
> cases.

> There is a vast difference be-
> tween the employment of troops
> under a specific statute to carry out
> a specific judgment of a court and
> the general powers of the United
> States to quell insurrection within
> this land. It should be unnecessary
> to dwell upon that difference. *Id.* at
> 12310.

(h) Conclusion on legislative purpose

The position that the repeal of sec. 1993 effectuated a legislative purpose to deny the President power to enforce judicial decrees under the civil rights act has little to recommend it. The position rests on these two elements:

> (1) The debate indicated a legislative policy against the use of military force to support court orders.

> (2) The statement of Senator Russell indicated the true legislative purpose.

Each of these elements is a weak reed. The terms of the amendment did not extend beyond sec. 1993 and so did not expressly repeal any other extant Presidential power. The legislative policy opposed to the use of military force did not culminate in express legislation denying such power to the executive. The only statement which would tend to justify an interpretation that other, duplicating Presidential powers were repealed by implication is that of Senator Russell, and since his voice is that of an opponent, it is no guide to the divining of the legislative purpose.[101] Furthermore the Senator's statement makes no legal sense. The distinction which he draws between general powers and specific powers is meaningless in the present context. When there exists a general power (10 U.S.C. 331–334) and a specific power parallel, and comprehended within it (42 U.S.C. 1993), and that special power is repealed, some statutory language is required before it can be argued that the general power has been diminished by the repeal of the specific power. The fact the Senator finds it "unnecessary to dwell upon that difference" would indicate that there is nothing to dwell on.

The other position, that repeal of sec. 1993 did not affect existing Presidential powers, seems correct (though it is not free from ambiguity). First, there are the floor statements which reveal that there was no purpose to take away existing, albeit duplicatory powers.[102] Second, it must be recognized that there is a distinction between a policy against enforcing decrees by military means, and its enactment into legislation. Although some statements by sponsors and advocates of the bill embraced policy, none went so far as to propose to enact it into legislation. No express statutory denial of power to the President was passed. Third, if there is anything to the idea of a "basic purpose," or of a legislative understanding at what "mischief" the legislative action was aimed to remedy, it then becomes evident that the basic purpose was a tactical one, and that was to narrow the debate to what were considered the more fundamental and immediate issues. The issue of whether or not all executive power to enforce judicial decrees in the area of civil rights was being repealed was not before the Senate when it voted on the Knowland-Humphrey amendment. Fourth, since the unanimity of the vote embraced many viewpoints, special weight must be given to the views of the sponsors of the amendment, and of the advocates of the main bill.[103] Their views do not reveal a purpose to have the repeal go beyond its express terms.

A DIFFERENT APPROACH

Although the Supreme Court has said: "Legislative materials . . . can scarcely be deemed incompent or irrelevant"[104] an analysis will be set forth which relies only partially on legislative history.[105]

To begin with, there is the text.[106] The Knowland-Humphrey amendment only repealed sec. 1993. It says nothing more. Since there is the duplicatory and more comprehensive executive authority under 10 U.S.C. 331–334, for the repeal to have any effect on these sections it must operate by implication.

Baldly stated the opposing argument is that "the express repeal of sec. 1993 also impliedly repealed those sections of Title 10 which authorizes the President to utilize armed forces to enforce judicial decrees dealing with civil rights. Therefore the President now is without such power. Congress has denied it to him."

The difficulty with the scope to be attributed to the repeal has been noted in a more general context by Justice Frankfurter:

> The difficulty in many instances where a problem of meaning arises is that the enactment was not directed towards the troubling question. The problem might then be stated, as once it was by Mr. Justice Cardozo, "which choice is the more likely that Congress would have made?" *Burnet* v. *Guggenheim,* 288 U.S. 280, 285 (1933). Frankfurter, *Some Reflections on the Reading of Statutes,* 47 Col. L. Rev. 527 (1947).

Congress did not squarely face up to the issue of what power the President would have left, after the repeal. It was really legislating on other matters. As to the choice Congress would have made, certain reliance can be placed on standard rules for construing legislation.

One such rule is that: "The courts will not ascribe to the legislature 'an intent to create absurd or harsh consequence, and so an interpretation avoiding absurdity is always to be preferred."[107] Applied, it means that Congress would not have acted so as to strip the Executive of the statutory authority he has under Title 10, leaving him power to use military force to enforce all judicial decrees, except those dealing with civil rights. That is, there was no reasonable distinction advanced during the debate as to why the President should by implication be denied this power with regard to civil rights decrees, and not with regard to all other decrees. To deny the President power in only one area when obstructionism may be as great with regard to civil rights as to any other subject matter creates an absurd result. Additionally, to construe such an implied repeal Title 10 would create an absurd result in the sense that Congress would have been deemed to have curtailed the executive power of art. II, sec. 1 and 3 of the Constitution. This interpretation can be avoided. All that is necessary is an interpretation that there was no repeal by implication.

Other rules of statutory construction that could be applied are:

(1) There is a presumption against the implied repeal of a statute.[108]

(2) A law is not presumed to be repealed by implication; conversely, the presumption is against an implied repeal.[109]

(3) It is a well established principle that a valid legislative enactment which contains an express provision repealing a particular act or part of an act is effectual to establish a repeal of the law it describes.[110]

(4) A single act may repeal former legislation, in part by a provision expressly repealing specified existing legislation, and in part by implication because of inconsistency with existing law. However, the existence of a specific repealer is evidence of an intent that further repeals (by implication) are not intended by the legislature.[111]

Putting aside the legislative purpose (if it should be deemed too ambiguous), and also these rules of construction (should they be deemed make-weights), nonetheless, there is a basic constitutional argument that can be made which would limit the effect of the repeal of sec. 1993. It is that the Constitution has prescribed certain steps for the enactment of legislation and unless these are satisfied, legislative silence cannot be taken as repealing previously enacted legislation. Cf. *Schwegmann Bros.* v. *Calvert Distillers Corp.,* 341 U.S. 384, 396 (1952) (Jackson, J. concurring).

A further consideration arguing for a narrow scope of application for the repeal is the contemporaneous and legislatively uncontested promulgation of the Little Rock executive orders.[112] On September 23rd and 24th, two months almost to the day from the repeal of sec. 1993, President Eisenhower issued two executive orders, one calling for dispersal of the mobs, and the other for the mobilization of the National Guard. Both were issued to enforce and to aid in the execution of judicial decrees. Both referred to the statutory power of Title 10 and to the constitutional power of the President.

(a) Conclusion

There is no convincing proof of a Congressional purpose that the repeal amendment was also to impliedly repeal 10 U.S.C. 331–334 as to matters dealing with civil rights. In fact, the legislative purpose, though slightly ambiguous, pointed the other way.

Normal rules of statutory construction for a situation where the legislature did not explicitly deal with a problem would construe the Title 10 provisions as being left unaffected by the Knowland-Humphrey repeal amendment.

It also seems doubtful that Congress can abridge the executive's constitutional powers to execute the laws.[113] Furthermore, contemporaneous executive action reinforces the conclusion that the prior statutory authority of Title 10 was unaffected by the amendment.

APPENDIX I

Some provisions from Title 50 (War and National Defense) Chapter 13 (Insurrection) sec. 205–226.

50 U.S.C. 205 Suspension of commercial intercourse with State in insurrection.

Whenever the President, in pursuance of the provisions of this chapter,[114] has called forth the militia to suppress combinations against the laws of the United States, and to cause the laws to be duly executed, and the insurgents shall have failed to disperse by the time directed by the President, and when the insurgents claim to act under authority of any State or States, and such claim is not disclaimed or repudiated by the persons exercising the functions of government in such State or States, or in the part or parts thereof are at any time found by the President to be in insurrection against the United States, the President may, by proclamation, declare that the inhabitants of such State, or of any section or part thereof where such insurrection exists, are in a state of insurrection against the United States; and thereupon all commercial intercourse by and between the same and the citizens thereof and the citizens of the rest of the United States shall cease and be unlawful so long as such condition of hostility shall continue; and all goods and chattels, wares and merchandise, coming from such State or section into the parts of the United States, or proceeding from other parts of the United States to such State or section by land or water, shall, together with the vessel conveying the same, or conveying persons to or from such state or section be forfeited to the United States.

(Derivation: Acts July 13, 1861, ch. 3, sec. 5, 12 Stat. 257; July 31, 1861, ch. 32, 12 Stat. 284)

Sec. 206 (Suspension of commercial intercourse with part of State in insurrection.)
Sec. 207 (Persons affected by suspension of commercial intercourse.)
Secs. 208–209 (Licensing to trade.)

Sec. 210 (Penalties for unauthorized trade.)
Sec. 211 (Investigation for abuses.)
Sec. 212 (Confiscation of Property employed to aid insurgents.)

Whenever during any insurrection against the Government of the United States, after the President shall have declared by proclamation that the laws of the United States are opposed, and the execution thereof obstructed, by combinations too powerful to be suppressed by the ordinary course of judicial proceedings, or by the power vested in the marshals by law, any person, or his agent, attorney or employee, purchases or acquires, sells or gives, any property of whatsoever kind or description, with intent to use or employ the same, or suffers the same to be used or employed in aiding, abetting, or promoting such insurrection or resistance to the laws, or any person engaged therein; or being the owner of any such property, knowingly uses or employs or consents to such use or employment of the same, all such property shall be lawful subject of prize and capture wherever found, and it shall be the duty of the President to cause the same to be seized, confiscated and condemned.
Sec. 213 (Jurisdiction of confiscation proceedings.)
Sec. 214 (Now 10 U.S.C. 7651(c)—property on inland waters.)
Sec. 215 (Institution of Confiscation Proceedings.)

The Attorney General, or the United States attorney for any judicial district in which such property may at the time be, may institute the proceedings of condemnation, and in such case they shall be wholly for the benefit of the United States: . . . .
Sec. 216 (Preventing transportation of goods to aid insurrection.)
Sec. 217 (Trading in captured or abandoned property.)
Secs. 218–226 (Ports of entry, vessels.)

APPENDIX II

LIBRARY OF CONGRESS

July 9, 1957

To: Hon. John A. Carroll
From: American Law Division
Subject: Use of Armed Forces to Enforce Civil Rights Bill (H.R. 6127; 85th Congress)

To suggest that under the terms of the proposed civil rights bill (H.R. 6127; 85th Cong.) entire armed might of the United States might be mobilized to enforce compliance with judicial law (namely the Supreme Court ruling that segregation is violative of the equal protection clause of the Fourteenth Amendment) but not to enforce other provisions of that bill pertaining to denial of the right to vote is to overlook existing statutory provisions authorizing employment of the Armed Forces by the President to fulfill his constitutional duty to see to the faithful execution of the laws (art. II, sec. 3). Under title 10, sections 332–333 of the United States Code, the President already is vested with ample authority to employ the Armed Forces to enforce obedience to any Federal law, whether that disobedience is directed at judicial and executive officers enforcing decrees issued pursuant to judicial interpretation of the Constitution, the supreme law of the land, or is manifested in the form of resistance to Federal officers attempting to execute statutory law. Moreover such resistance elsewhere is declared by statute to be a crime against the United States; and if the ordinary, judicial processes are inadequate to punish those found guilty of committing such offenses, suppression of disobedience to said statutory provision legally would warrant the President's use of troops consistent with his constitutional duty as chief law enforcer.

The applicable provisions of law hitherto cited are the following: [Citing 10 U.S.C. 332–333]

> Whoever forcibly assaults, resists, opposes, impedes, intimidates or interferes with any judge of the United States, any United States attorney, any assistant United States attorney, or any United States marshal or deputy marshal, or any officer or employee of the Federal Bureau of Investigation of the Department of Justice * * * (etc.), while engaged in or on account of the performance of his official duties shall be fined * * * (U.S.C. 18:111, 114).

The purpose of this presentation of the aforementioned statutory provisions is to demonstrate that independently of the proposed civil rights bill, the President already is vested with ample authority to deploy the Armed Forces to meet concerted popular resistance designed either to obstruct enforcement of judicial decrees issued pursuant to constitutional and statutory provisions or to interfere with enforcement of statutory law by Federal officers. It matters little, therefore, whether title 42, United States Code, section 1993 is to be viewed as expressly authorizing the use of military force to execute title 42, United States Code, section 1981 [1985?] as amended by part 3 of H.R. 6127, but not complementing execution of title 42, United States Code, section 1971 as amended by part H.R. 6127 and relating to the denial of the right to vote.

As a perusal of the first cited provisions will confirm, the President's right to use the Armed Forces is clearly circumscribed. Military forces cannot be mobilized to mow down private citizens merely because they have congregated together in the exercise of their constitutionally protected freedom to assemble. On the contrary, these forces can only be deployed for one purpose only: namely, to combat organized resistance to the enforcement of law. To condemn the use of armed forces without acknowledging the only legitimate occasion for its exercise is either to becloud the issue or to conceal behind such protest what amounts to an arrogation of a right to resist with impunity.

Norman J. Small
AMERICAN LAW DIVISION

Inserted by Senator Clark,
    103 Cong. Rec. 12306–07
    (1957) (July 22).

APPENDIX III

The Little Rock Executive Orders

Proclamation No. 3204, Obstruction of Justice in the State of Arkansas, Sept. 23,[115] 1957, 22 F.R. 7628. (From Newport, R.I.)

WHEREAS certain persons in the State of Arkansas, individually and in unlawful assemblages, combinations, and conspiracies, have willfully obstructed the enforcement of orders of the United States District Court for the Eastern District of Arkansas with respect to matters relating to the enrollment and attendance at public schools, particularly at Central High School, located in Little Rock School District, Little Rock, Arkansas; and

WHEREAS such willful obstruction of justice hinders the execution of the laws of that state and of the United States, and makes it impracticable to enforce such laws by the ordinary course of judicial proceedings; and

WHEREAS such obstruction of justice constitutes a denial of the equal protection of the laws secured by the Constitution of the United States and impedes the course of justice under those laws:

Now therefore, I, DWIGHT D. EISENHOWER, President of the United States, under and by virtue of the authority vested in me by the Constitution and statutes of the United States, including chapter 15 of Title 10 of the United States Code, particularly sections 332, 333, and 334 thereof, do command all persons engaged in such obstruction of justice to cease and desist therefrom, and to disperse forthwith.

❀❀❀❀❀❀❀❀❀❀❀❀

10 U.S.C. 334   Proclamation to disperse.

Whenever the President considers it necessary to use the militia or the armed forces under this chapter, he shall, by proclamation, immediately order the insurgents to disperse and retire peaceably to their abodes within a limited time.

Executive Order No. 10730, Assistance for Removal of an Obstruction of Justice Within the State of Arkansas, Sept. 24, 1957, 22 F.R. 7628. (From Washington, D.C.)

WHEREAS on September 23, 1957, I issued Proclamation No. 3204 reading in part as follows:

❀❀ [Operative parts are recited] & ❀❀

WHEREAS the command contained in that Proclamation has not been obeyed and willful obstruction of enforcement of said court orders still exists and threatens to continue:

NOW, THEREFORE, by virtue of the authority vested in me by the Constitution and Statutes of the United States, including Chapter 15 of Title 10, particularly sections 332, 333 and 334 thereof, and section 301 of Title 3 of the United States Code, it is hereby ordered as follows:

Section 1: I hereby authorize and direct the Secretary of Defense to order into the active military service of the United States as he may deem appropriate to carry out the purposes of this Order, any or all of the units of National Guard of the United States and of the Air National Guard of the United States within the State of Arkansas to serve in active military service of the United States for an indefinite period and until relieved by appropriate orders.

Section 2: The Secretary of Defense is authorized and directed to take all appropriate steps to enforce any orders of the United States District Court for the Eastern District of Arkansas for the removal of obstruction of justice in the State of Arkansas with respect to matters relating to enrollment and attendance at public schools in the Little Rock School District, Little Rock, Arkansas. In carrying out the provisions of this section, the Secretary of Defense is authorized to use the units and members thereof, ordered into the active military service of the United States pursuant to Section 1 of this Order.

Section 3: In furtherance of the enforcement of the aforementioned orders of the United States District Court for the Eastern District of Arkansas, the Secretary of Defense is authorized to use such of the armed forces of the United States as he may deem necessary.

Section 4: The Secretary of Defense is authorized to delegate to the Secretary of the Army or the Secretary of the Air Force, or both, any of the authority conferred on him by this order.

✻✻✻✻✻✻✻✻✻✻✻✻✻

10 U.S.C. 332   Use of militia and armed forces to enforce Federal authority.

Whenever the President considers that unlawful obstructions, combinations or assemblages or rebellion against the authority of the United States makes it impracticable to enforce the laws of the United States in any State or Territory by the ordinary course of judicial proceedings, he may call into Federal service such of the militia of any State, and use such of the armed forces, as he considers necessary to enforce those laws or to suppress the rebellion.

10 U.S.C. 333   Interference with State and Federal law.

The President, by using the militia or the armed forces, or both, or by any other means, shall take such measures as he considers necessary to suppress, in a State, any insurrection, domestic violence, unlawful combination, or conspiracy, if it

(1)   So hinders the execution of the laws of that State, and of the United States within the State, that any part of class of its people is deprived of a right, privilege, immunity or protection named in the Constitution and secured by law, and the constituted authorities of that State are unable, fail or refuse to protect that right, privilege, or immunity, or to give that protection; or

(2)   Opposes or obstructs the execution of the laws of the United States or impedes the course of justice secured by the Constitution.

Montgomery Improvement

NEGOTIATING COMMITTEE

Rev. Ralph D. Abernathy
Rev. L. Roy Bennett
Mr. Fred D. Gray, *Attorney*
Rev. H. H. Hubbard
Dr. Moses W. Jones*
Rev. Martin Luther King, Jr.
Mr. Charles Langford, *Attorney*
Mr. Rufus A. Lewis
Mr. E. D. Nixon
Mr. J. E. Pierce
Mrs. Jo Ann Robinson
Rev. S. S. Seay*
Mrs. A. W. West
Rev. A. W. Wilson

EXECUTIVE BOARD

Rev. Ralph D. Abernathy
Mrs. Euretta Adair
Rev. A. W. Alford
Rev. L. Roy Bennett
Rev. R. B. Binion
Mr. P. M. Blair
Rev. J. W. Bonner
Miss Ida Caldwell
Dr. James Caple*
Rev. J. H. Cherry*
Rev. H. A. L. Clement*
Mr. P. E. Conley

Mrs. Erna A. Dungee
Mr. Isaiah Ferguson*
Rev. U. J. Fields
Rev. E. N. French
Rev. R. J. Glasco
Rev. Robert Graetz*
Mr. Fred D. Gray, *Attorney*
Mr. Thomas Gray
Rev. J. W. Hayes
Rev. R. W. Hilson
Rev. H. H. Hubbard
Rev. H. H. Johnson
Dr. Moses W. Jones
Rev. Martin Luther King, Jr.
Rev. B. D. Lambert
Mrs. Charles Langford, *Attorney*
Mr. Clarence W. Lee
Mr. Rufus A. Lewis
Mr. E. H. Ligon*
Mrs. Jimmie Lowe*
Mr. R. L. Matthews
Rev. A. W. Murphy*
Rev. H. J. Palmer
Mrs. Rosa Parks
Mr. J. E. Pierce
Rev. W. J. Powell
Mrs. Jo Ann Robinson
Rev. A. Sanders
Rev. S. S. Seay
Rev. B. J. Simms*
Dr. Jefferson Underwood*
Mrs. A. W. West
Rev. A. W. Wilson

Association

OFFICERS OF THE MIA

Original

Rev. Martin Luther King, Jr., *President*
Rev. L. Roy Bennett, *Vice-President*
Rev. E. N. French, *Corresponding Secretary*
Rev. U. J. Fields, *Recording Secretary*
Mrs. Erna A. Dungee, *Financial Secretary*
Mr. E. D. Nixon, *Treasurer*

Current

Rev. Martin Luther King, Jr., *President*
Rev. W. J. Powell, *1st Vice-President*
Dr. Moses W. Jones, *2nd Vice-President*
Rev. Robert Graetz, *Secretary*
Mrs. Erna A. Dungee, *Financial Secretary*
Rev. A. W. Wilson, *Treasurer*
Mr. J. E. Pierce, *Parliamentarian*
Rev. Ralph D. Abernathy,

    Chairman of Executive Board

Rev. S. S. Seay, *Executive Secretary*

FINANCE COMMITTEE

Original

Mrs. Euretta Adair
Rev. R. B. Binion
Mr. P. M. Blair
Miss Ida Caldwell
Mrs. Erna A. Dungee
Rev. R. J. Glasco
Rev. J. W. Hayes
Rev. H. H. Johnson
Mr. E. D. Nixon
Rev. W. J. Powell

Current

Rev. H. H. Hubbard, *Chairman*
Rev. R. B. Binion
Mr. P. M. Blair
Mrs. Erna A. Dungee
Rev. H. H. Johnson
Mr. Clarence W. Lee
Rev. A. W. Wilson

TRANSPORTATION COMMITTEE

Mr. Rufus A. Lewis, *Chairman*
Mrs. Euretta Adair
Mr. P. E. Conley
Rev. R. J. Glasco
Rev. J. W. Hayes
Rev. H. J. Palmer
Rev. W. J. Powell
Rev. A. Sanders
Rev. B. J. Simms*

PROGRAM COMMITTEE

Rev. Ralph D. Abernathy, *Chairman*
Rev. L. Roy Bennett
Rev. H. H. Hubbard
Mrs. Rosa Parks
Mrs. A. W. West

    * Added after original formation.

Notes

STRIDE TOWARD FREEDOM

Montgomery Today

1 The author is grateful to Professor Lawrence Reddick of Alabama State College for his help in the preparation of this chapter.

STRENGTH TO LOVE

A Tough Mind and a Tender Heart

1 John 18:11.

Transformed Conformist

2 Philippians 3:20 (MOFFATT).

3 Luke 12:15.

4 Matthew 5:28.

5 Matthew 5:10.

6 Matthew 21:31.

7 Matthew 25:40.

8 Matthew 5:44.

9 *Hyperion*, Bk. IV, Chap. 7.

10 *Writings*, Vol. X, p. 173.

11 "Stanzas on Freedom" (extract).

12 Romans 12:2.

13 Daniel 3:17–18.

14 "The Declaration of Independence" (extract).

15 Matthew 26:52.

16 William Hamilton Nelson, *Tinker and Thinker: John Bunyan* (1928).

Love in Action

17 Matthew 18:21.

18 Exodus 21:23–24.

19 Sonnet XCIV (extract).

20 Romans 10:2.

21 John 3:19.

Loving Your Enemies

22 *Metamorphoses*, Bk. VII (*Video meliora, proboque; deteriora sequor*).

23 Romans 7:19.

24 Hymn by Isaac Watts (extract).

25 Extract from "No East or West," *Selected Poems of John Oxenham*, ed. by Charles L. Wallis. Reprinted by permission of Harper & Row, Publishers.

A Knock at Midnight

26 *Essays on Freedom and Power* (1948).

27 Quoted in *Deep River* by Howard Thurman (1955).

28 *Ibid.*

29 Psalm 30:5.

The Man Who Was a Fool

30 Matthew 6:8.

31 Matthew 6:33.

32 Psalm 46:1.

33 Abraham Mitrie Rihbany, *Wise Men from the East and from the West* (1922), p. 137.

34 Luke 12:15.

35 Luke 12:33.

The Death of Evil Upon the Seashore

36 "The Battle-Field" (extract).

37 *The French Revolution*, Vol. I, Bk. III.

38 Hebrews 12:11.

39 *Hamlet*, Act V, Scene II.

40 "The Present Crisis" (extract).

41 *In Memoriam* (extract).

42 Speech at the Mansion House, November 10, 1942.

43 Letter to John Holmes, April 22, 1820.

44 Annual Message to Congress, December 1, 1820.

45 *Douglass' Monthly*, January 1, 1863, p. 1.

46 Luke 17:21 (RSV).

47 *Literature and Dogma* (1883).

48 Psalm 139:7–12.

Three Dimensions of a Complete Life

49 2 Kings 5:1.

50 "The Ladder of St. Augustine" (extract).

51 "Meditation XVII" (extract).

52 Psalm 8:3–4.

53 *Confessions,* Bk. I, Chap. I, tr. by Watts.

54 Matthew 22:37.

Shattered Dreams

55 Hebrews 11:9.

56 Edward FitzGerald, tr., *Rubáiyát of Omar Khayyám,* Stanza XVI.

57 *Ibid.,* Stanza LXIX.

58 *Ibid.,* Stanza LXXI.

59 Jeremiah 10:19.

60 2 Corinthians 11:26.

61 Philippians 4:11.

62 Philippians 4:7.

63 John 14:27.

64 Romans 8:28.

What Is Man?

65 *Gulliver's Travels: Voyage to Brobdingnag,* Chap. VI.

66 *Hamlet,* Act II, Scene II.

67 Isaiah 53:6.

68 "The Ways," *Selected Poems of John Oxenham,* ed. by Charles L. Wallis. Reprinted by permission of Harper & Row, Publishers.

How Should a Christian View Communism?

69 Amos 5:24.

70 Luke 1:52–53.

71 Luke 4:18–19.

72 *The Jesus of History* (1917).

73 Isaiah 40:4–5.

Our God Is Able

74 "Hymn of Man" (extract).

75 "The Present Crisis" (extract).

76 "Life" (extract).

77 John 14:27.

Antidotes For Fear

78 *Hamlet,* Act III, Scene I.

79 From "Courage" in *Society and Solitude* (1870).

80 *Discourses.*

81 Proverbs 3:19.

82 Psalm 8:5.

83 Matthew 10:26, 28–31.

The Answer to a Perplexing Question

84 Exodus 14:15.

85 Ezekiel 2:1.

86 2 Corinthians 5:17 (RSV).

87 Revelation 3:20.

Paul's Letter to American Christians

88 Romans 12:2.

89 Galatians 3:28.

90 Acts 17:24, 26.

91 Romans 8:38–39.

92 Matthew 5:11–12.

AN APPEAL / SECTION I: PREAMBLE

1 Kennedy, John F. "Are We Up to the Task," *The Strategy of Peace,* Popular Library, N.Y., 1961.

2 *Ibid.*

3 Editorial, "Hotel Workers Union," May 29, 1961, p. 3.

4 Frederick Douglass, describing the mood and temperament of abolitionists and free Negroes who had convened in a church in Boston on the evening of December 31, 1862, wrote:

"We were waiting and listening as for a bolt from the sky, which would rend the fetters of four millions of slaves; we were watching, as it were, by the dim light of

the stars, for the dawn of a new day; we were longing for the answer to the agonizing prayers of centuries. Remembering those in bonds as bound with them, we wanted to join in the shout of freedom, and in the anthem of the redeemed."
Life and Times of Frederick Douglass,
N.Y. 1941, Pathway Press, pp. 387–89.

When the news that the Proclamation had officially become law was announced to the persons in the church assembled, it had an electrifying effect. Douglass described it thus:

> "The effect of this announcement was startling beyond description, and the scene was wild and grand. Joy and gladness exhausted all forms of expression, from shouts of praise to sobs and tears. My old friend Rue, a Negro preacher, a man of wonderful vocal power, expressed the heartfelt emotion of the hour, when he led all voices in the anthem, 'Sound the loud timbrel o'er Egypt's dark sea, Jehovah hath triumphed, His people are free.'"
> *Ibid.*

5 The speeches delivered by leaders of the Southwide Student Sit-In Movement before the national Platform Committees of the Democratic and Republican Parties in the summer of 1960 aptly summarized the more modern efforts to extend freedom:

> "We also represent the thinking of thousands of Negro and white Americans who have participated in, and supported student efforts that have been characterized, generally, as Sit-Ins, but which in truth were peaceful petitions to the conscience of our fellow citizens for redress of the old grievances that stem from racial segregation and discrimination. In a larger sense, we represent hundreds of thousands of freedom loving people, for whom our limited efforts have revitalized the great American dream of 'liberty and justice for all.'

. . . . .

> "The threads of freedom form the basic pattern in man's struggle to know himself and live in the assurance that other men will recognize this self. The ache of every man to touch his potential is the throb that beats out the truth of the American Declaration of Independence and the Constitution. America was founded because men were seeking room to become.

> "We again are seeking that room. We want room to recognize our potential. We want to walk into the sun and through the front door. For three hundred and fifty years, the American Negro has been sent

to the back door in education, housing, employment, and the rights of citizenship at the polls. We grew weary. Our impatience with the token efforts of responsible adult leaders were manifest in the spontaneous protest demonstrations which, after February 1, spread rapidly across the entire South and into the North as sympathetic students sought to display their own dissatisfaction with race relations in the United States."

6 "Because ours is a government under a Constitution, Negroes have secured through court action the enforcement of many of their rights. The judicial process is not, however, a valid substitute for political leadership. The courts can only guardedly look beyond the case at bar, and their decrees have limited application. Negro Americans, whose resources have been taxed severely in financing and manning what is in truth a defense of everybody's constitutional principles, have a just claim that the President and his administration give invigorating guidance toward real equality. The nation as a whole needs to feel the impulse of Presidential concern and activity. The free peoples of the world, who value the reputation of the United States, wait to see us act with fairness toward our own citizens."
The Federal Executive and Civil Rights,
Southern Regional Council, Jan. 1961,
p. 2.

7 163 U.S. 537 (1896).

8 347 U.S. 483, 74 S.Ct. 686 (1954).

9 Tourgee, Albion. *First Mohonk Conference On the Negro Question in 1890* (Boston 1890) p. 111.

AN APPEAL / SECTION II

10 *Brown* v. *Board of Education,* 347 U.S. 483.

11 *Ibid.*

12 *Steiner* v. *Simmons,* 111 A. 2d 574 (Del. 1955).

13 347 U.S. 497 (1954).

14 *Ibid.*

15 *Brown* v. *Board of Education,* 349 U.S. 300 (1955).

16 358 U.S. 1 (1958).

17 *Ibid*. at p. 4.

18 *Ibid*. at p. 17.

19 *Ibid*. at p. 7.

20 353 U.S. 230 (1957). A Negro lad had been denied admission to Girard College, operated and erected under a trust naming the City of Philadelphia as trustee and providing that the college was to admit "as many poor white male orphans, between the ages of six and ten years, as the said income shall be adequate to maintain." The trust was administered by a Board of Directors made up of judges and elected officials. No city funds were used, but the property was tax exempt. The U.S. Supreme Court rejected the argument that the city officials were acting in a fiduciary, not a governmental, capacity and were not, therefore, subject to the Fourteenth Amendment.

21 *Ibid*. at 231. The "1961 Report of the United States Commission on Civil Rights," Vol. 2, *Education,* summarizes the decisions of the U.S. Supreme Court concerning equal protection of the law in public education and the rules governing their implementation. It states:

"1. State-imposed racial segregation in public educational facilities creates inequality and therefore constitutes a denial of equal protection of the laws under the Constitution. All schools in which a State participates through any arrangement, management, funds or property are subject to this rule. All provisions of Federal, State, or local law requiring or permitting racial segregation in public schools are void.

"2. All school authorities operating segregated school systems have a duty to make a prompt and reasonable effort in good faith to comply with the Constitution. The primary responsibility for elucidating, assessing, and solving the problems of desegregation rests with the local school authorities.

"3. In many locations this duty would require immediate general admission of Negro children. In others, justification for not requiring immediate general admission of all qualified Negro children may exist. Hostility to racial desegregation is, however, not a ground for delay." *Ibid*.

22 Ala. Code Tit. 52 #61(4) *et seq.* (1957 Supp.)
Ark. Stats. Ann. #80-1519 *et seq.* (1957 Supp.)
Fla. Stats. Ann. #230.232 (1957 Supp.)
La. Rev. Stats. #17:18.1 *et seq.* 17:331 (1957 Supp.)
Miss. Code Ann. #6334-01 *et seq.* (1956 Supp.)
N.C. Gen. Stats. #115-176 *et seq.* (1957 Supp.)
S.C. Code #21-230(9) (1957 Supp.)
Tenn. Code Ann. #49-1741 *et seq.* (1958 Supp.)
Tex. Rev. Civ. Stats. art. 2901a(4) (1957 Supp.)
Va. Code #22-232.1 *et seq.* (1958 Supp.)
Significantly, these are all states in which there has been either no compliance with *Brown* or only a minimum. There are a total of 2,917 school districts in these ten states; 1,899 are bi-racial, only 172 are desegregated, with Texas having 132 school districts listed as desegregated.
Southern School News, June 1961.

The Alabama Assignment Law is fairly representative. Its express intent is to insure "an efficient educational program with public support and to maintain order and goodwill." The local school board is given the power and authority to assign students to particular schools on the basis of legislative criteria. The criteria include availability of space, teaching capacity, transportation, suitability of established curricula for particular pupils, "psychological qualifications" of the pupil for the type of teaching and association involved, the psychological effect upon the pupil of attendance at a particular school, the possibility of breaches of the peace or ill will or economic retaliation within the community, the morals, conduct, health and personal standards of the pupil.

If a student wishes to appeal the decision of the local school board, there is an appeal to the school board for a hearing, then to the local circuit court for a jury trial and finally to the state supreme court.

In its first court test, the Alabama Law was upheld as "not unconstitutional on its face." *Shuttlesworth* v. *Birmingham Board of Education,* 162 F.Supp. 372 (N.D. Ala. 1958), affirmed 358 U.S. 101 (1958).

The Alabama criteria are typical of those used in Arkansas, Florida, Tennessee, Texas and Louisiana. *Report of the U.S. Commission on Civil Rights* (1959) Ch.V, "Legal Developments of Resistance in the Southern States," p. 242.

The original Virginia Pupil Placement Law (1956) included as one criterion "the efficient" operation of the schools. The same legislature defined an "efficient" system of schools as one in which no white and colored children were taught together! The district court examined these two statutes together and declared the Pupil Placement Act unconstitutional on its face. *Adkins* v. *School Board of the City of Newport News,* 148 F.Supp. 430 (E.D. Va., 1957), affirmed 246 F.2d 325 (4th Cir. 1957) *cert. denied,* 355 U.S. 855 (1957).

The Act was amended and now orders placement "so as to provide for the orderly administration of such public schools, the competent instruction of the pupils enrolled and the health, safety, and general welfare of such pupils." This statute has yet to be tested, but if *Shuttlesworth* is followed it may well be upheld as constitutional on its face.

Similarly, the North Carolina Pupil Placement Law directs the local school boards to assign pupils so as to provide for the orderly and efficient instruction, health, safety and general welfare of the pupils. In *Carson* v. *Warlick,* 238 F.2d 724 (4th Cir. 1956), the United States Court of Appeals for the 4th Circuit found the Act not unconstitutional on its face.

23 Citing *Cooper* v. *Aaron,* 358 U.S. 1.

24 Excerpt from John F. Kennedy's acceptance speech of nomination for President.

25 Secretary Ribicoff announced that:
    1. As of September 1963, the federal government will no longer regard segregated schools as "suitable" for federal grants for the education of children whose parents live and work on federal installations.

    2. Where no desegregated schools are available to serve these installations, the commissioner of education "will be authorized to provide for the education of children on a nonsegregated basis on federal property or make other suitable arrangements."
    SSN.V.8 No. 10, p. 1 (April 1962).
[In 1961, more than $12 million in current school operating funds was furnished by the federal government in behalf of 65,000 pupils residing on federal government property in 17 Southern and border states (Ala., Ark., Del., Fla., La., Ky., La., Md., Miss., Mo., N.C., Okla., S.C., Tenn., Tex., Va., W.Va.,)] SSN.V.8 No. 10, col. 3, p. 1.

26 *Public Beaches: Lonesome* v. *Maxwell,* 123 F.Supp. 193 (D. Md. 1954) stated that *Brown* did not apply to public beaches and pools. The decision was reversed by the Fourth Circuit, 220 F.2d 386 (4th Cir. 1955) whose decision was affirmed *per curiam* by the U.S. Supreme Court in *Mayor and City Council of Baltimore City* v. *Dawson,* 350 U.S. 877 (1955).

Public Golf Courses: In *Holmes* v. *City of Atlanta, Ga.,* 223 F.2d 93 (5th Cir. 1956) the Court of Appeals had held that Atlanta's municipal golf courses could continue a program of "separate-but-equal." This decision was reversed by the U.S. S.Ct. in 350 U.S. 879, *per curiam,* with an order that the case be remanded to the district court and a decree entered in favor of petitioners in accordance with *Mayor* v. *Dawson, supra.*

Public Parks: In *Detiege* v. *New Orleans City Park Improvement Association,* 252 F.2d 122 (5th Cir. 1958) the Fifth Circuit ruled that a Louisiana law and New Orleans city ordinance requiring segregation in city parks was unconstitutional. Affirmed by the U.S. Supreme Court in 358 U.S. 54 (1958).

These same principles apply even though state-owned public facilities are leased to private persons. See *Derrington* v. *Plummer,* 240 F.2d 922 (5th Cir. 1956), *cert. denied,* 353 U.S. 924 (1957), and *Tate* v. *Dept. of Conservation,* 231 F.2d 615, *cert. denied,* 352 U.S. 838. Cities which manage their own facilities in a "proprietary capacity" are also forbidden to discriminate. *City of St. Petersburg* v. *Alsup,* 238 F.2d 830 (5th Cir. 1956), *cert. denied,* 353 U.S. 922 (1957).

Public Libraries: As far back as 1945, *Kerr* v. *Enoch Pratt Free Library* was decided by the Fourth Circuit, 149 F.2d 212. The defendant, a privately endowed library, governed by a self-perpetuating board of trustees appointed by the original donor, barred Negroes from its training school for librarians. Because of the importance of financial assistance given the library by the state and city, and because of the significant control over library activities exercised by the state, racial discrimination by the library was held violative of the Fourteenth Amendment. The U.S. Supreme Court denied *certiorari* in 326 U.S. 721 (1945).

27 245 U.S. 60 (1917). Buchanan, a white person, had brought an action in the Kentucky State Court to compel specific performance of a contract for sale of certain real estate in Louisville to a Negro. The State courts denied him relief because a Louisville ordi-

nance's stated purpose was to "prevent conflict and ill-feeling between the white and colored races in the City of Louisville" by forbidding Negroes to move into a block upon which a greater number of houses were occupied by white people.

28 *Ibid.* at p. 73.

29 273 U.S. 668 (1927).

30 281 U.S. 704 (1930).

31 *Hurd* v. *Hodges,* 334 U.S. 24 (1948), was decided on the same day as *Shelley.* The case involved the issue of judicial enforcement of restrictive convenants in the District of Columbia. The Court based its decision on 8 United States Code 342, derived from the Civil Rights Act of 1866:

> "All citizens of the United States shall have the same right in every State and Territory, as is enjoyed by white citizens thereof to inherit, purchase, lease, sell, hold, and convey real and personal property."

It concluded that, even in the absence of statute, judicial enforcement of restrictive covenants in the District of Columbia would be unconstitutional:

> "It is not consistent with the public policy of the United States to permit federal courts in the Nation's capital to exercise general equitable powers to compel action denied the state courts where such state action has been held to be violative of the guaranty of the equal protection of the laws."

32 346 U.S. 249 (1953).

33 *Ibid.* at 254.

34 See: *Banks* v. *Housing Authority of City and County of San Francisco,* 120 Cal. App. 2d 1, *cert. denied,* 347 U.S. 974.
Detroit Housing Commission v. *Lewis,* 226 F.2d 180.
Jones v. *City of Hamtramck,* 121 F.Supp. 123.
Vann v. *Toledo Metropolitan Housing,* 113 F.Supp. 210.
Askew v. *Benton Harbor Housing Commission* (W.D. Mich., C.A. No. 2512, Dec. 21, 1956).
Davis v. *St. Louis Housing Authority* (E.D. Mo., C.A. No. 8637, Dec. 27, 1955).
Ward v. *Columbus Metropolitan Housing Authority* (S.D. Ohio, C.A. No. 4299, Nov. 5, 1955).
Woodbridge v. *Housing Authority of Evansville* (S.D. Ind., Civ. No. 618, 1953).
Taylor v. *Leonard,* 30 N.J. Super. Ct. 116, 103 A.2d 632 (1954) (quota system and segregation violate 14th Amendment).
Miller v. *McComb,* Camden County, N.J. Super. Ct. 1955 (consent decree).

35 63 Stat. 413 (1949), 42 U.S.C. 1441 (1958).

36 FHA Underwriting Manual, Sec. 303 (Dec. 1949). The FHA is authorized to insure private lending institutions against losses on long-term, first mortgage, home loans, and on unsecured loans for home repairs.

37 *Report of U.S. Commission on Civil Rights,* Vol. 4, "Housing," p. 25.

38 *Ibid.*

39 12 U.S.C. Sec. 1750aa.

40 Excerpt from a transcript of the President's news conference, as reprinted on p. 14, Jan. 16, 1962, *The New York Times.* Anthony Lewis of *The New York Times,* commenting on the President's response to the question at his news conference, said:

> "The President indicated his feeling that it was important not to move too fast in the field of race relations so as not to get too far ahead of public opinion.
>
> ❋❋❋❋❋❋❋❋❋❋❋
>
> "There was some suggestion that Mr. Kennedy feared that issuance of the order (in Federally assisted housing) would hurt the chances of other legislative problems, notably his trade program, *because of possible resentment among key Southern Congressmen.*"
>
> *The New York Times,*
> Jan. 16, 1962, p. 1, p. 15.

41 *The New York Times,* Jan. 18, 1962, p. 16, in an article entitled "Kennedy Aides Report Nation is Dissatisfied With Status Quo," indicated that a Report released by the White House showed "The American people were far from satisfied with the 'status quo' and expressed 'a strong demand for Federal action in numerous areas.' "

42 *The Federal Executive and Civil Rights,* p. 10, 1960–61 Report of the Southern Regional Council. The words of the Southern

Regional Council are as appropriate today in 1962 as they were in 1960:

". . . the President of the United States in the 1960's ought carefully to decide what are the necessary conditions of national unity. We think they do not reside in the perpetuation of sectionalism. The white population of eleven Southern states is roughly 20% of the nation's total. These are people who, besides being numerous, have been a seed bed throughout our history of able statesmen, treasured writers, and valorous military men. They are not a people to be condemned and shunned. And there could be no greater mistake than to assume that this 20% is a monolith. A large proportion would welcome, or at least have no objection to a broadening of civil rights because, more keenly than do persons in other regions, they want to be emancipated from the heavy age-old weight. There are state governments which have given clear indication, in the language of political maneuver, of their willingness to be silent followers of a national consensus. There is, in short, within the ranks of white Southerners practical, effective support for reform which ought not to be undervalued."　　　*Ibid.* at pp. 6–7.

43　Article I, Section 8, Clause 3 of the U.S. Constitution provides:

"The Congress shall have power . . . to regulate Commerce with foreign Nations, and among the several states, and with the Indian Tribes."

44　325 U.S. 761 (1945).

45　328 U.S. 373 (1946).

46　The Court pointed out the lack of uniformity among states on segregation; 18 states forbade segregation while ten states required it; the definition of Negro varied from state to state which would cause passengers to be in a state of constant change during an interstate trip. Therefore the Court concluded:

"As there is no federal act dealing with the separation of races in interstate transportation, we must decide the validity of this Virginia statute . . . as a matter of balance between the exercise of the local police power and the need for national uniformity in the regulations for interstate travel. It seems clear to us that seating arrangements for the different races in in-

terstate motor travel require a single, uniform rule to promote and protect national travel. Consequently, we hold the Virginia statute in controversy invalid."

Ibid. at 386.

47　Columbia University Press, 1955.

48　*Ibid.* at p. 120. Greenberg's study of the application of the "Morgan rule" indicated that the Sixth Circuit has applied the *Morgan* rule to company regulations as well as state laws. Segregation ordered by a driver in Kentucky which had no bus segregation law was held to be an unreasonable burden on interstate commerce just as much as if it had been imposed by law. *Whiteside* v. *Southern Bus Lines,* 177 F.2d 949 (6th Cir. 1949). The Supreme Court of Virginia also applied the *Morgan* rule to rail travel when it held that buses and trains are indistinguishable as far as of burden to interstate commerce. *Lee* v. *Commonwealth,* 189 Va. 890 (1949).

49　49 U.S.C.A. 3 (1).

50　313 U.S. 80 (1941).

51　339 U.S. 816 (1950).

52　The Court commented on the principle of segregation, however, by criticizing "the curtains, partitions and signs (which) emphasize the artificiality of a difference in treatment which serves only to call attention to a racial classification of passengers."

Ibid. at 325.

53　364 U.S. 454 (1960).

54　On November 7, 1955, the Interstate Commerce Commission decided *NAACP* v. *St. Louis-San Francisco Ry. Co.,* ordering the end of segregation on all interstate rail travel. It also ordered that the Richmond Terminal take down "WHITE" and "COLORED" signs. Relying heavily on the *Brown* decision, the ICC stated:

"It is hardly open to question that much progress in improved race relations has been made. . . . We are, therefore, now free to place greater emphasis on steps 'to preserve the self-respect and dignity of citizenship of a common country' which this commission in 1887 balanced against 'peace and order.' "

On this same day as the ruling in the above case the ICC also declared that to require "Negro interstate passengers [to] occupy space or seats in specified portions . . . of buses, subjects such passengers to unjust discrimination, and undue and unreasonable prejudice and disadvantage, in violation of Section 216(d) [of the ICA] and is therefore unlawful."

64 M.C.C. 769 (1955) at 772.

55 The ICC issued a regulation on September 22, 1961, effective November 1, 1961, prohibiting carriers from segregating passengers on any bus operated interstate, and from maintaining or using any terminal any portion of which is segregated. The Department of Justice has moved quickly against localities which prevented bus terminals from obeying the regulation. Since November, 1961, eight suits were filed against the following cities: Alexandria, Baton Rouge, Monroe, and Rustin, Louisiana; Greenwood, Jackson, and McComb, Mississippi. Favorable decisions for the government have been made in all cases except Baton Rouge and Jackson which are still pending.

56 The 2nd Circuit Court of Appeals has held that the Civil Aeronautics Act outlaws racial discrimination in the air. *Fitzgerald* v. *Pan Am World Airlines,* 229 F.2d 499 (2nd Cir. 1956).

57 At the request of the Federal Aviation Agency, the Department of Justice filed a suit which led to the desegregation of the Montgomery Airport in January, 1962. Another suit, intended to desegregate the New Orleans restaurant at the airport, is awaiting judgment as of April 1962. The Department of Justice was able to desegregate the Columbus, Georgia, and the Raleigh-Durham, North Carolina, airports by negotiation.

58 142 F.Supp 707 (M.D. Ala. 1956), aff'd *per curiam,* 352 U.S. 903 (1956).

59 358 U.S. 202 (1958).

AN APPEAL / SECTION III

60 "Statistical Summary," Southern Education Reporting Service, November 1961.

61 *Ibid.*

62 *Ibid.*

63 *Ibid.*

64 *Ibid.*

65 *Ibid.*

Addendum to Notes 60–65

On August 12, 1962, the Sunday edition of the *New York Times* reported on page 80, column 1, the following:

"INTEGRATION GAIN LISTED FOR SOUTH Report Says 33 More School Districts will Desegregate

NASHVILLE, Tenn., Aug. 11 (UP) The Southern School News said today that thirty-three public school districts in seventeen Southern and Border states had announced policies of desegregation to begin when schools open in September.

The monthly publication of the Southern Education Reporting Service noted that only four of these districts were desegregating by court order. The others are acting voluntarily.

The News also said that increased Negro enrollments were expected in twenty-four previously desegregated districts.

The new districts bring to 948 the number of districts in the region desegregated in practice or in policy. Of the 6,368 school districts in the region, 3,047 have both white and Negroes enrolled.

In the field of higher education there were these developments:

Arlington State College in Texas and the Johns Hopkins Medical School in Baltimore announced they would admit their first Negro students this fall.

St. Andrews College, a Presbyterian institution in North Carolina, admitted its first Negro student in July.

LITIGATION IN MISSISSIPPI

In Mississippi, a Federal court order to admit a Negro, James Meredith, to that state's university remained tied up in a series of legal maneuvers.

Of the newly desegregated public school districts, Texas and Virginia have eight each; Tennessee, six; Kentucky, five; North Carolina, four, and Florida two.

Additional desegregation has been announced by twenty-four districts in eleven states: Arkansas, one; Delaware, one; Florida, three; Georgia, one; Kentucky, three; Louisiana, one; Maryland, three; North Carolina, four and West Virginia, one.

In three Maryland districts and one in Delaware that were formerly desegregated in policy only, whites and Negroes will attend classes there together for the first time this fall.

Prince Edward County in Virginia is under Federal Court order to present a plan by September 9th to reopen public schools closed since 1959 to avoid desegregation.

Fort Worth, Texas also is under Federal Court order to desegregate its public schools this fall, but is expected to wait until after its case is heard by the United States Court of Appeals in October.

There will also be desegregation of parochial schools of the New Orleans and the Atlanta archdioceses of the Roman Catholic Church in September.

66 Nine Negro children first entered the 11th and 12th grades of four former all-white high schools of Atlanta on August 30, 1961 by court order in *Calhoun* v. *Latimer*.

67 *Southern State News,* Oct. 1959, p. 13. The State of Mississippi stands out as the worst example of defiance of Federal law and human decency. It has innumerable statutes which are applied and enforced by various state officials, requiring racial separation in all areas of life, public and private.

68 Unpublished Manuscript by Charles Markham, Esq., of Battle, Fowler, Stokes & Kheel, New York City, New York.

AN APPEAL / SECTION IV

69 *Congressional Quarterly,* Weekly Report, July 22, 1960 Supp., p. 1301.

70 *Congressional Quarterly,* Weekly Report, July 22, 1960 Supp., p. 1301.

71 *Ibid.,* p. 1301.

72 *Ibid.,* p. 1296.

73 *The New York Times,* Jan. 17, 1962, p. 3.

74 James G. Blaine, leader of the Republicans and later Speaker of the House, described the "Black Codes" as follows:

"The trust was that his (the Negro's) liberty was merely of form and not of fact and the slavery which was abolished by the organic law of a Nation *was now to be revived by the enactment of a State*." (emphasis added)
Twenty Years in Congress, Vol. I (Henry Bill Publishing Co. 1886).

75 *The Civil Rights Cases; United States* v. *Stanley; United States* v. *Ryan; United States* v. *Nichols; United States* v. *Singleton; Robinson and wife* v. *Memphis & Charleston Railroad Company,* 109 U.S. 3, 203 S. Ct. 18, 28 (1883).

76 *Ibid.*

77 *The New York Times,* Jan. 12, 1962, p. 12.

78 State of the Union message, *The New York Times,* Jan. 12, 1962, p. 12.

79 *Ibid.,* p. 12.

80 *Ibid.,* p. 12.

81 *The New York Times,* Jan. 12, 1962, lead editorial "The Burden and the Glory."

82 *The President Office and Powers*—1787–1957, Edward S. Corwin, pp. 28, 39; New York University Press, 4th Edition (1957).

83 "America has no undeveloped resource comparable to the reservoir of human talent which, in our Negro population, is going to waste. We need manpower and we leave it untrained. We need brains and talents and we allow them to lie fallow. We need to restore the social health of our cities and we do little to prevent their greater infection with the virus of disorganization and spiritual deadness. We need to deepen our sense of purpose and our confidence in our country and its cause, and we allow prejudice to be institutionalized and our national values to be layered with hypocrisy. We need the friendship of the non-white peoples of Africa and Asia, and we subject our own non-white citizens to indignity."
The Federal Executive and Civil Rights,
Southern Regional Council

84 Rossiter, Clinton. *The American Presidency* (2nd Ed.) New York: Harcourt Brace & Co., Inc., 1960.

85 Article II, Sec. 1, #8.

86 Article VI.

87 Article III, Sec. 3.

88 See *Standard Computing Scale Co.* v. *Farrill,* 249 U.S. 751, 577 (1919); *In re Neagle,* 135 U.S. 1 (1889); *Williams* v. *Bruffy,* 96 U.S. 176, 183 (1877); *Stoffel* v. *W. J. McCahan Sugar Ref. Co.,* 35 F. 2d 602, 603 (E. D. Pa. 1929). Petition of the United States to intervene in Prince Edward County School Board case.

89 135 U.S. 1.

90 *Ibid.* at p. 59.

91 Roosevelt, Theodore. *An Autobiography.* pp. 388–389, New York 1913.

92 *New York Times,* Jan. 17, 1962, p. 3.

93 The history of 10 U.S.C. 332 goes back to the early days of our country when President Washington requested authority from Congress to handle the Whiskey Rebellion in Western Pennsylvania. Congress granted him broad authority to call forth the militia. It is illuminating for us today to see the various means Washington attempted to use until he felt compelled to resort to the militia as the final means of seeing that the laws of the country would be obeyed. He issued a proclamation on September 15, 1792, warning "all persons whom it may concern to refrain and desist from all unlawful combinations and proceedings whatsoever. . . ." 36 N.C. LR. p. 124. The Administration began legal proceedings against those who were violating the law. The Government purchased whiskey for the Army only from those farmers who obeyed the law. Attacks upon the revenue collector were followed by warrants for the arrest of those who had participated in the attacks. The U.S. Marshal was physically threatened by the western farmers and was therefore unable to serve process. President Washington still hesitated to use the militia and first appealed to the Governor of Pennsylvania to call forth the state militia. Upon the latter's refusal, Washington issued a second proclamation warning the insurgents that he was determined to "cause the laws to be duly executed." p. 127. He also appointed three U.S. commissioners to proceed to the scene of the trouble and a referendum was conducted in which the people voted against compliance with the Whiskey Tax. The President hesitated no longer to enforce the law. He issued a third proclamation in which he declared that the militia from four of the neighboring states would proceed to "the scene of the disaffection." When the militia arrived, it was met with complete submission.

As a result of this disobedience to the laws of the land, Congress passed the Act of 1795 to provide "means by which the Executive could come in aid of the Judiciary" by calling forth the militia to execute the laws of the United States whenever they "shall be opposed, or the execution thereof obstructed."

The Thomas Jefferson Amendment of 1807 gave the President the additional power of employing the land or naval forces of the United States. In *Martin* v. *Mott,* 12 Wheat 19 (1827), it was held that authority to decide whether the exigency had arisen to call the militia belonged exclusively to the President.

The Abraham Lincoln Amendment of 1861 to the George Washington 1795 Act authorized the President to call forth the armed forces "to enforce the faithful execution of the laws" whenever, in the judgment of the President, "It shall become impracticable" to enforce them by the ordinary course of judicial proceedings.

94 See Appendix A.

AN APPEAL / APPENDIX A

95 42 U.S.C. 1985 Conspiracy to interfere with civil rights.

(1) Preventing an officer from performing duties. If two or more persons in any State or Territory conspire to prevent, by force, intimidation, or threat, any person from accepting or holding any office . . . under the United States or from discharging any duties thereof; . . . or impede him in the discharge of his official duties;

(2) Obstructing justice; intimidating party, witness or juror. If two or more persons in any State or Territory conspire . . . for the purpose of impeding, hindering or obstructing, or defeating in any manner, the due course of justice in any State or Territory with intent to deny any citizen the equal protection of the laws. . . .

(3) Depriving persons of rights and privileges. If two or more persons . . . conspire, or go in disguise on the highway . . . for the purpose of depriving . . . any person . . . of the equal protection of the laws . . . the party so injured may have an action for the recovery of damages.

96 Hearings Before the Subcommittee on Constitutional Rights of the Senate Committee on the Judiciary, 85th Cong., 1st Sess., 214–217 (1957).

97 Congress probably acted under art. I, sec. 8, which states: "provide for calling forth the Militia to execute the Laws of the Union, suppress Insurrections and repel Invasions."

98 See Appendix I for the statutes.

99 The reference evidently is to the recodifica-

tion of 1956. 50 U.S.C. 201–204 on August 10, 1956 was recodified as 10 U.S.C. 331–334, ch. 1041, 70A Stat. 641.

100 See Appendix II.

101 "The fears and doubts of the opposition are no authoritative guide to the construction of legislation. It is the sponsors we look to when the meaning of the statutory words is in doubt." *Schwegmann Bros.* v. *Calvert Distillers Corp.,* 341 U.S. 384, 394 (1952).

102 See *United States* v. *San Francisco,* 310 U.S. 675, 186 (1951) (individual statements admissible when they seem to represent the understanding of the group).

103 Testimony of the draftsman as to the nature and effect of the bill is often treated as evidence of legislative intent. *Elder* v. *Brannan,* 341 U.S. 277, 284 (1951); see also, *NLRB* v. *Denver Bldg. Council,* 341 U.S. 675, 686 (1951) (weight of statements of Representative or Senator in charge of bill) and *Ahrens* v. *Clark,* 335 U.S. 188, 192 (1948) (Congressman who introduces bill).

AN APPEAL / A DIFFERENT APPROACH

104 *United States* v. *Dickerson,* 310 U.S. 554, 562 (1940), see, *United States* v. *American Trucking Assoc.,* 310 U.S. 534, 543 (1940).

105 "Spurious use of legislative history must not swallow the legislation so as to give point to the quip that only when legislative history is doubtful do you go to the statute. While courts are no longer confined to the language, they are still confined by it." Frankfurter, *Some Reflections on the Reading of Statutes,* 47 Col. L. Rev. 527 (1947).

106 *Ibid.* at 535.

107 I Sutherland, Statutory Construction · Sec. 2007 (3rd ed. Horack, 1943).

108 I Sutherland, Statutory Construction Sec. 2012, n.2 (3rd ed. Horack, 1943). The footnote cites: *Frost* v. *Wenie,* 157 U.S. 46 (1894); *United States* v. *Greathouse,* 166 U.S. 601 (1897); *United States* v. *Noce,* 268 U.S. 613 (1925).

109 *Ibid.* at Sec. 2014, n. 1.

110 *Ibid.* at Sec. 2008, citing *Bear Lake & River Waterworks & Irrig. Co.* v. *Garland,* 164 U.S. 1 (1896).

111 *Ibid.* at Sec. 2015, citing *Fay* v. *Dist. Ct. of Appeal,* 200 Cal. 522, 254 Pac. 896 (1927); *Buffurn* v. *Chase Nat'l Bank,* 192 F.2d 58 (1951).

112 See Appendix III.

113 Cf. *Youngstown Sheet & Tube Co.* v. *Sawyer,* 343 U.S. 579 (1952).

AN APPEAL / APPENDIX I

114 Although 50 U. S. C. 205 refers to "provisions of this chapter" the reference must be understood as applying to 10 U. S. C. 331–334 since they were formerly 50 U. S. C. 201–205. Aug. 10, 1956, ch. 1041, sec. 53, 70 A Stat. 641.

AN APPEAL / APPENDIX III

115 10 U. S. C. A. 334 has the Proclamation date listed as of Sept. 24, 1957. This is an error, as can be seen by the reference to the Proclamation in the subsequent Executive Order. The Federal Register has the correct date listed, Sept. 23, 1957.

Index

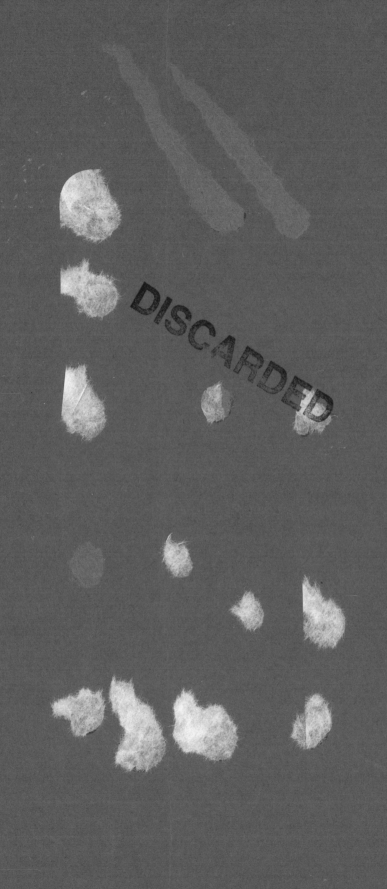